Music and Revolution

MUSIC OF THE AFRICAN DIASPORA

Edited by Samuel A. Floyd, Jr., and Rae Linda Brown

Music and Revolution

Cultural Change in Socialist Cuba

ROBIN D. MOORE

University of California Press
Berkeley Los Angeles London

Center for Black Music Research
Columbia College Chicago

University of California Press, one of the most distinguished
university presses in the United States, enriches lives around the
world by advancing scholarship in the humanities, social sciences,
and natural sciences. Its activities are supported by the UC Press
Foundation and by philanthropic contributions from individuals
and institutions. For more information, visit www.ucpress.edu.

University of California Press
Berkeley and Los Angeles, California

University of California Press, Ltd.
London, England

Center for Black Music Research
Columbia College, Chicago

© 2006 by The Regents of the University of California

Library of Congress Cataloging-in-Publication Data

Moore, Robin, 1964–.
    Music and revolution : cultural change in socialist Cuba / Robin D.
Moore.
        p.   cm. — (Music of the African diaspora)
    Includes bibliographical references (p.   ) and index.
    ISBN 0-520-24710-8 (cloth : alk. paper).—ISBN 0-520-24711-6 (pbk. :
alk. paper)
    1. Music—Political aspects—Cuba.   2. Music—Cuba—20th
century—History and criticism.   3. Socialism and music.   I. Title.
II. Series.
    ML3917.C9M66   2006
    780'.97291'0904—dc22   2005022138

Manufactured in the United States of America

15 14 13 12 11 10 09 08 07 06
10 9 8 7 6 5 4 3 2 1

This book is printed on New Leaf EcoBook 50, a 100% recycled fiber
of which 50% is de-inked post-consumer waste, processed chlorine-
free. EcoBook 50 is acid-free and meets the minimum requirements
of ANSI/ASTM D5634-01 (*Permanence of Paper*).

Qué rumbo al futuro más infortunado
qué nueva frontera hemos violado
qué camino más estrecho andamos
cuánto corazón juntamos

GERARDO ALFONSO, "Amiga mía"

Contents

Illustrations

Preface

In retrospect, the process of my growing interest in Cuban music and history over the past fifteen years has been somewhat fortuitous and deserves explanation. I grew up in Southern California, surrounded by Latin American culture, but, as in the case of far too many Anglo Americans, largely oblivious to it. My family and friends had virtually no contact with the large Hispanic population in the area aside from casual acquaintances. After entering college and deciding to pursue music, I was encouraged to take German, ostensibly the "best" language choice for my major in the conservative environment that prevailed. I did so and found that I enjoyed languages; shortly thereafter, I spent a year on exchange in Austria. The trip made a lasting impact in many ways, but perhaps most importantly changed my perspective on the United States, raising my awareness of cultural difference. After my return, I began for the first time to take serious note of Spanish speakers in the area. Continuing to study German seemed silly given the demographics of the Southwest. I soon made the decision to switch to Spanish.

In an attempt to combine the study of language, travel, and music, I entered graduate school at UC Santa Barbara in ethnomusicology, a new program there. My professors offered excellent courses on a variety of subjects but little specifically on Latin America. I felt strongly about pursuing work that would be relevant to the region I lived in, and for that reason eventually transferred to the University of Texas at Austin. There I began to play in a mariachi band, learned something about Andean music, and slowly became more familiar with Caribbean styles. The percussiveness and overall sound of Afro-Latin music in all its permutations (Brazilian, Colombian, Cuban, Puerto Rican, etc.) attracted me a great deal, as they have many North Americans. Undoubtedly this is because U.S. and Afro-Latin popular styles

ical, while to others it may appear "soft." I have tried to keep the analysis as balanced as possible and to create a book potentially useful to readers on and off the island. I consider myself sympathetic to the goals of socialism and believe that many of its basic precepts are more humane than those driving decision making in capitalist countries. However, this has not blinded me to the oppressiveness of many aspects of life in Cuba today. I hope that readers on the left and right of the political spectrum will agree that it serves no one's interest to gloss over mistakes made by any government. Political agendas, however well intended, are not furthered by mass rallies or flag waving, but rather by a careful examination of their successes and failures and attempts to improve them. Authors living in Cuba should be leading the way in discussing the long-term impact of cultural changes over the past forty-five years. Unfortunately, before the mid-1990s, they generated little in the way of self-reflective criticism. Visitors with an interest in Cuba, such as myself, thus have little choice but to raise some topics of discussion themselves. The primary goal of this book is not to have its interpretations proven "right" or "wrong," although I hope they will stand some scrutiny, but simply to broaden the dialogue about lessons to be learned from the revolutionary experience.

My attempt to synthesize major cultural trends over the past forty years has been a humbling endeavor, as the countless cultural initiatives, institutions, policy makers, performers, and musical styles involved are impossible to discuss comprehensively. I devote scant attention to important musical forms such as rock and rap, for instance; they will have to be discussed by others. Beyond this, factors derived from the tense political environment have complicated research considerably. Funding for work in Cuba remains difficult to obtain from institutions in the United States. Securing permission from the Cuban government to access information is also far from simple. Over the past eight years, state agencies have refused to offer me research visas that would allow direct access to their facts and figures and facilitate interviews. A great deal of statistical data from the Ministry of Culture on music education, recording, and performance that would have strengthened the study have been impossible to include as a result. One trip in 1996 had to be scrapped because of a Cuban attack on Brothers to the Rescue airplanes flying over Cuban airspace; in the controversial aftermath, my hosts felt it inappropriate to extend an invitation to any American. Raúl Castro's denunciation of the CEA (Centro de Estudios sobre las Américas) and the purging of that institution had a negative impact on academic relations for some time, as did the Clinton administration's suggestions that research on the island be used as a political weapon.[1] Political tensions have increased even further since 2000 with the election of George W. Bush. Finally, readers should be aware that most of my field research has been confined to the Havana area; though I attempt to discuss artists from other parts of the island, the study nevertheless reflects that bias.

Politics not only complicates the contexts for conducting research and the extent of access to publications but the very content of publications. The fact that the Cuban government has controlled domestic presses since the early 1960s means that information contained in books and journals is often incomplete or represents only one perspective. To the extent that such texts include rigorous analysis, they often avoid sensitive lines of inquiry. Sources from the United States and elsewhere vary similarly in quality and objectivity. In some cases, they are not based on extended fieldwork in Cuba;[2] in others, authors' political views shape the analysis. Those interested in Cuban history face a decidedly polarized literature, one filled with opposing opinions that are difficult to reconcile. Cubans on the island provide some of the best information on past events through interviews, yet many will not speak about them openly.[3] Others do not wish their conversations to be taped, making retention difficult. Foreigners who ask penetrating questions may be accused of spying, as I myself have experienced. This climate of distrust is the result of ongoing political antagonisms, covert and overt actions by the U.S. government, and the Cuban leadership's vilification of capitalist countries.

Polarized attitudes about Cuba abroad have their basis in the personal experiences and meanings that the revolution holds for various groups. People either love present-day Cuba with a passion because of what it represents to them (an alternative to capitalism, concern for the poor and disenfranchised, a symbol of all that should be criticized in the United States) or despise it because of the intense pain the revolution has caused them (harassment, jailings, loss of property, severed family ties). Researchers find themselves caught in this uncomfortable context from the outset. Pro-Cuba advocates have shouted at me merely for raising issues of limitations on personal freedoms. They assert that heavy-handed policies of media control are not the government's fault, that they represent a logical response to external aggression. Similarly, exiles often become antagonistic as soon as they find out that I travel regularly to the island and dismiss out of hand any criticisms I might raise about prerevolutionary Cuban society. Authors attempting impartiality thus walk a tightrope between constituencies and, despite their best efforts, usually fail to please anyone.

A few chapters of this publication have appeared in press before. Thanks are due to the *Canadian Journal of Latin American and Caribbean Stud-*

ies, Ethnomusicology, the *International Journal of Qualitative Studies in Education,* and Routledge Press for permission to reproduce earlier versions of the essays.[4] Support at various stages has come from the Rockefeller and MacArthur Foundations, the Center for Black Music Research, Temple University, and the National Humanities Center. Among the many friends and colleagues in the United States, Europe, and Latin America who provided information and commentary on draft essays, I must express my gratitude to David Brown, Ka'ala Carmack, Arsenio Cicero, Alejandro de la Fuente, Cristóbal Díaz Ayala, Rosario Espinal, Sujatha Fernandes, Nadine Fernandez, Raul Fernandez, Reynaldo Fernández Pavón, Ed Flanagan, Samuel Floyd, Agustín González García, Lara Greene, Katherine Hagedorn, Gisela Hernández, Narciso Hidalgo, John Kirk, Lisa Knauer, Lisa Lindsay, Enrique "Guajiro" López, Peter Manuel, Enrique Patterson, Marc Perlman, Paul Ryer, John Santos, Elizabeth Sayre, T. M. Scruggs, Chuck Silverman, Diane Soles, Piotr Sommer, Susan Thomas, Elio Villafranca, and Eric Zolov. Cristóbal Díaz Ayala and Peter Manuel deserve special mention for the extended amounts of time and support they have graciously offered. In Havana, special thanks are due to Yaroldi Abreu Robles, Leonardo Acosta and Margarita González, Saylín Álvarez, David Calzado, Walterio Carbonell, Rosa and Rosita Chang, Alexis Esquivel, Alberto Faya, Tomás Fernández Robaina, Melquiades Fundora Dino, Radamés Giro, Neris González Bello, Zoila Lapique Becali, Rogelio Martínez Furé, Pablo Menéndez, Helio Orovio, Pepe Piñeiro, José Reyes, Loipa Rodríguez and Julio Rimada, Lázaro Ros, Zoe Santos García, Cristóbal Sosa, Celso Valdés Santandreu, and María Elena Vinueza. I owe a tremendous debt to them—especially Leo Acosta—and to countless other musicians, visual artists, historians, authors, friends, expatriates, and revolutionaries who have contributed to this study.

INTRODUCTION

Music and the Arts in Socialist Cuba

> Our highest aspiration has been the promotion of relationships
> between artistic and intellectual movements and the political,
> social, and moral development of the country. That is, we reject
> the conception of art and culture as something added to or super-
> imposed on social life and instead attempt to situate them in their
> rightful place in the construction of socialism.
>
> ARMANDO HART DÁVALOS, *Adelante el arte*

Though the scope of its influence has declined in recent years, socialist
thought represents one of the most far-reaching conceptual developments
of modern times. It has resulted, directly and indirectly, in fundamental political changes throughout the world and has given rise to educational systems that produce artists of world-class status, in Cuba and elsewhere. This
introduction considers the prominent role that leaders in state socialist countries typically ascribe to culture. It includes a summary of the practical issues facing them as they attempt to inspire music making in a more utopian
world and some of the deficiencies they recognize in the music making of
non-socialist countries, including the United States.

Without doubt, the Cuban Revolution of 1959 has its roots in many ideological currents besides Marxism. These include anticolonialist and nationalist liberation movements throughout Latin America, writings by Simón
Bolívar and José Martí, the *arielismo* discourse of José Enrique Rodó, even
the pronouncements of right-wing figures such as Brazil's Getúlio Vargas.
A number of Cuban insurgents in the 1950s were themselves staunchly anti-
Communist. Nevertheless, Marxist literature has had strong influence in
the country since at least the early twentieth century. It has circulated in
the form of writings by Marx himself, by Cuban intellectuals at home and
abroad (Juan Marinello, Paul Lafargue), and by socialist-inspired authors
from Latin American neighboring countries (Mexican Felipe Carrillo Puerto,
Peruvian José Carlos Mariátegui, Argentine Aníbal Ponce) and of course in
the views of self-confessed Communists within Fidel Castro's revolutionary leadership itself: Alfredo Guevara, Ernesto "Che" Guevara, Raúl Castro,
and so forth. Significantly, most of the figures planning cultural policy in
revolutionary Cuba during its first decades came from the ranks of Cuban

Communist Party organizations such as the PSP, founded in the 1920s. International works on socialist aesthetics have influenced platform documents of the new Cuban Communist Party (established in 1965) strongly and continue to be a basis for arts policy. This literature establishes an important ideological frame within which musicians continue to live and work. Socialist discourse affects performers' lives in tangible ways, regardless of whether they consider themselves socialists or actively incorporate its philosophy into their compositions.

A central goal of this book is to explore the "slippage," or disconnect, between what state socialist societies ostensibly strive for through the arts and what they actually do, using Cuba as a case study. Most of the chapters focus on practice, describing government institutions, the ways in which they have been successful or unsuccessful, changes in policy, and how musicians work within and respond to their environment. To analyze this relationship between theory and practice, it is necessary to consider the discursive goals of policy makers. Socialist aesthetics does not provide the key to understanding all Cuban musical development since 1959. Rather, socialist theories of art, themselves far from codified and precise, are a point of reference from which to evaluate the rationale behind government positions at particular moments. They also help readers appreciate ongoing shifts in revolutionary ideology. Clearly, other factors have shaped Cuban arts policy over the past forty-five years nearly as much as Marxism: elitist and/or Eurocentric attitudes (manifesting themselves in exclusive support for classical repertoire), political tensions with the United States, the actions of individual government representatives, and the struggles of performers themselves to help define revolutionary art, to name only a few. These issues are discussed in later chapters.

The study as a whole consists of two interrelated sections. The first, chapters 1–3, provides a roughly chronological overview of cultural changes within Cuba since 1959. The second, chapters 4–7, represents a series of case studies considering particular individuals, groups, and music genres. Chapter 8 and the conclusion describe the transformation of Cuban socialism since the collapse of the Soviet Union. The combination of chapters focusing on larger processes and on more specific topics is intended to provide a feel for overall artistic tendencies while helping underscore the complexities of the revolution—its many phases, protagonists, policy reversals, the conflicting experiences of performers—and the tremendous amount of research on it that remains to be done.

Chapter 1 begins with a description of musical life in the 1950s. It considers the political climate of the late Batista era along with its social problems (wealth disparities, racism, government corruption) and cultural expression, especially the nightlife associated with Havana's renowned clubs and cabarets. Chapter 2 evaluates political changes initiated during the years immediately following 1959 and their impact on music making. Decisions to nationalize private businesses and standardize performer salaries, increasingly tense relations with the United States, and other factors affected performers significantly. Chapter 3 discusses the gradual creation of new cultural institutions and policies. It examines campaigns designed to bring art and culture more directly to the masses, the founding of specialized art schools, and the transition toward more government oversight of the arts.

Initiating the case study section, chapter 4 focuses on the history of dance entertainment since 1959. The countless *charanga* and *conjunto* bands of the late 1950s performed a mostly *son*-based repertoire, dominating commercial performance and recording. They remained very popular in later years and yet were never a terribly effective vehicle for conveying revolutionary values. This section considers the ambivalent attitudes of the revolutionary vanguard toward fun-loving, irreverent dance tunes; by extension it underscores the leadership's difficulty in determining the role of "fun" within a state cultural agenda that supported music with political content. Chapter 5 focuses on the history of the genre known as *nueva trova*. This music was a product of youth culture, of the first generation raised under a socialist education system. Analysis considers tensions between artists and officials in early years as well as the process by which *nueva trova* became an institutionally accepted form of revolutionary life.

Chapters 6 and 7 focus on Afro-Cuban traditions.[1] Chapter 6 examines the biases against genres that Cuba inherited from the colonial period and suggests that they resulted in tepid support for folkloric performance. Chapter 7 describes the history of religious music, a repertoire that received little public recognition within the atheist state until recently. Chapter 8 chronicles how the end of support from Eastern Europe has affected Cuba in material, ideological, and musical terms. To save the country's economy, the leadership began to encourage tourism and foreign investment in the early 1990s; this in turn has prompted a crisis of ideology and unease over the future of socialism itself. The chapter notes that economic crisis has actually led to the wider proliferation of Cuban music at home and abroad, contrary to what might be assumed. A concluding section ponders the future of Cuban music within an ongoing context of international political tension.

THE ORIGINS OF SOCIALIST THOUGHT

Karl Marx and Friedrich Engels began their influential writings in the context of mid-nineteenth-century industrialization in Europe and its labor practices. Viewing photos such as those in Eric Hobsbawm's *The Age of Empire* (1987), one sees firsthand the inhuman living conditions of the urban poor at that time. Mass production techniques, while slowly raising standards of living in Europe, had the initial effect of making workers miserable. They resulted in extended hours of employment with inadequate pay, forced children into factories, and condemned many to mindless, repetitive tasks. In response, Marx and Engels began to analyze history from a radically new perspective, one that emphasized the uneven distribution and control of economic goods. Marx contributed to their effort a mind well versed in history and philosophy, while Engels complemented this expertise with experience in the world of finance. Their ultimate goals were to make sense of the systemic problems facing Western society, to raise awareness about the exploitative nature of the Industrial Revolution, and to suggest alternatives for the future.

Marx and many of his contemporaries noted that capitalist modes of production created a surplus of goods. Businesses expanded whenever possible, searching to dominate new markets so as to maximize sales for wealthy investors. Marxists viewed the constant drive to generate new capital and profit as a force to be tamed in order to more effectively serve the needs of all citizens. The working classes too, they argued, deserved a share of the material gains they helped generate. They needed more leisure time, the "right to be lazy" (Lafargue 1907:107), to devote themselves to the pursuit of happiness and to intellectual and artistic fulfillment.

> In our days everything seems pregnant with its contrary. Machinery, gifted with the wonderful power of shortening and fructifying human labor, we behold starving and overworking it. The newfangled sources of wealth, by some strange weird spell, are turned into sources of want. The victories of art seem bought by the loss of character. At the same pace that mankind masters nature, man seems to become enslaved to other men or to his own infamy. . . . All our invention and progress seem to result in endowing material forces with intellectual life, and in stultifying human life into a material force. (Marx and Engels 1978:577–78)

Because it perpetuated inequality between owners and wage earners, Marx argued that capitalism contained the seeds of its own destruction. He suggested that conflict between them would eventually lead to revolution as laborers realized their plight, rose up against their patrons, and took control of businesses themselves. Marx envisioned the initial phase of the resulting revolutionary society, now known as socialism, as involving the equal allocation of material goods to every citizen by representatives of the working classes, a "dictatorship of the proletariat." He conceived a final, utopian phase, now referred to as Communism, as one in which the apportioning of goods by the government would no longer be necessary. Under Communism, equality would become such a basic organizational principle that the very concept of private ownership would gradually disappear. Man's naturally generous nature would emerge as the result of higher standards of living and education. This would hypothetically allow everyone to live harmoniously and to attain their full creative potential. It was believed that Communism would witness the gradual withering away of government institutions as individuals learned to act responsibly without their guidance.

Several key aspects of social change in the late nineteenth and twentieth centuries deviated from Marx's vision. His writings did not suggest that those promoting the welfare of the working classes would form political parties and fight for change through nonviolent means. By the 1870s, nevertheless, "workers' parties" influenced by his ideas had begun to emerge. This soon created schisms in the movement, with pacifists pressing demands through the legislature and more ardent revolutionaries supporting armed conflict as the only viable means of social transformation. Another surprise came when the first massive uprisings in the name of socialism took place in countries (Russia, China) whose populations were primarily rural and agricultural. According to Marx, the class conflicts leading to revolution should have been most intense in urban, industrialized regions. Finally and perhaps most problematically, the power structures that developed in state socialist countries such as the Soviet Union did not gradually disappear as he had suggested. On the contrary, they grew, retaining authority for themselves.

The values of socialism represent a radical shift in perspective for those raised in countries such as the United States. Classic capitalist discourse prioritizes the safeguarding of personal rights above all others and provides opportunities for financial gain on the part of individuals. Those influenced by socialist thought, however, conceive fundamental rights in collective terms. Note that while Cuba has adopted socialist principles in an especially aggressive manner, many countries in Latin America and elsewhere embrace similar principles and have reconciled them with capitalist market structures. As their first priority, governments influenced by socialism strive to guarantee everyone the right to a job, an affordable home, and free health care and education. Their leaders consistently identify these rights to be as fundamental as personal freedoms. In the same way, capitalists and socialists view the material needs of the population differently. Capitalist markets identify highly specific preferences among consumers and cater to them to sell a diversity of products. Socialism defines needs in much more basic terms: enough food to eat, an adequate pension, shoes, a warm jacket. The primary goal is not to determine which products are most desirable to the public but only to make sure that everyone has the most necessary items.

State socialist economies such as those in Cuba generally improve the lives of poorer citizens and eliminate wide disparities of income, but they can provide only limited consumer goods. Katherine Verdery (1996:22) associates them with "cultures of shortage" under the best of circumstances, plagued by chronic underproductivity and rationing. Job guarantees provided by the state often lead to complacency or poor performance among workers. Centralized economic control itself causes problems, as even the most carefully crafted five-year plan cannot anticipate and respond to consumer needs in a timely manner. Nonessential goods are difficult to find at any price. For this reason, life in modern-day socialist countries involves a constant search for limited resources, often clandestinely through informal networks of friends and associates. Of course, shortages in Cuba have been exacerbated significantly as a result of the United States trade embargo, which has contributed to widespread suffering.

In its attempt to equitably redistribute products and services, the state takes over most private institutions and centrally manages them. Government institutions thus proliferate in countless forms as a surrogate for civil society. This degree of centralization was not dictated by Marx but rather developed under leaders such as Stalin in the twentieth century. Much more than under capitalism, government intersects with the activities of the average citizen on a daily basis. Instead of private clubs or fraternities, one finds official organizations designed to facilitate an individual's activities as a child, an adolescent, a student, and a worker. There are groups to link those of similar ethnic backgrounds or interests, and even to facilitate socialization in one's neighborhood.[2] Through such groups, the state involves itself in the lives of nearly everyone. The fact that institutions are controlled by the government should not be taken to mean that individuals have no space to help define the boundaries of their activities, however, or even to contest their policies, only that the public sphere is defined by the state rather than nongovernmental factions.[3]

CULTURE AND SOCIALISM

Most books on the Cuban Revolution include scarcely a reference to music, and yet music and the arts have been central to the revolutionary experiment from the outset. Both Odilio Urfé (1982:165) and Fidel Castro himself (1961:12) make this point. Within months of taking power, leaders began passing legislation designed to establish new centers of music, film, theater, and literary production. In December 1960, the ICAP (Instituto Cubano de Amistad con los Pueblos [Cuban Institute of Friendship with Other Nations]) was established in an attempt to further cultural exchange between Cuba and other Latin American countries.[4] By 1961, a national arts school (ENA) had been created for the training of musicians, dancers, and visual artists (Ministerio de Cultura 1982:72, 75). In the same year, the government established a National Culture Advisory (El Consejo Nacional de Cultura, or CNC). Musicologist Radamés Giro (2001, interview) believes that Cuba invests more money per capita in the arts than virtually any other country, citing as one example a course of study offered free of charge to aspiring violinists that may last as long as eighteen years. Film professor Mario Masvidal (pers. comm.) similarly asserts that Cuba has invested resources in cultural programs disproportional to the country's small economy, creating a massive superstructure over an atrophied base. The work of other researchers, such as Ted Levin's studies in central Asia (Levin 1996), supports the view that one-party socialist states encourage artistic performance to a greater extent than their capitalist counterparts. In many respects they are forced to do so, since they must compensate for the absence of nongovernmental institutions that would otherwise contribute to cultural life.

The prominence of the arts is but one facet of the greater respect for ideas generally under socialism. Konrád and Szelényi (1979:179–80) note that although socialism implies rule by the working classes, as a political system it tends to encourage education and generates large numbers of artists and intellectuals. Often, they are not merely commentators or critics on the periphery of the political hierarchy but active participants and even leaders of their respective countries (e.g., Václav Havel in Czechoslovakia, Árpád Göncz in Hungary). Hernández (2003:119) likewise asserts that in Cuba the pursuit of knowledge has become more important since 1959. There are various reasons for this. Perhaps the most important is that the ultimate goal of the leadership is the transformation of society through the dissemination of ideas (Fagen 1969:7). Marx was critical of the status quo and envisioned himself and his followers as struggling to change social relations as

and goals of a national cultural apparatus developed by revolutionary leaders since 1959 and the ways in which such policies have impacted the lives of performers, how they have reacted to the ideological priorities of the revolution, and how they have come to create spaces for their individual concerns as part of such groups.

MARXISM AND AESTHETICS

State socialism as it existed in Cuba for many years attempted to centrally plan nearly all cultural activity. Those charged with such a task were confronted with many difficult questions: How should the arts be organized and supervised? How much money should be devoted to such endeavors? How many artists does the country need? Do specific kinds of performance deserve more promotion than others, and if so, which kinds? Who will determine which music to record and air in the media? Does some art have negative effects on society and require regulation? To be sure, those administering cultural policy were not always aware of the existing Marxist literature on such issues. Some, such as film institute director Alfredo Guevara, were highly educated intellectuals who knew a great deal about it. Others were political appointees who knew next to nothing about the arts and whose value lay primarily in their loyalty to Fidel Castro and his 26th of July movement. Their preparation consisted, in many cases, of six-month crash courses on Marxism, leaving them with little grasp even of its fundamental premises.

The difficulty in resolving debates over socialist aesthetics is that Marx and Engels never chose to examine the subject of art at length, leaving only "scattered comments and opinions" (Schwartz 1973:108) as their legacy. In part, this is undoubtedly due to the relative insignificance of cultural forms to economic processes in the nineteenth century, as opposed to their close links with the marketplace today. In general, Marx seems to have envisioned the ideal community as containing few professional performers but allowing many more individuals than before to develop their creative potential. His ultimate goal was decidedly populist: the reintegration of creative activity into daily life. To Marx, capitalists not only exploited their laborers economically, but—because of oppressive working conditions and lack of access to education—kept them from the cultural pastimes that made life fulfilling. Socialism would rectify this situation in various ways: through the elimination of poverty and the creation of more leisure time; by providing new opportunities for education; and ideally by letting workers think and act creatively on the job, regardless of their profession. Paul Lafargue is one of many who referred to the role of culture in an idealized future.

> Mechanical production, which under capitalist direction can only buffet the worker back and forth from periods of over-work to periods of enforced idleness, will when developed and regulated by a communist administration, require from the producer . . . only a maximum day of two or three hours in the workshop, and when this . . . is fulfilled he will be able to enjoy freely the physical and intellectual pleasures of life. The artist then will paint, will sing, will dance, the writer will write, the musician will compose operas, the philosopher will build systems . . . not to gain money, to receive a salary, but to deserve applause, to win laurel wreaths, like the conquerors of the Olympic games, to satisfy their artistic and scientific passion. (Lafargue 1907:102–103)

Vague references in Marx's writings to an artistic utopia of this sort are the only original sources leaders have had to use as the basis for policy. The strong encouragement of amateur performance in Cuba and elsewhere for many years reflects this goal, as discussed in chapter 2. Otherwise, Marx provided few specifics, and officials have experimented widely with the best means of achieving artistic excellence. Varied interpretations of Marx and of the appropriate role of the state in such activities have led to a variety of approaches through the years. Some of the more hotly contested topics that first surfaced in Europe are mentioned below. Again, the fact that many gained acceptance among the Cuban leadership for a time does not imply that all or even most artists embraced them. They represented guidelines that were frequently disputed or ignored.

Class Issues

Marxist theorists agree that revolutionary art should benefit the masses, but they are divided on whether to draw the inspiration for such art in the expressive forms of the working classes, the professional and elite classes, or both. The central issue is whether, under the rule of the proletariat, it is more appropriate to valorize and disseminate primarily folk and traditional expression, popular music, classical music, or some combination of all three. Tension surrounds this point because it represents the intersection of distinct and somewhat contradictory goals: the promotion of marginalized proletarian culture and a desire to "raise" the standards of the socially downtrodden. Art can cater to the aesthetic preferences of the masses at a given moment or it can attempt to widen their horizons, but it cannot always do both successfully. Complicating the issue further is the fact that socialist planners typically come from the middle classes; though they intend to represent the best interests of everyone, they may not personally identify with or fully appreciate all forms of working-class art.

Several revolutions have been associated with the wholesale rejection of elite culture and the promotion of exclusively working-class forms. China's leadership, under the supervision of Mao Tse-tung's wife, Chiang Ching, was notorious for its purging of "bourgeois" elements and artists during the Cultural Revolution, which lasted from 1964 through 1976 (Siegel 1992:18); similar phenomena plagued Russia in earlier decades, resulting in the banning of books by Pushkin and Dostoyevsky. Taking the opposite view, some leaders suggested that the poor in their respective countries had never developed cultural forms of significance and proposed massive campaigns of education to rectify the situation (e.g., Trotsky 1992:48). One notes in the works of many a desire to use art as a means of breaking down class division through the elaboration or modification of working-class culture. This goal is commendable but can lead to dramatic aesthetic changes. Examples include the dissemination of "improved" folk songs of greater harmonic or technical complexity such as in Bulgarian women's choirs (Buchanan 1995), the writing of complex symphonic compositions for traditional instruments such as the balalaika, and the creation of experimental modern dance presentations based on traditional Santería ceremonies (Hagedorn 2002).

In an alternate case, Levin (2002) found that the socialist government in Uzbekistan attempted to divest the local music of many unique ornaments, scale intervals, and other characteristics. Its goal was apparently to create a populist culture devoid of elements associated with the earlier emirate's elite and more similar to music in other regions of the Soviet Union. Planners believed that the creation of a common folk culture would foster a sense of unity and brotherhood among the international proletariat.

Nationalist Issues

The question of how strongly to support local, regional, or national forms as opposed to those from abroad has also been central to aesthetic debates in many countries. This is true despite the fact that Marx's overall philosophy spoke against nationalism, especially when it conflicted with class identification. Socialist governments in the developing world often assume power in the wake of colonialist aggression. Because their local forms have been belittled or repressed for years (or centuries) in favor of an imposed culture from abroad, the natural reaction of any new leadership is to dispense with internationalism and promote localism. Largely for this reason, the "rescue of cultural roots" has been a fundamental component of Cuban cultural policy since 1959 (Hart Dávalos 1988:23). Prevailing views contend, with some justification, that prior governments did little to support traditional music and that a barrage of products from abroad threatened to compromise, even destroy, much Cuban heritage. The danger of nationalist policies, as in the case of those related to class-based art, is that taken to extremes they can result in oppressive prohibitions.

It is difficult to determine what constitutes "local" and "foreign" culture within any society, but this is especially difficult in countries such as Cuba that developed as ports of call along international trade routes and whose expression has always incorporated diverse influences. Indeed, much of the strength of Cuba's culture derives from the fact that it has never been mono-ethnic, that its traditions do not derive from a single group but from many. Faced with these issues, the government for many years defined "foreign" primarily as North American or British and kept music from both countries out of the media. This had some positive effects. Isolationism helped local genres develop in unique ways. It may have also shielded the population from certain ideological influences related to consumerism or materialism, as intended. Yet blanket prohibitions against foreign culture also fostered a negative image of the revolution, since most viewed them as unnecessarily severe. By the late 1970s, the leadership itself eventually came to the same conclusion; progressive voices have argued since that any musical style (jazz, rock, funk, reggae, rap) can be "Cubanized" and that support of traditional music to the exclusion of other genres may be as detrimental to the country as the loss of its own folklore (Hernández 2002:73). At present, very few official restrictions remain on the consumption of foreign culture.

Aesthetic Issues

Marxist philosophy has often been used to advocate the creation of art with certain types of formal qualities as opposed to others. Debates over aesthetics speak to the central purpose of art, what it is trying to accomplish, and by extension how it might best achieve such goals. Some suggest that it should expose injustice or call the people to action. From this view, art and politics have the same goals: the betterment of society, the establishment of moral guidelines, and the regulation of civic activity. Mao Tse-tung appealed to artists observing suffering or oppression to use such anecdotes as their inspiration. They should concentrate on such things, he suggested, "typify the contradictions and struggles within them," and "produce works which awaken the masses, fire them with enthusiasm and impel them to unite and struggle to transform their environment" (Mao 1977:19). Castro made sim-

FIGURE 2. "Himno a la Demajagua" (Hymn to Demajagua), an example of the sort of sheet music with strong
political content printed by the revolutionary government
for many years. La Demajagua was a sugar plantation
near Manzanillo, originally owned by Carlos Manuel de
Céspedes. He helped organize the revolutionary wars
against Spain in 1868 and initiated the struggle at Demajagua, freeing his slaves and urging them to take up arms.
The lyrics of the song discuss the importance of patriot-
ism and liberty. Photo by the author, 2001.

ilar remarks during the First National Congress on Education and Culture
in 1971: "We valorize most those cultural and artistic creations that serve
a utilitarian function for the people, for humanity, that support the revin-
dication and liberation of humanity" (Castro in Leal 1982:242).[7] Miguel
Barnet has likewise asserted that Cuban art should "always contain an

ideological element" and "provide a body of cognitive social statements" (1983:58) to help orient the public (Fig. 2).

The ideal forms of socialist music would thus seem to be those that contain politicized messages. However, restricting art to the realm of political commentary risks downplaying a tremendous amount of the human experience—feelings of tenderness, cynicism, loneliness, impotence, melancholy, ambivalence, and so forth. It is also difficult to compose songs with overt political content that do not strike the public as dogmatic. Other compositions tend to be fresher but deviate from the aesthetic goal. Questions also surface about the role of abstraction and experimentation in a theory of socialist art. Are metaphorical texts, images, or sounds something to strive for to enrich experience, or are they to be avoided as confusing and potentially subversive? What about humor?

Again, various attitudes have prevailed through the years. In the Soviet Union, abstraction received support for a time but under Stalin came to be interpreted as a form of decadence. Leaders denounced those interested in nonspecific sounds or images as "profoundly alienated" from society and thus forced to fall back upon their own subjectivity (Dupré 1983:268). The trend reached maximum expression in the social realism movement, especially influential from the mid-1930s through the 1950s. Instigated by Stalin's friend Andrei Zhdanov, social realism involved prohibitions against modernist styles of art. It advocated instead grandiose representations of the "new socialist man" and new social prerogatives in an idealized context.[8] Within Cuba, social realism is most closely associated with the *ofensiva revolucionaria* of the late 1960s and early 1970s, though its merits were discussed by the leadership as early as 1961.[9] One interviewee related a story from the *ofensiva* about a young painter whom teachers expelled from his art program because in a work depicting the death of Ernesto Guevara he chose to paint the fatal bullet yellow rather than a more "natural" color (Díaz Pérez 1996, interview). This sort of aversion to abstraction is no longer a concern. Artists are much freer to pursue a diversity of stylistic trends, musical and otherwise, and intellectuals have spoken out openly against earlier dogmatism (e.g., Otero 2001:55).

Issues of Regulation and Control

Policies restricting artistic activity are difficult to investigate for various reasons. Little documentation exists on particular examples of censorship and the reasons for them. Additionally, wide discrepancies often exist between official pronouncements on the subject and the day-to-day experience of the people. And some policies may impact particular sectors of the culture indent and unhealthy, a nation with a history of colonial exploitation made rotten by excessive consumption (Partido Comunista de Cuba 1977:62). They question whether capitalism, as a form of economic organization geared toward the single-minded pursuit of financial gain, is well suited to support the arts. They argue that it does not encourage sufficient intellectual or cultural development since it prioritizes materialistic over humanistic pursuits. This often puts artists at a disadvantage, restricts their impact, and isolates them. Most members of society struggle with unappealing day jobs, perhaps hoping someday to achieve recognition in fields such as theater, music, or visual art but with few such opportunities. Those fortunate enough to secure employment as performers may find that they have to compromise their tastes in order to satisfy the demands of the marketplace. It may also be that knowing how to promote and publicize their artistic efforts becomes more important to their success or failure than the act of artistic creation itself. The capitalist artist can find "his temperament oppressed, his creation coopted, his right to glory and happiness suffocated" (Mariátegui 1967:14). While socialist cultural systems are not without flaws according to this critique, they provide valuable professional support for artists and help teach the public to appreciate the importance of their work.

Industrialization and urbanization in the eighteenth and nineteenth centuries led to the dissolution of rural communities as well as many of the forms of music and culture with which they were associated. Socialists suggest that, in their new roles as urban laborers, the working classes often lack both their earlier sense of cultural connectedness and the time to explore the arts. Capitalism supports only a relatively small group of professional musicians who entertain a passive, alienated majority. Performers of classical repertoire do not often disseminate their art to the masses (Guevara 1965:85), nor do they valorize the expression of other groups. Adding insult to injury, the magnates of industry appropriate the urban popular musics of the poor created in this difficult context—blues, R&B, reggae, rap—and return them to the people as a market product that must be paid for (León 1985:411).

Capitalist systems prioritize the exchange value of music, typically in recorded form, rather than its use value among performers and the public (Gramatges 1983:127). Big business contracts and promotes musicians based on their revenue potential; it tends not to consider other issues, such as the appropriate level of artistic diversity in the media or whether the public should be made aware of less familiar styles (Faya et al. 1996:75). Few policies regulate the dissemination of music aside from those based on supply and demand. Today, even more than in Marx's time, art in capitalist society has become a corporate investment. Educational programming on TV and the radio is marginalized, relegated to undesirable time slots or channels when it appears at all.

Theorists since Adorno have critiqued music making in capitalist countries as a stylistically controlled space, one that permits certain kinds of expression and excludes others. Adorno, paraphrasing Marx, suggested that popular music was a sort of sonorous "opiate of the masses" (Adorno 1992:21–38). By this he meant that industry leaders partially determine public taste, often deciding for themselves what music should circulate in the media and choosing not to promote material that is socially engaged or otherwise controversial. These actions are motivated by the desire to sell recordings, to find a musical "lowest common denominator" that appeals to the largest possible consumer group. For this reason, companies may release yet another Elvis Presley or Beatles anthology rather than focus consumer attention on newer talent. In the past fifteen years, as the result of mergers, the executives of a mere four or five corporations have become responsible for determining the substance of roughly 93 percent of all (legal) commercially available music on the planet (Feld 1992:4). This has resulted in a homogenization of music, with media programming becoming increasingly less varied.

Local folkloric expression, to the extent that it is performed in public, tends to be marginalized from the central currents of the media. Record companies may ignore folk music because the consumer group interested in it is too small to be profitable (Barnet 1983:43). Folk genres often become exoticized, turned into minor, picturesque forms doomed to be heard only at specialty events or in museums. Those who perform them remain at the margins of society, it is argued, victims of exploitation who are kept from taking part fully in its progress and benefits (Martínez Furé 1979:258).

Musical trends can develop as genuine forms of grassroots expression (e.g., 1920s calypso, 1950s R&B, early New York salsa), but they can also be imposed and maintained artificially through promotion (the twist, the lambada). As the result of corporate manipulation, popular expression in capitalist societies is often associated with artificially rapid changes in style. Industry instigates fads as a marketing ploy. Industry can also help "make" stars or hits through promotional mechanisms. Díaz Pérez (1994:18–19) criticizes the music establishment's tendency to generate an endless succession of young, attractive teen idols (Jennifer Lopez, Ricky Martin, Britney Spears); the emphasis placed on their physical beauty rather than their artistry and the romantic topics they sing about to the exclusion of others strike her as a ploy to distract youth from more pressing concerns.

To Acosta as well, the youth market promotes rebelliousness but in fruit-to the country that served as its original source of inspiration. Authors complain that the marketing of such transformed culture can result in the deformation and loss of traditions in the developing world. Examples of stylized quasi-Cuban works from the mid-twentieth century include Percy Faith's LP *North and South of the Border,* Morton Gould's *Jungle Drums,* and Richard Hayman's *Havana in Hi-Fi.* Leonardo Acosta refers to them as "pseudopopular." He considers them offensive, evidence of how big business caters shamelessly to U.S. preferences. Similar processes of stylization have appeared in the U.S. domestic market, for example in the emergence of "sweet jazz" and "city blues" of the 1920s and "schlock rock" of the late 1950s (Acosta 1982:50–55). All represent alterations of black, working-class expression in an attempt to make them more palatable to urban professionals.[16]

Businesses can have disastrous effects on developing nations even without producing pseudopop. The power of first-world industry and its ability to distribute to every corner of the globe means that it can easily saturate and engulf smaller countries in particular sounds. Without specific legislation to protect them, small nations are often defenseless against this onslaught (Wallis and Malm 1984). In the Cuba of the 1950s, for example, U.S. companies heavily influenced radio, television, and record production, using Cuban media to disseminate North American songs.[17] And though major record labels distribute North American products abroad with a vengeance, they are frequently unwilling to promote third-world artists because they don't consider them to have the same market potential (León 1985:426). This leads to a "back-of-the-bus" phenomenon, a hierarchy of cultural prominence, with developed nations towering over all others. Cultural inundation from abroad can lead to "grayout," the decline or disappearance of local practices (Feld 1988; Goodwin and Gore 1990). More broadly, it can also impose Western ideals and values associated with rampant consumerism, what Cuban critics often refer to disparagingly as the "American way of life."

The mass dissemination of foreign culture within developing nations can lead in some cases to a rejection of local forms. Postcolonial nations receiving sophisticated musical products from abroad may view their own expression as inferior. José Ardévol has suggested that Cubans of the 1950s rejected many local genres because they had come to believe that only European and North American culture deserved their consideration. Even classically trained Cubans performed few of their own works because local audiences had no interest in them. They refused to consider Cuban-born conductors for their own symphony orchestra, believing them incapable (Ardévol 1966:97, 112–19). In the same way that Frantz Fanon (1967) describes negative views about blackness emerging in the French Antilles as the result of the inculcation of European values, cultural impositions from abroad can lead to feelings of artistic inferiority.

> The creations of the oppressor nation are presented as objects of universal value, a standard against which the cultural products of the exploited country are measured. The latter are valued on the basis of how closely they conform to established foreign models. Those that diverge from them are deprecated and considered simple or inferior products. Dominant interests would have the oppressed country believe that the language, customs, habits, and arts of the oppressor are in every way superior to its own and that, in consequence, it will renounce its own nature, content itself with imitating, and distance itself from the forces that could contribute to its liberation. In so doing, it would not only impoverish itself but also leave itself spiritually and materially at the mercy of the enemy. (Partido Comunista de Cuba 1977:91)[18]

Socialist critics argue that colonialist biases can be found in other places, including the educational practices of the Western conservatory. Textbooks often characterize third-world arts in a patronizing or inadequate manner. Their implicit conception of what music is worth teaching continues to be limited in many cases to the works of a European elite between about 1750 and 1900. Yet Western composers have hypocritically availed themselves of non-Western repertoire as raw material for countless new compositions. Their own works of "exotic" inspiration, far from being disparaged, are hailed as exciting contributions to "universal" literature. Some of these pieces are inspired by the traditional music of foreign countries (Bizet's arias in *Carmen* based on the Cuban *habanera*, Messiaen's *Harawi* with its Andean themes) or may derive from the music of "interior colonies," marginal enclaves within the developed world (Edward MacDowell's *Indian Suites*, Stravinsky's *Ragtime*), but the dynamic is largely the same. Acosta describes these works as a sort of "imaginary folklore" that implicitly attempts to supplant the original (1982:40). Without necessarily intending to, they create cultural hierarchies, classical works perceived as more important than those they take inspiration from. By extension, they legitimate the cultural dominance of the developed over the developing world.

·　·　·　·　·

This section provides an introduction to socialist aesthetic principles, discussing the motivations of policy makers influenced by them and the importance of culture to the new societies they construct. Cuba has always been home to many forms of music and dance; the revolutionary government supports traditional expression but also encourages new kinds of performance and creates new contexts for it. Leaders resist letting laws of supply and demand freely determine what music the public will hear. They exhort musicians to think about their society and its values and to write pieces that reflect such values. Ideally, they believe that art should not only appeal aesthetically but contribute actively in some way to making the world a better place. One of Fidel Castro's appeals to the Union of Young Communists (UJC) applies equally well to performers: "This is what we ask of future generations, that they know how to make a difference."[19] The specific institutions created to support the arts and the most important musical genres that have developed since 1959 represent the focus of following chapters.

In the same way that Marxist perspectives help us view capitalist society in a new light, Marxist-influenced theories of art help us view music itself in new ways. The critiques of the entertainment industry discussed earlier represent views from various countries but especially developing nations that have been affected in negative ways by first-world culture commerce. We need to evaluate this discourse with care and determine where the rhetoric ends and the truth begins. Many critiques ring true, in part. Of course, they often refer to music abstractly, avoiding references to specific performers, audiences, or historical periods. Note that younger Cubans expressing such views often have limited firsthand experience with capitalism. Unable to travel easily and with little financial support for research, they may base their conclusions only on commercial music heard within their own countries or on the impressions of others. Authors intimately familiar with market-based economies may have more nuanced opinions.

Marx's vision, while brilliant, has been problematic in various respects. By advocating a "dictatorship of the proletariat," his writings have led to the concentration of political power in monolithic institutions that often abuse their authority. And his assertion that violent revolution is the only means of instigating meaningful social change is not supported by history. If alive today, he might be surprised that nominally capitalist countries (Sweden, Finland, Switzerland) have adopted laws guaranteeing many of the rights associated with the socialist future he envisioned. One might argue that these countries actually have drawn closer to the social utopia Marx envisioned than those that took up arms in his name. Of course, progressive European nations represent the exception rather than the rule from a global perspective; capitalist governments and businesses continue to make decisions that have dire international consequences. Many of the world's ongoing conflicts derive ultimately from class stratification and disparities in wealth perpetuated by capitalism. Even the United States, despite its vast wealth, has never managed even to provide adequate health care or educational services to its own population.

Marx's work has proven especially limited in its applicability to the arts. As a result, policies under state socialism have been erratic, with officials struggling to map political and economic ideals onto cultural agendas by trial and error. The history of almost every revolutionary society reflects this lack of orientation; initiatives change frequently because of new leadership, the establishment of new administrative structures, or unrelated external events. Views of "appropriate" revolutionary art may be inclusive or decidedly restrictive at any given time. At least as important, those managing cultural affairs may be highly qualified or decidedly unqualified; their level of expertise affects the state's efforts to effectively promote culture. Further research is needed on the origin and nature of state policies, their relationship to orthodox Marxism, and the relationship between socialist discourse and the practice of its institutions.

CHAPTER 1

Revelry and Revolution

The Paradox of the 1950s

> It is possible that other epochs of our history may have produced
> works of greater quality. But in terms of sheer volume there is no
> period associated with more musical performance or production than
> the decade of the 1950s. . . . The vast majority of the music listened
> to in Cuba for years afterward and almost all of what continues to
> be heard in Cuban exile communities comes from that same music.
> And a majority of the new music made abroad, among Cubans and
> Latinos more generally, has been influenced by those same recordings.
>
> CRISTÓBAL DÍAZ AYALA, *Música cubana del areyto a la nueva trova*

Memories of Cuba in the 1940s and 1950s vary widely; they represent a
point of tension between those sympathetic to the socialist revolution and
others ambivalent or opposed to it. From the vantage of the present, prerevolutionary memories can be used to justify the actions of revolutionaries or to criticize them and thus retain discursive significance. Authors often
discuss the period in essentialized terms. Supporters of socialist Cuba have
tended to characterize the "pseudo-republic" as one of the darkest periods
of the country's history. To them, midcentury life was fundamentally
marred by the effects of government corruption and political violence as well
as by widespread social ills—racism, class division, organized crime, gambling, prostitution, unemployment—and deficiencies in public education and
other social services.[1] They stress Cuba's subservience to North American
interests and the fact that it had never achieved the autonomy aspired to in
1898 and 1933.

Cubans in exile, by contrast, often ignore or downplay the period's problems. They instead emphasize its many positive features, including its large
professional class, cosmopolitan intelligentsia, nightlife, media stars, and
world-renowned performers. Cuba was undeniably one of the most affluent
Latin American countries in the 1950s, and North Americans were not alone
in considering it an unlikely site of socialist revolution (Llenera 1978:11).
Its standard of living was high, roughly equal with that of poorer European
countries such as Spain and Italy (Goldenberg 1965:120). The growth of its

entertainment and mass media industries in the mid-twentieth century was absolutely phenomenal. By 1958, the island already boasted 3 television channels and over 145 radio stations, including 5 national broadcasters, 45 shortwave stations, and 7 FM stations (Díaz Ayala 1981:213).[2] Cuba had more TV sets per capita than any other Latin American country (Fagen 1969:23). Cuban music became astoundingly popular during this decade at home and abroad, generating tremendous revenues. Curiously, the years of the bloodiest clashes with Batista's forces in the late 1950s were also those in which domestic musical entertainment achieved an absolute peak. Batista's final years in power are thus associated simultaneously with pleasure and political repression, hedonism and terror (Rojas 1998:68).

It is difficult to reconcile these distinct realities and to understand what life was actually like for local residents. Did most citizens recognize the social and political problems that existed around them? If so, did such things predominate in their daily experience? Did they appreciate their relative affluence as a country or chafe at the inequity of its distribution? Rosalie Schwartz, whose work focuses on representations of Cuba in the foreign and national media, has described presocialist Cuba as various things for various groups, "a holiday paradise in the midst of a political hell" (1997:167). She demonstrates that conflicting visions of the nation competed in the media even at that time. Especially after 1957, coverage of bombings, assassinations, and violence shared newspaper space with descriptions of carnival festivities, yacht races, golf championships, and openings of new cabarets. In many respects, debates over the 1959 revolution have manifested in a struggle over representations of the past, the editing and foregrounding of historical data.

This chapter provides an overview of the 1950s and examines the apparent disconnect between the growing political anarchy of the period and the artistic life with which it was associated. It focuses not on why revolution took place in Cuba or how the primarily reformist agenda of most rebels was quickly radicalized into a Marxist-Leninist position, as these paradoxes have been the focus of others (e.g., Ruiz 1968). Instead, it asks how a country with many social problems, and one eventually in a state of civil war, could have simultaneously been the site of amazingly vibrant musical development. Analysis suggests that the political conflicts of the period did not originate with Batista but reflected long-standing tensions related to foreign dominance and political corruption. The prominence of music resulted from the society's orientation toward tourism, its support of stage entertainment of virtually any kind, and the relatively direct access of Cuban performers to U.S. markets. The extent of artistic creativity also reflected a nation with

toward rule by constitutional law had been "unceremoniously shunted aside" (Luis Pérez 1999:446) by Batista's actions. Beginning a year or so later, groups vying for power abandoned political discussion in favor of violence. The process begun in the 1940s in which disputes increasingly came to be resolved by warring gangs of gunmen, policemen, ex-ministers, officers, and students (Thomas 1971:886) became even more pronounced.

This spirit of anarchy and growing radicalism is what fueled the famous attack organized by Castro on the Moncada garrison in Santiago on July 26, 1953. His 26th of July movement failed resoundingly in this initial effort, yet its very audacity brought Castro to national attention. The remainder of the decade witnessed an intensification of acts of violence against the government. It also saw the return of Castro, who had been exiled, and a group of supporters who eventually initiated guerrilla raids against military targets in Oriente. Wayne Smith (1987:38) mentions particular songs that the public came to associate with Castro's *barbudos* (bearded soldiers), including the Mexican *ranchera* "La cama de piedra," civil war songs from Spain, and "Son de la loma" by Miguel Matamoros. Cristóbal Díaz Ayala recalls others such as "Clave a Martí," a favorite of Esther Borja's, and the children's song "El ratoncito Miguel" by Félix Caignet (pers. comm.). Batista eventually banned "Son de la loma" from the radio because of its associations with the insurgents and their "Radio Rebelde" broadcasts.

By 1957, random bombings and other sabotage were commonplace across the island, and the regime became more ruthless in its attempts to retain political control. Several of Batista's military leaders gained notoriety for their bloody tactics: Carlos Tabernilla Doltz and Alberto Ríos Chaviano in Santiago and chiefs of the Secret Police Ugalde Carrillo and Captain Esteban Ventura in Havana, among others. By 1958, perceiving that Batista was absolutely discredited among Cubans of every political affiliation and class, the United States finally imposed an arms embargo against him. In May 1958, his army failed in a final offensive against the guerrillas and began losing territory. On New Year's Eve 1958, Batista fled the country with a few of his closest supporters, leaving revolutionary forces free to take control of the capital.

MIDCENTURY SOCIETY

Guillermo Cabrera Infante's *Tres tristes tigres*, written by an admirer of 1950s Cuba, provides a window on what it was like to live in Havana at that time. The novel depicts a city with a large, well-educated, cosmopolitan pro-

FIGURE 3. The impoverished Havana barrio of La Timba, 1951. Parts of this neighborhood still exist, but much of it was torn down to construct what is now the Plaza of the Revolution. Political leaders in Cuba since 1959 have employed images like this one as a means of characterizing the prerevolutionary era as plagued by severe social problems; *Bohemia* magazine reprinted countless similar photos in its "La Cuba de ayer" series. Archives, the Cuban Heritage Collection, University of Miami.

fessional class, enamored of its cabarets and clubs, given to sensual pursuits and the full enjoyment of life. This group, primarily of white/Hispanic origin, lived well and chose for the most part to ignore problems in the countryside and in marginal urban neighborhoods (Fig. 3). Ruiz (1968:153) describes the society as one "in which rich and poor lived in separate worlds." Cuba had more telephones and cars per capita than virtually any other Latin American country, yet a large underclass could not afford them. Educational levels varied widely, with school enrollment in urban areas reaching nearly 70 percent but less than half that amount in rural areas. Many of those in smaller towns—about 40 percent of the population—had less than a third-grade education and lived in severe poverty (Pérez-Stable 1993:28).[5] Land ownership tended to be concentrated in the hands of a small number of wealthy investors. Underemployment represented a pervasive problem, with about one-quarter of the labor force unable to secure adequate income. The

ated high profits, required little initial investment, and created a buffer against fluctuating sugar prices. It did, however, attract organized crime as well. Cubans themselves, no strangers to shady business dealings, found that North American mobsters extended such activities far beyond the realm of government contracts. Mob activities in the 1920s focused on illegal liquor shipments during Prohibition. They became more extensive in the mid-1930s after Batista and figures such as New York's Meyer Lansky reached "incredibly profitable" (Hinckle and Turner 1981:25, 288) business agreements.

Crackdowns on crime under Senator Estes Kefauver beginning in 1950 made gaming illegal in much of the United States. This led to the eventual bulk sale of slot machines and other equipment to Cuba and increased the incentives for gangsters to relocate there. The Havana gambling industry grew rapidly by offering services to Americans that had been prohibited at home. In the mid-1940s, mobster Charles "Lucky" Luciano took control of the Jockey Club and Casino Nacional. Others arriving shortly thereafter included Sam Tucket and Moe Dalitz, Norman Entratter, and Santo Trafficante Jr. Together, they controlled a majority of high-profit tourist businesses (Schwartz 1997:128), sharing earnings with Batista. Luis Pérez (1999:197, 471) describes Cuba of the late 1950s as supporting "a far-flung economy of commercialized vice," noting that gambling receipts alone exceeded $500,000 monthly. Of course, the mob's investments in hotels, casinos, racetracks, and the like simultaneously enhanced nightlife and contributed to the attractiveness of Havana for visitors (Benjamin 1990:125). Batista's profits through links to organized crime, though significant, represented only a small part of his network of graft that functioned in many other sectors.

MIDCENTURY MUSICAL LIFE

Cuba offered its first institutionalized music instruction to the public with the founding of what became known as the Conservatorio Nacional in the 1880s (Orovio 1992:55). A series of additional schools appeared shortly thereafter, most notably the Conservatorio Municipal de La Habana in 1903. It received significant government subsidies and offered instruction at no charge to all who passed the entrance exams (Gramatges 1982:124–25). The primary barrier to enrollment for most working-class students, therefore, seems not to have been the cost of matriculation but rather factors related to the difficulty of finding work as a classical performer upon graduation. Additionally, the school provided no stipends or loans to students to support them while enrolled. Nevertheless, a surprising number of performers from poor families, white and black, managed to train and graduate alongside members of the middle classes. Initially directed by Guillermo Tomás, the Conservatorio Municipal passed under the control of Amadeo Roldán in 1936 and eventually gave rise to an important national school of composition, the Grupo de Renovación Musical. Prominent individuals associated with it in the 1940s and 1950s include the group's founder, José Ardévol, along with Hilario González, Harold Gramatges, Gisela Hernández, Argeliers León, and Julián Orbón. Mario Bauzá, Juan Blanco, Paquito D'Rivera, and Chucho Valdés are but a few of the renowned figures who completed their studies at the Conservatorio Municipal prior to 1959.

By the late 1920s, approximately thirty-five additional conservatories had been established in Havana alone, many opening branches across the island. The city's Pro-Arte Musical Society (established in 1918) and Sociedad Liceum and Lawn Tennis Club regularly sponsored a variety of classical events.[8] Cuba boasted an excellent symphony orchestra as of the early 1920s and later featured world-class guest artists and conductors such as Kleiber, Stravinsky, and Villa-Lobos.[9] In 1931, María Muñoz de Quevedo established a choral society, with José Ardévol creating a professional chamber orchestra shortly thereafter. Eduardo Calero Martín's 1,100-page compendium, *Cuba musical* (1929), with lists and photos of over 160 smaller music schools and approximately 1,850 music teachers, makes apparent the extent of interest in music at the time. The government encouraged involvement in the arts with the establishment in 1934 of a cultural division within the ministry of education (Weiss 1985:119). Its influence, however, was limited, as was its patronage, though it did offer nominal funds to classical ensembles.

Music education and performance continued to face financial limitations in subsequent decades. José Ardévol's chamber group received only meager support from patrons, in part because its members wished to promote early music and twentieth-century composition in addition to more-standard European repertoire; it disbanded in 1952 for lack of funding.[10] The Havana Philharmonic faced a similar crisis a few years later (Acosta 2002:12, 53–58). José Lezama Lima's literary magazine *Orígenes* also ceased publication in 1956 because of insufficient funds, owing to the withdrawal of support by José Rodríguez Feo. Little if any music by twentieth-century Cuban composers was published within Cuba before 1959 (Ardévol 1966:74). In general, salaries offered to performers in the symphony were meager, averaging about one hundred pesos a month and paid only for half the year.

Nevertheless, throughout the 1940s and 1950s the numbers of formally trained performers continued to grow. Census data from 1943 indicates that out of a total population of 4,800,000, 3,402 Cubans identified themselves as

audiences by providing accessible entertainment. In general, they avoided issues of social critique in favor of lyrics foregrounding humor or romance. Dance pieces and boleros dominated their repertoire. The music industry of the 1950s placed great emphasis on the physical appearance of artists and strove to make their stage presentations memorable. Cabaret spectacles reached an absolute peak at this time, replete with sequined gowns, elaborate group choreographies, and flashy arrangements for large orchestras. Growth in the tourist sector through 1956, increased income from gambling, an expanding local economy, and other factors led to a dramatic rise in commercial music making. Because of the number of performers, their professional options, and the extent of their influence abroad, the "fabulous fifties" (Díaz Ayala 1981:205) represented a period of phenomenal opportunity for popular musicians. By contrast, performers of folk music had relatively few options. Biases against African-derived genres especially meant that those involved with such repertoire could rarely perform in public or record. Music schools included very little instruction related to traditional music of any sort (Lino Neira, pers. comm.). Folklore flourished in the black working-class neighborhoods of major cities and in rural towns but did not often appear on the radio or television. Its status might be likened to that of black gospel in the United States, given its strong influence on popular music but its near total invisibility for years in the marketplace.[12]

Noncommercial folk music traditions of many kinds existed, however. Examples include the songs of regional *santorales* (patron saint festivals); improvisational *música guajira* events with their varied string instruments; traditional rumba; *comparsa* carnival bands of distinct sorts in various cities; Haitian-influenced folklore such as *gagá* and *tumba francesa* in the east; Kongo *tambor yuka* and Palo ceremony; Abakuá processional music and other religious songs and drumming derived from various parts of Africa; and the *pregones* (songs) of street vendors. Few studied or wrote about folklore at this time, and government agencies were no exception. The only center dedicated to such endeavors was the Instituto Musical de Investigaciones Folklóricas, created through the efforts of Odilio Urfé in 1948 (Barnet 1983:133). Owing to its meager resources and the lack of middle-class interest in the subject, the institute had little impact on prerevolutionary cultural life. Singers with a background in folklore who did achieve commercial success tended to adapt their music to the marketplace by performing *música guajira "de salón,"* such as that written by Guillermo Portabales, or dance repertoire based on Afro-Cuban religious themes as popularized by Celina González and Reutilio Domínguez, or by incorporating elements of folk traditions into cabaret acts.[13]

Poets, novelists, and classical musicians worked in the shadow of the surrounding commercial culture just as folk musicians did, playing for a circumscribed public. To be an academic or intellectual in prerevolutionary Cuba was to be largely ignored by the local population (Machover 1995:18). It was almost impossible to make a viable living as a conservatory artist or in the humanities; almost everyone who chose such a career was independently wealthy or held additional jobs in unrelated fields. Carlos Alberto Montaner, by no means a Castro supporter, describes the Cuban bourgeoisie of the 1950s as decidedly shallow in cultural terms (see Montaner 1985:145). Others agree that before the revolution writers Virgilio Piñeira, Alejo Carpentier, and Lydia Cabrera, painters Wifredo Lam and Amelia Peláez, and composers Harold Gramatges and José Ardévol were practically unknown within Cuba itself (Kirk and Padura Fuentes 2001:21, 96; de la Vega 2001:55). Ardévol commented in 1956 that there was perhaps no other place in Latin America where classical composers received less moral and material support than Havana (Ardévol 1966:70). To the extent that an audience for classical music existed among the middle class, it supported nineteenth-century European repertoire rather than Cuban composers.

Yet despite their relative anonymity at home, these and other cultural figures thrived and often became internationally recognized. Ballet and theater, too, had modest domestic audiences. Alicia Alonso's government-subsidized dance troupe performed to enthusiastic audiences in the Teatro Auditorium, though some middle-class families refused to let their daughters take part because they considered sweating unseemly (Kirk and Padura Fuentes 2001:45). Nearly a dozen acting troupes staged presentations in 1950s Havana and included works of a decidedly international character by Sartre, Ionesco, and others (Víctor Batista, pers. comm.). The frequency of classical music recitals, though modest, continued to grow during the 1950s in university settings, in middle-class *sociedades de recreo*, and on concert stages. The cultural society Nuestro Tiempo sponsored performances of works by Aurelio de la Vega, Juan Blanco, Julián Orbón, and other contemporary composers. De la Vega wrote the first pieces of serial music in Cuba in 1957 (Machover 1995:199).

The only exceptions to the relative marginality of classical artists were individuals who wrote "light" pieces for the musical theater or the piano. Opera and *zarzuela* (nationalist opera) compositions by Rodrigo Prats, Gonzalo Roig, Ernesto Lecuona, and others consistently generated large audiences. Many of the arias from their stage works were further popularized through sheet music sales. The number of internationally renowned vocalists who interpreted Cuban *zarzuela* works is striking: Ester Borja, Miguel

such as *Show* and *Gente*, one cannot help but note with amazement the magnitude and extravagance of entertainment in urban areas (Fig. 4). The number of internationally recognized artists and groups emerging at this time is almost beyond belief: singers Celia Cruz, La Lupe, and Benny Moré; *filin* artists Ángel Díaz and Omara Portuondo; traditional *soneros* Guillermo Portabales and Francisco Repilado; the *charangas* of José Fajardo, Antonio Arcaño, and the Orquesta Aragón; the *conjuntos* of Arsenio Rodríguez, Félix Chappottín, and the Sonora Matancera; Dámaso Pérez Prado with his mambo; and the jazz bands Orquesta Riverside and Orquesta Siboney, to mention only a handful. The 1950s was a decidedly internationalist period in which bands toured constantly throughout the Americas and Europe, and foreign pop stars—Josephine Baker, Nat "King" Cole, Xavier Cugat, Carmen Miranda, Pedro Infante, the Trio Los Panchos, Ima Sumac, Libertad Lamarque—appeared just as often on Cuban stages.

Havana was the unquestioned center of nightlife, offering diverse entertainment options for locals and visitors alike. Bars and restaurants could be found everywhere, among the most famous being the Floridita, said to have been frequented by Hemingway, and Sloppy Joe's on Zulueta Street. Clubs and cabarets existed in all sizes, from smaller, intimate, and bohemian (the Alí Bar, the Las Vegas, the Palermo, the Alloy) to lavish and expansive (the Montmartre, Salón Rojo, the Sans Souci).[15] Some were located in the heart of the city, for instance in the hotels of Vedado and Habana Vieja, while others (the Bambú, Johnny's Dream Club, Club 66, at least a half-dozen on the beaches of Marianao) operated at a discreet distance.[16] Interestingly, Cubans themselves represented the majority of the patrons rather than foreigners (Díaz Ayala 1981:212). The vast majority of entertainers performed to live musical accompaniment.

Perhaps the most well-known cabaret was the Tropicana, opening its doors for the first time in 1939. After its acquisition by Martín Fox in 1941, the establishment expanded considerably, opening a casino and featuring an extravagant dinner show (Lam 1999b). The latter presented acts ranging from blackface comedy with Alberto Garrido and Federico Piñeiro to singers and musicians to the legendary dance choreographies of Roderico "Rodney" Neyra, often with as many as seventy dancers in elaborate costumes. Bandleaders working in the Tropicana over the years included pianists Alfredo Brito and Armando Romeu. Other renowned instrumentalists filled the house orchestra: pianist Bebo Valdés, arranger Chico O'Farrill, trumpeter Chocolate Armenteros, and saxophonist Paquito D'Rivera (D'Rivera 1998:61). Schwartz estimates that this establishment, in conjunction with the cabarets in the Riviera, Nacional, and Capri Hotels, generated $50,000 weekly in gross

FIGURE 4. Floor show in the Cabaret Montmartre, Havana. This image comes from the December 1955 issue of *Show* magazine. Soprano María Marcos appears center stage in black as part of the revue "Midnight in Paris." Supporting singers and dancers include Olga Navarro, Teté Machado, Ofelia Gómez, Carmita González, Ada Armil, and Emy de Mendoza. The thousands of photos from *Show* and related publications testify to the splendor and extravagance of Cuban nightlife at this time, even as the country moved closer to open civil war.

revenues by the mid-1950s (Schwartz 1997:197). Revenues from gambling subsidized the floor shows and made opulent stage presentations economically viable.

Some authors (e.g., Luis Pérez 1999) emphasize the strong influence of foreign, especially North American, culture on midcentury Cuba and suggest that local traditions were in the process of being diluted or lost. Certainly foreign influences abounded in Cuba, from Christmas trees to pancakes to rock and roll. Nationalists on the island have noted this since at least the turn of the twentieth century (Linares 1970:106–107), associating North American culture with political and economic dominance; such criticisms appear even more frequently after the 1959 revolution. However, Cuba as an island has always been a nexus of influences; this diversity contributes to the richness of its art forms. The *contradanzas* and *danzas,* for instance, which constitute Cuba's earliest national music genres, could never have developed without strong influences from France, Haiti, and Spain. It is probable that foreign influences would have increasingly become a liability rather than an asset had Cuba remained part of the capitalist world after 1959. Yet one thing is certain: some of the decade's most characteristic forms of expression—the jazz-influenced big band music of Benny Moré

case because of its origins among working-class blacks (Torres 1995:209). On the other hand, younger Cubans no longer danced the traditional *danzón* enthusiastically or even learned to execute all of its varied steps. Faced with this dilemma, *charangas* adopted the chachachá instead of the *danzón* as a means of attracting a wider audience. The new music was essentially a slower and less syncopated version of the *son*. Its bass patterns emphasized the downbeat rather than weak beats, and its timbal bell patterns marked steady quarter- and eighth-note rhythms. Chachachá choreography was similar to that of the *son* as well but included a shuffle step every four beats. The sound of this shuffle apparently inspired the name of the genre.

Violinist and composer Enrique Jorrín (1926–87) wrote some of the most popular early chachachás beginning in about 1953. At that time, he formed part of the Orquesta América. It was this ensemble that made famous the unison vocals and overall sound of the new genre that would be further promoted by José Fajardo (1919–2001), the Orquesta Aragón, and others. Example 1 comes from the final vamp of "Que nos separa" by José Fajardo. The instruments notated are accompanied by congas, timbales, and *güiro*. The relatively straight bass line and slow tempo of "Que nos separa" make the piece easy to dance, yet it retains the chord sequence, call-response format, syncopated *guajeo*, and improvisational emphasis associated with the *son*. Unison vocals alternate in this example with Fajardo's flute solo.

Mambo has been used in various ways over the years and merits clarification. The word comes from a Kongo term meaning "conversation," "message," or "chant" and originally referred to acts of magic projected through song during religious events (Ortiz [1950] 1965:235, 244).[18] Since then it has acquired new meanings, but in reference to popular music it has two common usages. The first is simply a *montuno*-like sectional interlude within a composition, during which one or more syncopated melodic riffs is repeated many times by strings, horns, or both. This kind of mambo usually represents a climax point within a composition, just as the original mambo did in a sacred context. One can understand why Orestes López chose to give his modified *danzón* of 1937 the title "Mambo," given the nature of the looping violin phrases in the final vamp. Various Cuban dance bands have referred to "mambos" in this sense since that time (Acosta 1983:69). The practice may have originated with Orestes and Israel López or in the *conjunto* of Arsenio Rodríguez (he later claimed to have invented the genre),[19] or it may have caught on among several groups more or less simultaneously.

The second, related meaning of *mambo* refers to a distinct musical genre (not just a section) for Cuban jazz band based exclusively on the final sec-

EXAMPLE 1.   Excerpt, final segment of the chachachá "Que nos separa," recorded by José Fajardo and his orchestra (Fajardo 1995).

tion of the *danzones de nuevo ritmo*. This is the meaning that has gained the most recognition internationally, in large part because of the success of recordings by bandleader Dámaso Pérez Prado beginning in 1949. The "big band mambo" draws on North American culture nearly as much as Caribbean sources; perhaps not surprisingly, it has been performed in Mexico, the United States, and elsewhere at least as often as in Cuba itself. The primary exponents of this mambo represented an artistic vanguard that wanted to "stretch" the sound of dance repertoire to include new harmonies and new forms of orchestration. Aside from Pérez Prado, others who contributed to its development included pianists Bebo Valdés and René Hernández. They all experimented with the big band format, searching for new ways to reconcile its sonorities with the rhythms of Afro-Cuban folklore. Cuban audiences reacted tepidly to their compositions at first, perceiving them as too experimental. Yet the mambo had a strong impact on domestic dance bands in later years, including the wildly popular *banda gigante* of Benny Moré.

The sound of mambo bands was distinct from North American jazz bands despite their use of similar horn and rhythm sections. To begin with, Cuban groups incorporated the conga drums in addition to the drum set, and in the late 1950s, some used the bongo and timbales as well. Percussion featured more prominently in the overall mambo mix than was common in jazz at that time. Melodic lines played by the saxophones, trumpets, and trombone(s) tended to be more repetitive and syncopated than in jazz. The formal structure of most mambos consisted of infinite variations on a single repeated section in the same key rather than a progression through finite sections in different keys. Perhaps most strikingly, the texture of the mambo was created through a process of layering melodies against one another instead of foregrounding a principal melody against supporting harmonies. Acosta (2000:167–68) describes the sound in this way:

> In the face of the predominant tendency in jazz since the 1930s to fill up ever more completely the sound of the orchestra, fusing instruments from different sections . . . [Pérez Prado and other composers of the mambo] do exactly the opposite, establishing distinct planes of sound in two basic registers: one high with the trumpets and another low with the saxes in constant counterpoint. Additionally, the function of the horn sections is more typically "melodic-rhythmic" rather than "melodic-harmonic."

This kind of structure, involving interlocking hocket melodies and recurrent ostinato figures lending themselves to improvisation, reflects the influence of African aesthetics. Not surprisingly, other genres such as the folkloric rumba and the *guaracha* are structured in essentially the same fashion and seem to have been used as a conceptual model (consciously or unconsciously) for the creation of the genre. One should note that mambo choreography as popularized by Pérez Prado was distinct from that of the Cuban *son*. Dancers' appropriation of the word *mambo* over the years has been as confusing as musicians', since they use it to describe the basic international salsa step (a fusion of choreography derived from the *son* with influences from swing), a specific New York variant of salsa choreography (also referred to as "mambo on two"), and the original step without distinction.

The importance of Dámaso Pérez Prado (1916–89) to the development of the mambo genre can hardly be overemphasized; it is he who should be given credit for defining it. Pérez Prado grew up surrounded by Afro-Cuban folklore in his native Matanzas. His mother was a schoolteacher, and his father sold newspapers. As a child he studied classical piano with Rafael Somavilla at the Principal School of Matanzas, and as a young man he played organ and piano in local cinemas and clubs.[20] In 1942, Pérez Prado moved to Havana; he began performing in local cabarets such as the Kursaal and Pennsylvania and soon thereafter became a pianist and arranger for the Orquesta Casino de la Playa. His arrangements and piano solos as part of that group demonstrate an interest in melodic syncopation, dissonance, and extended harmonies, including tone clusters.[21] His tendency to write repeating horn figures is also evident.

In 1948, the composer moved to Mexico, where he found more freedom to experiment with Latin jazz. The following year his group made its first recordings with RCA Víctor, which included his hit single "Que rico el mambo" (Pérez Firmat 1994:84). Characteristics of the Pérez Prado band include (1) a tendency to contrast extremely high trumpet lines against low, sustained pedal tones for the trombone; (2) having entire instrumental sections (the trumpets, the saxes) play unison lines against one another; (3) prominent use of the ride cymbal and cowbells throughout compositions; (4) the adoption of stylistic elements from jazz bands such as shakes, bends, glissandi, and (5) incorporation of the North American drum set. Acosta (1991:34) notes that Pérez Prado eventually developed two mambo styles, a slower mambo *caén* and the more typically rapid mambo *baitirí*. In later years, he recorded primarily non-mambo Latin standards that still incorporated many mambo elements.

Singer and songwriter Benny Moré (1919–63) was one of many musicians to perform with Pérez Prado and to incorporate elements of the mambo into the repertoire of Cuban dance bands. His biography is perhaps even more typical of popular musicians at the time. One of twenty children, Bartolomé Maximiliano Moré grew up in a poor black neighborhood named Guinea on the outskirts of San Isabel de las Lajas, near Cienfuegos. The town had been founded at the turn of the twentieth century by former slaves of the sugar plantation Caracas who were of Kongo origin; others arrived later of Yoruba ancestry (Díaz Ayala 1981:229). Leaving public school at age eleven in order to help support his family in agricultural work, Moré listened to a wide variety of music from an early age: *Regla de Palo* drumming and dance in the Casino Congo de Lajas, *bembé* rhythms, rumba, *tambor makuta*, Spanish-derived *punto* and *décima*, Mexican *rancheras, sones,* and boleros, and U.S. popular music. As a teenager he taught himself to play the guitar and began performing in small groups near the Central Vertientes sugar plantation. In 1940, he moved to Havana and spent years in poverty, singing for tips on street corners and in cafés. In 1945, the Conjunto Matamoros offered him his first professional contract, asking him along on a tour of Mexico. He accepted and stayed in the country for years afterward, singing with the ensemble Son Veracruz, in duet appearances with singer Lalo Montané (Orovio 1981:253) and in the big bands of Arturo Núñez and Rafael de la Paz. Shortly thereafter, Moré began rehearsing with the Pérez Prado orchestra, singing over sixty songs with them for the RCA Victor label. It was in Mexico that Moré made the first hit recordings of his own, notably "Bonito y sabroso" and "Pachito Eché" (Gurza 2003).

In 1950, Moré returned to Cuba and sang for a time in the orchestras of Bebo Valdés and Mariano Mercerón. By 1953, he had formed his own group that in its various incarnations included musicians who later established themselves as prominent solo artists (Chocolate Armenteros, Rolando La Serie, Generoso "El Tojo" Jiménez). Unable to read music, Moré nevertheless became a competent composer, singing the phrases of his pieces to arrangers Eduardo Cabrera, Pedro "Peruchín" Justiz, and Generoso Jiménez; they in turn notated them and created the scores. Moré's primary gift, however, lay in his ability as a vocal improviser. Recordings have captured some of his *soneos* that demonstrate amazing melodic creativity. As in the case of Pérez Prado's band, Moré worked essentially with Cuban jazz band instrumentation: numerous horns and a percussion section featuring drum set, congas, and bongo (Acosta 2002:42).

Music performed by the Moré orchestra is similar in some respects to that of the Pérez Prado band. It is less experimental, however, and includes more influences from traditional *son.* Many faster pieces are in binary form, with a strophic *canto* or verse followed by the cyclic *montuno* favored by Pérez Prado. Yet others, such as the famous "Mi sacoco," are essentially identical to the mambo (Ex. 2). "Mi sacoco" is constructed of a repeating eight-measure phrase over a major I–IV–V–IV progression. The vocal line consists of a call-response dialogue between the chorus and Moré, who improvises responses to their refrain. Trumpets, saxes, and trombones each have distinct melodies that enter and layer upon the next when cued by the director. Conga drums play a typical *tumbao* rhythm, and the timbales a *cáscara,* or shell pattern, derived ultimately from the *rumba guaguancó.* The result is an open-ended ostinato of interlocked elements that serves perfectly as a

EXAMPLE 2. Representative ostinati in Benny Moré's "Mi sacoco," a mambo-influenced composition from the 1950s *(Gran Serie Benny Moré Vol. II)*.

vehicle for spontaneous improvisation by vocal or instrumental soloists in the African tradition.

· · · · ·

Cuba in the 1950s remains difficult to comprehend in light of its many opposing representations and realities. Socially, the country was divided into a surprisingly large group of affluent urban professionals on the one hand and a mass of rural farmers and urban immigrants struggling to make ends meet on the other. It boasted one of the highest levels of per capita income in Latin America, yet the concentration of economic development in Havana as well as problems with discrimination deprived many of education, social services, and adequate employment. Politically the nation was in chaos, lorded over by dishonest presidents and military men. Fulgencio Batista is one example of the sort of opportunist who established control over the

51, no. 6 [February 8, 1959]: n.p.; archives, Cristóbal Díaz Ayala). Others joined clandestine resistance groups (the 26th of July movement, the Directorio Revolucionario) in an attempt to topple the government. Saxophonist Leonardo Acosta attests to having been part of these efforts, as was singer Manolo Fernández (Acosta, pers. comm.; Cristóbal Díaz Ayala, pers. comm.).[22] Dance bands such as the Orquesta Sublime and Orquesta Aragón as well as conductors and composers—Juan Blanco, Carlos Faxas, Adolfo Guzmán, Nilo Rodríguez, Rafael Somavilla—played secret fundraising benefits for the revolutionary cause or composed music with revolutionary themes (Melquiades Fundora Dino, Leonardo Acosta, pers. comm.; Ardévol 1966:200). Work for dance bands became less frequent in the late 1950s, especially outdoor community events. Members of the resistance contacted *sociedades de recreo*, cabarets, and other institutions, urging them not to celebrate as tensions escalated (Orejuela Martínez 2004:35–38), though this appears to have been effective only in smaller venues.

Among the most chilling of insurrectional acts were those carried out in cabarets themselves. While infrequent, they received significant media attention and negatively affected all facets of entertainment. On October 28, 1956, for instance, members of the Directorio Revolucionario entered the cabaret Montmarte and killed colonel Blanco Rico, chief intelligence officer under Batista, as he attempted to leave the building (Cirules 1999:19). Colonel Marcelo Tabernilla, son of Batista's notoriously ruthless chief of staff, was also wounded along with his wife. The event forced club manager Mario García to close down for a time and to take his entertainers on tour in South America. On New Year's Eve in 1956, Javier Pazos and other members of the 26th of July movement set off bombs in the Tropicana, blowing off the arm of a seventeen-year-old girl, injuring the daughter of a former police chief and half a dozen dancers and causing other damage (Thomas 1971:910). The Havana Hilton delayed its opening several months in 1958 because of a similar event (Acosta 2002:67).

Perhaps the paradox of the 1950s is less difficult to explain than it might first appear. The musical impact of the period was due to the increasing affluence of the country overall, the emphasis placed on nightlife and tourist entertainment within the national economy, and the existence of a large middle class with money to support a diversity of leisure activities and of a larger underclass with musical talent. Batista's coup of 1952 and the resulting political crisis were unrelated events that did not negatively affect the country's entertainers. On the contrary, it appears that political instability, rather than suppressing performance, functioned to encourage it in certain respects. Music and dance remained more popular than before, serving as a refuge from social concerns. Whether in Havana or in areas far from the capital, military offensives against the revolutionaries rarely kept José Fajardo, the Orquesta Aragón, and Celia Cruz from animating guests (Rojas 1998:68). Friendly relations between Cuba and the United States continued to encourage the growth of tourism and investment through at least 1957, leading to new opportunities for performers. Batista's links with organized crime and the spread of gambling directly supported the arts as well. Every new hotel or casino represented an additional source of revenue for the state and mafia at the same time that it created stage space. The hedonistic world of the Tropicana, Salon Rojo, and Hotel Nacional flourished, at least in part, because they served such interests as well as those of popular musicians. Gaming that supported Havana's nightlife provided much of the revenue for their self-serving activities.

idea that would have been inconceivable before 1959 (Kirk and Padura Fuentes 2001:46). Legislators initiated a series of other sweeping measures designed to benefit poorer working Cubans. They cut phone rates significantly, reduced rent prices by as much as 50 percent, lowered federal taxes, and protected domestic industries with new tariffs. All of this resulted in greater buying power and increased standards of living for the masses, making the new authorities very popular indeed. Pérez-Stable (1993:74), in commenting on the first months of the revolution, notes that no other leadership "had done so much to improve popular living standards in so short a time." Somewhat more controversial were initiatives involving the forced sale of large agricultural properties to the government with the goal of redistributing them to farmers.

The end of the Batista dictatorship served as a source of inspiration for many music compositions such as "Fidel ya llegó" (Fidel Has Arrived) by Rolando La Serie, "Como lo soñó Martí" (As Martí Dreamed It) by Juan Arrondo, and "Los barbudos" (The Bearded Ones) by José Fajardo.[1] Eduardo Saborit wrote "Cuba, que linda es Cuba" shortly thereafter on a trip to Austria, part of a delegation to the World Festival of Youth and Students sponsored by the Soviet Union. Celia Cruz recorded songs in support of the agrarian reform and similar initiatives, as did most everyone else (Orovio 2001, interview). Classical composers Hilario González, Harold Gramatges, and Juan Blanco wrote instrumental works inspired by the insurrection. Others—Leo Brouwer, Carlos Fariñas, Nilo Rodríguez—scored music for films that documented the positive social changes taking place since Batista's departure. Foreign musicians raised their voices in support of the victorious *guerrilleros* as well. Daniel Santos, long known for his support of the insurgents, traveled to revolutionary Cuba and performed there; Spaniard Pablo del Río recorded the *paso doble* "Alas de libertad" (Wings of Freedom). The government itself soon began to sponsor mass music celebrations, such as the First National Art Festival in May of 1959, and outdoor dance events in conjunction with carnival in April (Orejuela Martínez 2004:57, 61).

Singer and composer Carlos Puebla (1917–89), from the small eastern town of Manzanillo, is one of the most widely recognized musical figures of the early revolution. His father, José María Puebla, distinguished himself as a *mambí* fighter at the turn of the century and contributed to his son's political leanings. Carlos began playing guitar at informal gatherings where he earned a reputation early on as a talented lyricist (Suardíaz 1989). His compositions from the 1940s ("Quiero hablar contigo" [I Want to Speak with You], "Qué sé yo" [What Do I Know], "Te vieron con él" [I Saw You with Him]) foregrounded romantic subject matter, but later works became

ing as a refuge from social concerns. Whether in Havana or in areas far from the capital, military offensives against the revolutionaries rarely kept José Fajardo, the Orquesta Aragón, and Celia Cruz from animating guests (Rojas 1998:68). Friendly relations between Cuba and the United States continued to encourage the growth of tourism and investment through at least 1957, leading to new opportunities for performers. Batista's links with organized crime and the spread of gambling directly supported the arts as well. Every new hotel or casino represented an additional source of revenue for the state and mafia at the same time that it created stage space. The hedonistic world of the Tropicana, Salon Rojo, and Hotel Nacional flourished, at least in part, because they served such interests as well as those of popular musicians. Gaming that supported Havana's nightlife provided much of the revenue for their self-serving activities.

CHAPTER 2

Music and Social Change in the First Years

> I am convinced that we have chosen a path that will take us far. I be-
> lieve there will be no turning back, for the first time in our history,
> in the conquest of our complete sovereignty; that the full dignity of
> man will be a reality among us; that many of the dreams that we have
> warmly, agonizingly nurtured in the depths of our being will now
> be possible, converted into a beautiful presence; that possibilities that
> never existed before will open for the work of artists and intellectuals.
> JOSÉ ARDÉVOL, speech in the Municipal Conservatory of Havana, 1959

The sudden departure of Batista in the final days of 1958 and the occupa-
tion of the capital by opposition forces represented significant events to
Cubans in several respects. Those who had fought against the dictator did
so without significant external assistance; their success bolstered faith in the
country's ability to manage its own affairs. Revolutionary victory brought
an end to a period of undeniable political oppression and suggested that responsible constitutional rule soon would be restored. Beyond this, the
struggle represented the culmination of Cuba's many attempts to achieve
complete autonomy. Overtly, the battle had been against Batista, but for
many it also revolved around questions of independence from the United
States.

Batista's defeat caught the forces allied against him off guard; they had
few concrete plans to shape the political future of the nation, let alone a cultural agenda. Some of this lack of vision derived from the factional nature
of the resistance itself. Urban resistance fighters and officials of the preexisting Communist Party did not necessarily approve of Castro's leadership
but did not retain central positions in the new government. The first months
of the revolution witnessed a period of intense maneuvering that resulted
in the consolidation of power in the hands of Castro's 26th of July movement (Pérez-Stable 1993). It was this group that proceeded to formulate
most new policies.

The years following Batista's second coup, as we have seen, gave rise to
a politically illegitimate government that nevertheless supported an amaz-

56

ingly vibrant artistic life. The period immediately after 1959, by contrast, witnessed the emergence of a less corrupt government and a more egalitarian society with fewer social vices. Yet it was also one in which musical performance and recording became less prominent over time. There are various reasons for this, including the militarized state of the country, the onset of the U.S. embargo, the overall decline of the national economy, and Cuba's increasing isolation. Above all, the early revolutionary period was characterized by fundamental social, political, and economic change that disrupted infrastructures supporting the arts. While in many cases motivated by the best of intentions, these changes nevertheless had unexpected, often negative consequences. This chapter describes some of the early decisions of revolutionary leaders and their impact on entertainment. It provides background on political changes and documents the financial crisis soon faced by the music industry and the increasingly politicized context of music making.

IMMEDIATE POLITICAL AND CULTURAL CHANGE

As in the case of most revolutions, the first weeks witnessed a violent backlash against anyone believed to have associated with the previous leadership. Mob justice imposed itself on the more infamous figures of the secret police, as documented in issues of *Bohemia* magazine. Discredited officials quickly lost their jobs and in some cases were arrested and imprisoned. Purging of state agencies led to the firing of hundreds, perhaps thousands of employees (Thomas 1971:1068). Reorganization of the military became a priority, with garrisons passing into the hands of the victors and trials commencing for those who had been in charge of Batista's troops. Castro assumed a central role at this time in winning over the masses to new initiatives. He proved a brilliant statesman, appeasing the concerns of every group, refusing to associate himself with the Communist inclinations of Che Guevara and his brother Raúl, declaring the right of dissent and opposition to be fundamental, and meeting informally with Vice President Nixon and other members of the Eisenhower cabinet.

From its first months in existence, the provisional government began passing legislation that put an end to corruption of various sorts. They declared prostitution illegal and began programs to find alternate professions for women in the sex industry. They outlawed segregation, opening many beaches, cabarets, hotels, and private clubs to Cubans of color. The same period witnessed the integration of Alicia Alonso's ballet troupe for the first time. Alonso has noted that an integrated troupe was a truly revolutionary idea that would have been inconceivable before 1959 (Kirk and Padura Fuentes 2001:46). Legislators initiated a series of other sweeping measures designed to benefit poorer working Cubans. They cut phone rates significantly, reduced rent prices by as much as 50 percent, lowered federal taxes, and protected domestic industries with new tariffs. All of this resulted in greater buying power and increased standards of living for the masses, making the new authorities very popular indeed. Pérez-Stable (1993:74), in commenting on the first months of the revolution, notes that no other leadership "had done so much to improve popular living standards in so short a time." Somewhat more controversial were initiatives involving the forced sale of large agricultural properties to the government with the goal of redistributing them to farmers.

The end of the Batista dictatorship served as a source of inspiration for many music compositions such as "Fidel ya llegó" (Fidel Has Arrived) by Rolando La Serie, "Como lo soñó Martí" (As Martí Dreamed It) by Juan Arrondo, and "Los barbudos" (The Bearded Ones) by José Fajardo.[1] Eduardo Saborit wrote "Cuba, que linda es Cuba" shortly thereafter on a trip to Austria, part of a delegation to the World Festival of Youth and Students sponsored by the Soviet Union. Celia Cruz recorded songs in support of the agrarian reform and similar initiatives, as did most everyone else (Orovio 2001, interview). Classical composers Hilario González, Harold Gramatges, and Juan Blanco wrote instrumental works inspired by the insurrection. Others—Leo Brouwer, Carlos Fariñas, Nilo Rodríguez—scored music for films that documented the positive social changes taking place since Batista's departure. Foreign musicians raised their voices in support of the victorious *guerrilleros* as well. Daniel Santos, long known for his support of the insurgents, traveled to revolutionary Cuba and performed there; Spaniard Pablo del Río recorded the *paso doble* "Alas de libertad" (Wings of Freedom). The government itself soon began to sponsor mass music celebrations, such as the First National Art Festival in May of 1959, and outdoor dance events in conjunction with carnival in April (Orejuela Martínez 2004:57, 61).

Singer and composer Carlos Puebla (1917–89), from the small eastern town of Manzanillo, is one of the most widely recognized musical figures of the early revolution. His father, José María Puebla, distinguished himself as a *mambí* fighter at the turn of the century and contributed to his son's political leanings. Carlos began playing guitar at informal gatherings where he earned a reputation early on as a talented lyricist (Suardíaz 1989). His compositions from the 1940s ("Quiero hablar contigo" [I Want to Speak with You], "Qué sé yo" [What Do I Know], "Te vieron con él" [I Saw You with Him]) foregrounded romantic subject matter, but later works became

FIGURE 5.   Carlos Puebla and his quartet, Los Tradicionales, in El Boguedita del Medio restaurant, Habana Vieja, 1967. In the first years of the revolution, compositions by Puebla in support of government initiatives received heavy airplay, effectively becoming anthems of political change. Even today, they constitute some of the best-known songs from Cuba among international audiences. Photo Archive, Ministry of Culture, Cuba.

more socially engaged after his move to Havana in 1952 and the outcry over Batista's coup. Puebla performed at that time with La Clave Azul ensemble on live radio shows and later established himself in the Boguedita del Medio restaurant with a trio under his own direction, Los Tradicionales (Fig. 5). He sang and played lead guitar, accompanied by Santiago Martínez (rhythm guitar), Nero Guada (voice and maracas),[2] and Rafael Lorenzo (*marímbula* and bass). The quartet became known for pieces that satirized or criticized the government such as "Los caminos de mi Cuba" (The Pathways of My Cuba), "Ya tenemos hospital" (Now We Have a Hospital), "Plan de machete" (Machete Plan), and "¡Ay! pobre mi Cuba" (Oh, My Poor Cuba) (Sauri Olivia 1990:5). Díaz Pérez discusses the lyrics to "Ya tenemos hospital" in her work on Cuban protest song (1994:79). Puebla took inspiration for it from the Topes de Collantes Hospital project, one of Batista's public works initiatives. Planned as an institution devoted to tuberculosis research, its construction halted on multiple occasions as the result of embezzlement or cuts in funding. Topes de Collantes became a symbol of the rampant corruption of the period and the apparent disinterest of Batista in the welfare of the Cuban people in later years (Vázquez 1987).[3]

On January 3, 1959, Puebla became one of the first musicians to hail the triumph of the revolution with his composition "En eso llegó Fidel" (That's When Fidel Arrived). The song was followed in short order by others: "La reforma agraria va" (The Agrarian Reform Continues), "Canto a Camilo" (Songs to Camilo), and "Todos unidos" (Everyone United) (Vázquez 1987). His works received widespread airplay, converting them into revolutionary anthems. Puebla wrote his most famous piece, "Hasta siempre" (Until Forever), in 1965, inspired by the "Letter of Farewell" written by Che Guevara to Castro before heading to Bolivia in a fatal attempt to organize revolutionary activity there (Zaldívar 1983:3).

Almost all of the songs in Los Tradicionales's repertoire are based on slow, bolero- or *son*-derived dance rhythms and simple harmonic progressions influenced by rural styles. Indeed, in musical terms, the songs are rather formulaic. They begin with an instrumental introduction featuring florid melodies played on lead guitar. This is followed by a verse sung by Puebla alone and then a choral response in thirds sung by other members. Each of these three sections repeats several times in alternation. The musical style is best described as *son-guajiro*, one that uses a slow *son* as the basis for storytelling, primarily in four-line couplets. It is similar to that of other performers of the period from rural areas (Ñico Saquito, Joseíto Fernández, Guillermo Portabales). Puebla performed in cafés and other intimate venues in the style of turn-of-the-century *trovadores*, creating a sound intended primarily for listening rather than dancing. He was a master at textual improvisation; this was the single most important factor contributing to his popularity. His lyrics could be humorous, poking fun at opponents of the revolution ("Mucha cordura" [Much Wisdom], "La OEA es cosa de risa" [The OAS (Organization of American States) Is Laughable]), or stern but were unswervingly nationalistic.

During the first years of the revolution, Puebla took advantage of the new educational opportunities for popular musicians. He attended lectures on Cuban music organized by Odilio Urfé in Havana's Iglesia de Paula. Eventually he learned to read notation and studied music theory in a School of Professional Improvement. Los Tradicionales toured Latin America several times beginning in 1960. At home, they performed for factory workers and at union meetings as well as on the radio show *Traigo de Cuba un cantar* (From Cuba I Bring a Song) that used Puebla's eponymous composition as its theme (Suardíaz 1989).

CABARETS IN CRISIS

The angry mobs that roved the streets of Havana in the first days after Batista's departure targeted not only government collaborators but also large cabarets and casinos. Many of these closed their doors for a time as a result. Beginning on January 6, revolutionaries announced that no more violence or looting would be permitted and that such institutions could reopen, but the gaming areas of the Hotel Plaza, the Deauville, and the Sevilla had all suffered too much vandalism to do so immediately (Díaz Ayala 1981:267). Casinos seem to have been a special focus of mob attention because they contained cash and valuables.[4] Before most could repair the damage, leaders announced a national prohibition against gambling. The formal legislation appeared on February 11, as part of law 73, with the following commentary: "The previous regime, . . . with the intention of diverting public attention from its illicit activities, countenanced organized gambling in all of its manifestations to unimagined extremes, converting the Republic into a veritable den of gaming, an international center of the criminal underworld."[5]

Generally, the public supported the closure of casinos, despite the thousands of workers who found themselves unemployed as a result and the significant losses in federal revenues that followed. Legislation passed at approximately the same time closed *academias de baile* because of their associations with prostitution. A further casualty of the campaign to make Havana less vice-ridden were jukeboxes; they were considered noisy and were often used in red-light districts and neighborhood bars. Though jukeboxes were banned in February, outcry against the decision resulted in a policy reversal a few months later.[6] None of the pronouncements suggested that cabarets should close, and many did manage to reopen beginning in February. The most lavish, however, had always relied upon gambling to subsidize their stage acts and found it difficult to remain economically viable. Some cabaret owners made voluntary contributions to the government in support of revolutionary goals,[7] but most expressed concern over the severity of gambling legislation and its implications, fearing a loss of tourist revenue. Cabaret employees staged protests, trying to moderate the new policies (Fig. 6).[8]

By July, the entertainment industry as it had existed under Batista entered a stage of crisis. The combination of sharp decreases in tourism due to political instability and the closure of casinos made it nearly impossible for large cabarets to remain profitable. An unsigned article in *Bohemia* noted that the Palermo, Las Vegas, and a host of others shut their doors. "Havana

FIGURE 6.   Striking workers protest the closure of gambling casinos in Havana shortly after the triumph of the revolution. The sign reads: "We Beg That They Reopen. Artists of the Casino Parisien, Hotel Nacional." *Show* 61 (March 1959), p. 50.

has become as sad as a tango. The shows in the Sevilla Libre have been suspended. The Cabaret Nacional, Sans Souci, Colonial, and Deauville remain closed, and the El Río doesn't dare open. The Copa Room, Night and Day, and Sierra have been nationalized; the Tropicana is begging to be taken over as well" (*Bohemia* 51, no. 28 [July 12, 1959]: 142; see also *Bohemia* 51, no. 35 [August 30, 1959]: 122). By August, the Cabaret Montmartre, Habana 1900, and El Panchín in Marianao (previously owned by Panchín Batista, Fulgencio's brother) had shut down as well, though some eventually reopened. Many smaller clubs remained unaffected, however, and the Ministry of Tourism made sure that admission prices remained low enough in clubs it managed so that all Cubans would have access (Díaz Ayala 1981:284).

Toward the end of the year it became clear that most entertainment venues would need government support in order to survive; the state decided to nationalize all of them and put their workers on the payroll. In October, authorities began managing the Capri, Tropicana, Casino Parisién, and Salón Caribe cabarets, followed in January of 1960 by the Club El Río. Large hotels such as the Riviera and Sevilla had accrued debt as the result of high vacancy rates and soon lost their independent status as well (Schwartz 1997:203). In order to manage so many enterprises, the provisional government created a National Institute of Tourist Industries (El Instituto Nacional de la Industria Turística, or INIT) in November of 1959 under the direction of Juan Bradmann.[9] Its primary focus at that time was to coordinate stage entertainment and manage the largest hotels. By 1962, the same agency began overseeing entertainment in smaller clubs such as El Taíno and El Karachi.

INIT did much to resuscitate nightlife for a time, creating new jobs by organizing musical jam sessions and additional cabaret events (Thomas 1971:1352). Nevertheless, the inexperience of revolutionary leaders in this area created problems in the quality and organization of performances. After 1961, conflicts emerged between club managers and bureaucrats because of the latter's desire to dictate the content of shows.[10] The nationalization of cabarets was followed by private *sociedades de recreo* that year and the following year. They came under state control for various reasons: because they lost wealthier members to the exile community and were no longer economically viable; because the state appropriated their property as part of urban reform legislation; because they were believed to contribute to racial divisions; and because leaders feared counterrevolutionary activities might be organized in such institutions (Fundora Dino 2001, interview).

THE NEW CULTURAL ENVIRONMENT

Many artists and intellectuals living through the first years of the revolution describe the environment as exhilarating, with a great deal of room for experimentation and creativity (Kirk and Padura Fuentes 2001:56–57). Government representatives organized numerous events and initiatives, as did private citizens. The appearance of *Lunes de Revolución,* a weekly literary supplement directed by Carlos Franqui, Guillermo Cabrera Infante, and Pablo Armando Fernández, represents one example. From March 1959 through November 1961, the supplement appeared in the newspaper *Revolución,* offering readers exposure to some of the best nationally and internationally known authors of the day (Kirk and Padura Fuentes 2001:27). It featured relatively unknown Cubans—Antón Arrufat, Rine Leal, Ambrosio Fornet, Heberto Padilla, Lisandro Otero—as well as articles on film, music, dance, and plastic arts. Contributors expressed in the first issue a belief that the revolution had destroyed barriers dividing artists and intellectuals from the public and suggested that they wanted to integrate themselves more fully into national life (García 1980: vol. 1, 525).

Individuals across the island spontaneously offered lectures, concerts, dances, and other events at no charge. Mario Rodríguez Alemán helped organize a film series on the history of the medium (Fernández Pavón 1998, interview). Guillermo Cabrera Infante coordinated lectures in the National Museum of Art and invited Pablo Neruda and Jean-Paul Sartre to the country to take part. Arranger and bandleader Chico O'Farrill arrived from Mexico at the request of the Club Cubano de Jazz to organize free concerts in a newly inaugurated Workers' Palace.[11] Odilio Urfé organized presentations of traditional *son, makuta* drumming, and Abakuá music and multiple festivals (Orejuela Martínez 2004:100, 125–26). The government gave visibility to modern classical performance on television, airing Amadeo Roldán and Alejo Carpentier's ballet *La rembambaramba* in March of 1960 (see *Bohemia* 52, no. 13 [March 27, 1960]: 91), presenting educational broadcasts on radio station CMZ hosted by José Ardévol or Harold Gramatges, and inviting composers from neighboring Latin American countries to discuss their works at the Casa de las Américas. It even took symphony orchestras and virtuoso cellists out into the countryside to play for campesinos (Ardévol 1966:142, 215).

Labor and political organizations promoted tours of folklore ensembles across the country, something that had never been done before 1959.[12] Women of color (Gigi Ambar, Fredesbinda "Freddy" García, Gina León, Celeste Mendoza, Lupe Yolí) gained new prominence in the music industry as the country attempted to promote and revalorize its local heritage. Performers of traditional music from North India, China, and the Soviet Union played for Cuban audiences, adding new dimensions to local cultural offerings. Musicians who had been living abroad returned to Cuba in order to take part in the new environment: Aurelio de la Vega, José Antonio Méndez, Armando Oréfiche, Guillermo Portabales, Ñico Saquito, Gilberto Valdés, Armando Valdespí, and Pucho Escalante.[13] Writers abroad returned as well: Alejo Carpentier, Heberto Padilla, Pablo Armando Fernández, and so forth. Numerous dance forms emerged between 1961 and 1964, suggesting the fecundity of the popular music scene: Enrique Bonne and Pacho Alonso's *pilón*, Dámazo Pérez Prado's *dengue*, Pedro Izquierdo's *mozambique*, Juanito Márquez's *pacá*, and Félix Chapottín's *guarapachanga*.

The importance of culture in all its manifestations seems to have been recognized to a greater extent than before by revolutionaries. Performers and authors reveled in the opportunity to refashion artistic life, dedicating themselves to such pursuits with little concern for personal gain. Anton Arrufat remembers the period as a decidedly idealistic. "What had been important before no longer was. Morals began to change. People started to support each other, at least in human terms. The mental structures changed, people began to lose interest in money . . . [they] also lost interest in the clothes they wore. It was enough to have one pair of pants, a shirt, and a pair of boots. And people liked these changes" (as quoted in Kirk and Padura Fuentes 2001:26–27).

Beginning in the summer of 1961, the government undertook a massive campaign to eradicate illiteracy, sending nearly every high school student into rural areas at the end of the academic year to accomplish the task. Leaders took advantage of their departure to nationalize and reorganize all educational institutions, public and private. Catholic schools complained bitterly about the takeovers, to be sure, and many found fault with the new curriculum implemented in the fall that avoided religion and contained heavy doses of Marxism. Yet the changes had a number of positive results. School enrollment increased 20 percent by 1962 (Thomas 1971:1340), and of course all classes were offered free of charge. The poor benefited from access to new schools constructed in rural areas as well as to higher education.

Testimonies from musicians suggest that working conditions improved for them in the early years of the revolution. Melquíades Fundora Dino (2001, interview) remembers that municipal commissions (JUCEI) in charge of funding dance events paid more after 1959 than had their counterparts previously.[14] He believes that government officials were less corrupt and thus had more to spend. JUCEI's higher salaries applied to performers working in urban areas as well as in the *verbenas* (patron saint festivals) and theaters of smaller interior towns. Classical composers received significantly more financial support from the new government as well. Carlos Fariñas and Enrique Ubieta left to study at the Tchaikovsky Conservatory in Moscow in 1961 on full scholarship (Machover 1995:199; Orovio 1981:139). José Loyola studied shortly thereafter in Warsaw. Harold Gramatges, a more established figure, played a central role in elaborating the government's new cultural and educational policies, becoming ambassador to France between 1961 and 1964 before returning to work for the CNC. The only exception to early salary increases involved high-profile artists hired by nationalized venues. In general, the state curtailed the salary range of performers on its payroll. This meant that stars could no longer determine their own fees and had to content themselves with a more modest income.

The early 1960s gave rise to a surprisingly vibrant jazz scene in Havana. Paquito D'Rivera recalls that during the first three or four years of the revolution, "there was jazz everywhere you looked: in clubs like El Pigalle, La Red, El Pico Blanco, and one in Neptuno street called El Descarga-Club" (1998:95–96). The latter often featured Kike Villalta on piano and guitar,

Tomasito Vásquez on tenor sax, and Luís Quiñones on bass. Guitarists Martín Rojas and Carlos Emilio, pianist Frank Emilio, and trombonist Pucho Escalante distinguished themselves as prominent figures. The Quinteto de Música Moderna included percussionist Tata Güines, bassist Papito Hernández, and other phenomenal artists who established their reputations at this time. Jazz represented only one of a surprising number of North American influences that continued to manifest themselves in Cuban culture despite the increasingly tense political relations between Cuba and the United States. Shop owners sold miniskirts and Elvis Presley records in the same areas where anti-imperialist political demonstrations or militia exercises were organized. Beginning about 1963, nevertheless, hard-liners began to discourage the performance of jazz, especially on television and in radio broadcasts.[15] Their attitudes resulted in less support for *filin* because of its North American musical influences (Orejuela Martínez 2004:70–71, 161–63); in some cases, revolutionaries even accused *filin* proponents of "decadence" or even counterrevolutionary sentiment.[16] By 1967, the Orquesta Cubana de Música Moderna was one of very few jazz-influenced ensembles receiving coverage in the media (Acosta 2002:136).

CONSOLIDATION OF POLITICS AND MEDIA

The final months of 1959 gave rise to the first major political controversies associated with the revolution. Castro and others remained overwhelmingly popular, yet their increasingly close ties to Communist groups began to generate concern. In July of 1959, Castro forced President Urrutia to resign because of his anti-Communist statements and replaced him with the more pliant Osvaldo Dorticós. Commander Huber Matos lost his commission in Camagüey province and served twenty years in prison for expressing similar views. Oppositional voices in the provisional cabinet gradually lost their jobs or found themselves excluded from decision making. Camilo Cienfuegos, a hero of the revolutionary struggle known for his inclusive vision, disappeared in a plane crash during the Huber Matos affair under conditions that suggested foul play (Franqui 2001). In October, Raúl Castro assumed command of the army (Pérez 1988:324). Shortly thereafter, the leadership reorganized Cuba's trade unions and dismissed faculty at the university who did not support the new government. By mid-1960, no institution remained to rival Castro; in fact, very few independent organizations of any sort existed besides the church.

On the eve of the revolution, Cuba boasted many independently owned newspapers, radio stations, and television stations. A year and a half later, all presses and radio and television stations had either been placed under government control or ceased operation. Privately owned newspapers began to close as well, not because they were forced to but because the independent businesses that had supported them through advertising no longer existed (Nicols in Brenner et al. 1989:219). The last two to shut down in 1961 were the *Diario de la Marina* and *Prensa Libre*. Thomas (1971:1268) notes that while their demise was regrettable, the reputations of major newspapers had been tarnished in the mid-1950s: all accepted bribes from Batista in order to remain silent on controversial subjects.

Major theaters and concert halls passed into government hands in 1960. Pro-Arte's prominent Teatro Auditorium on Calzada and E was taken over in December, for instance, and later renamed the Teatro Amadeo Roldán. The motivation seems to have been populist, a desire to give the masses direct access to all forms of art in what had once been a bastion of the bourgeoisie. "It cannot be denied that, prior to the triumph of the Revolution, enjoyment of the highest manifestations of art were only the patrimony of a privileged minority. These groups, organized into exclusive institutions, denied poorer sectors of the population—who constitute the vast majority—access to the events that they patronized."[17] In the coming years, this venue would host Benny Moré's dance band and *comparsa* drumming ensembles in alternation with concerts of symphonic music, a truly populist change (Orejuela Martínez 2004:141).

Appropriations of private lands and properties and movement on the part of government toward closer ties with the Soviet Union led to counterrevolutionary activity by mid-1960. This was limited primarily to the professional classes and elites, however, as well as to Catholics. Nevertheless, by October of 1960, approximately ten thousand political prisoners filled Cuba's jails (Thomas 1971:1348). Counterrevolutionaries (some of whom had previously belonged to the 26th of July movement) began to commit acts of sabotage, including the arson fires that ravaged the El Encanto and La Época department stores. In March of 1960, President Eisenhower began funding domestic agitation of this sort covertly as well as arming Cuban exile groups (Pérez 1988:324). Violent opposition and intervention by the United States made the revolutionaries take an even harder line. They resisted holding elections, asserting that massive funding of antigovernment campaigns from abroad would influence voting and preclude a fair referendum on their government. On October 13, Washington cut off all normal diplomatic relations. On February 7, 1962, they initiated a total trade embargo against the country as well.[18]

ARTISTS AT HOME AND IN EXILE

The increasingly tense political context in Cuba soon led to an exodus of artists, part of a larger overall trend. Between 1960 and 1974, Cuba lost an average of about thirty thousand citizens a year to exile, not to mention the hundreds of thousands more who left subsequently (Domínguez 1978:140). No one has ever made an exhaustive study of the number of musicians who left, the dates of their departures, or their reasons for doing so. The Cuban press of the early 1960s is not much help in this regard, containing surprisingly few references to defections. Apparently the leadership felt that the emigration would reflect badly on it and instructed the media not to discuss the issue. One of the best sources on the departure of performers is *Bohemia Libre*, a magazine that appeared in New York in 1960 under the direction of Miguel Angel Quevedo. It followed artists' careers abroad in roughly the same way that *Bohemia* had previously. *Bohemia Libre* existed through 1965 but eventually lost financial support and ceased publication.

Among the first individuals to choose exile from culture-related professions were media executives such as Goar Mestre. Entertainers who opted for exile shortly thereafter include Xiomara Alfaro, Blanquita Amaro, Bobby Collazo, Celia Cruz and the Sonora Matancera, the orchestra of Ernesto Duarte, José Antonio Fajardo, composer Osvaldo Farrés, *negrito* comedian Alberto Garrido, Blanca Rosa Gil, Olga Guillot, Rolando La Serie, Ernesto Lecuona, and La Lupe.[19] Figures in other fields (critic Jorge Mañach, folklorist Lydia Cabrera, classical composer Aurelio de la Vega, etc.) left at approximately the same time. They chose exile for a mixture of reasons, both economic and political. Performers with multiple homes (Olga Guillot, Ernesto Lecuona) expressed outrage over property lost as the result of urban reform laws enacted in 1960. The legislation permitted individuals to own only a single residence and authorized the confiscation of others so they could be distributed to the poor.[20] Others left Cuba because of the autocratic style of the Castro leadership or out of fear of Communism itself. Political differences frequently led to conflicts within the same music ensemble; Helio Orovio (2001, interview) remembers that the band he played in, Los Trovadores del Cayo, fell apart in 1963 after half the members opted to leave the country.[21]

Those in charge of the media typically blacklisted artists if they left the country. The government never seems to have passed legislation to this effect, yet it advised managers of radio stations to stop playing their music and not to mention their names in print.[22] Yet the managers did not always know who had defected and had to constantly revise their record collections and cull the hits of performers who had left based largely on hearsay. Some defectors, such as Eduardo Davidson (the so-called inventor of the *pachanga*) in 1961, created special headaches because of their popularity (Díaz Ayala 1981:278). On occasion, media outlets continued playing the music of defectors if their groups stayed behind, but they usually changed the name of the ensemble. Such was the case with the band Fajardo y sus Estrellas, which became known as Estrellas Cubanas after José Fajardo's departure and passed under the direction of violinist Félix Reyna (Leonardo Acosta, pers. comm.).

The exile of disaffected citizens benefited the revolutionary cause to an extent, distancing many who might have criticized the government. The U.S. policy of accepting exiles with open arms, while intended to debilitate Castro, thus seems to have had the reverse effect, creating more domestic political unity (Domínguez 1978:137). The only major disadvantage caused by the departures was that those leaving were primarily professionals whose skills were difficult to replace. In the United States, the influx of refugees created logistical problems yet also proved beneficial. Most were highly educated and could be absorbed with relative ease into the economy. Their presence served as good propaganda, proving that Castro's Cuba did not represent an attractive option for everyone.

Travel abroad became more difficult for performers in Cuba as political relations with the capitalist world worsened. This was another factor that upset musicians and led to defections. Tense relations with Washington meant that obtaining a visa for a visit to the United States became nearly impossible, and the exile community organized boycotts of Cuban nationals who attempted to perform in any capitalist country (Fundora Dino 2001, interview). Thus, even if they were fortunate enough to receive an invitation abroad, Cubans could rarely play music in Western Europe or North America without creating an incident.

Laws regulating travel within Cuba appeared in the second half of 1960, requiring that formal permission be requested in advance from the government.[23] Initially this was not difficult to obtain, but later, in an effort to curb the flow of currency out of the country and monitor the movement of suspected counterrevolutionaries, the procedure became more complex. After the Bay of Pigs attack in April 1961, only the most well-known artists traveled abroad for several years. Touring began again in the mid-1960s but less consistently. Artists received permission to do so only if they arranged the trip through a state agency. Favorable political relations with nearby Mexico made that country an attractive place to perform; Bola de Nieve, Los Papines, Enrique Jorrín, José Antonio Méndez, Omara Portuondo, and others visited there frequently (Díaz Ayala 1981:309). Increasingly, artists traveled as part of large multigroup ensembles rather than alone, visiting socialist countries more than those in Europe or Latin America and accompanied by government representatives.[24]

Established musicians found themselves subject to more travel constraints than the average Cuban because their defections could prove embarrassing. The fact that many had left the country in 1960 before stringent regulations were established meant that those remaining constituted a precious resource. Officials tended to view travel, therefore, as a reward to bestow upon loyal revolutionary musicians, not an intrinsic right (Acosta 2001, interview). In this way, the normal movement of performers in itself became a statement about one's relationship to the cultural hierarchy. Attempting to discourage defections, the government began to restrict performers' access to foreign currency while abroad. It provided only enough for per diem expenses and paid the balance of their salaries in Cuban *pesos*, essentially worthless on the international market after about 1967.[25]

These infringements on travel and international contact did not mean that performers as a group lost faith in the revolution. On the contrary, many viewed them as a relatively small price to pay for the new benefits they enjoyed. Working-class artists and Afro-Cubans, especially, continued to support the new government enthusiastically because they had been the immediate benefactors of its progressive social policies. As a result, they came to hold an even more central place in national music making than they had before. Examples of musicians and dance bands that continued to perform actively within Cuba include the *charangas* of Elio Revé and the Orquesta Aragón; singers Paulina Álvarez, Ester Borja, Barbarito Diez, and Celeste Mendoza; composers Ñico Saquito and Sindo Garay; *tresero* Niño Rivera; Ignacio Piñeiro and his newly reconstituted Septeto Nacional; *conjunto* artists Miguelito Cuní and Félix Chappottín; folklore ensembles such as Los Muñequitos de Matanzas and Los Papines; *filin* artists José Antonio Méndez and César Portillo de la Luz; *décima* singer El Indio Naborí (Jesús Orta); and the vocal ensembles Los Modernistas and Los Zafiros. The island continued to host a wealth of talent.

Nevertheless, the decision of many businessmen and performers to leave, the state of managerial disorganization within the entertainment sector, and the increasingly militarized state of the nation resulted in less over-all musical performance after 1961. In response, the National Culture Advisory began organizing and promoting festivals of all sorts, an approach that has remained central to arts policy to this day. Organizers enlisted the support of musicologists and presented a broad array of local musical styles, past and present. One event in the Teatro Roldán in September 1962, for instance, provided an overview of three centuries of repertoire beginning with the famous "Son de la Ma Teodora" of colonial times. It recreated vernacular theater sketches from the 1920s, turn-of-the-century art song, and traditional *trova* and included presentations by dozens of folklore troupes (Sánchez Lalebret 1962). State-sponsored events of this size had no precedent before the revolution. Other annual or biannual celebrations began at approximately the same time, such as the Festival of Cuban Song (Festival de la Canción) in November 1965 and the International Festival of Protest Music (Encuentro Internacional de la Canción Protesta) in 1967. They often took place in beachfront areas such as Varadero, as planners intended them to attract foreign audiences and foster a positive image of the revolution.

GIRÓN AND RADICALIZATION

The Bay of Pigs attack (known in Cuba as the battle of Playa Girón) that began on April 17, 1961, led to an immediate radicalization of the revolutionary climate. The invasion force, consisting of Cuban exiles trained by the CIA, severely underestimated Castro's popularity. Lacking external military support and with a poorly conceived offensive plan, they failed miserably. Within three days, the Cuban military put an end to all resistance and took over twelve hundred prisoners. Far from initiating revolt against Castro, the invasion did much to bolster his support. The most striking domestic change resulting from Girón was a marked increase in the imprisonment of suspected counterrevolutionaries, as Castro used the threat to justify their roundup. Between April 15 and 17, the armed forces detained as many as one hundred thousand individuals (Thomas 1971:1365). Public theaters that had recently come under government control, such as the Blanquita in Miramar, served as temporary holding facilities for them (Valladares 1986:89). Some remained in jail only a short time, others for extended periods.

One of the only options open to revolutionaries as they attempted to withstand military aggression from the United States was to ally themselves with the Soviet Union. Large quantities of Soviet weapons and military advisors began arriving in Cuba in the summer of 1961. In November, Castro declared that he had always been a socialist and affirmed that the Cuban Revolution would model itself in part after the example provided by East Bloc nations. Some months later, U.S. reconnaissance photographs indicated that Russian nuclear missiles had been shipped to Cuba and soon would be ready for launch. This alarming state of affairs led to the October Missile Crisis, perhaps the closest the world has ever come to nuclear disaster.

The Bay of Pigs created a wave of nationalist sentiment that manifested itself in popular song. Many who had never written on political subjects before wrote lyrics in support of the revolution and the island's sovereignty. The Cuarteto Las D'Aida recorded a version of the Mexican *son jarocho* "La bamba" with lyrics praising socialism (*Bohemia* 53, no. 34 [August 6, 1961]: 88). Carnival floats promoted similar messages. Floor shows with socialist themes appeared in the Tropicana. Racially mixed fiestas took place in the aftermath of the invasion in what had formerly been the most exclusive recreational clubs of the aristocracy (Orejuela Martínez 2004:121). The valor of the military at Playa Girón inspired countless pieces, especially among Cuban youth (Díaz Pérez 1994:82). In the wake of the missile crisis, a ditty circulated in Havana criticizing the Russians in rather crude terms for removing their nuclear weapons from the island. The song, discussed by Vázquez Montalbán (1998:261), included the lyrics "Nikita, mariquita, lo que se da no se quita." This might be translated roughly as "Nikita [Khrushchev], you little faggot, what has been given cannot be taken back."

Confrontations between Cuba and the United States also took place on the radio. As early as 1960, the Eisenhower administration authorized broadcasts of anti-Communist messages to Cuba in an attempt to influence domestic politics. Between 1960 and 1969, what began as Eisenhower's Radio Swan (later known as Radio Americas) continued to broadcast to Cuba from Honduras. During final preparations for the Bay of Pigs invasion, Swan's transmissions extended to twenty-four hours a day (Hernández-Reguant 2004c: 430). Cuban stations effectively jammed Radio Swan with their own broadcasts. Beginning in May 1961, Cubans took the offensive and initiated shortwave broadcasts from a new station, Radio Habana Cuba (RHC), in order to provide an alternative perspective on domestic politics to other countries. "Throughout the 1960s and 1970s, RHC also offered a voice to leftist movements, from Colombian guerrillas to U.S. black nationalists like Bobby Seale and Stokely Carmichael" (Hernández-Reguant 2004c: 430). Improved U.S.-Cuba relations under Jimmy Carter (1976–80) brought about a "radio armistice" of sorts, but the election of Ronald Reagan in 1980 led to a return to the use of radio as a political weapon on both sides.

MUSIC RECORDING AND PUBLISHING

The first years of the revolution witnessed dramatic changes in the domestic record industry. As mentioned, the late 1950s had been a period of rising LP production, with many new labels established. During 1959 and 1960, this trend continued largely unabated; new labels established included Rosy, Neptuno, Maype, Mambí, Velvet, Sonolux, Modiner, Minerva, and Meca (Díaz Ayala 1981:276). Toward the beginning of 1961, the government nationalized RCA Victor's studios as well as those of Cuban-owned Panart, the largest single domestic producer. Panart became an early candidate for intervention apparently because of its close ties with Columbia Records in the United States (Reyes 2001, interview). Its properties and assets served as the basis for the creation of the first state record company, the Imprenta Nacional de Discos, directed by composers Adolfo Guzmán (1920–76) and Rafael Somavilla (1928–80). The musical activities of the Imprenta Nacional represented only a fraction of its overall activities, which were devoted primarily to book publishing. Early records featured songs with revolutionary themes. An LP from November 1961 with interpreters Pío Leyva, Pacho Alonso, and Ramón Veloz included titles such as "Enseñar a leer" (Teaching to Read) and "Avanzar más y más" (Advance More and More) (*Bohemia* 53, no. 48 [November 26, 1961]: 122). Other novel LPs offered to the public at that time included *balalaika* performances and music from Poland, in addition to more standard repertoire.

In 1964 the government created EGREM (Empresa de Grabaciones y Ediciones Musicales), the Enterprise of Recordings and Musical Editions, separating sound recording from the Imprenta Nacional and conferring more autonomy on musical directors. The first chief executive of EGREM was Medardo Montero, who made decisions in conjunction with an advisory board consisting of composers and performers (Reyes 2001, interview). Unfortunately, record production in the early years of EGREM's existence experienced sharp declines and did not quickly recover. There seem to have been many causes for its poor performance. Perhaps most significantly, the U.S. economic embargo made sales of Cuban music to countries abroad more difficult. Foreign markets had always been the largest and most lucrative; Guillermo Álvarez Guedes noted that for every LP he sold in Cuba in the late 1950s he sold seventeen abroad (Díaz Ayala 2002). Foreign demand slipped independently of the embargo because Cuban performers no longer played abroad as frequently and lost the international profile they had enjoyed earlier. Raw materials for record production (petroleum products, shellac, replacement parts for mechanical equipment) became more difficult to obtain as well; this problem was especially acute after 1963. The policy of blacklisting artists in exile also had a negative impact on recording. In some cases, because of the shortages of materials, EGREM took existing inventories of LPs by exiles and melted them down, using the vinyl to print new material (Díaz Ayala 1981:286).

Another reason for the decline in record production derived from the government's decreasing interest in making a profit. It had less need to do so after establishing subsidized trade relationships with the Soviet Union in 1962. Beyond this, leaders tended to view music as an art form that should be promoted and distributed on the basis of its value to the people rather than its profitability. They did not believe songs that sold well necessarily represented the ones they should produce in greatest quantity. From the outset, EGREM's directors put little faith in public opinion, relying more on their own judgment in terms of which albums to release. "The state confiscated the catalogues of private music companies but in the initial years did very little with them for various reasons. Many artists had left the country and the government wanted to show that the best forms of cultural expression were being created during the socialist period. In general, the music of earlier times was belittled, especially that of the 1950s" (Cristóbal Díaz Ayala, pers. comm.).

Finally, declines in record industry output reflect broader economic woes that have plagued the revolution since its earliest years. Castro and his close associates knew little of finance and economics. Idealistic and confident of their own abilities, they assumed that collective hard work would be enough to make the nation's economy flourish. Indeed, a cornerstone of Ernesto Guevara's approach to finance as president of the National Bank was that monetary transactions be deemphasized and the use of money itself should end in short order. Exacerbating problems of inexperience was the defection of midlevel managers and businessmen, leaving few experienced economists to run Cuba's Central Economic Planning Board (JUCEPLAN). In general, the disassociation of production from profit in the new economy and a lack of accountability on the part of individual factories led to inefficiency and waste (Mesa-Lago, Arenas de Mesa, et al. 2000:175). The growth of the military adversely affected business as well, draining cash from civilian projects.[26] Impulsive decisions on the part of Castro's inner circle resulted in confusion and policy changes midstream.

As a result, record production declined from a peak of millions of records a year in the late 1950s to one hundred forty thousand in 1966 (Díaz Ayala 1981:286).[27] The decline was so dramatic that articles appeared even in state-controlled magazines noting that few LPs of any sort were available for purchase (*Bohemia* 55, no. 16 [April 19, 1963]: n.p.; archives, Cristóbal Díaz Ayala). In a technological sense, record manufacture also experienced setbacks. On a more positive note, José Reyes (2001, interview) asserts that the decline in production was compensated for to some extent by a greater diversity of recordings released by EGREM. He cites the choral music of the Amateurs' movement, discussed in the following chapter, and classical piano releases by Frank Fernández as examples. As opposed to the 1950s, in which, with the exception of *zarzuelas*, almost all recordings were of popular music, the revolutionary period would witness the increasing promotion of experimental classical music, folkloric traditions, compositions by less-well-known traditional artists, political song, and music of other kinds.

Book publishing received far stronger government support than music recording from the outset because of its associations with the literacy campaign and attempts to bring educational opportunities to the masses. Novelist and music critic Alejo Carpentier took charge of this facet of the National Press's activities in 1961. The government released large quantities of political material (collected speeches by Castro, Lenin, and Marx, Blas Roca's *Fundamentals of Socialism in Cuba*) but also works of a nonpolitical nature by Tolstoy, Voltaire, Cervantes, and other international figures. Approximately 70 percent of these books were distributed free to interested readers through the late 1960s (Thomas 1971:1467). Support for academic publications increased significantly, including those related to music and folklore. Since state institutions concerned themselves more with the dissemination of particular kinds of knowledge than with making money, they published things that had never appeared in print. The journal *Actas del folklore*, established in 1961, represents one example. In 1963, the Editora Musical de Cuba was created, a press devoted exclusively to sheet music under the direction of Niño Rivera, Rey Díaz Calvet, and others. One of its important contributions was the creation of editions of the music of Cuban composers, past and present.

The 1960s witnessed dramatic changes in copyright and royalty payments that affected music making. Commentators note that most artists in the 1950s received only minimal royalties, if any. As in the United States, composers often signed away all rights to their songs after recording them, hoping that the wider dissemination of the music would bring them exposure (Orovio 2001, interview). Copyright thus tended to serve the interests of big business, not those of the individual. The only exceptions were nationally known figures (Ernesto Lecuona, Gonzalo Roig) who had more bargaining power; they helped establish the Sociedad Nacional de Autores Cubanos (SNAC) and thereby received better financial representation.

On August 8, 1960, the revolutionary government dissolved SNAC, accusing Lecuona and Roig of embezzlement, and created a new agency, the Cuban Institute of Musical Rights (Instituto Cubano de Derechos Musicales), in its place.[28] This organization fought for royalties owed to domestic record labels by international companies; since some of the former had been nationalized and many of their owners were in exile, the ICDM took over the management, distribution, and licensing of their catalogs. Within a few years, however, contact with foreign copyright agencies dwindled. The increasing isolation of Cuba meant that maintaining international ties of any kind became more difficult. For their part, executives considered musicians to have less need of royalties in a socialist society given that they were guaranteed a higher wage, free health care, and pensions (Reyes 2001, interview). Additionally, the concept of paying artists extra royalty income clashed with Marxist ideals of egalitarianism and Che Guevara's drive to orient Cuban society around moral rather than material incentives. Leaders felt art should be offered freely to the people, that it should not exploit them with fees that would end up in the pockets of a single composer, that it should be a spontaneous gift. Copyright, from such a perspective, represented everything that was wrong about the capitalist system.

These issues came to a head in 1967. Following a series of declarations on the subject by Castro while in Pinar del Río, artists in the Unión de Escritores y Artistas Cubanos (UNEAC) voted to support the abolition of copyright altogether (Borges Suárez n.d.; Thomas 1971:1465). The primary concern at the time was to make printed matter available for students in Cuban schools and universities that the government could not afford to purchase. Castro insisted that textbooks should be free for everyone and called for their distribution in all centers of learning (Cantor 1998a: 30). He instructed national presses to make copies of any foreign books needed for schools without compensation to their publishers, a move that resulted in the suspension of royalty payments from other countries.

The government eventually lost a great deal of money as a result of the termination of licensing agreements. By the late 1960s, companies abroad began reissuing Cuban LPs without compensating their Cuban authors or even formally recognizing them because they were no longer required to do so. Foreigners recorded their own versions of Cuban standards in the same way, keeping royalties for themselves. Even if they had wished to send money to Cuba, such transactions would have been difficult if not outright illegal from the United States, owing to the economic embargo.

The abolition of copyright resulted in further artistic defections. Composers had grown accustomed to special financial recognition for their creative work during the capitalist years. They could not all be persuaded that someone capable of writing hit songs deserved the same salary as a secretary or accountant, for instance, or a less talented musician (Orovio 2001, interview). Additionally, the government had created full-time jobs for composers in various facets of the entertainment industry and guaranteed them a monthly salary whether they wrote songs or not; without a financial incentive to be productive, they tended not to write as much music. The number of new compositions, especially in the realm of popular music, declined sharply in the mid-1960s. While the state attempted to reverse this trend through national competitions and one-time cash prizes, it did not immediately create a system attractive to songwriters.[29] Not until the mid-1970s did officials begin the process of changing policy back to one that allowed for greater financial recognition of artistic excellence. Representatives at the First Party Congress in December 1975 (Partido Comunista de Cuba 1977:129) debated the matter and concluded that cultural effort deserved special compensation.

As part of reforms authorized shortly thereafter, the newly created Ministry of Culture permitted visual artists to sell their works privately in galleries for profit once again (Benítez-Rojo 1990:173). Municipal agencies reestablished modest fees for entertainment such as sporting events. They created a system of salary bonuses for exemplary workers (Pérez 1988:352). All of this had positive effects on the economy. Formal legislation reauthorizing copyright appeared in the *Gaceta Oficial* on December 30, 1978, in the form of law 14.[30] While recognizing the ultimate goal of completely "socializing" the production of all intellectual goods—that is, making them an unremunerated gift on the part of artists to the people—it also noted the need to protect the rights of artists themselves and to support them adequately. Copyright compensation in more recent years has been overseen largely by ACDAM (La Asociación Cubana de Derechos de Autores Musicales), the Cuban Association of Musical Copyright. Domestic royalties typically come in the form of a single modest payment for a given work, however, and are not directly linked to radio play or sales figures. State agencies retain the right to use pieces copyrighted through ACDAM as frequently as they choose without additional remuneration.

·   ·   ·   ·   ·

Regardless of their arguable errors, Cuba's revolutionary leaders had the best interests of the people in mind as they nationalized businesses, slashed utility rates, initiated programs of agrarian and urban reform, and in other ways radically refashioned society. Their policies did much to eliminate class stratification and endemic social ills. The new government quickly put an end to the "seductive and hierarchical" Havana associated with the mid-1950s, one "open to all the world's voices and saturated with pleasures" (Rojas 1998:68). But by eliminating institutions such as casinos that had supported music making, it radically altered the country's cultural landscape.

The early 1960s witnessed cultural turmoil and experimentation on a magnitude that rivaled the period's political changes. Revolutionaries who took charge of television, radio, and print publications had significant resources at their disposal and made decisions with little regard for the dynamics of capitalist markets. Poets and novelists (Nicolás Guillén, José Lezama Lima, Alejo Carpentier), classical composers (Juan Blanco, Harold Gramatges, Argeliers León), and others became prominent members of government organizations. Under their guidance, the state published new literary supplements, books, and sheet music, conducted academic research on folk traditions, and developed other exciting initiatives explored in chapter 3. The works of conservatory artists received broader recognition and dissemination than ever before (Vázquez Montalbán 1998:354). The state organized foreign tours of popular artists as goodwill ambassadors. It "democratized" formerly exclusive cultural spaces, making them available to working-class artists and performers of color.

Changes in the political sphere had negative effects on culture as well. Visas for travel became more difficult to obtain. The exodus of large segments of the middle class resulted in a lack of qualified entrepreneurs to oversee the business of music making. Employees in charge of sound recording after 1964 demonstrated little interest in promoting artists abroad and produced fewer albums. Economic instability, campaigns of salary regulation, and the abolition of copyright and royalty payments all functioned to suppress nightlife and song composition and to encourage the departure of many performers.

Just as in the 1950s, the experiences of individual artists in the early years of the revolution vary to a surprising degree. Many of those who remained remember the period as *un vacilón*, a tremendously exciting time in which a wide variety of artistic activity flourished. For the most part, the government allowed individuals to pursue initiatives of their own creation and in some cases financially supported them as they did so. National cultural policy took some time to codify, with priority given instead to military, economic, and political reorganization. This created space for performers and intellectuals themselves to define the cultural agenda. On the other hand, those unwilling to embrace the goals of socialism found the revolutionary experience decidedly less agreeable. Well-known stars (Osvaldo Farrés, Olga Guillot, Ernesto Lecuona) lost property and income, suffered personal humiliations, and felt compelled to leave the island. Separated from family members and friends and with little professional support, these artists did not always weather the dislocation. Their fate has generated bitterness toward the revolutionary government that remains alive to this day.

CHAPTER 3

Artistic Institutions, Initiatives, and Policies

For years, essayists in Cuba avoided critical evaluations of domestic arts institutions. Some considered it counterproductive to focus on negative aspects of the revolutionary experience. Others may not have felt at liberty to express critical views or have had access to the sorts of information that would substantiate them. Authors consistently found fault with music making in the capitalist world yet discussed local initiatives only in the most positive terms.[1] In retrospect, their unwillingness to evaluate revolutionary initiatives objectively may have done more harm than good, placing the credibility of many publications in doubt. Commentary on exactly what problems have existed at particular moments, how they have affected certain groups, and how they might be resolved can only strengthen the national agenda. As Abel Prieto noted (Díaz and del Pino 1996:9), open and inclusive cultural debate is vital to Cuba's future.

This chapter considers a few of the most visible programs that have emerged since 1959. After outlining broader social and political changes, it discusses the centralization of cultural activities under institutions such the Consejo Nacional de Cultura (CNC) and the Ministry of Culture. It documents the rise of the Amateurs' movement and the creation of specialized music schools. Later, the chapter discusses the formation of management agencies designed to coordinate musical performance. It ends with commentary on some of the advantages and disadvantages of being an artist in a state socialist society, including issues of artistic freedom.

POLITICAL AND SOCIAL TRANSFORMATION

The processes of change in revolutionary Cuba are enormously complex and merit further reading.[2] One of their most obvious manifestations has been

80

the emergence of a single political party. Plurality in this sense largely disappeared in 1965 when Castro fused an amalgam of semiautonomous institutions, known collectively as the Organizaciones Revolucionaries Integradas (ORI),[3] into a new Communist Party under his direction (the PCC). In social terms, the state greatly expanded networks of health care. As mentioned previously, officials took steps to eliminate segregation and racial division, especially in the workplace. Crime indexes dropped precipitously; between 1959 and 1968, the homicide rate on the island fell an astounding 600 percent, for example (Domínguez 1978:493). Women eventually had greater professional opportunities. The national literacy campaign cut in half the numbers of those unable to read and write by 1970 (Mesa-Lago, Arenas de Mesas, et al. 2000:225) and led to the construction of many new schools. The number of students in higher education doubled between 1959 and 1969; it climbed to over 235,000 by the mid-1980s (Mûjal-León 1989:407–13).[4]

Kirk and Padura Fuentes (2001) make evident the large number of present-day cultural figures from humble origins who in all likelihood would never have been able to excel in the arts without access to free higher education. Poet Nancy Morejón grew up in a working-class family; her mother was a seamstress, her father a stevedore. Classical pianist Frank Fernández came from a poor rural home in Mayarí; visual artist Roberto Fabelo was born into the same background in Guaímaro, Camagüey. The revolution has cultivated the extraordinary gifts of many underprivileged individuals such as these, often from the Afro-Cuban community. The strong nationalist orientation of the government has resulted in support for research on folklore. Publications available on local performers and genres far exceed the relatively scanty research conducted on such themes in Puerto Rico, the Dominican Republic, and other islands.[5]

Equally impressive are Cuba's losses during the revolutionary period. It has lost more than 10 percent of its population to exile as well as much of the contact it enjoyed with neighboring countries. It has suffered from shortages of goods and services, with all but the poorest sectors of society experiencing declines in their standard of living. Cuba has lost an independent press and judiciary. Its citizens can no longer elect national leaders who do not belong to the Communist Party. They have had other liberties infringed upon, such as the right to travel freely and to have access to the media. Losses are evident in terms of musical activity as well. Cuba lost thousands of family-run music schools along with other forms of private enterprise. Many religious songs, performed in patron saint festivals or during the Christmas season, are no longer heard. *Parrandas campesinas,* country music parties associated with the harvest season, have become less frequent since the incorporation of individual farmers and their properties into state enterprises (Fernández Pavón, March 18, 1998, interview).

STATE CULTURAL INSTITUTIONS

As mentioned, the first months of the revolution demonstrated the government's willingness to support a wide variety of musical ensembles and institutions. Some of these were new; others had existed previously but underwent transformation. The Havana Philharmonic Orchestra (La Filharmónica) remained intact, though leaders changed its name to the National Symphony (La Sinfónica Nacional), doubled its budget, and offered performers substantially higher salaries (Ardévol 1966:162–65). Supervision of municipal bands and orchestras became the responsibility of the armed forces (Gramatges 1982:42). The Ministry of Education continued to support broadcasts by the classical radio station CMZ but placed additional instrumental ensembles and a professional chorus at its disposal. Live performances and radio broadcasts on CMZ became more varied, featuring twentieth-century works by Boulez, Stockhausen, Xenakis, and others. Cuban composers José Ardévol, Juan Blanco, Harold Gramatges, and Nilo Rodríguez took an active part in these programming decisions. New institutions included the Teatro Nacional (National Theater), opening its doors on June 12, 1959, and the Casa de las Américas (Americas House), inaugurated in July of the same year (Gramatges 1982:133).[6] Both became important sites for a wide variety of musical performance. This was especially true in the Casa de las Américas after 1965, when a music division was created there under the initial direction of Harold Gramatges.

The ICAIC (Instituto Cubano de Artes e Industrias Cinematográficas), the agency responsible for film production, dates from 1959 as well (Otero and Hinojosa 1972:38) and has become one of the most successful cultural initiatives of the revolution. As mentioned, cinema did not exist as a vital industry in the 1950s but gained international recognition thereafter (Brenner et al. 1989:498). The first years of the revolution witnessed the release of *Memories of Underdevelopment, Lucia, The Other Francisco, Death of a Bureaucrat,* and other important movies. Prominent composers wrote scores for many of them. Documentaries represent a significant percentage of the ICAIC's releases since its inception, including a surprising number devoted to traditional music: Sergio Giral's *¡Qué bueno baila Usted!* on the life of Benny Moré; Octavio Cortázar's *Hablando del punto cubano* on campesino traditions; Héctor Veitía's *Sobre la conga* and *Congas trinitarias;* Oscar

Valdés's *Sobre la rumba* and *Rompiendo la rutina*, the latter about the orchestra of Antonio Arcaño.[7] In 1979, the ICAIC established the Festival of New Latin American Cinema, which continues to be an important international event. Celebrities from around the world attend the yearly festival; those participating in years past include Francis Ford Coppola, Robert Redford, Harry Belafonte, Gregory Peck, Jack Lemmon, Pedro Almodóvar, Constantin Costa-Gavras, and Fernando Trueba.

The earliest institution created to oversee and support macro-level cultural activities across the island was the National Culture Advisory, or CNC, dating from January 1961. It represented an expanded and more dynamic version of the Dirección de Cultura, formerly part of the Ministry of Education. As opposed to other areas of government, members of Castro's 26th of July movement did not figure prominently in the CNC. They chose to take charge of military, economic, and financial sectors, leaving what were perceived as less vital interests such as culture to "old-guard" Communist leaders. When the revolution triumphed, the PSP (Partido Socialista del Pueblo) was one of the few viable political groups from the past with a national infrastructure and a codified ideology. Castro took advantage of this by affiliating himself with its members. Among other things, he charged it with the formulation of a cultural agenda (Joaquín Ordoqui, pers. comm.).

Prominent figures in the CNC during its early years included Juan Marinello, Carlos Rafael Rodríguez, Vicentina Antuña, and Edith García Buchaca.[8] Of these, perhaps the most important were Antuña and García Buchaca; the latter became its first president. With support on the highest levels, she embarked on the "ambitious sponsorship of painting and sculpture, concerts, music, dancing, and theater" (Thomas 1971:1342). It was García Buchaca who conceived a majority of new national initiatives of the early 1960s, coordinated the Amateurs' movement, created early centers for artistic instruction, helped establish the UNEAC (Unión de Escritores y Artistas Cubanos, or Union of Cuban Writers and Artists),[9] and provided support for symphonic music performance. Subsequent directors of the CNC included diplomat and journalist Carlos Lechuga, psychiatrist Dr. Eduardo Muzio (together with writer Lisandro Otero), and Luís Pavón Tamayo.[10] Mirta Aguirre directed theatrical and dance activities in the first years; Marta Arjona, expositions of plastic arts; Alejo Carpentier and José Lezama Lima, written publications; and María Teresa Freyre de Andrade, the formation of libraries (Duarte Oropesa 1993:342). When establishing policies related to music, García Buchaca relied heavily on the advice of composers José Ardévol and Harold Gramatges (the latter shown in Fig. 7). Both served for extended periods as principal advisors (Ardévol 1966:191; Orovio 1981:191).

FIGURE 7.   A gathering of some of the most important cultural figures from the first decades of revolutionary Cuba. From left to right in the front: Haydée Santamaría, Harold Gramatges, Argeliers León, and Leo Brouwer. In the back stands composer and author Edgardo Martín. Photo Archive, Ministry of Culture, Cuba.

The creation of the Ministry of Culture in 1976 came about as part of the restructuring of Cuba's economic and political institutions under the influence of the Soviet Union. It intended to streamline bureaucracy and standardize institutions of all sorts nationally. The Ministry of Culture represented only one of twenty-three ministries established at that time (Domínguez 1978:236). Lawyer and 26th of July movement leader Armando Hart Dávalos (1931–) became the first minister of culture in 1976. He was not an artist or intellectual and never risked much independent leadership in the realm of creative expression. Nevertheless, he contributed to a diverse array of cultural activities in the ministry's initial years. The publication *Perfiles culturales* (Flores 1978) provides an overview of events organized by the ministry in the mid-1970s. These include coordinating national and international conferences and festivals, staging concerts, overseeing touring ensembles abroad (Irakere, Los Papines, the Orquesta Aragón, *nueva trova* artists), releasing music documentaries, and hosting visits by music and dance troupes from Eastern Europe and Africa, to name only a few.

The current minister of culture, Abel Prieto (1950–), took office in February of 1997 after having served as president of the UNEAC. In contrast to

Hart, Prieto is a talented writer, an authority on the works of José Lezama Lima, and has demonstrated an ability to make decisions about culture independently of other government figures. He is a member of the Political Bureau of the PCC and has a voice in key policy decisions. Many perceive his appointment as a trend toward liberalization (Cantor 1999:18). Prieto has supported the greater international mobility of artists and extends them more autonomy in the licensing of their works abroad. He has stood up for the free circulation of controversial films such as *Guantanamera* and the creation of statues to figures such as John Lennon. On several occasions he has publicly come to the aid of artists and performers that run afoul of the state bureaucracy.

THE AMATEURS' MOVEMENT AND OTHER MASS INITIATIVES

One of the more interesting and successful cultural programs of the 1960s, the Amateurs' movement (Movimiento de Aficionados) was a utopian attempt, based on Marx's writings, to directly involve as many people as possible in the arts. Some of its most visible manifestations included neighborhood mural projects and the formation of theater and dance troupes, choruses, and amateur music ensembles. The initiative began in 1960 and reached a peak in about 1965, though it persisted for decades. Countless institutions sponsored events associated with it: work centers, labor unions, the armed forces, the CNC itself, student groups, agricultural collectives, and neighborhood CDRs (Comités en Defensa de la Revolución). *Bohemia* magazine provides documentation on many types of music that appeared early on under the auspices of this program. One finds references to groups such as the vocal quintet "Los Guamá," created by workers in Havana prisons; the "Conjunto de mozambique from the CDR San Francisco de Paula"; a "Vocal Ensemble of the Syndicate of Public Administration," and "Theater Group of the Gastronomic Union."[11] Directors of the army (FAR) and Ministry of the Interior (MININT) supported the creation of rock combos and created other cultural opportunities for the tens of thousands of young people serving their country at this time.

At the heart of the amateurs' initiative was the implicit idea that capitalism had created an unhealthy division between professional performers and workers; the CNC attempted to compensate for this by training approximately three thousand new arts educators in seminars offered at the Habana Libre and Comodoro hotels. These individuals then headed across the island to stimulate grassroots artistic expression (Bulit 1972). In 1962, the government began organizing multiday festivals in every province to celebrate amateurs (Fig. 8). It sent delegations of them abroad as ambassadors of the revolution and tried to ensure that all forms of expression were as collective and participatory as possible (Cristóbal Díaz Ayala, pers. comm.). It commissioned ensembles to perform in factories, psychiatric hospitals, and recreational areas. Work centers encouraged employees to become involved in noontime or after-hour shows. In many respects, the movement represented a challenge to the very concept of the artist in capitalist society, encouraging collective composition and downplaying the role of the star. Linked to Che Guevara's vision of a society driven by moral prerogatives rather than money, amateurs tended not to charge for their services. Leonardo Acosta (pers. comm.) remembers that many considered the thought of making money from art at this time immoral and antisocialist. Figure 8 reproduces a newspaper advertisement for an early series of amateur concerts.

It is difficult to gauge the overall extent of the Amateurs' movement. Published statistics on the number of participants are unreliable, as educators often exaggerated their numbers in order to impress provincial authorities (Orovio 2001, interview). Nevertheless, the movement had a strong positive impact for some time.[12] Its ensembles served as an especially important vehicle for Afro-Cubans interested in representing their heritage. Indeed, prior to the 1990s, they were virtually the only means of doing so.[13] The same could be said of rock bands. Amateur musicians entertained Cuban troops in Angola, Ethiopia, and other countries (Portuondo 1989). A surprising number of current performers first became involved in the arts in this way, including members of the *nueva trova* group Moncada, the Sierra Maestra dance band, and singer Albita Rodríguez (Rivero García 1990). As of the 1980s, however, amateurs began receiving less support. In part this was due to the gradual recognition that not everyone had a strong interest in or propensity for art. It was also due to broader economic difficulties. Since the 1990s, the Amateurs' movement has largely disappeared as a nationwide effort.

Criticisms of the amateurs' events appeared occasionally in newspapers and magazines following major festivals, especially in the 1980s. One of the most typical comments was that the heavy emphasis on mass participation, frequently by those with little motivation, resulted in disappointing performances (Díaz Rosell 1989). Nancy Morejón noted such failings, suggesting that the movement often supported "mediocrity . . . in the name of a supposed form of equality" (Kirk and Padura Fuentes 2001:116). The phenomenon known in Cuba as *festivalismo*—support for performance only on high-profile occasions such as festivals rather than on a day-to-day

FIGURE 8. A page from the newspaper *Hoy,* September 21, 1962, announcing the first festival of amateur artists in the province of Havana. Various events appear in the schedule including a stage play, instrumental music concerts, choral concerts, exhibitions of visual art, and dances.

basis—also became a problem (Ruiz Ruiz 1990). One critic published the following challenge in the wake of a concert: "Ask any [participant] . . . 'are you performing consistently in municipal or provincial theaters, in officially programmed youth activities, or for school organizations? Do you record your music and have it aired on the radio?' The majority of the answers to such questions will be 'no'" (Carbó 1990). Acosta has similarly cautioned that amateur festivals were often representative of a certain falseness because they did not "correspond to a real base, emerging as the culmination of sustained effort" (Acosta 1983:213). Successful amateurs who fought for years against mediocrity and eventually sought recognition as professionals also faced difficulties. Their attempts to change status were often frustrated because professionalization ran contrary to the stated goals of the movement itself.

This initiative represented one facet of a broader attempt to develop the musical potential of the average Cuban. Between 1963 and 1967, the state supported multiple lecture series known as the Popular Music Seminars (Seminarios de Música Popular), which broadened performers' understanding of the repertoire they played and its history (Gramatges 1983:32). Organized by the CNC, most of the seminars took place under the direction of Odilio Urfé in the Iglesia de Paula. The program offered sixty fellowship awards at a time, permitting selected performers to take time off from work and devote themselves to the study of music. Instructors attempted to raise the technical level of musicians of popular music, to provide them with ear training and a background in harmonic theory, and to expose them to classical repertoire. Lecturers on music history and theory included some of the best-known cultural figures of the day: Antonio Arcaño, Alejo Carpentier, Félix Guerrero, Manuel Moreno Fraginals, Eduardo Robreño, and Vicente González "Guyún" Rubiera (Orejuela Martínez 2004:167).

More beneficial still were the Professional Improvement Schools (Escuelas de Superación Professional), which allowed musicians of any age or background to learn musical notation, harmony, and theory. Little information is available on exactly how many of these schools existed or continue to exist or how many musicians took classes in them over the years. Yet countless personal testimonies suggest that a significant number did so, especially in the 1960s and 1970s. In the case of many performers who had been active before the revolution, access to these schools represented their first opportunity for formal study (Fundora Dino 2001, interview). As early as 1962, multiple Escuelas de Superación existed in Havana with hundreds of students enrolled;[14] more were created in 1968. Following the advent of formal pay scale formulations for performers, discussed below, the Escuelas became especially important; enrollment represented one of the only means by which professionals could demonstrably improve their abilities and receive a higher salary.

Professional Improvement Schools today primarily train working artists rather than amateurs. Havana's school, the Escuela Ignacio Cervantes, is located in La Víbora and overseen by the Instituto Cubano de la Música. Its six full-time and nineteen part-time instructors offer beginning and midlevel music instruction to approximately four hundred students at any given time. A full course of study requires approximately six years to complete; areas of specialization include violin, piano, guitar, bass, trumpet, trombone, saxophone, flute, voice, and percussion. Occasional informal courses on rapping are also offered now for members of the Asociación Hermanos Saiz (the youth wing of the UNEAC). The Ignacio Cervantes schedules most of its class work in the mornings so as not to conflict with the professional duties of its students. Directors cannot accept everyone; applicants must take entrance exams, and only the most promising enroll. Some students come from other, more prestigious music schools. Others come from municipal bands, military ensembles, or choral groups. The administration schedules annual music competitions to which the public is invited. Since 1997, they have also sponsored Festivals of Identity that feature neighborhood amateurs playing a wide variety of folkloric and popular styles.

Perhaps the most widespread of the state's arts programs for the masses was the National Choral Movement (MNC). This initiative began in 1959 with *santiaguero* Electo Silva as one of its main protagonists. It incorporated thousands of individuals across the island and led to ensembles of surprisingly high quality (Orovio 2001, interview). In work centers, schools, and universities, the MNC helped organize singing of various kinds, often in collaboration with unions. The ensembles provided a means of involving large numbers of people in music as well as fostering a sense of national pride and socialist consciousness. Members sang a variety of material: revolutionary marches, Soviet hymns, traditional *trova* scored for multiple voices, and so forth. Political issues surfaced in the repertoire, such as agrarian reform or the sugar harvest of 1970. One representative work is Electo Silva and Mirta Aguirre's "Canción a Che Guevara" (1978), scored for children's chorus, flute, oboe, two violins, and piano. Songwriter Tania Castellanos (1920–88), wife of labor activist Lázaro Peña, wrote many pieces for amateur choruses, as did others (Fernández Pavón 1999, interview). This program began to lag in the 1970s, due largely to changing goals of the leadership.

Classical music had largely been taught by middle-class Cubans in the 1950s, many of whom later fled the country and abandoned their private schools. In response, the government created new institutions. The Alejandro García Caturla Conservatory in Marianao and the Guillermo Tomás of Guanabacoa opened their doors in 1960, joining Havana's Municipal Conservatory in Centro Habana (subsequently called the Amadeo Roldán) as an option for aspiring performers. In the following year, similar schools for midlevel music education appeared in every province (Gramatges 1983:32,

125). Many appropriated large abandoned residences that had formerly belonged to the bourgeoisie, as in the case of the Conservatorio Esteban Salas in Santiago (Navarro 1964:8). For many years these institutions fostered exchanges with East Bloc nations, organized international festivals for the performance of aleatoric works including mixed-media "happenings," and the like (Brouwer 1989:22). They likewise sent Cuban instrumentalists and musicologists to study in the music schools of East Berlin, Moscow, and elsewhere. Jesús Gómez Cairo noted that in the 1980s, the Cuban government had approximately fourteen hundred classical musicians on its payroll, performing in six different symphony orchestras as well as in a host of smaller ensembles (Pola 1989:343).

Perhaps the government's most ambitious initiative for mass cultural diffusion involved a plan in 1978 for ten distinct arts institutions within every community across the island (Robbins 1990:119). They were to consist of a brass band, a choir, a museum, a library, a *casa de cultura*—neighborhood "culture houses" for informal performance and instruction of various kinds—a store selling handmade crafts, a theater troupe, a cinema, a bookstore, and an art gallery. As in the case of the Amateurs' movement, no critical statistics on the implementation of the program exist, and it is impossible to know how effective it actually was. The idea for the *casas de cultura* apparently came from models in the Soviet Union (Weiss 1985:124; Olson 1994:48–49); they represent one of the most important of the ten institutions mentioned. The Ministry of Culture did manage to establish a *casa de cultura*, at least, in virtually every community. They filled a significant need, creating new spaces for community socializing. The *casas* continue to exist, though are sometimes oriented toward dance music and other events attractive to tourists.

PERFORMERS AS GOVERNMENT EMPLOYEES

During the first half-dozen years of the revolution, state regulation of musical events and performer salaries only affected certain sectors of the entertainment industry. Some groups in clubs received pay on a set scale from the government; others negotiated their salaries and hours of employment. All of this changed with the complete prohibition of private enterprise in 1968. At that time, the CNC required performers to coordinate all performance and to receive all payment through their agencies. As part of the initial restructuring, each individual underwent a series of evaluations supervised by conservatory-trained panelists. They determined whether the musician's expertise was sufficient to justify ongoing professional employment in the field. Those failing the evaluation were redirected to other jobs (Orovio 2001, interview). The evaluation and rating process seems to have begun as early as 1963 for those in the employ of state agencies such as the Instituto Nacional de la Industria Turística (Orejuela Martínez 2004:165).

If performers passed, panelists assigned them an overall skill classification level of A, B, or C. Each letter corresponded to a fixed monthly salary, with A-level performers receiving the most and C-level performers the least. Musicians then proceeded to work in the locations and on the schedules specified by the state. Ratings proved difficult to change, but in theory everyone had the option of retaking their test and striving for a higher score. Some note that the evaluations made no allowance for the popularity of the artists in question and tended to favor those with formal training. Folk performers often received lower scores despite proficiency in their respective styles because they did not know how to read Western notation (Vélez 1996: vol. 1, 74).

Since 1968, aspiring professional musicians have been required to graduate from conservatory programs; successful completion of their course of study often guarantees them the right to a job in their field. The approach has advantages, producing technically accomplished instrumentalists who play many different kinds of music well. However, not all performers are accepted into music institutions or manage to complete their degrees. The only option open to those not selected for professional status through the educational system is to perform on an ad hoc basis in clubs, hotels, or restaurants. They prepare an act in their spare time (while holding down a different job) and look for venues interested in contracting them. Musicians working under these conditions perform without compensation. If they manage to sign enough contracts to consistently play about twenty shows a month, they can apply for status as professionals. Achieving such recognition allows them to receive a steady salary from the government as entertainers. It is comparable to, though usually somewhat less than, that of conservatory-trained professionals.[15]

As full-time staff *(plantilla)* employees of a particular artistic agency, or *empresa*, musicians receive a monthly wage in return for a set number of performances (generally between six and sixteen). I have been unable to access information on the precise numbers of music groups supported by the government through the years, the kinds of music they play, and their locations. It is apparent, however, that the CNC and Ministry of Culture have supported a wide variety of ensembles: experimental electronic music, municipal brass bands, campesino groups, *charangas*, and more. For many years, the Centro Nacional de Contrataciones Artísticas (CNCA) coordinated all of them. Though it provided vital work opportunities, the CNCA created problems for musicians because it could not effectively manage so many groups. Leonardo Acosta (interview, 2001) described the situation as "a disaster." "Just imagine, it would be like having a single manager, a single impresario, for every artist in California, or in New Jersey. There was no way, they couldn't do it." Thankfully, policy makers eventually split the CNCA into a number of distinct organizations. The decision seems to have been part of larger processes of decentralization spearheaded by Central Committee member Humberto Pérez (Pérez-Stable 1993:126).

The resulting auto-financed enterprises, dating from the late 1980s, continue to coordinate most domestic music making. In Havana there are now four agencies of this sort. They are the *empresa* Benny Moré, in charge of dance music; the Ignacio Piñeiro, which coordinates traditional and folkloric ensembles; the Adolfo Guzmán, which contracts pianists, singers, guitarists, and other solo artists; and the Agrupación de Conciertos, in charge of classical music. In more sparsely populated parts of Havana province, the *empresa* Antonio María Romeu oversees musical activity (Orovio 2001, interview). Similar agencies exist in other fields, managing the careers of actors, comedians, and dancers. Regional economic planning boards, the JUCEPLAN and JUCEI network, also schedule some performances.[16] Since the 1980s, INTUR, which coordinates entertainment for tourists, has become an increasingly important patron. The breakup of the CNCA helped decentralize music making and create more cultural events in eastern Cuba and across the island than had existed before. Mass organizations, student groups, the military, and various branches of government (the Ministries of Education, Communication, and Labor) all contract artists through the *empresas* (Robbins 1990:48).

After 1968, the salaries of professional musicians remained consistent for decades. Salary ranges were small, with those in the lowest brackets receiving approximately 128 pesos a month and those in the highest, approximately 450. By Cuban standards, this represented a respectable sum; pay for other fields averaged 180 (Robbins 1990:99). Some of the best-known classical composers (Leo Brouwer, Carlos Fariñas, Harold Gramatges, Roberto Valera) received even higher pay—as much as 700 pesos a month—because of their simultaneous roles as institutional directors or teachers and as creative artists (Giro 1997, interview). For musicians who had survived on minimal and inconsistent income in the 1950s, the standardization process represented a highly positive change. Headline artists, however, had to content themselves with more modest lifestyles. Celso Valdés Santandreu of the Orquesta Aragón remembers that before 1968 he and other band members received approximately 3,000 a month; suddenly he found himself living on one-sixth that amount (2001, interview). Established groups complained as well that despite their years of experience, they received the same pay as musicians just beginning their careers.

Socialist Cuba deserves credit for the creation of multiple research institutes dedicated to musical study. One of the first was the Institute of Ethnology and Folklore (IEF), established in 1961 under the direction of Argeliers León. The IEF specialized in Afro-Cuban traditions, having among its goals that of confronting the prejudice of the public toward sacred repertoire (González Manet 1962). Many of the country's best-known investigators worked there: Miguel Barnet, Isaac Barreal, Armando Bermúdez, Pedro Deschamps Chapeaux, Teodoro Díaz Fabelo, Rogelio Martínez Furé, and Alberto Pedro Sr., among others. Articles in the institute's journal, *Actas del Folklore,* include analyses of African sculpture, instruments, theology, aesthetics, and history. Unfortunately, it ceased publication after only one year. The IEF continued to generate a considerable amount of research but eventually closed its doors toward the end of the decade, the result of internal power struggles and an intellectual climate less open to critical inquiry on the topics of religion and race.

Important research on music and the arts has appeared in the *Revista de Música* of the José Martí National Library (1960–61), the *Boletín de Música* from the Casa de las Américas (1969–), the journal *Clave* (1986–), published by the Ministry of Culture, and others. León played a central role in the founding of both the *Revista de Música* and *Boletín de Música* and directed musical activities in the National Library and Casa de las Américas in the 1960s (Domínguez Benejam 2000:57). Several serials, such as *Clave* and the *Boletín de Música,* disappeared for a time in the 1990s but have since resumed publication. After the opening of the University of Las Villas in the 1970s, Samuel Feijóo founded the journals *Islas* and *Signos,* which contain articles on folklore. The government began underwriting Odilio Urfé's Instituto Musical de Investigaciones Folklóricas in the early 1960s. In 1971, it founded a national music museum (along with a museum in Remedios to composer Alejandro García Caturla) and in 1978 created the Centro de Investigación y Desarrollo de la Música Cubana (CIDMUC, or Center for the Investigation and Development of Cuban Music).[17] New music journals have appeared in recent years that focus primarily on popular music, such as *Música Cubana, Salsa Cubana,* and *Tropicana Internacional.*

SPECIALIZED MUSIC EDUCATION

Communist Party documents from the 1970s continued to insist that efforts in the realm of culture should be based on a program of work with the masses, contrary to the tendencies of capitalist countries (e.g., Partido Comunista de Cuba 1977:51). In practice, however, the 1970s and 1980s saw the gradual decline of mass arts education and gave rise instead to programs geared toward the formation of an artistic elite. National conservatories attempted, with increasing success, to produce world-class artists who could compete successfully with those from other countries, especially the United States and Europe. The tendency has been to select students with exceptional musical gifts at an early age and to train them intensively in boarding schools. Limited amounts of music are taught in all schools, but most professional performers since that time have gained their expertise through a process of intensive, specialized instruction in classical music over many years.

There are ironies inherent in this approach to pedagogy. Perhaps most obvious is the fact that the programs have not only used the music of Europe's aristocracy as their core repertoire, but for years did not allow much room for the performance of local folkloric or popular music. According to Robbins (1990:504), revolutionary music curricula "blatantly contradicted" the ostensible values of the PCC and resulted in a situation in which the least distinctively "Cuban-sounding" groups (wind bands, chamber ensembles, symphonies) were in the most privileged position with respect to state support, while the most autochthonous (carnival groups, religious folklore, rumba ensembles) tended to suffer. A substantial cultural and educational divide often separated policy makers from those who performed in folklore groups. In general, the former viewed folklore from poorer communities as less sophisticated and less deserving of support than European repertoire. José Ardévol, perhaps the most important musical figure in the government during the first decade of the revolution, falls in this category. An ardent supporter of twentieth-century Cuban classical composition, he nevertheless failed to appreciate African-influenced forms and made clear distinctions in his publications between "culture" and "folklore." Additionally, many of the instructors who came to Cuba to establish conservatory programs were from Eastern Europe and had little knowledge of local traditions, thus deemphasizing their study.[18] Since approximately 1979, folk and traditional music have gradually achieved a foothold in music schools, especially in percussion programs.

The first institution devoted to the training of classical musicians in socialist Cuba was the ENA, or Escuela Nacional de Arte (National School of Art). The ENA opened its doors in 1962 on the grounds of a former elite resort, the Havana Country Club, where Richard Nixon and Gerald Ford had played golf only a few years before. Programs of study included drama, theater, music, ballet, and visual art, with approximately three hundred students enrolled. Revolutionaries converted guest rooms into practice space and offices and constructed additional buildings to provide dormitory space. Pablo Menéndez (1996, interview) notes that on festive occasions, the students still use the country club's fancy china and silverware. The architectural designs of the ENA's new buildings, conceived by Ricardo Porro, were highly innovative, with curved, flowing lines; they have received international acclaim (González Manet 1964).[19] Cubans from across the island received full scholarships to study at the ENA, as did many foreign students from the Caribbean, Latin America, Africa, and the East Bloc (Giro 1986:14). Nilo Rodríguez and Carmen Valdés directed the music program during the first four years, followed in 1966 by Alicia Perea and Radamés Giro, and in 1970 by Virtudes Feliú and Miriam Concepción (Unión de Escritores y Artistas Cubanos 1998:18). It continues to produce outstanding performers (Fig. 9).

During the first decade and a half of the ENA's existence, it could not provide advanced instruction in instrumental performance or musicology; students pursuing such careers did so on scholarship in Russia, Bulgaria, Poland, and East Germany. Beginning in 1976, however, enough graduates had returned from foreign programs to found the ISA, or Superior Art Institute (Gramatges 1997:36), an extension of the ENA. From this point on, fewer students went abroad, since they could receive comparable expertise at home. The ENA and ISA continue to offer comprehensive training in solfège, music theory, music history, harmony, instrumental performance, and composition. National composers—Saumell, Cervantes, White, Roldán, García Caturla—are studied alongside European figures. Argeliers León (Unión de Escritores y Artistas Cubanos 1998:19) suggests that for many years a certain aesthetic tension was apparent at the ENA and ISA. Directors of the individual programs—typically artists themselves—strongly promoted the study of twentieth-century experimental repertoire. Students, for their part, often demonstrated interest in traditional and popular music and desired at least some incorporation of it into degree programs. Finally, PCC members assigned to oversee the curriculum promoted socially conscious art.

Neighborhood *casas de cultura* now provide interested children with their first formal music education when they reach six or seven years of age. The

FIGURE 9.   Clarinetists Pedro Cancio (left) and Jesus Rencurrell (right) playing
a student recital in the recently founded National School of Art (ENA), 1964.
Behind them stands one of the music program's first administrators, Carmen
Valdés. The ENA stands on the grounds of what had been the exclusive Havana
Country Club; this room previously housed a formal dining area. Photo Archive,
Ministry of Culture, Cuba.

casas typically offer two- to three-hour after-school programs during the
week. Older students who wish to continue study beyond this point take a
series of tests. If they perform well, they enroll in specialized arts boarding
schools. At the conclusion of this second phase, students take a more rigorous series of tests; those passing once again continue on to arts high schools.
From the 1960s through the mid-1980s, performers across the island came
to the ENA at this point, but now such schools exist in the provinces as well
(Hart Dávalos 1988:26). After completing study at an arts high school, students take yet more tests, with the best and brightest advancing to the ISA.
It is thus possible for exceptional performers to receive specialized training
for many years at no expense, as well as housing and a small stipend for living expenses (Cantor 1997:20). The nationwide division of music education
into elemental, midlevel, advanced, and superior education first took place
in 1974, represented by the *casas de cultura* and the three levels of specialized music schools described above (Giro 1986:87).

Socialist countries inevitably have more applicants for arts programs than
they can accept; the faculty must weed out a majority of aspirants and redi-

rect them to other careers. David Calzado (1996, interview) remembers that the year he applied to the ENA in the early 1970s, the school accepted only 20 new students out of 240 (approximately 8 percent). Those accepted encounter additional obstacles. Military service is typically required before they can pursue their degree. In the 1960s and 1970s, this involved three years of active duty; in recent decades it has been reduced to one or two. School curricula include subjects unrelated to the arts that must be passed satisfactorily in order to remain in the program. Manual labor in the countryside (working in *escuelas del campo*) is also a requirement. This involves planting or picking crops on weekends or during vacations for a total of forty-five days year. Attendance at political meetings of various sorts also constitutes an obligation. Extracurricular responsibilities often take valuable time away from practicing and other homework. Ernesto Cardenal published the following quote from an anonymous student describing a typical day at the ENA around 1970.

> We leave at six in the morning for a ceremony at which I read the announcements and we salute the flag. We have breakfast and come to art classes. In the afternoon we have our academic classes: philosophy, history of philosophy, literature, French, art history. . . . We can leave on weekends, unless they hold up our passes because of some breach of regulations. On Tuesdays we have study groups where we discuss texts: speeches by Fidel, writings of Che, Martí, Lenin. . . . The "politician" of the [student dorm] is the one who directs these studies. The materials are chosen by the [Union of Young Communists]. (Cardenal 1974:56)

Reynaldo Fernández Pavón studied at the Escuela Nacional de Arte beginning in 1962, part of the first generation to do so. He recalls, "When we didn't have to go to a political rally, it was a mandatory mass mobilization in the Plaza de la Revolución with Fidel, or something else; so many extracurricular activities that had nothing to do with music! I have come to the conclusion that those who finished their degrees had extraordinary talent, because they were fighting constantly against many factors that conspired to halt their progress" (February 2001, interview). Following completion of their degrees, artists generally perform "social service." This involves accepting a job at reduced pay and often in a less than desirable location such as a rural town or neighboring province. After completion of the assignment, they may return home and look for other positions at full pay.

During the first ten or fifteen years of its existence, the ENA was associated with militaristic discipline. This was a tense moment for the country, one that witnessed violent conflicts with exiles. Some directors appointed to oversee the school felt that Cuba needed soldiers more than musicians and instituted policies that bordered on the extreme. Berta Serguera, appointed director in approximately 1966, and her 1968 successor, Mario Hidalgo, seem to have been among the worst offenders. They called upon students to practice extended marching drills and to train with rifles between classes. The smallest infractions of policy could result in expulsion. Grounds for dismissal included failure to comply with extracurricular responsibilities, "confrontational attitudes" of any sort, or involvement in jazz or other kinds of music against the wishes of one's instructors.

By contrast, the experiences of percussionist and pianist Elio Villafranca are illustrative of music education as it existed in the late 1970s and 1980s, perhaps the best period for such study. Villafranca began learning to play music in a *casa de cultura* at age eight, and at ten was selected to enroll in an arts boarding school in Pinar del Río, the Escuela Vocacional Raúl Sánchez (2000, interview). He remembers that at first it was very difficult to be away from home at such a young age; many students felt homesick. Gradually, however, they became accustomed to the routine. In the morning, all 120 students studied normal subjects, devoting their afternoons to artistic disciplines. Villafranca spent three years at San Luis, graduating at age thirteen. The state provided housing, meals, and classes; his family sent him 35 pesos a month for other expenses. Toward the end of the program, he and others took tests to determine who would continue on to the ENA. The pressure was considerable because failure to gain acceptance meant the end of one's professional future in the arts. Villafranca remembers that in the year he entered the ENA there were only six openings for percussionists (his specialty) from all of the provinces combined. The total number of matriculated students in the ENA at that time was about 650 (Giro 1986), a marked increase from previous decades.[20]

Students enrolled at the ENA understood that upon graduating they would become performers or educators of some kind. Villafranca's general classes continued in the mornings: Spanish literature, history, introduction to Marxism, physical education, military preparation, and so forth. Musical instruction became more focused and intense, including advanced courses in pedagogy, form and analysis, counterpoint, percussion history, and performance. During the final two years of his training, he was assigned to teach music at an elementary school in Marianao. During those years, Villafranca met Carlos Varela, who was studying acting; the two began playing rock music together in their spare time. Villafranca anxiously hoped to be accepted into the ISA and to continue studying in Havana. This would mean better job opportunities and would also allow him to postpone military and/or social service duties. Fortunately, he managed to do so.

Overall, Villafranca describes his musical education as excellent and is grateful to the government for the training it provided him. His only complaint is that arts-related careers did not receive as much support as other fields in the 1980s. Ambitious students avoided music, choosing more "upwardly mobile" careers in law, economics, medicine, or international relations. The attitude of the leadership seems to have been that "artists always cause problems" (Villafranca 2000, interview). For that reason, they kept program enrollments down and did not always provide adequate facilities or instruments. Nevertheless, students at the schools developed such dedication that they overcame all difficulties.

There are many advantages to musical training in socialist Cuba as compared to capitalist countries. The education is of consistently high quality, and enrollment comes at no cost to the student. Participants can devote considerable time to their discipline because they do not have to work to support themselves. The primary focus on classical repertoire, while confining, provides a strong technical foundation for performance of any sort.[21] No comparative statistics exist, but Cuban performers today believe that the number of highly trained musicians is greater in socialist Cuba than in pre-revolutionary times (Calzado 1996, interview). Those fortunate enough to attain recognition as full-time musicians receive steady, competitive salaries. They also devote themselves to composition and rehearsals without the need to look for other means of support. Before the 1990s, especially, they presented their work in concert for a modest fee or free of charge, ensuring broad public access. They participated in an environment in which cultural activities of many sorts proliferated.

The socialist cultural environment is not without problems, however. One is the difficulty of getting work as a *plantilla* musician. Few positions exist, meaning that countless performers are unable to perform in this capacity. Among those that do become full-time performers, complacency has often been an issue, just as in other sectors of the economy; those guaranteed a salary do not always strive to play their best. The *plantilla* system has created situations in which musicians sabotage their instruments or invent excuses in order not to travel to small, out-of-the-way towns, knowing that in any case they will make the same amount of money (Orovio in Fornet et al. 2001:175). For their part, musicians complain about not being able to freely choose where to play and whom to work with; their relationship to the *empresas* compromises this aspect of their profession. Even superstars of the stature of Silvio Rodríguez have spent decades trying to form backup ensembles of their own choosing, for instance (Acosta 2001, interview). Groups often feel inefficiently managed and promoted. They have little recourse if their representatives do not offer them attractive engagements or touring options. Government help with transportation of personnel and equipment is often unavailable or inadequate.

Centralized bureaucracies create problems beyond the level of individual performers and groups. The reshuffling of cultural institutions under new directors and umbrella organizations can be detrimental to productivity (Domínguez 1978:237). Performances are canceled frequently because of power outages or equipment failure (Robbins 1990:111). José Pola has collected perhaps the most comprehensive commentary on the Cuban music establishment in his book *Entrevistas: Temas relacionados con la cultura* (1989). Complaints raised include comments on the difficulty of getting permission to record music; allegations that ensembles in the provinces receive less support than those in Havana; descriptions of inadequate performance facilities and sound equipment; and frustrations over limited production of sheet music and other supplies.

All of the music *empresas* mentioned above continue to function, but since the late 1990s they serve more as agencies of taxation than service providers. Music groups now have more freedom to determine their own work schedules and fees, as will be discussed in chapter 8, but often suggest that *empresas* abuse their authority by charging inordinately high administrative fees. This is a noteworthy problem given that Cubans are not used to paying income tax of any sort. Jerry Ferrer Aponte, director of Habana Ritmo, describes the Antonio María Romeu agency to which his group belongs as "a vampire that sucks your blood and won't let you live" (2004, interview). The agency requires him to surrender approximately 65 percent of all earnings. Government inspectors circulate constantly in an attempt to assure that groups do not perform without notifying and paying their *empresa*. Bands caught doing so are subject to a 1,500 fine in dollars (virtually impossible for most to pay) and often have their instruments confiscated. Nevertheless, bands continue to perform illegally in order to make ends meet.

Administrators for many years did not consider popular tastes when determining what music to promote and record (Manuel 1987:168); they scrapped polls, top ten charts, and other means by which public opinion had at least some effect on airplay. Popular culture of all kinds received less support for a time because bureaucrats considered it a "low" form of expression, an impediment to cultural advancement. "The revolution was proposing to raise the cultural standards of the country. The leadership felt that . . . letting musicians continue to play *son*, *guaracha*, boleros, and chachachás was not going to contribute to this goal, but instead to the perpetuation of the status quo. They were interested in converting Cuba, as quickly as possible, into the most cultured country in the Americas" (Orovio 2001, interview).

Given this goal, it is striking that among the combatants in the Sierra Maestra, only a handful were college educated. As demonstrated in an article from *Carteles* in 1959, most did not even know how to read (*Carteles* 40, no. 12 [March 22, 1959]: 38–39). For years, 80 percent of the PCC membership had less than a sixth-grade education (Pérez-Stable 1993:119). Most university students fighting against Batista belonged to the Revolutionary Directorate in Havana; for political reasons, they tended to be passed over for prominent jobs in favor of those in the 26th of July movement (Montaner 1985:30). This resulted in situations in which appointees chosen to enforce cultural policy did not have sufficient training. To the extent that they were trained, leaders tended to come from law or other fields rather than the humanities. José Llanusa, for example, became minister of education in the 1960s with only the most minimal of qualifications. Mario Hidalgo worked as a baker before joining the revolutionary effort and eventually becoming director of the ENA. He described himself as unprepared for such a position and asked repeatedly to be replaced (Guillermoprieto 2004:135). Figures such as Berta Serguera often clashed with students and professional performers for similar reasons (Cardenal 1974:55). Campaigns of rectification since the late 1970s and increasing levels of education across the country have resulted in more professional oversight of culture in recent years.

LIMITATIONS ON ARTISTIC FREEDOM

> In every moment of history and in every society, the relationship between artists and the government or those in power is never an easy or enjoyable one.
>
> ANTÓN ARRUFAT, "Pequeña profesión de fe"

An analysis of music making in socialist Cuba would be incomplete without addressing issues of artistic freedom in more detail. Cuba continues to struggle with a number of problems related to limitations on personal liberties. In fairness, we should recognize that virtually all other nations do as well, regardless of their political orientation. The mistreatment of artists and intellectuals at particular moments in Argentina, Chile, the Dominican Republic, and Nicaragua has been comparable to and in some instances much worse than in Cuba. Many forms of censorship also existed in Cuba before 1959.

When queried, government representatives do not deny that they impose limitations on artistic expression. Instead, they counter that mass media in every country have administrators who decide what should and should not be included in programming (Hernández-Reguant 2002:125). They note that representatives of the PCC serve this purpose in Cuba and stress the necessity of such controls in light of ongoing antagonism with the United States and exile groups (e.g., Partido Comunista de Cuba 1977:62). Officials describe their country as existing in a state of war and suggest that extreme measures are necessary to safeguard the revolution. Castro has noted, for instance, that if one considers the Bay of Pigs invasion and all subsequent violent acts committed against the country since the early 1960s, approximately thirty-five hundred Cubans have lost their lives to foreign aggression.[22] As mentioned, the CIA sent saboteurs to the island for years and helped fund anti-Castro elements living there (Smith 1987:166). This was especially prevalent in the 1960s and 1970s, the period of Cuba's most severe limitations on artistic expression. "Paramilitary missions were organized to destroy sugar mills, sugar and tobacco plantations, farm machinery, mines, oil refineries, lumber yards, water systems, warehouses, and chemical plants. Communication facilities were attacked; railroad bridges were destroyed and trains derailed. The United States [government] was successful in disrupting Cuban trade initiatives with Western Europe by blocking credit to Cuba and thwarting the sale of sugar products" (Pérez 1988:347).

The infamous Operation Mongoose of the 1960s, a CIA-funded initiative with a budget of approximately $500 million annually, coordinated many of these activities. Employing between six hundred and seven hundred personnel, it organized hundreds of covert missions in Cuba (Hinckle and Turner 1981:113). In addition to sabotage, the United States government attempted for years following the Bay of Pigs attack to assassinate Castro through alliances with the mafia, the exile community, and others.[23] Radical Cuban exiles working with the CIA committed additional violent acts. The terrorist bombing of a civilian Cuban jet near Barbados in 1976, the planting of explosives in a Cuban embassy in Lisbon, and attempts to kill members of the Cuban delegation to the United Nations represent only the most well-known examples (Stubbs 1989:xv). Events of this nature continue with the capture of the Betancourt commandos on the island in 1991 and the bombing of Cuban tourist hotels in 1997.[24]

Such conflict is important to bear in mind because it provides the context for policies that often strike the outside observer as heavy-handed. To historian Graciela Chailloux, the survival of the Cuban Revolution in the face of external aggression is nothing short of amazing and has required close regulation in order to keep the public focused on their goals and responsibilities. "The most potent force that the revolution has in the face of the political will of the United States is force of a moral and ideological nature. Our preoccupation with anything that threatens that force often results in policies that violate freedom of expression" (1996, interview). Justification for prohibitions against the discussion of political reform derive from this issue: the government considers a united front necessary in the face of aggression and suggests that discourse with the potential to create internal divisions cannot be permitted.

State publications insist that foreign culture threatens local folklore in the same way that people are threatened by physical attack. As mentioned, they characterize the 1950s, a period of strong U.S. influence, as leading to the "destruction and mutilation" of national traditions (Otero and Hinojosa 1972:13). One finds constant references in official literature to the facile, commercial, and escapist nature of music from the period. Cultural imports such as Elvis Presley and the Beatles came to be viewed as symbols of a capitalist way of life that Cuba wanted to distance itself from (Díaz Pérez 1996, interview; Ministerio de Cultura 1982:71). This is congruent with a fundamental goal of the Cuban Revolution: to free the country from foreign control. National music and culture represented weapons in the struggle to reorient public opinion but also a means of resisting "the penetration of the enemy" (Partido Comunista de Cuba 1977:57).

The promotion of local genres represents a centerpiece of national cultural policy. Pronouncements in favor of the "rescue of cultural roots and values" are found in the conclusions of the First National Congress on Education and Culture (1971) and in countless other publications (e.g., Hart Dávalos 1988:23). One of the ways such initiatives manifest themselves is in guidelines requiring at least 70 percent of all music played on the radio and television to be Cuban rather than foreign (Acosta 1996, interview). Wallis and Malm (1984) note that smaller capitalist nations such as Sweden have created similar policies in order to safeguard their national culture. From the late 1960s through the mid-1970s, these views also led to a suppression of the performance of rock and other music associated with the United States and Britain in the Cuban media (Acosta 2002:97, 163).

Given the tensions between Cuba and the United States, some regulation of the media by the government is clearly necessary. Yet few can dispute that the Cuban government has aggressively regulated the press, the publishing industry, and all other media as well as access to national and international opinion, sometimes in counterproductive ways. It limits the dissemination of many foreign news publications. Critical, independent journalism is virtually nonexistent, with daily reports carefully screened before being printed. Artists and others who are critical of the government risk professional complications.

The period most closely associated with crass censorship was the *quinquenio gris,* or "five-year gray stretch," extending from approximately 1968 to 1973. Lisandro Otero, vice president of the CNC, appears to have been responsible for many abuses, with the blessing of Minister of Education José Llanusa. Later, Tony Pérez Herrero, director of cultural affairs in the PCC's Central Committee, began to take an active role in censorship of the arts as well. This was a horrendous moment that restricted virtually all forms of cultural expression, musical and otherwise. It derailed the careers of many individuals and sidelined others for years. John Kirk (pers. comm.) recounted that in discussions with novelists for a recent publication, Antón Arrufat and Pablo Armando broke down crying when recounting their experiences at this time. Others have refused to discuss the *quinquenio* at all. I personally know musicians who suffered internment, loss of employment, loss of party membership, and other humiliations.[25] In the late 1970s, artistic freedoms expanded dramatically and have continued to improve in the last ten years. Yet problems remain. Musicians continue to have songs taken off the air if officials perceive them to be inappropriate. Their ability to record and perform domestically likewise depends upon favorable relations with state organizations.

The censorship of artists can take many forms, often subtle. Officials may restrict their access to radio and television in order to limit their exposure and thus their popularity, deny them access to performance space, or withhold visas for travel (Perna 2001:92). Midlevel bureaucrats typically make these decisions, not those at the highest levels of government. Managers in charge of radio and television stations, for instance, have considerable autonomy in determining whom to support and whom to ignore. Self-censorship should also be mentioned as an important factor affecting artistic creation. This involves decisions on the part of performers or writers to avoid sensitive subjects even if they have not expressly been asked to do so. Put simply, the tendency of the state to marginalize those believed to espouse controversial ideas creates fear in the artistic community and elsewhere (Rosendahl 1997:159). Not knowing where the state will draw the line on a given subject, many choose to restrict the content of their own work and "play it safe."

Recent decades have witnessed some liberalization. The gradual move toward greater cultural freedom—not without significant setbacks at times—has been due to multiple factors. The Carter administration's politics of engagement with Cuba in the late 1970s helped create a somewhat more relaxed environment. Visits by the exile community, which began in earnest at that time, brought alternate views of capitalist countries to Cuban nationals; these in turn invited comparison and led to reforms. In the aftermath of the Mariel exodus of the early 1980s, the government tried to make Cuban society more attractive to its citizens in the hopes that they would choose to stay. This was the first period since the mid-1960s in which television stations began to show video clips of foreign rock groups, for instance (Agustín González, pers. comm.). Many TV producers living on the island such as Manolo Cuervo, director of *Colorama* from 1980–85, contributed to liberalization trends by fighting for a wider selection of programming. The 1990s has given rise to a generation of younger, confrontational individuals who create "ironic art," in many cases transforming visual imagery or political discourse as a means of critiquing local representations of power (Zeitlin 1999:27). Their freedom to do this suggests that tolerance has increased significantly.

Censorship is an important tool of any nation engaged in a struggle for survival but must be used with care. Overly rigid limitations can prove counterproductive, fostering alienation and antigovernment sentiment. Marx himself spoke out against censorship, believing that it should never restrain critical inquiry (Solomon 1973:71). The prohibitions that existed for years against foreign culture, for instance, tended to provoke negative reactions, especially on the part of younger Cubans. Even staunch supporters of socialism such as composer Silvio Rodríguez voice concern about this aspect of their country's reality:

> One of the things that has always bothered me is the lack of communication and of information in Cuba. . . . Why can't I have access to what other people say? I would like to learn more about the opinions of people who don't think along the same lines as myself, because that helps me to reflect, and maybe it will help to improve me, to make me understand things. . . . One of the defects that all socialist systems have had is precisely that. Why do people say that there is more freedom in a capitalist system than in a socialist one? It is precisely because, whatever the reason may be, there always exists in socialism [a] pretext that can be used to restrict certain freedoms. I am a complete socialist. But I would be far happier if we who live in a socialist system could really say that we are freer than those who live under different systems. That is the sort of socialism that we should be constructing. (As quoted in Kirk and Padura Fuentes 2001:14)

. . . . . .

Beginning in the late 1960s, revolutionaries made cultural activity a concern of the state. Members of the National Culture Advisory promoted the Amateurs' movement as one of its early initiatives, attempting to bridge the divide between worker and artist. The ICAIC Film Institute, the National Theater, the Casa de las Américas, and the ENA all represent fruits of their labor. As time passed, more individuals than ever attended a variety of cultural events and had access to arts education. Officials gave thousands of musicians professional status and a guaranteed salary. They cultivated the gifts of promising performers in specialized schools.

Sandra Levinson (in Brenner et al. 1989:488) notes that Cuba in the late 1980s had two thousand libraries and hundreds of museums, most of which did not exist during the capitalist years. Prior to 1989, it printed almost fifty times more books a year than it had by year in the 1950s. Even in the current period of economic crisis, the country sponsors international festivals of jazz, film, ballet, guitar, popular music, electro-acoustic music, modern dance, as well as conferences on literature and art. More than two hundred *casas de cultura* still function across the island. By the same token, artists complain that bureaucracies stifle their creative initiatives and take critical decisions about performance out of their hands. They acknowledge that inefficiencies inherent in centralized planning lead to delays and problems with equipment, transportation, and travel. They frequently feel poorly represented and promoted. In some cases, they find their work censored.

This overview of Cuba's cultural establishment raises many more questions than it answers. This is largely because the Ministry of Culture does not afford foreign academics easy access to information on its day-to-day workings. The history of the Cuban Revolution indicates that governments can have a decidedly positive effect on many aspects of cultural life and that other countries stand to gain by imitating many of its initiatives. By the same token, certain aspects of the revolutionary experience are less satisfying and at particular moments have been highly repressive. It is unclear how the advantages of state management, such as its generous educational opportunities and salary guarantees, might be retained while eliminating unnecessary bureaucracy, providing for additional freedom of expression, or empowering artists in new ways.

CHAPTER 4

Dance Music and the Politics of Fun

> At the dances I was one of the most untiring and gayest. One
> evening . . . a young boy took me aside. With a grave face, as if he
> were about to announce the death of a dear comrade, he whispered
> to me that it did not behoove an agitator to dance. Certainly not with
> such reckless abandon, anyway. It was undignified. . . . My frivolity
> would only hurt the Cause.
> I grew furious at the impudent interference. . . . I did not believe
> that a Cause which stood for a beautiful ideal . . . should demand the
> denial of life and joy.
>
> EMMA GOLDMAN, *Living My Life*

When Ernesto Guevara described Cuba in the early 1960s as having given
rise to a revolution with *pachanga* (the ambience of a party), he perhaps
unknowingly touched upon a subject that has generated controversy for
many years: the place of fun, humor, sensuality, and irreverence within the
lives of concerned socialists. Marxist leaders often strike the public as somewhat puritanical; the society they strive for, while humane, is not necessarily one in which fun plays a central role. Abel Prieto has recognized the problem in Cuba, describing the cultural establishment of the 1970s and early
1980s as "impregnated with a strange solemnity" (as quoted in Díaz and
del Pino 1996:6). Critics did not always support dance music because they
perceived it as unaligned with, or even opposed to, political initiatives. Marxism encourages the dissemination of new values and ways of thinking. Its
artistic forms frequently intend to "edify," limiting their use for pleasure.
Beyond this, critics may have sensed the rebelliousness implicit in popular
music, the fact that much of its pleasure derives from the transgression of
social norms of various kinds.

Ambivalence toward the classical arts has rarely been evident in socialist Cuba, but controversy over dance repertoire surfaced in the mid-1960s.
Leaders associated it with the extravagant nightlife of the prerevolutionary
period and considered it antiquated, a throwback to times of decadence, inappropriate in a society rethinking itself and its values. At best, dance music was unimportant; at worst, it represented a form of escapism and false
consciousness. Under Soviet influence and in the throes of the cold war, the
government made decisions that resulted in decreasing support for such en-

tertainment. This chapter analyzes the history of dance repertoire and its use as a form of social critique, especially among Afro-Cuban youth. The first section describes a gradual decrease in dance performance as of the late 1960s. The next section discusses two groups, Los Van Van and Irakere, in order to illustrate changes in dance band aesthetics and comments on controversy over the international salsa craze. The final section documents the revival of dance activity in Havana as of the mid-1980s and the prominence of so-called *timba* bands in the new tourist economy.

DANCE MUSIC IN THE EARLY YEARS OF THE REVOLUTION

Dance music continued uninterrupted in 1959 and 1960 more or less as it had under Batista. In hotels, nightclubs, and the scores of *sociedades de recreo* across the island, Cubans continued to party, viewing political change as a cause for celebration rather than solemnity. Beginning in April 1961 with the Bay of Pigs invasion and the missile crisis in October 1962, nightlife became more subdued. University students and younger professionals who had attended dances began to devote themselves to political concerns. Many joined military or civilian militia groups as a safeguard against further aggression; others volunteered in the national literacy campaign. In 1963, political tensions receded once again and cabaret life continued relatively unabated for another four years (Acosta 2001, interview).[1] Campaigns to desegregate the country led to new opportunities for many dance bands to perform in exclusive venues. The Conjunto Chappottín, the Conjunto Modelo, and the Estrellas de Chocolate that had formerly played almost exclusively for Cubans of color found themselves invited to the Tropicana and Habana Libre (Orejuela Martínez 2004:122). The multiracial audiences that listened to them there represented a novelty as well.

Cabarets and nightclubs represented a dilemma of sorts for policy makers. On the one hand, they were associated with the excesses of the late Batista years, and the entertainment they provided was apolitical in the extreme; few considered them a priority. In fact, some derided cabaret enthusiasts as early as 1961 as "marginal," "lumpen," and on the fringes of the revolutionary endeavor (Otero 2001:53). The banning of the Sabá Cabrera Infante film *PM* at that time derived largely from the belief that it distorted the image of Cuba by glorifying Havana's hedonistic nightlife while failing to discuss important government initiatives (the literacy campaign, volunteer militias, housing reform, etc.). José Ardévol also expressed his lack of enthusiasm for many cabaret shows, describing them as cheap, crude, and working against the CNC's attempts to educate the public about "high" culture.

> We agree that entertainment spectacles are not especially destined to improve, educate, or instruct. In a certain sense, they function like an escape valve, as a parenthesis of superficial diversion, and that is how it should be. But, if in addition to being an amusing pastime they contribute to crudeness, bad taste, insolence, cheap sensualism, or sexual ambiguity, it is evident that they can be a significant negative factor. They may become a form of spreading habits and preferences that, although it may not appear so at first glance, conspire openly against revolutionary goals. What the public gains in cultural understanding through our educational work is lost, with interest, in the most profound of their modes of being or feeling, in terms of ideology. (Ardévol 1966:135–36)[2]

On the other hand, the Cuban public was enamored of its stage artists. It had come to expect lavish venues that featured them and did not want these venues closed. The problem became more acute after the state closed private recreational *sociedades* in 1962 that had served as alternate centers for dance activity. State-controlled cabarets and clubs thus represented an especially important space—one of the few remaining—for listening to a *conjunto* or *charanga*.

Many bands continued to receive government support and airplay in the mid-1960s and beyond: the Orquesta Aragón, the Riverside, Estrellas Cubanas, the Sensación, the Conjunto Roberto Faz, the Melodias del 40, Pacho Alonso, and so forth. Gradually, however, the directors of radio and television called upon performers to express their sympathies with socialist issues through their compositions and/or in live verbal segments between songs. It became difficult to remain neutral, unassociated with the new Communist Party or with political issues of the moment, and be a viable entertainer. As codified a decade or so later in position papers of the PCC, government leaders pressured artists toward the linking of art with "the lives of the masses and their most vital interests" and the rejection of "outdated, antihumanistic literary or artistic manifestations derived from capitalism" (Partido Comunista de Cuba 1978:90). Moralizing initiatives were common, involving attempts by government-controlled unions to impose "decency and good manners" in theaters and cabarets (*Bohemia* 52, no. 8 [February 21, 1960]: 110).

Beginning in 1962, state institutions began using dance music as a means of rewarding those in support of revolutionary ideals and endeavors, as they continue to now (Ardévol 1966:213). One of my first experiences with a Cuban dance event in 1992, as an example, was at a government-sponsored party thrown for factory workers. They had been selected for their high output and quality standards maintained over a period of months. Dance music may also be used to ensure a strong public turnout for socialist holidays, such as outdoor block parties celebrating the anniversary of the founding of the Comités en Defensa de la Revolución each fall. Dance bands may accompany volunteers in agricultural work brigades or as part of the annual sugarcane harvest. David Calzado suggests that PCC members do not have a high opinion of dance music—often they consider it "low class" *(música baja, sin nivel, de la hampa)*, vulgar, and a *cosa de negros*, associated primarily with poorly educated Afro-Cubans—but nevertheless recognize its utility as a tool to further particular ends.

> Popular Cuban [dance] music has always been a marginal music
> [in revolutionary Cuba]. What happens is that it has been strongly
> supported [by the masses]. It has endured because the public wanted
> it that way. If you try to have an assembly in the Plaza of the Revolu-
> tion, or a mass rally of the national UJC, well if you don't invite Paulito
> and his Elite . . . the Charanga Habanera, or Los Van Van, or others
> that I haven't mentioned, no one will attend. That's reality. Our work
> as musicians has been recognized only because [the government] was
> obligated to do so. (Calzado 1996, interview)

Calzado's comments suggest that dance music represents a potentially oppositional space, one in which politics and Marxist ideology are generally deemphasized and pleasure, physicality, and other factors predominate.

DECREASING SUPPORT FOR DANCE MUSIC

Various factors impeded the development of dance music in the late 1960s, even after the exodus of major performers tapered off. The constant shuffling and reorganization of music events under centralized agencies as well as abrupt shifts in government policy toward culture led to disruptions. A lack of access to replacement parts, resulting from the embargo, meant that when recording or amplification equipment broke down it could not easily be repaired. Hundreds of artists put down their instruments and took part in the massive "Cordón de La Habana" agricultural effort in 1967, a movement to plant coffee on the outskirts of the city.

Even more important, the attitude of leaders began to shift more decisively against dance bands and cabarets. In a *Bohemia* article from 1967, one author refers to cabarets as "commercial structures designed to exploit frustrations and vices . . . a mere ostentatious exhibition of butts and thighs"

(Muñoz-Unsain 1967:34). It stresses that nightclubs are characteristic of a capitalist "society of exploitation" in which art serves as an opiate, keeping the public from thinking about more important issues. "In a society that, on the contrary, tries to elevate not only the economic but also the moral and cultural level of its members," it suggests, these establishments lose their meaning. "Because in such a society—like ours today—it is important that the people think deeply about things" (Muñoz-Unsain 1967:34).[3]

Reflecting such values, policy makers lent their strongest support to music with overtly political, or at least socially conscious, lyrics. This led to new sorts of composition from the outset of the revolution: marches dedicated to the 26th of July or the departure of the *Granma*, traditional *sones* discussing agrarian reform, and choral works calling for socialist unity.[4] The same tendency led to eventual support of the protest song movement, with compositions denouncing the U.S. war in Vietnam, colonialist aggression, and related topics. Widespread promotion of this music eclipsed dance repertoire for a time (Hernández 2002:70). Ideological pressures convinced some musicians to play danceable tunes that reflected the goals of the revolution. As of the 1970s, one finds happy, upbeat recordings whose lyrics make reference, somewhat incongruously, to civil war in Angola ("De Kabinda a Kunene un solo pueblo" by Los Karachi) or the revolutionary campaign of the Sandinistas in Nicaragua against the Samoza dictatorship ("El son de Nicaragua" by the Orquesta Chepín).[5]

In the final analysis, a combination of economic crises and political decisions combined to adversely affect Cuban nightlife. The government's well-intentioned but unproductive agricultural efforts such as the *cordón* plan resulted in a significant drop in the country's GNP. Its decision to nationalize all small businesses as part of a hardening of socialist policy—part of the *ofensiva revolucionaria*—also proved detrimental to economic activity across the board. Acosta 2002:137 describes 1968 as "the most disastrous year ever for popular Cuban music," noting that the ramifications of decisions made at that time are still being felt. The mass mobilization of workers in an attempt to boost sugar production in 1969–70, the *zafra de los 10 millones,* contributed to this slump. As Cuba struggled with its finances and devoted all possible resources to the harvest, reducing support for nightlife seemed justifiable. In 1969, officials shut down thousands of the clubs it had just nationalized across the country to keep people focused on the task at hand (D'Rivera 1998:120); afterward, many never reopened.

Dance venues closed after 1968 and that's when the big crisis began.
The Tropical and Polar beer gardens, almost all the places where they

offered big dances were shut. After [the harvest of 1970], the Salón
Mambí opened to one side of the Tropicana. It was the only place that
presented shows continuously after that time. Even it was a mess . . .
events inevitably ended in fights, arguments, police intervention.
Almost the only nightlife left [in Havana] was in Vedado in the high-
profile hotel spots, and in the Tropicana. (Acosta 2001, interview)

Approximately 40 percent of popular entertainers had nowhere to perform
during the early 1970s. They continued to receive their salaries but remained
idle, without viable work options. Cabarets and dances all but disappeared
from public social life for a time.

Recording proved difficult as well. Melquiades Fundora Dino, a member
of the Sublime and the Sensación orchestras, remembers that although his
groups received support and continued to perform through the 1970s and
1980s, they were unable to make records for almost sixteen years (Fundora
Dino 2001, interview). Tellingly, the record the Sublime finally produced
resulted from the efforts of a West German entrepreneur, not the support
of EGREM. The Orquesta Aragón experienced similar difficulties, making
a record in the Dominican Republic for its fiftieth anniversary only due to
the efforts of a Cuban music lover in exile, Eduardo Hernández (Cristóbal
Díaz Ayala, pers. comm.). Similar problems kept bands from making frequent television appearances. Popular music recordings and airplay in the
early 1970s seem to have been dominated by Hispanic pop styles rather than
local genres (Orejuela Martínez 2004:221–24).

Through the late 1980s, it was virtually impossible to study dance music at National Art Schools. Calzado (1996, interview) remembers that in
the ENA "you could only talk about Beethoven, Bach, Mozart, you couldn't
even mention popular music. If they found someone playing Cuban pop at
school they could be expelled because [the teachers] thought of it as a cheap
music, a third-class music." Numerous students clashed with administrators over these issues, including guitarist Pablo Menéndez, now the leader
of the fusion group Mezcla, and the recently deceased Emiliano Salvador,
one of Cuba's best jazz pianists. Both were expelled because of their refusal
to focus on the European classical canon. Menéndez now regrets his unwillingness to study classical guitar, believing that it would have improved
his abilities as a performer (Menéndez 1996, interview). Happily, in the mid-
1990s he became part of the ENA's faculty as its first instructor of electric
guitar.[6]

One result of the classical emphasis in the ENA's curriculum is that countless individuals graduated from the school lacking a basic familiarity with

dance music (Calzado 1996, interview). They had admirable technical skills but knew next to nothing about the *son, comparsa,* or mambo. Some continued playing this repertoire on their own and were able to combine traditional rhythms with their newly acquired classical technique. But the lack of direct exposure to the popular performance styles of earlier decades resulted in significant changes. The music personified by pianist Rubén González, *timbalero* Amadito Valdés, bassist Orlando "Cachaito" López, trumpeter Félix Chappottín, and others ceased to be a dominant model after the mid-1970s. It was left to younger performers graduating from conservatories to reinvent Cuban dance music with their own experiences and tastes.

THE EMERGENCE OF A NEW GENERATION

Without much local repertoire to listen to, aspiring dance band musicians after 1968 often turned their attention abroad, listening in the evening to radio broadcasts from Miami. This is one reason that influences from jazz, rock, funk, bossa nova, and other genres appear increasingly in recordings from the period. Given the difficulty of travel, incorporating foreign influences represented a way to mark new compositions as modern and cosmopolitan, as well as somewhat hip and "subversive." Cuba's isolation from the international community fed local musicians' desire for such music, yet it also created space for them to freely interpret and refashion it. Along with genres from other countries, local folkloric drumming also served as an increasing source of inspiration because of its greater prominence.

The history of Los Van Van, one of the most important dance bands to emerge in the late 1960s,[7] demonstrates the creativity of ensembles at that time (Fig. 10). The band, created by bassist Juan Formell (b. 1943) in 1969, might be considered the Rolling Stones of Cuba, given its enduring popularity. Its name derives from slogans on TV suggesting (incorrectly) that the country would attain its goal of producing ten million tons of sugar in the harvest of 1970, that "los diez millones van, señores, van . . ." Formell received early musical instruction from his father, a pianist and flutist, and listened to *filin* music played near his home in the Callejón de Hamel. As a teenager he studied guitar, then concentrated on bass after receiving job offers in the Revolutionary Police Band and in the house orchestra of the nationalized Havana Hilton (Salado 1985:71). His early influences included Elvis Presley, the Beatles, compositions by Juanito Márquez, as well as the music of traditional dance bands: the Conjunto Chappottín, Orquesta Aragón, and the dance band of Benny Moré (Peláez 1988:5). In 1967, Formell

FIGURE 10.   Los Van Van posing for a promotional photo, 1984. Members seated in the front row, from left to right: Pedro Calvo, lead singer; Manuel Leyva (violin); Lázaro González (violin); Manuel "Manolo" Labarrera (congas). Middle row (L–R): Juan Linares (violin); Orlando Canto (flute); César "Pupy" Pedroso (piano); Edmundo Pina (trombone); and Julio Noroña (güiro). Top row (L–R): José Luis "Changuito" Quintana (timbales/drum set); Mario "Mayito" Valdés (vocals); Juan Formell (director/bass); Cristóbal González (trombone). Photo Archive, Ministry of Culture, Cuba.

joined the *charanga* of Elio Revé and remained there until forming Van Van with *timbalero* Changuito (José Luis Quintana), singer Pedrito (Pedro Calvo), pianist César "Pupy" Pedroso, and others. Changuito and Pupy contributed greatly to the group's success as well, the latter through his many compositions, the former with his rhythmic innovations and unique performance style.

Members of Van Van are part of the progressive movement whose experiments helped create the sound of *timba*, modern Cuban dance music. The anthology *Los Van Van: 30 aniversario* (Formell and Los Van Van 1999b) provides a good overview of the group's stylistic development. Early pieces such as "Marilú" are influenced by British invasion rockers (whose music is referred to as "beat"), fusing R&B-style percussion with multipart vocals and extended harmonies. Later songs strike the listener as more grounded in a 1950s-style *charanga* format, albeit with variations. Formell added trombones to his orchestra in addition to the flute and violins, apparently inspired by Fania-era *salseros* from New York. His was the first band to incorporate the drum set alongside the timbales, another manifestation of rock influence, and to modify the traditional *güiro* pattern so that it emphasized an "and-1," "and-3" rhythm. More recently, the band has experimented with rap elements. Van Van has consistently adopted the role of modernizer, blending Cuban music with foreign styles (Perna 2001:45).

Changuito's use of the kick drum, snare, and synthesized percussion made a strong impression on younger artists (Villafranca 2000, interview), especially in early hits such as "El buey cansado" (The Tired Ox) (Salado 1985:71). This and later pieces represented a conspicuous incorporation of funk music into the *son*. The most well-known rhythm popularized by Van Van, *songo*, has existed in many permutations through the years, some of which contain influences from Yoruba folkloric drumming (Salado 1985:71) as well as from rock. Raul Fernandez (pers. comm.) notes that *songo* developed at least in part from attempts on the part of other *charangas* such as Ritmo Oriental, Maravillas Florida, and Elio Revé y su Charangón to emulate the dense, syncopated rhythms popularized by Pedro Izquierdo in the 1960s;[8] Ritmo Oriental's *timbalero* Daniel Díaz and others began adding new accessories to their timbales kits as well as incorporating the U.S.-style drum set in order to create new layers of texture.[9]

One of the common ways that Van Van played *songo* in the early 1970s is transcribed below (Ex. 3). The group's drum set was minimal, consisting only of tom-toms, bass drum, and snare; later high hat and cymbals were added. A straight right-hand pattern on the timbales' wood block apparently imitates what a rock drummer might play in a British invasion band (Abreu Robles 2003, interview). Congas play a fast pattern against this, creating a double-time feel. Note that in the conga transcription of Example 3 and in other conga parts notated subsequently in this work, the note heads on lower lines indicate those played on a second, lower-pitched drum; those with downward stems are played by the weak hand, up-stems with the strong hand. Normal note heads in the conga part denote open tones; "x" note heads denote slaps. Slash heads are used to indicate light strokes. A "T" above a slash head means a light touch with the fingers and a "P" a light touch with the palm.[10]

Changuito has incorporated elements from a host of sources into his repertoire over the years, including music from neighboring Caribbean islands, Brazil, and the United States. In terms of the latter, he notes the drumming of jazzers Art Blakey, Buddy Rich, and Elvin Jones as contributing to

EXAMPLE 3.   Early *songo* rhythmic sketch as played by Los Van Van.

his style, as well as the groove of Blood, Sweat and Tears drummer Bobby Colomby (Quintana and Mauleón Santana 1996) and the group Chicago. The *bota* rhythm he popularized in the 1970s has strongly influenced the rhythms heard in modern *timba* bands, especially on the conga. Other notable experiments by Changuito include the *merensongo* rhythm, incorporated into pieces such as "Nosotros de Caribe." At present, Van Van's *songo* style incorporates a unique *cáscara,* or shell pattern, on the timbales and an expanded conga *tumbao* that spans four measures.

Van Van lyrics tend to be lighthearted; Formell attributes much of his success to them and emphasizes that humor has not always been effectively used by Cuban entertainers (Salado 1985:72). References to wild dancing is a common theme, as are bawdy subjects, for instance "La fruta," which discusses a *fruta bomba,* or papaya, synonymous with "pussy." Other pieces ("La Habana no aguanta más" [Havana Can't Take Any More]) address social concerns more directly, in this case urban housing shortages, or stress the importance of Afro-Cuban heritage ("Soy todo" [I Am Everything], "Appapas del Calabar" [Appapas from the Calabar]). Van Van's development of new sounds seems to have contributed to the longevity of the band; it continued to perform to enthusiastic audiences even after Pupy Pedroso, Pedro Calvo, and other members left to pursue solo careers. The band won a Grammy in 2000 for their release *Llegó . . . Van Van* (Van Van Has Arrived), distributed by Time Warner (Formell and Los Van Van 1999a: 58).

As should be clear, a tendency toward experimentation has characterized Cuban dance music of the socialist period. Perhaps no band epitomizes this tendency more than Irakere, founded in 1973 by Jesús "Chucho" Valdés (b. 1941), son of Tropicana pianist Bebo Valdés (b. 1918). "Irakere" is Yoruba, meaning "jungle" or "lush place." The band's cadre of amazingly virtuosic musicians (initially Valdés himself, trumpeters Arturo Sandoval and Jorge Varona, saxophonists Carlos Averhoff and Paquito D'Rivera, guitarist Carlos Emilio Morales, percussionist Enrique Pla), its creative, playful reper-

FIGURE 11. The group Irakere photographed in a recording session in Havana, early 1970s. Director Chucho Valdés is at the piano. Other members depicted from left to right: Jorge "El Niño" Alfonso (cowbell), Armando Cuervo (tambourine), Paquito D'Rivera (flute), Carlos Averhoff (piccolo), Carlos Emilio Morales (guitar), Jorge Varona (trumpet), and Arturo Sandoval (trumpet). Photo Archive, Ministry of Culture, Cuba.

toire, and its overall excellence have long been recognized internationally (Fig. 11). Valdés completed his musical education prior to 1959 in the Municipal Conservatory of Havana, but most other members studied in socialist schools. Some have defected—D'Rivera in 1980 and Sandoval in the 1990s—but new talent of similar caliber continues to join the ensemble.

Several founders of Irakere played together in an experimental jazz group as early as 1963 known as Chucho Valdés y su Combo; they offered concerts without government recognition or salary (Valdés in Seguin 1997:44). Many also played in the Orquesta Cubana de Música Moderna (OCMM), a progressive, jazz-fusion ensemble established in 1967, and in the more conventional Army Band through approximately 1975. The OCMM created countless logistical problems for dance band performers; bureaucrats pulled the best musicians out of more than a dozen preexisting groups, weakening all the rest to form a "super-orchestra" (Raul Fernandez, pers. comm.). This sort of intervention would only have been conceivable in a centrally planned economy. Directed by Armando Romeu and Rafael Somavilla, it performed avant-garde jazz compositions by Leo Brouwer and Juan Blanco, Gershwin jazz standards, and progressive arrangements of Cuban dance tunes.

Founding members of Irakere struggled to separate from this and other state-organized groups in order to have complete control over their repertoire and to increase opportunities for travel (Kirk and Padura Fuentes 2001:70). They also wished to write music that would appeal more directly to Cuba's youth. Directors of the OCMM had attempted this as well by including drum set and electric guitar in their ensemble but only managed to score hits with an occasional piece, such as a Cubanized version of the Jimmy Smith R&B tune "One Mint Julep."[11] Separating from the OCMM proved difficult, as its directors did not want to lose their best instrumentalists (Acosta 2002:151). In the face of significant obstacles, Irakere has managed to become independent and flourish, creatively blending influences from mainstream jazz, funk, Cuban *son*, Afro-Cuban religious repertories, classical pieces, and other sources. Diverse artistic tendencies among members contributed to the group's vitality: percussionists such as Oscar Valdés championed experimentation with folklore and dance rhythms, and Paquito D'Rivera simultaneously explored creative fusions of jazz and classical music (Orejuela Martínez 2004:285).

Known internationally as an experimental jazz band, Irakere has consistently played dance music as well; within Cuba, dance music constitutes its primary repertoire. The group achieved widespread popularity in 1972 with the Valdés composition "Bacalao con pan" (Codfish and Bread), based on a traditional *pregón*, followed by "Luisa" and "Moja el pan" (Wet the Bread; D'Rivera 1998:180). "Misa negra," a piece written a few years earlier, predates repertoire of the following decade by incorporating entire *toques* (rhythmic sequences) and liturgical melodies from Santería ceremony. Irakere's music from the 1970s also experiments with the incorporation of *batá* drums and *chéquere*. In "El coco" and "Juana" one can hear the antecedent of the 1980s *timba* sound—funk bass lines, prominent drum set, jazz-influenced instrumental melodies—along with picaresque lyrical inferences typical of Cuban dance tunes.[12] Irakere, like Van Van, has created highly original grooves including *batum-batá* (D'Rivera 1998:180). In this style, the group's original percussionists, Tato Alfonso, Enrique Pla, and Oscar Valdés, performed *iyesá* patterns on the *batá* in tandem with Jorge "El Niño" Alfonso's wildly elaborated *tumbao* on five different congas and a simultaneous bell pattern (Paquito D'Rivera, John Santos, pers. comm.). Since

1990s, the group has recorded dance music on albums such as *Indestructible* (Valdés 1999).

It took years for the members of Irakere to achieve critical recognition at home; before 1977 they received little institutional support and could rarely record. The fact that the ensemble's music was influenced by styles from the United States, especially funk and jazz, and that not all members had strong socialist convictions complicated the approval process (Orovio 2001, interview). Most functionaries at this time still considered jazz "music of the imperialists."[13] The group performed wherever they could: in vocational schools, off nights in the Club El Rio, and for dancers in the Salon Mambí (D'Rivera 1998:194). Cultural policies of the 1970s obliged them to play less-desirable sites outside Havana as well and to modify their repertoire. "We had to play in many *escuelas al campo*, for other 'voluntary' work efforts, to record songs composed by Commander [Juan] Almeida, accompany political activities, and write music dedicated to the efforts of the revolution as in the case of a lovely *danzón* composed by Chucho, 'Valle de Picadura,' inspired by an agricultural plan of [Fidel's elder brother Ramón Castro]" (D'Rivera 1998:182–83). D'Rivera also describes playing in parties of high military officers such as Commander Curbelo.

Despite such concessions, opposition from Medardo Montero, Jorge Serguera, and others in control of the media made commercial success elusive; only through personal connections did they eventually triumph. In 1976, Irakere traveled to Bulgaria and Poland as well as to neighboring Jamaica as part of Carifesta. The latter trip came about after the election of leftist Michael Manley to the presidency, which improved relations between the two islands (D'Rivera 1998:199). In 1977, during the Carter administration, band members took part in concerts with North Americans in Havana and participated in the Newport and Montreux Jazz Festivals.[14] The international recognition they achieved as a result created additional opportunities for touring and recording.

THE SALSA CONTROVERSY

"Salsa" is commonly understood to be a marketing term that developed in 1960s New York to denote certain kinds of Cuban-influenced dance music. New York City has been an important center for the development and dissemination of Latin genres since at least the 1940s, but its importance increased dramatically in the aftermath of the U.S. trade embargo imposed on

Cuba in 1962. The history of salsa in New York and its ties to various immigrant communities there are beyond the scope of this study. I would only emphasize that many of the Latin dance crazes sweeping Europe and the United States prior to 1959—ballroom rumba, chachachá, conga—derived from Cuba rather than New York. The rupture of ties with Cuba created an artistic vacuum in North America and elsewhere, with countless enthusiasts unable to purchase the music they loved. This demand paved the way for the preeminence of Fania and other North American entrepreneurs.

The emergence of New York salsa, coming as it did only a few years after the onset of the embargo, assassination attempts against Castro, extreme tensions between Cuban nationals and the exile community, and the height of ideological radicalism among socialist leaders, inspired controversy from the beginning. The alteration and remarketing of music based on traditional Cuban genres as "salsa" by Fania and other labels without clear recognition of its origins angered musicians.[15] Many, including Antonio Arcaño, Rafael Lay, and Rosendo Ruiz, denounced the term immediately (Acosta 1997:27–28). More than a few suggested that salsa was a plot designed to further marginalize and disenfranchise revolutionary artists (Acosta 1996, interview).

Salsa as an economic phenomenon does raise troubling issues. The fact that North Americans implemented an embargo policy prohibiting Cubans from selling their music abroad and then proceeded to market much the same music themselves seems unethical. Manuel (1987:170) notes that "since the United States has made a particular effort to isolate Cuba economically, diplomatically, culturally and ideologically, the commercially successful recycling of Cuban music under the 'alienating and mystifying slogan' (Torres 1982) of 'salsa' is seen as especially duplicitous."

One might counter that the Cuban government created much of the problem for itself by refusing to adhere to international copyright agreements, leaving the legal door open for Jerry Masucci and others to record songs without compensating the composers. But Cuba's tepid support for dance music after 1968 undoubtedly contributed to the decision by foreign businesses to market such music as well. Even without the U.S. embargo, less *conjunto* and *charanga* repertoire would have been available, given that its production was no longer a priority. Responding to demand, companies like Fania simply provided what consumers wanted.

Many of the complaints raised by Cuban nationals about salsa were and are legitimate. U.S. firms amassed a fortune in revenues during the 1970s and 1980s by brazenly appropriating songs of Cuban origin; access to widespread networks of distribution in the capitalist world has allowed Fania,

RMM, and others to dominate the international Latin music trade ever since. Even today, producers abroad frequently print the letters "D.R." (*derechos reservados*, or "copyright reserved") after particular titles as a means of claiming legal rights while avoiding use of Cuban composers' names (Díaz Ayala 1981:339). In other cases, songs are brazenly copyrighted under entirely new authors and titles.[16]

Cristóbal Díaz Ayala believes that the term *salsa* was consciously adopted as a means of obscuring the roots of the music, but not for political reasons. Rather, adopting it allowed artists and producers to avoid references to Cuba during a politically volatile period and to sell their music to a broader sector of the public. "Earlier they used the term 'Cuban music,' but [after 1959] Cuba turned into an ugly four-letter word . . . one of those guys had the bright idea, instinctively, of creating a new name, making a cosmetic change: 'salsa.' And of course, in time salsa itself has become aesthetically richer, more distinct and innovative in its own right, separating from its origin and roots" (Cristóbal Díaz Ayala, pers. comm.). Izzy Sanabria (1992) largely supports this view. He suggests that the term, which he helped popularize, did function to obscure the roots of the music and was chosen because of its appeal as a catchy marketing label. Sanabria does not believe, however, that the failure to reference Cuba directly was conscious or malicious.

It is ironic, given the heated controversy surrounding salsa on the island, that most Cuban nationals remained oblivious both to the term and to the New York artists associated with it. An entire generation of listeners grew up without ever hearing names like El Gran Combo, La Sonora Ponceña, the Fania All Stars, or Pete "El Conde" Rodríguez. This was due in part to the inability of consumers to freely purchase music from abroad but primarily to national media censorship—the "autoblockade"—that excluded salsa from domestic airplay (Acosta 1997:28). Party ideologues went as far as to prohibit mention of "salsa" on the radio or in print (Orovio 2001, interview). Journalist Cristóbal Sosa (2001, interview) remembers that merely by playing an LP of New York *salsersos* at home one risked denouncement by local CDR members. "The salsa music from New York, of Eddie and Charlie Palmieri, all that, was considered the enemy." In referring to domestic dance music they used other terms, most often *son* or *música bailable.*

Beginning in the late 1970s, government policy began to move toward reconciliation with foreign salsa artists. It may be that the strong popularity of the music abroad forced bureaucrats to reevaluate the importance of dance repertoire and to begin recording it domestically once again. In the late 1970s, EGREM created an ensemble known as the Estrellas de Areíto, or Areíto All Stars, taking their name from the regional state-owned recording label in Havana. This group, consisting of highly regarded musicians Tata Güines, Rafael Lay, Niño Rivera, Félix Chappottín, Carlos Embale, Miguelito Cuní, and others, represented a direct response and challenge to the Fania All Stars of Jerry Masucci. It attempted to draw attention away from New York and to underscore again their belief that "salsa" came from Cuba.

Policies of engagement with Cuba under the Carter administration (1976–80) contributed to a gradual thawing of the "cold war" over salsa; this is the same period that saw the reestablishment of diplomatic ties between the two countries for the first time since 1961 and a new allowance for cultural exchange. CBS Records successfully invited Irakere to record and perform in the United States. At roughly the same time, the Fania All Stars themselves visited Cuba. Politically oriented salsa compositions by Rubén Blades, Willie Colón, and others sympathetic to socialist issues eventually caused those in charge of cultural policy to amend their long-standing biases.

The changing attitudes of the establishment may also have been shaped by a desire to foster stronger relations with other Latin American countries. Many remember Venezuelan Oscar de León's visit to Cuba in 1984 as a watershed moment in terms of salsa's acceptance, for instance (Alexis Esquivel, pers. comm.). León, the first internationally recognized *salsero* from the developing world to perform in Cuba, had always acknowledged his debt to Benny Moré, Barbarito Diez, the Trío Matamoros, and others; for that reason, his presence was less problematic. León's dynamic stage presence and strong promotion of prerevolutionary repertoire drove home to Cuban audiences how little music of that sort they typically heard. Bureaucrats interpreted the decision by the Central Committee to air and promote his music as a signal that salsa could now be played on the radio; this remained true even after statements he made against socialism (apparently incited by Miami politicians) generated new polemics.

Dance music on Cuban television continues to be performed largely by national rather than international artists, however. The year 1979 saw the emergence of the *Para bailar* show; from 1990 through 1999, the program *Mi salsa* appeared (Hernández-Reguant 2002:160). Others of the early 1990s such as *Todo el mundo canta* and *Sabadazo* included dance music segments. Since 1989, popular music of all types has received strong support because of its ability to generate foreign currency. At present, performing dance music offers Cubans potentially higher salaries than they could hope to achieve in virtually any other way.

SALSA VERSUS *TIMBA*

New York salsa music—considering primarily the "classic" pieces of the 1970s and 1980s—is associated with a number of distinct musical characteristics that distinguish it from *timba*. The incorporation of Puerto Rican *bomba* and *plena* rhythms in many pieces, as well as those from Colombia and elsewhere;[17] the use of *güiro* patterns and entire melodies derived from Puerto Rican *seis*; the foregrounding of instruments such as the *cuatro*; the development of hybrid genres incorporating influences from North American pop of the 1960s (e.g., bugaloo) and more recently African American style vocal melisma; and a preference for particular timbral/orchestrational blends emphasizing strident percussion and prominent trombone riffs represent only a few examples. These significant factors notwithstanding, the essence of the musical style is taken from the Cuban *son* and specifically *conjuntos* of the 1940s and 1950s. Features derived from Cuba include characteristic percussion instruments (clave, bongo and conga drums, timbales, cowbell), a number of distinct rhythms (the basic *tumbao* pattern on the conga; *cáscara* rhythms derived ultimately from Cuban rumba; interlocking bell rhythms performed on the timbales and bongo bells; the clave rhythm itself), anticipated bass figures, and piano *montunos* derived from melodies on the *tres*.

In contrast to New York groups, modern Cuban *timba* bands typically do not use a bongo drum, replacing it with drum set (often playing a funklike groove), a second keyboard, and sometimes a drum machine. Drums, timbales, and congas combine with the bass and the two keyboards to create a very dense and syncopated texture. Bass lines are more unpredictable than in salsa, incorporating fast runs, sustained notes, glissandi, chromatic passages, and slaps. Horn sections tend to be large, foregrounding trumpets and saxophones rather than trombones. The instrumentation of most groups is closer to that of Cuban jazz bands of the 1950s than the *conjuntos* of the same period (Perna 2001:118). Jazz melodic influences are prominent, especially in the instrumental arrangements. Horn lines, while fast and complex, are often scored in unison rather than multiple voices, as this is believed to create a "harder," edgier sound. Bands such as Earth, Wind and Fire and P-Funk seem to have influenced *timbero* composers heavily, as discussed by Bamboleo's director Lázaro Valdés (Robinson 2004:87). Pianist Elio Villafranca (2000, interview) notes additionally that each group has its own arranger who tends to write for it exclusively over an extended period. In this way, bands strive for a unique sound consisting of characteristic "sig-

EXAMPLE 4. Standard and *timba*-style piano *montuno* patterns, the latter from Delgado 1999.

nature breaks," or *sellos*, innovative *montuno* patterns, and other elements that define their style.[18]

Example 4 contrasts a standard New York salsa-style keyboard pattern over a i–IV–ii–V progression against a pattern with the same changes representative of Cuban *timba*. Note the freer use of rhythm, the extended melodic range, and the longer phrase length. The second example comes from Issac Delgado's rendition of the Pedro Flores song "Obsesión" (Delgado 1999).[19]

Modern *timba* compositions often begin with a funk-influenced introduction—as in NG La Banda's "Santa palabra" (Cortés 1994), one of the first *timba* pieces recognized as such—rather than the ballad-like introductions common in modern Puerto Rican salsa. *Timba* songs also place greater emphasis on the *montuno* than the verse; the *montuno* is usually the longer section and may contain as many as five or six distinct choruses. Each band uses multiple singers who alternate inventing improvised responses to them. The transition from the verse to the *montuno* is often marked by a *bomba* or *masacote* "breakdown" interlude in which percussion continues but horns, keyboards, and bass drop out (González Bello and Casanella 2002). Van Van initially popularized the breakdown, now imitated by almost everyone (Drake 2000). It is accented by occasional downward slides on the bass strings and strong beats on 3 and 4 of the 4/4 measure by the floor tom of the drum set.

Finally, the dance style accompanying *timba* music is also different from that of salsa in New York, Puerto Rico, or South America. Puerto Rican dancing usually emphasizes fast successions of complicated turns and spins that focus attention on couples' arms. When dancing individually, couples execute kicks and slides reminiscent of the lindy and jitterbug. *Timba* dancers, by contrast, execute turns less frequently and quickly, placing more emphasis on round, independent motion of the hips and shoulders. *Timberos* dance individually quite often, especially as part of *despelote* exhibitionism associated with the breakdown (Drake 2000). This section often features women who execute virtuosic and/or sexually explicit movements. Specific choreography associated with *despelote*, which derives ultimately from Afro-Cuban folklore, includes *la batidora* (rapid pelvic rotation) and *tembleque* (making the entire body quiver or tremble).[20] *Rueda de casino*, another distinct form of Cuban choreography, consists of group dancing in which multiple partners stand in concentric circles, men on the outside and women on the inside. It first developed in the late 1950s as a fusion of *son* and chachachá with jitterbug (Orejuela Martínez 2004:231) and became a national craze in the mid-1960s. Designated leaders call out moves which are then executed simultaneously by all participants. They often involve passing partners or moving to a new partner so that everyone gradually rotates around the ring.

Musicologist Danilo Orozco describes *timba* as an "inter-genre" because it so aggressively references and mixes elements from a diversity of local and international sources and maintains them in "permanent internal conflict or tension" (as discussed in González Bello and Casanella 2002:4). Many elements derive from African American subculture (rapped vocal lines, clothing reminiscent of hip-hop artists such as baggy pants and baseball caps, the funk and jazz elements mentioned earlier). *Timba* is performed primarily by black Cubans; in a stylistic sense, the music creates an aesthetic perceived by local audiences as decidedly "black" yet also modern and cosmopolitan. Indeed, some suggest that its construction of blackness contains a decidedly oppositional edge: "Under a political regime that rejected displays of identity based on race, religion and the like, timba boldly paid tribute to Afro-Cuban heritage, both religious and secular" (Hernández-Reguant 2004a:33). By means of Yoruba exclamations or the incorporation of ritual melodies from Santería; constant musical and verbal "riffing" off of national repertory of past decades; references to local people, places, or events; the creation of entirely new rhythms; the "quoting" of distinct Afro-Cuban folkloric traditions on percussion instruments; and with other playful elisions of music across boundaries of time and genre, musicians of color assert their ties to a unique and dynamic heritage.[21]

Example 5 illustrates how breaks in the song "Santa palabra" (Sacred Word), mentioned previously, imitate the sound of sacred *batá* drums. The middle line represents a traditional *iyesá* entrance rhythm on the *batás* as played by the larger *iyá* drum. Lower notes indicate those played on the *enú*, or larger head; higher notes indicate those played on the *chachá*, or

EXAMPLE 5. A traditional *iyesá* entrance rhythm on the *batás* and a timbal rhythm imitating it.

smaller head. This religious rhythm is imitated in variation on the timbales and floor tom. The break can be heard at 3:24" and 3:35", and at 6:18" (Cortés 1994).[22]

DANCE MUSIC IN THE 1990S AND BEYOND

The period extending from the late 1970s through 1989 gave rise to a number of campaigns of rectification within Cuba that had important implications for dance repertoire. New policies of decentralization, including the creation of independent musical *empresas* designed to direct and promote dance orchestras, proved beneficial to performers. Older groups, such as Van Van, Irakere, Son 14, La Original de Manzanillo, and Sierra Maestra, began to perform in more-attractive venues. Traditional *charangas, septetos,* and *conjuntos* (the Conjunto Chappottín, the Gloria Matanzera, the Conjunto Roberto Faz, etc.) recorded once again. New groups formed and rose to prominence: Adalberto Álvarez y su Son, Dan Den, Issac Delgado, NG La Banda. Cristóbal Díaz Ayala includes a useful summary of the approximately 650 LP titles issued by EGREM in the 1980s in his publication *Música cubana del areyto al rap cubano* (2003b:388–90). He notes that the Cuban recording industry at that time produced more LPs than in the 1960s and 1970s. Though it supported many different sorts of music—jazz, *nueva trova,* lyric vocalists, and experimental classical music—its largest number of releases is devoted to dance repertoire.

Since the mid-1990s, the prominence of dance music has skyrocketed, driven by strong international interest, the importance of such entertainment to tourism, and the relatively large salaries earned by performers.

Countless new ensembles have appeared: Anacaona, Azúcar Negra, Bamboleo, La Charanga Habanera, Girardo Piloto and Klímax, Dany Lozada y su Timba Cubana, Manolín "El Médico de la Salsa," Opus 13, Paulito FG y su Elite, Pupy Pedroso y los que Son Son, Sello L.A., Tamayo y su Salsa AM, Son Damas, and so forth. Over the last few years, the dance music scene has become so vibrant as to rival that of the 1950s once again. Variance exists between the styles of these groups, yet most demonstrate the influence of *timba*. The music has provided much-needed diversion for youth living in the difficult post-Soviet era.

One of the most influential bands of the early 1990s was NG (Nueva Generación) La Banda, directed by flutist José Luís Cortés, "El Tosco." More than any other ensemble, NG helped define the emergent sound of *timba*. Established in 1988, NG represented an all-star group of sorts that drew members from other important bands. Singer Tony Calá had previously played violin in Ritmo Oriental; singer Issac Delgado and the legendary *conguero* Juan "Wickly" Nogueras began their careers with Pachito Alonso; alto saxophonist Gérman Velazco played with the Orquesta Revé; he, together with trumpeter José "El Greco" Crego, tenor saxophonist Carlos Averhoff, and trumpeter José Munguía had also played in Irakere. Cortés himself performed previously in both Irakere and Los Van Van. Other initial members of NG included drummer Giraldo Piloto and keyboardist Rodolfo "Peruchín" Argudín. Groups of the mid-1990s, such as La Charanga Habanera, Klímax, and Paulito FG, owe much of their style to NG. The latter began with primarily jazz-oriented repertoire but soon shifted to dance music and solicited audiences in poorer, predominantly Afro-Cuban neighborhoods. The eclecticism of the group's sound, drawing from rock, jazz, chachachá, mambo, salsa, samba, and rap, set it apart immediately. NG was the first to expand the role of the chorus, playing down the role of instrumental improvisation while foregrounding vocal *soneos* (Perna 2001:61).

Modern dance music performance remains male-dominated, yet several female singers have emerged. Probably the best known is Haila (Haila María Mompié González), whom some refer to as "the diva of *son*." Born in 1974, she began her career in the early 1990s in the Septeto Tradición of Jacqueline Castellanos and later in the group Habana Son. In 1995, she gained popularity singing in the newly created group Bamboleo, often sharing the stage with vocalist Vania Borges. The use of two female singers to front a driving, top-notch *timba* orchestra represented a novelty and helped Bamboleo define its sound. Their first two albums, *Te gusto o te caigo bien* (1996) and *Yo no me parezco a nadie* (1997), were both well received. In 1998, Haila left the group together with Leonel Limonta and other members to form a new band,

FIGURE 12.   Singer Liena Hernández Senteno performing with the *timba* band Bamboleo in a free outdoor concert for local fans. Behind her stands bassist Osmani Díaz; conguero Lipsael Jiménez is also visible on the right. Note the singer's religious necklaces and white clothing, characteristic of new Santería initiates. Bamboleo tries to balance commercial performances in dollar venues with shows the public can more easily attend. This event took place in the predominantly Afro-Cuban neighborhood of Manglar, Havana, July 2004. Photo by Brunella Battista.

Azúcar Negra. She continues to perform with them and as a solo artist. Bamboleo has employed various new singers, including Liena Hernández Senteno and Tanja Pantoja (Fig. 12). The group's successful experiments with female vocalists have created new opportunities for women within *timba* bands.

It is interesting to compare *timba* lyrics with those of *nueva trova*, the youth music of a generation earlier. *Timba* is written in the direct parlance of the street, of the less educated, while *nueva trova* is mostly written by college-educated performers. *Timba* does not often allude to subjects found in *nueva trova*, at least directly: socialist struggle, international politics, existential issues. Its songs are much more grounded in local experience, often including slang words and phrases from poorer black neighborhoods. Lyrical themes are often ironic, humorous, bawdy, and irreverent. Many songs deprecate women, describing them as shallow, vain, and mercenary in their use of sexuality (Hernández-Reguant 2004a:35). Despite their frequently uncouth *(chabacana)* associations, and their condemnation by many music critics for that reason, commentators consistently cite *timba* lyrics as fundamental to the genre's popularity.[23] In the early and mid-1990s, they discussed subjects that did not appear in news reports: illegal business dealings, the detrimental effects of tourism, and the lack of basic consumer goods, to mention only a few examples. For this reason, the public perceived *timba* as more relevant and meaningful than other popular music.

> Lyrics had a great deal to do with the sudden popularity of *timba*. Many were written from the perspective of the socially marginal; they included very vulgar wording that reflected the crude realities of the moment, things that the press wouldn't cover, for example the *jineteras*,[24] the hunger many were experiencing, the legalization of the dollar and its effects, the material concerns of the people. . . . Initially, because of their vulgarity, there was a wholehearted rejection of such music by intellectuals. But the choruses of the songs were phenomenal . . . and the phrases that they incorporated became the refrains that everyone used on the street. (Saylín Álvarez, pers. comm.)

Examples of *timba* compositions of this nature include Los Van Van's "Un socio para mi negocio" (A Buddy for My Business Deal), which alludes to private enterprise and black market dealings; NG's "La bruja" (The Witch) and Manolín's "Te conozco, mascarita" (I Recognize You, Little Masked Girl), about female hustlers who reject the advances of Cuban men, preferring foreigners; and the Charanga Habanera's "Yuya la Charanguera" (Yuya the Party Girl), about a government vigilante associated with CDR organizations. Perna (2001:203) suggests that *timba* songs were controversial in the 1990s not primarily because of their "crude" lyrics or even their often-pejorative depictions of women, but because they focused on severe social problems and implicitly on the failings of revolutionary life. The attitude of *timba* composers toward the social phenomena they discuss is often ambiguous, but in many cases their lyrics seem to celebrate hustling and prostitution rather than condemn them. The locally grounded meanings of *timba* lyrics help explain both the popularity of the music within Cuba and the difficulty *timberos* have had generating audiences abroad.

One example of sociopolitical commentary from NG's repertoire worthy of mention is "La soya," or "Soy" (Cortés 1994). The song was inspired by a meat substitute, *picadillo de soya*, or soy hamburger, distributed across the island for several years at a time in which the government could provide virtually no real meat to the population. It consisted of soy mash mixed with animal blood and entrails so that it tasted vaguely like meat; in fact, everyone hated the taste and officials eventually discontinued its distribution. Open criticism of this food item was impossible in the state-controlled media, so Cortés chose instead to praise its virtues in a highly exaggerated manner. Using this approach, discussion of the *picadillo* became a form of parody.

> Señoras y señores,
> lo que les estoy contando es una cosa sabrosa.
> El picadillo de soya tiene 1, 2, 3, 4, 5, 6 7, 8, 9, 10,
> diez puntos sobre la alimentación mundial.
> En China comen la soya, en Bélgica, en Suiza, en Holanda,
> en Japón comen soya, la MacDonald e' de la soya también . . .
>
> Porque la soya es un alimento que tiene a todo el mundo en talla.
> Las mujeres están sabrosas,
> unas cinturas terribles, unas piernas que se caen.
> Yo no sé lo que pasa pero,
> caballeros, la soya está en ta-, ta, ta-ta, ta-ta, talla, talla, talla, talla,
> tremenda talla e' lo que tiene la soya, caballeros, ¡uh!
> ¡Vale Peruchín! ¿Oyó? ¡Prepárense a comer!
>
> Ladies and gentlemen,
> what I'm telling you is great news.
> Soy hamburger has 1, 2, 3, 4, 5, 6 7, 8, 9, 10,
> ten advantages over most global diets.
> In China they eat soy, in Belgium, in Switzerland, in Holland,
> in Japan they eat soy; Cuban hamburger is made of soy too . . .
>
> Because soy is a food that gets the whole world in shape.
> Women look wonderful,
> lovely waists, legs that make you fall over.
> I don't know what's going on, but, man,
> soy is for good sha-, sha-, sha-sha, sha-sha, shape, shape, shape, shape,
> great shape is what soy offers, man.
> Peruchín, hear that? Get ready to eat!

Perhaps the most notorious and controversial *timba* composition of the decade was the Charanga Habanera's "El temba" (Calzado 1996). This song popularized the term *temba*, meaning a middle-aged man, usually in his forties, who has plenty of money and is willing to share it with young women in return for sexual favors. *Tembas* are usually thought of as foreign tourists but can also be wealthier Cubans. *Guaniquiqui* from the same piece, meaning money, has also become part of everyday speech. The chorus of "El temba," performed in a highly rhythmic, semi-rapped style, tells young women: "Búscate un temba que te mantenga . . . pa' que tú goces, pa' que tú tengas" (Go find a *temba* that will support you . . . so you can enjoy yourself, so you can have things). A later phrase ("para que tengas lo que *tenías* que tener") parodies the final section of Nicolás Guillén's famous poem "Tengo," denoting the benefits the revolution brought to Cubans of color. Calzado (1996, interview) recounts that in political meetings held subsequently by the UNEAC, fellow artists denounced the song, believing that it incited young women to prostitute themselves. He countered that he only wrote about what he saw happening around him. Despite its popularity, the song was taken off the air for a time.[25]

Government reaction to *timba* lyrics has varied widely, from acceptance to indifference to a calculated suppression of particular tunes. Censorship was most common in the early and mid-1990s, prior to the music's popularization abroad. Recently the government has taken a more mercenary approach, letting compositions that generate high sales revenues circulate with relative freedom. Of course, dance music titles and chorus phrases are often short or ambiguous and can be interpreted in a number of ways. In some cases, their meanings may be altered or elaborated during live performances by means of improvised *soneo* vocals; alternately, they may be interpreted by the public in particular ways, regardless of what the authors intended to say. Stubbs (1989:78) notes that the title of Irakere's "Bacalao con pan" from the 1970s was charged with significance for listeners because at the time little else besides codfish was available to eat in Havana. Even apparently "normal" lyrics may have political connotations, such as "Green Mango" by Charanga Habanera. This song brought Castro to mind among many listeners because of the green military fatigues he typically wears (Perna 2001:245).[26] Artists are still far from free to discuss many issues, but the references to political issues in *timba* have proven more effective in disseminating their message than most other forms of music.

Increasing support for dance repertoire has resulted in the reopening of many clubs in the 1990s that had been closed for years. Radio and television now feature dance music constantly, and scores of new recordings are available. The domestic prominence of this music has been mirrored by growing interest in *timba* in the United States and Europe. All Cuban music has experienced an increase in foreign sales. International artists such as David Byrne and Ry Cooder have shown their interest through the creation of the *Cuba Classics* CD anthologies, the *Buena Vista Social Club* documentary, promotion of the Cubanismo ensemble, and in other ways.

The "*Buena Vista* phenomenon" deserves brief mention because of its almost unbelievable international success and the relatively cool response to the project within Cuba. Cuban commentators criticized the *Buena Vista Social Club* documentary when it appeared in 1997. Some derided Ry Cooder because of his ignorance of Cuba, its history, and of the Spanish language;

they considered him a poor choice as the film's central figure. Others expressed concern over the lack of political references in the work and the fact that no one had mentioned the negative impact of the U.S. embargo on artists and the public (Fornet et al. 2001:165). Filmmakers attacked it as dishonest, shallow, and "semiotically vulgar" (Rufo 2001:137). Musicologist María Teresa Linares took offense at scenes depicting dilapidated buildings in Havana but only the most pristine and well-maintained sections of Manhattan's business district. Others questioned why filmmaker Wim Wenders and Cooder chose to showcase prerevolutionary artists rather than the musical innovations of the *timba* generation. Ariana Hernández-Reguant has taken this last critique a step further, suggesting that *Buena Vista* evokes what might be described as "imperialist nostalgia" for prerevolutionary Cuba. She suggests that it recreates a colonial past devoid of political and economic inequalities and of the role of the United States in perpetuating them. By focusing on only selective aspects of Cuban history, she argues that the film contributes to an image of the country that Americans choose to remember: not one of right-wing dictatorships, American weapons, and bloodshed, but of smiles, music, *mulatas*, and cigar-smoking peasants (Hernández-Reguant 2000).

These commentaries effectively illustrate how cultural forms can perpetuate misrepresentations of particular groups and the ideologies that give rise to them. By the same token, commentators on the island have overlooked the complicity of domestic policies in the decline of prerevolutionary dance music. Performers of the 1940s and 1950s were consistently undervalued and underpromoted for years. They could rarely record or perform on television, and many of the clubs in which they established their careers were shut down. EGREM's archives undoubtedly contain better and more-representative recordings of midcentury dance music than those selected by Wim Wenders and Ry Cooder, but administrators chose not to market them until recently, abroad or at home. As a result, the Rubén Gonzálezes of Cuba remained in obscurity until "discovered" by visitors such as Cooder. *Timba* artists themselves struggle under adverse conditions, but they have the advantage of appealing strongly to the present-day Cuban public. This is something that earlier generations of dance band musicians cannot always achieve.

. . . . .

Dance traditions under socialism never disappeared but underwent changes as the result of revolutionary arts policies. Beginning in the mid-1960s, support for dance entertainment gradually declined. Those interested in studying and performing the traditional *son* struggled within a new cultural reality, one that promoted classical music instruction and strongly supported works with political messages. After 1970, the government reduced the available performance space for dance music and chose not to promote existing bands strongly. Its attitudes derived at least in part from bias against expression associated with poorer black communities that it considered simplistic or backward. By the mid-1980s, however, it began to support dance music once again, often as a means of drawing crowds for political events. Former Unión de Jóvenes Comunistas leader and Minister of Foreign Affairs Roberto Robaina had much to do with this change.

The new space created for dance bands since the late 1980s has been filled primarily by innovative artists associated with *timba*. Antecedents of this style can be traced to groups, such as Los Van Van and Irakere, that experimented with the fusion of foreign influences and local folklore with the Cuban *son*. As a fully developed style, *timba* first achieved recognition in the compositions of José Luis Cortés and his influential group NG La Banda. *Timba* represents a stylistic "blackening" of dance music traditions, revealing their close association with the tastes of Afro-Cuban youth and poorer communities generally. Its eclectic blend of local and international influences is perhaps a metaphor for the transnational spread of the Cuban population, the country's movement toward a market economy, and its increasing contact with foreign visitors (Noble 2001:50). *Timba* manifests a rejection on the part of younger Cubans of socialist rhetoric; its repertoire embraces sensuality, hedonism, and materialism.

Because of its appeal to tourists and its ability to generate hard currency, dance music has prevailed over other forms in recent years. Dance bands are more active abroad than at any time in the past forty years. New groups continue to appear: Los Ángeles de La Habana, Dayron y su Boom, Dennis y su Swing. It now appears that *timba* may have oversaturated the domestic market, however. Bands remain popular but compete for attention with other styles—rock, folkloric groups, rap, reggae, flamenco-influenced repertoire—and are perceived by many as being too commercial, too oriented toward foreign markets, less grounded in local social realities. A few artists have also gained considerable popularity performing traditional *son* music in a style similar to that of the pre-*timba* era, such as the recently deceased Polo Montañez (1955–2002) and the *tresero* and composer Pacho Amat.

The history of Cuban dance music teaches lessons about the central role of fun, humor, and sensuality in many forms of popular culture. Emma Goldman, quoted earlier, expressed feelings typical of many Cubans who struggle within a sometimes restrictive context to keep Cuban music playful and irreverent. They recognize that music's value often lies in the pleasure it brings to its listeners and that such pleasure cannot be compromised without affecting the vitality of the medium. *Timba* represents movement away from dogmatism and toward "fun" in a number of senses. It represents the triumph of grassroots traditions over those of the conservatory. As dance repertoire it represents liberation of the body. Its foregrounding of Afro-Cuban traditions brings the pleasures of marginal communities into the mainstream. Finally, its focus on sexuality, its unabashed embrace of material pleasure, and its avoidance of socialist "political correctness" constitute a good-natured yet forceful challenge to established values.

CHAPTER 5

Transformations in *Nueva Trova*

> There is no revolutionary art as yet. There are the elements of this art,
> there are hints and attempts at it, and, what is most important, there is
> the revolutionary man, who is forming the new generation in his own
> image and who is more and more in need of this art. How long will it
> take . . . to manifest itself clearly? It is difficult even to guess. . . . But
> why should not this art, or at least its first big wave, come soon as the
> expression of the art of the young generation which was born in the
> revolution and which carries it on?
>
> LEON TROTSKY, *Art and Revolution*

Despite its broad impact, surprisingly little of substance has been written
about *nueva trova*,[1] the music most closely associated with the Cuban Revolution. My primary interest in this repertoire concerns its changes in status through the years. *Nueva trova* began as an oppositional form of expression in aesthetic terms and sometimes in political terms. During its early
years it was referred to as *canción protesta* (protest song) and provided a
unique perspective on the revolution for those willing to listen. As a result
of their nonconformity, young *trovadores* often ran afoul of the police and
cultural organizations through about 1971. After that time, attitudes toward
them began to change. Within a few years they had received dramatically
increased exposure on radio and television, eventually becoming international symbols of a new socialist culture.

Since then, first-generation artists have tended to work within government institutions rather than outside them. While many remain creatively
active and influential, they no longer represent the same constituency or
issues as they did in the 1960s, and in their place new generations have
emerged. This essay provides information on the history of *nueva trova*,
examining the conflicts of early artists with authorities and the process by
which the movement was transformed from a voice of marginality into a
component of state-supported music making. Younger *trovadores* of the
1990s and beyond now distinguish their songs from those of past decades
by referring to them as *novísima trova*. Whether written on the island or
abroad, they continue to demonstrate a degree of freshness and irreverence
that characterized the movement when it began.

DEFINING *NUEVA TROVA*

Nueva trova cannot be understood without considering the turbulent political conditions of much of the developing world in the mid-twentieth century. In large part, this resulted from challenges to colonialism by groups who had been under political or economic domination for as long as three and a half centuries. Political agitation reflected a radicalization of the disenfranchised, a violent struggle for more equitable distribution of wealth and property within states that had achieved independence. Examples are plentiful; one has only to consider the Chinese Revolution or the campaigns to free Indonesia and India from the Dutch and British in the 1940s to recognize their magnitude. Similar events took place shortly thereafter in North Africa and French Indochina, as well as protests of a distinct but related nature in the United States in conjunction with the Civil Rights movement. Activism in all of these countries was roughly contemporary with the campaign that Fidel Castro began against Fulgencio Batista in 1953.

In Central and South America, the 1950s and 1960s witnessed land reform campaigns in Guatemala, leftist guerrilla warfare in Peru, Bolivia, Colombia, and Uruguay, independence movements in Jamaica and Puerto Rico, and the development of *negritude* and *noirisme* in the French Caribbean and of a popularly elected socialist government in Chile. Even the appearance of brutal right-wing dictatorships in Brazil and elsewhere can be viewed as part of this same process, a reaction against the increasing demands of the working classes and rural poor for political change. Revolution in Cuba was thus far from an isolated occurrence, and in fact members of many constituencies cited above developed their own song repertories similar to *nueva trova* in an attempt to represent their experiences. It was in this overarching context, beginning in the mid-1960s, that "the political lid came off the pot" as one singer has described it (Feliú 1997:9–10) and new forms of musical expression emerged to complement new social orders.

Nueva trova owes a debt to the efforts of folklorists and musicians in Chile, Argentina, and Uruguay, where Latin American protest song first achieved widespread popularity. Authors frequently cite Argentine Atahualpa Yupanqui (Héctor Roberto Chavero, 1908–92) and Chilean Violeta Parra (1918–67) as early influential composers who championed the arts of indigenous peoples and other marginal groups as well as the social issues pertinent to them. *Nueva canción* in South America developed in part out of reactions to the onslaught of consumer culture from the United States and Europe after World War II as well as heavy foreign investment in local economies. Its early songs were implicitly political in that they incorporated indigenous instruments *(charangos, zampoñas, quenas, bombos)* and folkloric styles *(huayno, milonga, zamba, chacarera)* largely ignored by the South American media. In this way, *nueva trova* was preceded by *nueva canción* and represents part of a host of related movements throughout the Spanish-speaking world and beyond.[2] However, significant musical differences exist between the movements. *Nueva canción* represented an attempt to valorize folk traditions that were absent in the national media. By contrast, early *nueva trova* represented something different, a conscious break with local influences and an effort to create a cosmopolitan blend of local and international genres (Kirk and Padura Fuentes 2001:5).

Nueva trova is the best-known form of Cuban protest song today but is far from the first. The origins of socially conscious music stretch back in time as far as documentation exists, well over one hundred fifty years. Certainly the stage presentations of the *teatro vernáculo* were notorious for their references to contemporary politics, especially issues related to the revolution against Spain beginning in the 1860s (Moore 1997:43–45).[3] Later works by individual *trovador*-artists of the early twentieth century included praise of war heroes Antonio Maceo and Máximo Gómez and outcry over policies of U.S. military intervention and foreign control of Cuban farmlands (Mateo Palmer 1988:136–67). Similar works date from the Batista years. One might suggest that an unbroken legacy of protest song stretches back into Cuba's past and that the prominence of *nueva trova* owes as much to its eventual promotion by the government as to any inherent "newness" in lyrical terms.

Publications from Cuba often suggest that the most direct predecessor of *nueva trova* is *vieja trova*. This is the name for the music of individual singer-songwriters and guitarists from the turn of the century such as Pepe Sánchez (1854–1918), Sindo Garay (1867–1983), Alberto Villalón (1882–1955), and Rosendo Ruiz Sr. (1885–1983). Robbins (1990:443) notes that both styles are intended to be listened to rather than danced, a fairly atypical characteristic of Caribbean popular music, and are performed by small groups in informal settings. Both emphasize the importance of song texts and convey emotional messages. More problematically, *vieja trova* is associated with the urban poor—semi-literate tobacco workers, tailors, and barbers, often black and mulatto—while their counterparts in the 1960s and 1970s were university educated (Benmayor 1981:20). Related to *vieja trova* is the *filin* (or feeling) repertory of the 1950s, whose exponents include César Portillo de la Luz, José Antonio Méndez, and Ángel Díaz. *Filin* is characterized by intimate, romantic pieces employing ample use of modulation and chromaticism, a fusion of the Cuban *canción* (romantic song) tradition with influences from North American jazz. Prominent *nueva trova* artists, most notably Pablo Milanés and Martín Rojas, began their careers as interpreters of *filin*. Others, including the group Los Cañas, made jazzy, multipart vocals in the style of the Swingle Singers a prominent component of their music.

Another influence on the musical substance of *nueva tròva* comes from rural dance repertoire. As a matter of fact, the first compositions embraced by government officials as "revolutionary" after 1959 bore little resemblance to the innovative *trova* of younger artists. They sounded instead almost exactly like prerevolutionary music, differing only in lyrical content. Older, established figures such as the duo Los Compadres sang songs of admiration about the lives of Fidel Castro and Camilo Cienfuegos, praised literacy campaigns, and discussed housing reform policy using the *son* and *son guajiro*.[4] This group, founded in 1949, initially included Lorenzo Hierrezuelo (1907–93) and Francisco Repilado (1907–2003), better known as Compay Segundo. In 1959 the two quarreled, and Lorenzo Hierrezuelo began singing instead with his younger brother, Reynaldo (b. 1926). Typically, Lorenzo played rhythm guitar and Reynaldo, a double-stringed lead guitar with a sound similar to the *tres* (a small, guitarlike instrument used to play melodies rather than to strum). The example below is a lyrical excerpt from the Los Compadres *son* composition "Se acabarán los bohíos" (The Rustic Hovels Will Be Gone). It is taken from the final *montuno* section and is sung in traditional call-and-response style. Vocals by the soloist and chorus are punctuated with flourishes on the bongo drum, claves, maracas, and guitar.

> Una vivienda *mi compay*
> Un apartamento *mi compay*
> Para cada familia *mi compay*
> En la Sierra Maestra *mi compay*
> En toda Cuba *mi compay*
> Se acabaron los bohíos *mi compay*
> Con mucho trabajo *mi compay*
> Con la microbrigada *mi compay*
> De la construcción *mi compay*
> Quedará algún bohío *mi compay*
> Para el museo *mi compay*
> En la Sierra Maestra *mi compay.*

> A dwelling place *my friend*
> An apartment *my friend*
> For every family *my friend*
> In the Sierra Maestra *my friend*
> All across Cuba *my friend*
> The rustic hovels are finished *my friend*
> With our hard work *my friend*

With the microbrigades *my friend*
Helping in the construction *my friend*
Perhaps a few huts will remain *my friend*
As museum pieces *my friend*
In the Sierra Maestra *my friend.*

> (Hierrezuelo and Hierrezuelo n.d.;
> italics indicate choral response)

Instrumental string traditions and *copla* and *décima* poetry derived from Spain have also had a significant impact on *nueva trova*.[5] Alfredo Carol, Pedro Luis Ferrer, and Alberto Faya (the latter from Grupo Moncada) are but a few of the writers known for incorporating such elements into their songs. A tension between the creation of works based on traditional genres and of other works with cosmopolitan influences has characterized *nueva trova* virtually since its inception.

Finally, rock and folk rock from the United States and Britain arguably represent the most important influence on the development of *nueva trova*, a fact that is rarely discussed at length in Cuban literature and which contributed to the movement's controversial reception in its formative years. Indeed, some assert that *nueva trova is* the equivalent of Cuban rock. Rock performance began on the island in the late 1950s with Elvis Presley imitators featured in Havana nightclubs. Singers Danny Puga, Jorge Bauer, and Luis Bravo began copying the style shortly thereafter (Manduley López 1997:136–38). The popularity of rock increased steadily over the next decade, and by the early 1970s it had become more popular among Cuban youth than any other music (Calzado 1996, interview). Los Astros, Los Dada, Los Vampiros, and a host of other bands flourished despite the fact that they never received recognition or support from the government and in many cases were forced to play on homemade instruments. In the later 1970s and 1980s, Cuban rock lost some popularity. This was due to many factors, including strong interest in *nueva trova*, a resurgence in dance music, and the departure of prominent *rockeros* as part of the Mariel exodus (Manduley López 1997:136–38).

Interest in rock varied somewhat among first-generation protest singers, but in general they were avid fans who incorporated influences from British and North American songs directly into their music. Noel Nicola and Vicente Feliú began their musical careers in the mid-1960s playing Elvis and Beatles covers and emulating rock combos such as Los Gnomos and Los Kent (Díaz Pérez 1994:143); eventually they wrote similar *nueva trova* music. Pedro Luis Ferrer performed for a time with Los Dada (Orejuela Martínez 2004:264). *Trovador* Alejandro "Virulo" García (b. 1955) also began as a rock entertainer in the band Los Sioux (Piñeiro 1989). Though Cuba's cultural

EXAMPLE 6.   "Son de Cuba a Puerto Rico." Pablo Milanés, *Pablo Milanés cantautor: No me pidas* (1997).

establishment was unsupportive of rock at the time, it was oddly in the homes of PCC members that it first flourished.

> The children of the politicians were rock fanatics, and in the houses of
> the leadership the same people who were prohibiting rock on the TV
> and the radio in many cases paid rock combos to play in their kids' parties.
> It was the leadership who brought back LPs from abroad. . . . They were
> the ones who traveled, and their kids asked them to bring back music of
> the Rolling Stones, Beatles, Bee Gees. The children in turn lent the discs to
> friends who copied them onto cassettes, and thus everyone could listen
> to the groups via a sort of musical underground. When they walked in
> the street with the records they'd sometimes put them in [a] slipcover
> of a record by Beethoven or Benny Moré. (Acosta 1996, interview)

One can hear the influence of 1960s rock and folk rock in a majority of *nueva trova* from that period. Nicola's "Para una imaginaria María del Carmen" strikes the listener as more reminiscent of Phil Ochs than of any Cuban musical antecedent, while Silvio Rodríguez's "Oleo de mujer con sombrero" takes its picking style directly from Bob Dylan's "Boots of Spanish Leather."[6] Rodríguez, more than any other early figure, championed the fusion of foreign musical elements, primarily from the United States and Britain, into Cuban popular song.

Since *nueva trova* performers blend styles, many of the best-known pieces don't sound overtly Cuban but instead strike the listener as cosmopolitan and eclectic. One might describe *trovadores* as the "culture brokers" of international music trends (Robbins 1990:435), strongly influenced by foreign pop and yet invariably changing and personalizing it for local audiences. Listeners unfamiliar with these performers who would like to experience the musical eclecticism of *nueva trova* need only contrast the following pieces: Silvio Rodríguez's "Unicornio," a slow, lyrical ballad that uses the image of a blue unicorn as a metaphor for fantasy, nostalgia, and desire; satirical political commentary by Alejandro "Virulo" García set to recycled fragments of international repertoire such as rococo-style harpsichord, the Mexican folk song "Cielito lindo," and "The Charleston"; and guitar pieces by Pablo Milanés such as "Son de Cuba a Puerto Rico," based on transformations of rhythms associated with Cuban dance music.[7] In the latter, Milanés's syncopated picking style imitates the anticipated bass of the *son* as well as its accompanying *tres* melodies (Ex. 6).

Lyrics are a central feature of *nueva trova*, but the lyrical themes with which it is associated are nearly as difficult to generalize about as its musical style. Some artists have been strongly influenced by internationally recognized poets (José Martí, Nicolás Guillén, César Vallejo, Pablo Neruda) to the point of imitating their work or setting their poems to music (Acosta and Gómez 1981:12).[8] Most typical, however, is the use of fairly simple and direct original verse. Writers tend to avoid machismo and the objectification of women as well as stereotypically romantic imagery, though love remains a prominent subject (Manuel 1987:174). Many works are political, contemplating the valor of insurgents at Moncada or paying homage to activists of past decades.[9] Others are entirely tender and personal, while in yet others one finds a powerful linking of public and private spheres. Examples of the latter include Silvio Rodríguez's "Aurora, Clara y Felicia," a love song dedicated to three women, one fighting in the Angolan civil war, or Carlos Varela's "Foto de familia," which ponders empty spaces at the dinner table representing loved ones separated through political exile.

Perhaps due to the heterogeneity of *nueva trova* and the degree to which its sound varies from one artist to the next, it has been defined less in musical terms and more by the generation that created it and its meanings.

Acosta and Gómez (1981:6) define *nueva trova* as "a phenomenon that arose among the youngest generation . . . a deliberate rupture with music that had come before, a certain 'return to the roots' combined with the scent of renovation, and finally . . . the adoption of social and political consciousness."[10] Danilo Orozco characterizes *nueva trova* as "a creative attitude, a manner of approaching song composition, an aesthetic sense, a sum of dissatisfactions [*inquietudes*]" (Hernández 2002:64).

Others place more emphasis on opposition, defining the movement as a "culture of contestation" among the young and disenfranchised (Faya 1995:389). The elements of innovation and contestation were both a self-conscious part of most participants' music. Players strove from the outset to create a different sort of art, to challenge the past musically and textually, to interpret and express the revolutionary experience in personal terms of their own choosing (Benmayor 1981:13). The entire lifestyle and persona of the protest singer represented a testing of boundaries. By growing long hair, wearing torn "hippie" clothing, performing on sidewalks or other nonstandard venues, and participating in other forms of nonconformity in addition to song writing, artists implicitly challenged social and artistic norms on multiple fronts.

THE FIRST ARTISTS

The generation associated with the emergence of *nueva trova* were in grade school when the revolution came to power. They were the first to be educated in a country attempting to radically alter the consciousness of its citizens. In addition to reading the works of Marx and Engels, these children debated questions of social justice from an early age. They were products of the drive to create an *hombre nuevo,* or idealized "new socialist citizen." *Granma,* the state newspaper, defined the new citizen as an individual with "a profound consciousness of his role in society and of his duties and social responsibilities, a [person] capable of constructing Communism and living with it" (Fagen 1969:17). Visitors to Cuba such as Ernesto Cardenal have noted the profound effects of such education on the young. My own experiences confirm that, regardless of their ultimate acceptance or rejection of socialism, most Cubans have been forced to confront a range of issues and have a much higher degree of political awareness than their counterparts in countries such as the United States.

In addition to domestic educational changes, international social trends of the 1960s heavily affected protest artists. Along with others in Europe and the United States, the musicians questioned established patterns of sexual behavior, dress, and social relationships. They were truly products of the revolution—most assisted in voluntary community service projects, joined the newly formed Asociación de Jóvenes Rebeldes (Association of Revolutionary Youth) as teenagers, completed military service after 1964—and yet didn't hesitate to raise their voices in criticism when necessary. They considered themselves patriotic and rebellious at the same time, ready to defend Cuba despite the fact that it might not always give them reason to feel proud. Perhaps because of this independent attitude, the first individuals who began singing protest songs in public were referred to disparagingly by PCC members as *los conflictivos*, "the troublemakers" (Rodríguez 1996:10).[11]

Most of the early *trovadores* were men, but several women such as Sara González (b. 1951) and Marta Campos also had a significant impact in the 1970s. Composer Teresita Fernández (b. 1930), though of an earlier generation, also deserves recognition as a seminal figure. She participated in the International Festival of Song with Silvio Rodríguez in 1967 and organized various *peñas* (informal artistic gatherings) as a means of encouraging younger artists to compose and play. Her Sunday afternoon gatherings in Lenin Park, probably her most famous *peña*, began in 1974 and continued for seventeen years. A surprising number of *trovadores* have recorded songs by Fernández, including Rodríguez himself, Noel Nicola, Miriam Ramos, Heidy Igualada, and Jorge García (Elizundia Ramírez 2001:58, 67, 94).

For many aspiring performers, the educational opportunities afforded them as part of the Amateurs movement proved important to the improvement of their musicianship and their contacts with peers. *Trovadores* Tony Pinelli, Jesús del Valle, and Carlos Mas emphasize the importance of these classes as providing a venue for the performance and critical evaluation of their work (Díaz Pérez 1994:168). Miriam Ramos (b. 1946) also studied music as an amateur in the early 1960s (Orovio 1981:320) before beginning to sing in the National Chorus. Amateur talent festivals hosted by the Revolutionary Armed Forces (FAR) represented another early performance opportunity for *trovadores*, one of the only public spaces available before they received government sponsorship. The informal nature of musical training among *trova* singers is significant, since it is one factor that made their music difficult for the cultural establishment to accept (Acosta 1995b: 375).

Because they had such a tremendous impact on the early years of the movement and continue to make a mark as composers today, some mention should be made of Pablo Milanés and Silvio Rodríguez. Their musical interests are distinct and complementary, underscoring the individualistic nature of *nueva trova*. Similarly, their careers, which have been more thor-

FIGURE 13.   A very young-looking Pablo Milanés taking part in inaugural events of the sixth Festival de la Trova, March 1969. Photo Archive, Ministry of Culture, Cuba.

oughly documented than most, demonstrate the changing relationship between artists and the government.

Pablo Milanés, a *mulato* (light-skinned Afro-Cuban) performer, was born in 1943 in Bayamo in eastern Cuba. His first musical experiences involved playing *son* and *vieja trova;* many of his compositions have been strongly grounded in Cuban folklore, and he has consistently promoted the work of traditional entertainers.[12] As a teenager in the 1950s, Milanés was already singing on Cuban television with José Antonio Méndez and Marta Valdés (Acosta and Gómez 1981:10). He later performed in Havana dance orchestras, in the Cuarteto del Rey (a group dedicated to interpreting North American spirituals), and in the jazz vocal group Los Bucaneros, directed by Robertico Marín (D'Rivera 1998:119). Milanés's early solo repertoire is noteworthy for its engaging lyrical quality, the influence of jazz harmonies, his adaptation of folkloric rhythms into unique fingerpicking patterns on the guitar, and his straightforward but engaging lyrics discussing intimate relationships, love of country, and political matters. More than any other figure, Milanés is credited with bridging the generational divides that separate *nueva trova* from popular song of the 1950s (Acosta 1995b: 378). He wrote the first piece recognized as *nueva trova* by historians, "Mis 22 años," in 1965 (Fig. 13).

If Pablo Milanés is an innovative traditionalist, extending and adapting local genres, Silvio Rodríguez (b. 1946) might be described as an internationalist, patterning his early musical style loosely on songs by Bob Dylan and Paul McCartney. Rodríguez, a Hispanic Cuban, was born in San Antonio de los Baños on the outskirts of Havana. Prior to 1959, he had no professional performance experience. During his formative teenage years he volunteered as a teacher in literacy campaigns, in military service, and in other revolutionary activities. He too performs principally on the guitar but more often strums in a folk-rock style. His music is harmonically complex but is also noteworthy for its asymmetrical phrases, abrupt key changes, and high vocals. The lyrics of Rodríguez's songs are especially daring, incorporating surrealist imagery and powerful extended metaphors so that the literal meaning of the text is far from transparent. Indeed, many consider him to be a poet first and a musician second. Rodríguez began composing about 1967 and quickly developed a following. He was the first to achieve national recognition in 1968 and remains *nueva trova's* most internationally renowned artist (Fig. 14).

While not absolute, there are distinctions between the admirers of Silvio Rodríguez and Pablo Milanés. Silvio's fans tend more often to be white, college-educated, and cosmopolitan, preferring rock and international pop music to the music of traditional Cuban performers. One gets the impression that some subtly associate Cuban dance music and other genres with poorly educated blacks and thus consider them less interesting (Robbins 1990:440). Pablo's fans, by contrast, are more consistently black or racially mixed and are more sympathetic to domestic music of all kinds. The racialized associations of each singer are perhaps clearest when one considers the performers that they have chosen to associate with. Silvio Rodríguez is best known for having given Hispanic Cuban rockers Carlos Varela and Santiago Feliú their first opportunities to perform and record, while Pablo Milanés chose to promote Afro-Cubans Gerardo Alfonso, Alberto Tosca, Xiomara Laugart, and Marta Campos and the folk drumming ensemble

FIGURE 14.   Silvio Rodríguez performing in the Festival
Internacional de la Canción, Varadero, 1982. Photo
Archive, Ministry of Culture, Cuba.

Yoruba An-dabo (Alexis Esquivel, pers. comm.). Likewise, Silvio established
close professional ties with white Brazilian Chico Buarque in the mid-1970s,
while Pablo collaborated with Afro-Brazilian Milton Nascimento (Leonardo
Acosta, pers. comm.).

EARLY PROTEST SONG

Singer Noel Nicola noted in 1971 that the deeds of socialist leaders implicitly exhort Cubans to rebellious acts, but that they have tended to be intol-

erant of rebellion in others (Cardenal 1974:51). The government has consistently supported progressive positions in terms of its social agenda but has proven conservative in its attitudes toward long hair (worn by men), homosexuality, religious expression, and other personal liberties. This was especially true in the late 1960s, as *nueva trova* protagonists found to their dismay. They gathered informally whenever they could (Coppelia, the Parque de los Cabezones at the university, the breakwater along the *malecón*) and shared songs that expressed a new vision of what Cubans should think about and strive toward. Ironically, their questions about the nature and substance of socialism came at a time when similar debates were occurring at the highest levels of government, debates that would result in the suppression of *nueva trova* for a time.

Supporters and critics of the Cuban Revolution alike recognize the late 1960s as a period of conflict. Díaz Pérez (1994:157) uses the metaphor of an enormous forge to convey a sense of how opposing goals and viewpoints were being fused into a unified political consensus, often at the expense of those unwilling to conform. Medin (1990:16) describes the country as moving toward "a new, Soviet-oriented phase of orthodoxy," implementing programs that extended Marxist principles more deeply into the social fabric. Such trends resulted in a more intrusive government presence than had existed previously. The change was most apparent in the area of economics. Beginning with the *ofensiva revolucionaria*, the government outlawed private business activity down to the fruit carts of street vendors and manicures offered by individual women in their homes. The extent of such centralization made many uncomfortable and resulted in new waves of exiles.

Along with this drive toward economic purism came an ideological movement, one that demonstrated less tolerance toward those unwilling to accept PCC doctrine. Increasingly, space for diversity of opinion about what Cuban socialism should be was replaced by a demand for uncompromising adherence to a single position. Most policy makers at that time could not conceive of promoting youth protest music as part of their political agenda. In a country that was striving to create a utopia for all citizens and that had the concerns of the masses constantly in mind, music of protest seemed inappropriate, even seditious. Just as leaders decided there was no need for complete intellectual freedom if it endangered socialist goals, "so there was no need . . . for protest songs within the revolution" (Medin 1990:126).

Fortunately for the *trovadores*, some leaders retained the will and the political clout to define revolutionary expression on their own terms. One such person was Haydée Santamaría, a survivor of the Moncada garrison attack led by Castro in 1953 who directed cultural activities in the Casa de las Américas (Americas House). A music lover and admirer of South American protest song, Santamaría created an early haven for *nueva trova*. She made efforts to expose younger performers to socially conscious repertoire from abroad and invited foreigners to Havana for events such as the Encuentro Internacional de la Canción Protesta (July 1967) and the Festival de la Canción Popular in Varadero (December 1967; de Juan 1982:51). These included guests from the United States, such as Barbara Dane, as well as others from Latin America and Europe. In 1968, Santamaría scheduled presentations of protest song at the Casa de las Américas on the first Tuesday of every month, many of which were televised. Only an individual with the impeccable revolutionary credentials of Santamaría could have done so at that time.[13] Featured performers in addition to Pablo and Silvio included Noel Nicola, Alfredo Martínez, Maité Abreu, and Ramón Díaz. Established *filin* artists Elena Burke, Omara Portuondo, and Maggie Prior also participated (Orejuela Martínez 2004:244).

In the first months of 1968, planners at one of Cuba's two national television stations authorized a half-hour show on Sunday evenings called *Mientras tanto* (In the Meantime) that featured Silvio Rodríguez and others. The title of the show was taken from a Rodríguez composition that served as its theme song. Younger artists mixed with more established figures such as Burke, Portuondo, and poet Guillermo Rodríguez Rivera. Even so, the program proved controversial at the Instituto Cubano de Radio y Televisión (ICRT) because of its inclusion of "hippies."[14] By mid-April, Director Jorge Serguera decided to cancel *Mientras tanto* (Correa 1997; Díaz Pérez 1994:134–37).[15] He had never liked the idea of featuring protest singers but felt pressured to give the Cuban youth a program that would appeal to them. This was especially urgent since broadcasts of U.S. and European rock groups had ended (Fernández Pavón 1999, interview). A few radio presentations of *trovadores* aired on Radio Habana Cuba at approximately the same time organized by Estela Bravo, and in 1968 the Casa de las Américas recorded at least one limited edition LP anthology of protest songs (Díaz Pérez 1994:164–67).

CONFLICTS WITH AUTHORITIES

Y así tengo enemigos que me quieren descarrilar,
haciéndome la guerra porque me puse a cantar.
Pero pongo la historia por encima de su razón

y sé con qué canciones quiero hacer Revolución,
aunque me quede sin voz,
aunque no me vengan a escuchar . . .

I have enemies that want to derail me,
at war with me because I began to sing.
But history is superior to their truths,
And I know the songs I want to make Revolution with,
even if I lose my voice,
even if they don't come to listen . . .

CARLOS VARELA, "Jalisco Park"

The reasons for the onset of the revolution's harshest period of ideological repression, what Ambrosio Fornet labeled *el quinquenio gris*, have yet to be fully explored. Beginning in 1968 and continuing through the early 1970s, as mentioned, Cuban artists and intellectuals experienced serious professional difficulties. Most who were active at that time tell horror stories involving public condemnation of their work, blacklisting, time served in jail or in "voluntary" labor camps (*granjas de castigo*, literally "punishment farms"),[16] and the like. Clearly, the so-called gray period represents the worst of the Cuban Revolution in terms of limitations on expression. It is characterized by excessive authoritarianism, "a deformity of official thought that rendered impossible everything from the free circulation of ideas to the legitimate right to make a mistake" (Alberto 1996:34; Dumont 1970:81).[17]

It is possible that economic difficulties and increasing reliance on Soviet aid contributed to these changes. Domínguez (1978:153–59) notes that the final years of the 1960s saw Cuba's GNP plunge to its lowest levels since the revolution had come to power. The economy hit its absolute low in 1970 during an unsuccessful attempt to produce ten million tons of sugar in a single harvest. Soviet aid arrived to make up much of the difference, but at the price of greater centralization of labor and an imposed reorganization of the government under foreign guidance. The Chinese Cultural Revolution, which reached a peak of intensity in 1966 and 1967, may have influenced Cuban leaders as well. "Red guard" youth organizations ascribed to fundamentalist interpretations of Marxism that rejected many forms of activity as bourgeois. Their belligerent actions against intellectuals and artists included jail sentences, beatings, and public humiliation of perceived counterrevolutionaries (Hinton 2003). Finally, the Soviet invasion of Czechoslovakia in 1968 also had ideological repercussions internationally. Major tensions surfaced in the PCC over whether to publicly condemn this act.

Ambivalent himself, Castro eventually chose to endorse the invasion in or-der to keep receiving economic aid. Among figures in the Central Commit-tee who had spoken out against the invasion, forty-three were arrested, nine were expelled from the party, and twenty-six were imprisoned before the year ended (Domínguez 1978:162).

Though the leadership of the late 1960s remained concerned about coun-terrevolutionary activities on the part of the CIA and Cuban exiles, they came to view military invasion of the island a less likely option as time went on.[18] In place of this concern, they instead focused on culture and the me-dia as the most central sites of future conflict with the capitalist world. As a result, they began to condemn music associated with the United States and Western Europe as corrupted or contaminated (Arias 1982:28); this is the period that witnessed the censorship of most rock and jazz. In a speech from 1980, Castro verbalized attitudes toward foreign influences that had circulated in party documents for over a decade. His primary point was that Cuban culture had been "deformed" as the result of external meddling.

> The profound deformation . . . at which imperialists have worked
> for [some time], using a corrupt press, radio, and television networks
> that they often manage to make serve their interests, the films they
> introduced here, the habits, customs, prejudices, etc. with which they
> infected our country: all this could not but create difficulties. . . . We
> know, for example, that years after the triumph of '59, after the victory
> at [the Bay of Pigs], in Cuba we still had to set ourselves the urgent goal
> of struggling against cultural colonialism, which survived the defeat of
> political colonialism and economic colonialism. . . . It is a long struggle
> and we are still engaged in it. (As quoted in Medin 1990:17)

The ideological initiatives of the late 1960s affected every sphere of cul-tural activity, but officials paid special attention to rock music, given its cen-trality to youth culture. Rock-influenced songs were viewed as implicitly subversive on many levels: because of their associations with the "decadent" ways of the United States and other capitalist countries, because of their En-glish lyrics, and because of their association with alternative dress and lifestyles that did not conform to established norms. Officials viewed rock as transcending sound and embodying an entire way of life that often re-sulted in an unwillingness to integrate into the revolutionary process (Sosa 1996, interview). To the leadership, the implicit aesthetic of all rock, with its emphasis on transgression, physical gratification and liberation, excess, and pleasure, ran contrary to the development of a disciplined and self-sacrificing socialist mentality. From their perspective, truly revolutionary artists should not adopt any of the physical trappings of a *rockero* or use rock music, even as a vehicle in support of socialism. Any affiliation with it implied *desviaciones ideológicas,* ideological drift.

By the late 1960s, a climate of fear permeated the intellectual community, young and old. Limitations on the exchange of ideas first surfaced during the Congreso Cultural de La Habana in January of 1968 and were most apparent in discourses surrounding the Congreso de Educación y Cultura in 1971 (Alberto 1996:33). Artists found that in many instances they could no longer voice their true opinions; as a result, they began avoiding controversial issues in an attempt to protect themselves. Media officials scrutinized song lyrics from this period and altered many of them or banned the pieces outright. Paquito D'Rivera (1998:121) recounts a conversation with Pablo Milanés in which the composer said, "Damn it, every time that I come up with a new song, [radio and television administrator] Papito [Serguera] has to listen to it first along with the folks on the commission of revolutionary ethics. The Party makes me change pieces of the text if they believe this or that section might be misinterpreted. . . . No, no, to hell with Papito and his television station!"

The internment of Cuban youth judged unsupportive of the country's socialist agenda occurred on a massive scale in the late 1960s and early 1970s. No reliable statistics exist, but one interviewee told Ernesto Cardenal that hundreds of thousands had been detained at least briefly as of February 1970: "Young men who fled from military service or school, or who have been brought there for other reasons, hippies, long-haired ones, malcontents . . . they are in rehabilitation farms or camps" (Cardenal 1974:50). This astounding figure has been supported by some of my interviews with Cuban exiles; poet and composer Reynaldo Fernández Pavón, for instance, estimates that about one-third of the adult male population spent at least brief periods in detention at this time. Sentences included manual labor in the countryside, prison, or assignment to "reeducation" sessions. Yet another potential destination were the *minas del frío* (literally mines of cold) area, a region in the Sierra Maestra. Many nonconformists served time there, including Pablo Labañino Merino, the painter who designed the covers of several early *nueva trova* albums. The year 1969 marked the peak of police activity of this sort, probably because of concern over the outcome of the mammoth sugar harvest (Sosa 1996, interview).

Because of the suspect image of protest singers, they experienced frequent difficulties. Pablo Milanés, one of the first to be jailed, suffered an especially harsh sentence. The circumstances leading to his arrest remain unclear and may have been unrelated to his song writing. In approximately 1966, officials accused him of being a homosexual and sentenced him to a UMAP (Unidades Militares para la Ayuda a la Producción) prison in Camagüey, where he remained for over a year (Giro 1996, interview; Golendorf 1977:48).[19] Thankfully, Milanés's confinement was cut short as a result of the growing popularity of songs such as "Para vivir," "Ya ves," and "Mis 22 años." Elena Burke and Omara Portuondo recorded and promoted these pieces and others by the composer in the mid-1960s. Burke is said to have sung them for visiting intellectuals at the Casa de las Américas; their enthusiasm for the music and repeated demands to meet the composer eventually facilitated Milanés's release (Fernández Pavón, March 18, 1998, interview).

Other musicians experienced similar difficulties. Documentation is scanty and, to the extent it is available, tends to focus only on the best-known figures. The case of Silvio Rodríguez may be typical. He is known to have had minor clashes with the police and administrators such as Jorge Serguera beginning in 1967. According to one source, he dedicated the piece "Te doy una canción" to a girlfriend who was the daughter of a prominent military leader. The girl's father did not approve of Rodríguez and eventually took it upon himself to impede his career (Sosa 1996, interview). Rodríguez exacerbated such problems with his combative nature: getting a tattoo, wearing hippie clothing, and making statements about the importance of foreign rock on his musical development. The police detained him on various occasions in the late 1960s, and at least once sent him to the countryside with other youths to an *encampamiento* where they lectured him on the importance of fuller integration into the revolution (Orovio 1996, interview). Intervention by Haydée Santamaría invariably led to his release before long, however.

The low point in Silvio Rodríguez's career came in 1969 when he was fired by the ICRT and had no options for artistic employment. At this point the composer accepted a job working on a fishing boat named after the Playa Girón, site of the Bay of Pigs invasion in 1961. His voyage on this ninety-four-meter craft with one hundred other young men began in September of 1969 and lasted through January of 1970 (Rodríguez 1996:9). Contemporaries viewed the trip as a form of punishment, a decision not made of Rodríguez's own free will; many thought he would never regain prominence as an artist. Rodríguez himself notes that during the year or two prior to leaving on the boat the "thread" on which his professional existence hung "had become dangerously tense" (Rodríguez 1996:12). He describes the individuals who fired him from the ICRT as "bosses who said one thing and did another, squares, those who didn't trust the young, guys with all the perks, enemies of culture, the establishment, cowards who were ruining the revolution that I carried inside of me" (Rodríguez 1996:12). Surprisingly, the months aboard the *Playa Girón* proved incredibly productive for Silvio from a musical standpoint. He wrote many of his most beautiful and internationally renowned compositions, including several that openly challenge the government, at sea.[20]

Conditions began to improve dramatically for younger musicians beginning only a few years later, and yet more subtle problems persisted. Radio programmers allowed them only limited access to the mass media for many years. Representatives of the CNC continued to closely monitor the ideological content of their song lyrics. They occasionally prohibited controversial pieces from being recorded and sent police to concerts to ensure that they were not performed live (Oppenheimer 1992:265). Even today, those with a history of oppositional compositions may find their careers thwarted. The PCC continues to determine on occasion that some performers should not appear on the radio or television despite their popularity.[21]

It should be clear by now that what came eventually to be called the *nueva trova* movement gained popularity in the 1960s not because of government policy but in spite of it. In fact, performers had to fight against a cultural bureaucracy in order to be heard at all. Castro himself nearly admitted as much in remarks made in the mid-1970s: "Did we, the politicians, conceive of [the *nueva trova*] movement? Did we plan it? No! These things arise, like so many others, that none of us can even imagine" (Díaz Pérez 1994:131). The eventual prominence of Vicente Feliú, Sara Gónzalez, Noel Nicola, Pablo Milanés, and Silvio Rodríguez and the nationwide promotion of younger artists were due to a conscious and abrupt shift in policy. In the space of only a few years, *nueva trova* moved from the margin to the mainstream of socialist music making. The state heralded its proponents as spokespersons of the revolutionary experience rather than berating them as insolent malcontents.

THE MNT AND INSTITUTIONALIZATION

The first government organization that employed *trovadores* and allowed them to produce music as professionals was the ICAIC cinema institute. Under the direction of classically trained composer Leo Brouwer, the ICAIC established a working group of young musicians with the intention of training them and letting them create film scores. The members, known collectively as the Grupo de Experimentación Sonora (GES), or Sonic Experimentation Group, first assembled in 1969; they continued working with various changes of personnel through 1978. Musicians involved at some point in the GES during these years include singer-songwriters Pablo Milanés, Noel Nicola, Silvio Rodríguez, and Sara González, saxophonist Leonardo Acosta, bassist Eduardo Ramos, guitarists Pablo Menéndez and Sergio Vitier, and percussionist Leo Pimentel (Orovio 1981:137). Under Brouwer's guidance, a number of the performers learned to read music for the first time, were exposed to the fundamentals of harmony and counterpoint, and developed the ability to work collectively as well as individually.[22]

The formation of the GES did not imply broad acceptance of *nueva trova* on the part of the establishment but rather a truce or compromise with younger performers. It offered them a creative outlet, but not entirely on their own terms. Silvio Rodríguez notes that Alfredo Guevara, the founder of the ICAIC, pushed through the idea of the group's formation mainly as an excuse to offer a few of the many disenfranchised *trovadores* a job (Rodríguez 1996:11). Much of the music the ICAIC asked them to produce was instrumental, quite distinct from the songs they had initially composed. Perhaps the most important result of the GES was that it legitimized the status of *trovadores* and supported their creative activities over a sustained period. As professional film scorers, they were more respectable and still had time to compose songs of their own choosing. The recordings they made at the ICAIC (e.g., Brouwer n.d.), while hailed in certain artistic circles and sparking a degree of interest elsewhere in Latin America, never received much local popular recognition. The group eventually disbanded as the result of problems such as lack of technical equipment, low salaries, and aesthetic differences among members. Leo Brouwer also devoted less time to the GES in later years, pursuing his own career as a conductor and composer (Acosta 2002:147).

The government's desire for closer political relations with the Allende administration in Chile and that of other Latin American countries undoubtedly contributed to the growing acceptance of *nueva trova*. Protest music gained widespread recognition in Chile half a dozen years earlier than in Cuba and was already an organized political force by 1969 (Morris 1986:121). Cuban singers had firsthand exposure to their counterparts in South America because the CNC began sponsoring pan–Latin American song festivals in Havana as early as 1965 (Díaz Pérez 1994:85).[23] By 1971, Víctor Jara himself came to perform in the Casa de las Américas; others visiting shortly thereafter included Daniel Viglietti, Isabel and Angel Parra, Tania Libertad, and the group Inti Illimani (Díaz Ayala 1981:310; Díaz Pérez 1994:229). In the same year, the First National Congress on Education and Culture called explicitly for the study of "the cultural values of our fraternal Latin American countries" (Orejuela Martínez 2004:269). Members of the Cuban group Manguaré, created through the direct sponsorship of the CNC and the UJC, received an invitation to fly to Chile and study Andean folklore (Benmayor 1981:23), becoming the first of several ensembles to do so.

The early 1970s represents a pivotal period in official reevaluation of protest song. With ever-greater frequency, state cultural institutions invited *trovadores* to take part in international festivals throughout Latin America, Spain, and Soviet Bloc countries and to play in more prominent settings domestically. Policy makers must have recognized the widespread appeal of the music and the fact that similar traditions now existed in numerous countries. They may still have found the protest singer persona and the foreign musical elements in many songs unpleasant but chose not to criticize. *Trova* had proven an effective tool in public relations and was certainly less controversial than the electrified rock bands that many listened to clandestinely on late-night Miami broadcasts. Gradually, songwriters found they had more opportunities to make recordings. Initially asked to play in relatively low-profile contexts—grade schools, factories, neighborhood theaters, parks—they soon moved to more prominent settings. In a short time, pieces by Silvio Rodríguez and others that had been considered counterrevolutionary had become the unofficial anthems of the country.

The peak years of *nueva trova*'s popularity, as well as that of protest song in many other Latin American countries, extend from 1973 through approximately 1985. During that time, it became the principal form of music targeted at younger domestic audiences and was often featured in annual festivals (Benmayor 1981:22). It should be remembered that the term *"nueva trova"* itself achieved widespread recognition only in the mid-1970s (Nicola [1975] 1995:365). The very label can be viewed as a move by authorities to link what many considered a suspect form of expression to artists and genres of the past, and in this way to take away some of its oppositionality. Calling rockers such as Vicente and Santiago Feliú *trovadores* linked them discursively to Sindo Garay and Alberto Villalón, performers whose compositions had never been controversial. It obscured the fact that their *trova* actually represented a form of counterculture heavily influenced from abroad.

In November 1972, *nueva trova* became part of an official movement across the country, inaugurated by performance events in Manzanillo (Orejuela Martínez 2004:278). By 1973, the *Nueva Trova* movement (MNT) had a national registry of members, a board of directors, centers for performance in every province, and annual festivals. This provided additional support to artists, though it also meant that they were required to audition and receive approval before being recognized as bona fide members.[24] The number of professional, salaried groups increased dramatically, and new names rose to prominence: Alfredo Carol in Sancti Spiritus; Lázaro García in Villa Clara; Alejandro García ("Virulo") and Miriam Ramos in Havana; Freddy Laborí ("Chispa") and Augusto Blanca in Oriente; the groups Canto Libre (based in Camagüey), Manguaré, Mayohuacán, Moncada, Nuestra América (Matanzas); and others. The first widely disseminated *nueva trova* LP, Silvio Rodríguez's *Días y flores,* appeared in 1975. Young acoustic players reappeared on television in 1978 as part of the show *Te doy una canción,* where they remained for many years.[25] Groups performing electrified rock began to appear as guests about 1982 (Acosta 1996, interview), though it took longer for that style to be fully accepted. In general, the drive to institutionalize what had been such an eclectic and personal phenomenon proved difficult. In the first years after the National Congress on Education and Culture, MNT officials made attempts to dictate the content of *nueva trova* composition, with disappointing results (Díaz Pérez 1994:22). They also continued to suppress songs deemed inappropriate, such as Pablo Milanés's "La vida no vale nada" (Life Is Worth Nothing).[26]

In a musical sense, the institutionalization of *nueva trova* offered more resources to performers than had been available previously. The government gave them access to recording studios and producers and facilitated the dissemination of their work. One begins to find more elaborated compositions on the market in the mid-1970s as a result; solo guitar pieces are still heard but contrast with others incorporating synthesizer, electronic special effects, instruments such as the piano or violin, formally scored arrangements for larger groups, collaborative recordings featuring other national and international performers and their ensembles, and so forth. Changes in *nueva trova* recordings may reflect the increased musical training and expanded aesthetic horizons of artists as they became professional entertainers. It may also represent the bias of a classically oriented musical establishment trying to make the repertoire sound more "sophisticated."

Lyrically, *nueva trova* repertoire began to change as well. During the 1960s, *trovadores* freely wrote about virtually any subject. Because they had little access to the media, they performed largely among themselves; their compositions never represented a significant threat. After 1972, this began to change. Musicians found themselves in the spotlight, invited to receptions by the president of the UNEAC, greeted personally by members of the Central Committee and even Castro himself as they returned home from tours,[27] and written about extensively in the media. Suddenly all of their actions, musical and otherwise, were subject to scrutiny. They could only critique domestic politics at the risk of losing the supportive relationship that now existed between themselves and the Ministry of Culture.

Trovadores thus walked an ever more delicate line between fidelity to a government that now supported them and fidelity to themselves and their own points of view. Songs about housing shortages in the city or references to censorship and restrictions on artistic freedom, for instance, become less common and were replaced by other themes: references to figures from Cuba's long anti-imperialist struggles; nationalism; international politics; or personal relationships.[28] Pablo Milanés wrote "Amo esta isla" in 1980 in response to the Mariel crisis, as one example. It represented a call to stay on the island and support the revolution (González Portal 2003). The case of Silvio Rodríguez's later works is more difficult to evaluate since his texts are so highly metaphorical. One might suggest that it is their very ambiguity that has enabled much of his music to avoid criticism from the state while still being read as subversive by fans.

Journalist Cristóbal Sosa suggests that the political pressures facing performers as of the mid-1970s are similar to those facing all artists and intellectuals in Cuba. Cultural figures must belong to state organizations. These affiliations facilitate one's career in many respects but also elicit and prohibit certain kinds of activity.

> Here there's a music institute and one must be in agreement with that institute to accomplish many things. Then there's the UNEAC, which also has its regulations. You belong to the UNEAC, fine, but you can't do anything you'd like such as adopting independent positions that cross [those of the PCC]. When there's an important cultural event that is judged to be contrary to the interests of the Revolution, a call goes out in the UNEAC so that all the intellectuals come together and sign declarations against it, as happened in the case of the Helms-Burton legislation. (Sosa 2001, interview)[29]

Without necessarily intending to, Milanés and Rodríguez have become *nueva trova* superstars who generate tremendous sympathy for socialist Cuba. In recognition of their contributions (and, undoubtedly, in order to make sure they won't defect), the government permits them to purchase large houses; provides them with domestic help, cars, and chauffeurs; provides access to foreign currency, free license to travel abroad, the right to establish their own artistic foundations; and other perks—all of this in a country in which many families still live on inadequate rations of rice and beans and can't afford to buy enough hand soap. By Cuban standards, these singers have, ironically, become bourgeois. Both Pablo and Silvio are masterful artists and deserve special financial recognition, but their new status compromises their ability to act as a "voice of protest." Even analysts on the island admit that their lives now are completely divorced from the day-to-day realities of the average person (Díaz Pérez 1996, interview). To the extent that songs by Silvio and others since the 1990s address pressing social issues (e.g., prostitution, crime), they tend to be marketed for foreign audiences, receiving little airplay within Cuba.[30]

PASSING THE MANTLE OF PROTEST

By the mid-1980s, the music of first-generation *nueva trova* singers had become less attractive to younger listeners. Only a few of them continued playing regularly for local audiences. Some found their talents inadequate compared with stars like Pablo or Silvio and gradually changed careers. Others opted to live abroad rather than at home. Virulo now performs in Mexico, Martín Rojas in Venezuela, Xiomara Laugart in New York, Donato Poveda in Miami (Acosta 1995b:21). Carlos Gómez and Admed Barroso Castellanos have left the country as well, the former a founding member of the MNT, the latter a former musician in Silvio Rodríguez's backup band (Ojito 1987). Increasing support of commercial dance music, as well as of rock, and the resulting proliferation of new groups has also meant that more listening alternatives are available than in previous decades and more competition for those that remain.

For the most part, the declining appeal of *nueva trova* stems from the changing social meanings and functions of the repertoire. In the minds of those under twenty-five, middle-aged performers represent the establishment, not the voice of an outsider with a fresh perspective. Even more important, political change in Eastern Europe has resulted in widespread disillusionment with socialism, a cause with which *nueva trova* is now associated. Earlier songs inspired by the martyrs of Moncada ring hollow in an era of uncertainty about the future. In large part, the mantle of Alberto Faya's "culture of contestation" has passed from early protest singers to a newer generation of *trovadores, rockeros,* and rap artists. Most receive far less recognition and occupy relatively marginal social positions, similar to those held by *trovadores* in the early 1970s.

A few older figures continue to write music with an edge. Pedro Luis Ferrer (b. 1952) represents one of the most well known; born in Las Villas province, he has gained a following both for his musicianship and his penchant for insightful social critique. He also stands out for promoting the *guaracha* and *décima* poetry at a time when many consider traditional forms passé. Ferrer worked in various *nueva trova* groups in the 1970s but later formed his own band. The albums for which he first gained national popularity such as *Espuma y arena* date from that time. According to one Spanish journalist, Ferrer's recent music contrasts sharply with that of the "establishment trovador" (P.P. 1994:42). Denounced by some, the composer nevertheless considers himself a critical but supportive socialist and lampoons the Miami exile community in song and interviews as ruthlessly as he does politics in Havana.

Lyrics in Ferrer's music address a diversity of subjects and underscore the imposed limits on social commentary in mainstream *trova*. Whether joking or serious, he has voiced concern about religious intolerance, racism, homophobia, restraints on freedom of expression and travel, and the need for political reform. Listeners unfamiliar with Ferrer's work who are interested in an introduction to it might begin with "Mariposa" (Butterfly). The song was recorded in the United States by Latin jazz artist Claudia Acuña (2002) and also included in the soundtrack of the film *Before Night Falls* about the life of poet Reynaldo Arenas. The accompaniment to "Mariposa" is stark in the original version (Ferrer 1995), consisting only of acoustic guitar. Ferrer strums rather than picks in a relentless pattern emphasizing the and-of-two and -four in every 4/4 measure, imitating the anticipated bass of the *son*. Chords include dissonant pedals and minor sevenths and ninths; the ambiguous harmonies parallel Ferrer's polysemic and metaphorical lyrics. His emphasis on the top strings of the instrument and the lack of prominent bass tones nicely support the central imagery of a butterfly in flight. With masterful language, Ferrer tells a story in ten-line *décima* poetry that alludes simultaneously to erotic love, fantasy, aspiration, agony, and the search for freedom.

> Mariposa, cual llorosa
> Canción que en tí se hace calma
> Vienes calmándome el alma
> Con tu volar, mariposa
> La libertad de una rosa
> Es vivir en la verdad
> Yo seguí felicidad
> En cada flor que te posas
> Me lo dijeron las rosas
> Eres tú su libertad
>
> Ay, mariposa
> Contigo el mundo se posa

En la verdad del amor
Sé que en el mundo hay dolor
Pero no es dolor el mundo.

Butterfly, just as a tearful song
Grows calm in you
You calm my soul
With your flight, butterfly
The freedom of a rose
Is to live in truth
I sought happiness
In every flower you rested on
The roses have told me
You are their freedom

Oh, butterfly
With you the world alights
On the truthfulness of love
I know that there is pain in the world
But the world is not pain.[31]

The metaphorical references in "Mariposa" to the quest for personal freedom have never generated much controversy in Cuba and are subject to a variety of interpretations. Two of Ferrer's best-known compositions, however,
"100% cubano" (100% Cuban) and "El abuelo Paco" (Grandfather Paco), are
more directly critical of current realities. The first draws attention to special
privileges afforded tourists and foreigners, emphasizing that Cubans themselves have frequently become second-class citizens in their own country. The
second implicitly likens Castro to an irritable old man who builds his family
a lovely house and then lords over them using implicit threats of violence. In
both songs, Ferrer demonstrates his quick wit and biting sense of humor.

Ten paciencia con abuelo
Recuerda bien cuanto hizo
No contradigas su afán
Pónle atención en su juicio
Gasta un poco de tu tiempo
Complaciendo su egoismo

No olvides que Abuelo tiene
Un revólver y un cuchillo
Y mientras no se lo quiten
Abuelo ofrece peligro

Aunque sepas que no, díle que sí
Si lo contradices, peor para tí.

Be patient with grandpa
Remember how much he's done
Don't contradict his enthusiasm
Pay attention to his views
Spend a little time
Flattering his ego

Don't forget that gramps has
A revolver and a knife
And as long as they're not taken away
He poses a threat

Even if you know the answer is no, say yes
If you contradict him, it will go badly for you.[32]

Not surprisingly, the last time EGREM agreed to produce an album for Ferrer was over fifteen years ago, though they have re-released his early compositions on compact disc for the tourist market. Ferrer recorded "El abuelo Paco" independently in Miami with the help of his brother during a visit there and in a home studio in Havana. Authorities continue to limit diffusion of his more political songs and, at least in the 1990s, would not allow his concerts to be taped. Ferrer is aware of the price of nonconformity but has decided to speak his mind: "If you understand that no one has the right to administer liberty to you in the manner that the state bureaucracy in Cuba does, you have to resist and act like a free person to the extent that you can" (Ferrer in Niurka 1996).

Economic conditions have improved somewhat in recent years, but younger Cubans still have few attractive job opportunities, few possibilities for travel or study abroad, and limited access even to clothing, food, and domestic goods. The loss of support from the Soviet Union has created "a mass of educated youths whose expectations [clash] sharply with Cuba's desperate conditions" (Oppenheimer 1992:263). Dissatisfaction has led to an even stronger interest in foreign rather than national music. In the early 1990s, for example, Che Guevara's grandson Canek was known as a heavy metal rock fan whose favorite groups included Slayer, Death, and Kreator (Oppenheimer 1992:267). He and others have used rock as a symbolic tie to an international artistic community they feel separated from and as a reaction to government policies still considered too constraining.[33]

Younger *trovadores* tend to play songs with an aesthetic identity distinct from that of earlier times. They recognize their debt to past repertoire but refer to their own music as *novísima trova* in order to underscore its unique qualities. Some members of the newer generation (Gerardo Alfonso, Heidy Igualada, Lázara Ribadavia, Rita del Prado) rose to popularity playing acoustic guitar, but others have adopted electrified rock as their medium of choice, fuse elements of Cuban traditional repertoire with influences from abroad (jazz, Brazilian pop, rap), or some combination of both. Most *novísima trova* sounds even more modern and cosmopolitan than the music of earlier generations for this reason. Its artists tend to move with ease between styles from diverse locations and ethnic origins, including Afro-Cuban religious music and Hispanic *música guajira*. Since 1998, the Pablo de la Torriente Brau Cultural Center in Habana Vieja has become an important performance venue for *novísima trova*.

Carlos Varela stands out as one of the most articulate social commentators of recent years. Despite occasional clashes with bureaucrats, he has managed to negotiate a fairly stable position for himself as a critic who supports the socialist government even as he finds fault with it. As in the case of other rockers (Polito Ibáñez, Frank Delgado), Varela was unable to pursue his musical career through the existing education system. He eventually opted to study acting, forming an unofficial band while enrolled at the ISA in the mid-1980s. Involvement with the theater seems to have contributed to his musical success; Vilar (1998:17) notes that he was among the first to concern himself with lighting, stage effects, and other visual components of performance, a clear break with the tendency of older *trovadores* to appear in public as informally as possible. Early venues for Varela's band included live radio shows hosted by Ramón Fernández Larrea on Radio Ciudad de La Habana (Evora 2000).[34] Beginning about 1986, as mentioned, the state gradually began accepting rockers as musical professionals (Manduley López 1997:138). In this context and with the help of Silvio Rodríguez, Varela was eventually invited to play for larger audiences. The turning point in his career was a concert in the Karl Marx Theater in 1990 that converted him overnight into one of the most popular musicians of the day.[35] Despite this acclaim, he has never recorded within Cuba; his five studio albums, produced between 1988 and 1998, were all recorded in Spain or Venezuela.[36]

Varela's work typifies that of *novísima trova* figures who have opted for an international pop/rock sound virtually indistinguishable from that of performers in the United States and Europe, in this case artists such as U2 or Sting. His pieces vary from sweet, lyrical ballads employing a lone keyboard or other instruments ("Memorias," "Bulevar," "Jalisco Park") to minimalist R&B grooves and half-spoken vocals reminiscent of Dire Straits ("La política no cabe en la azucarera") to raunchy, driving rock with heavy percussion and distorted electric guitar ("Soy un gnomo"). Example 7 demonstrates these tendencies. "Cuchilla en la acera" (whose lyrics are quoted be-

EXAMPLE 7.   Excerpt from the opening of Carlos Varela's "Cuchilla en la acera" (Varela 1993a).

low) is a 1980s-style alternative rock piece harmonically similar to Randy Newman's "Short People." It opens at a slow tempo, but the voice and piano eventually accelerate and are joined by bass, electric guitar, and lively set drumming. In other songs, Varela incorporates occasional elements of more "Cuban-sounding" *timba* dance music (e.g., in "Tropicollage") to allude to issues related to tourism and commercialism.

Clearly a gifted musician, Varela nevertheless has gained widest recognition for his lyrics. They address domestic social concerns with a directness and bite that is striking. Examples include the text of "Guillermo Tell" (William Tell), written from the perspective of Tell's son, who is tired of being a target and asks his father to put the apple on his own head. The allegorical quality of the story is typical of Varela; in this case he alludes to generational conflicts between youth and older members of Cuba's power structure. Another example, "Cuchilla en la acera" (Razor on the Sidewalk), graphically describes violent street assaults typical of mid-1990s Havana:

> Le pusieron la cuchilla en el cuello
> Y después le quitaron la ropa
> Los transeúntes que lo vieron viraron la cara
> Y se callaron la boca
>
> Y aunque no le encontraron dinero
> Lo dejaron tirado en la vía

Y a pesar de la sangre, los gritos, y Dios
Nunca llegó la policía.

They put the razor to his throat
And then they took all his clothing
The passers by that saw him turned their faces
And kept their mouths shut

And although they didn't find any money
They left him sprawled on the street
And despite the blood, the cries, and God
The police never arrived.

One well-known song, "Monedas al aire" (Coins in the Air), makes an impassioned call for political change. During the peak of Varela's popularity, his concerts became associated with antiauthoritarianism to such an extent that they frequently ended in violence and intervention by the police (Vilar 1998:22–24).

To the extent that they perform traditional music, younger *trovadores* alter it substantially. The group Gema y Pável (named after principal members Gema Corredera and Pável Urkiza) is representative of this trend and is one of my personal favorites (Fig. 15). Their music is nearly as irreverent as that of Varela, but in a decidedly musical sense. Rather than foregrounding sociopolitical critique, their compositions instead redefine Cuban culture in more inclusive, hybridized terms. The style of the performers is highly individualistic. They eventually decided to leave Cuba, preferring to sing about past experiences while residing in Spain, as have a number of their contemporaries.

Gema and Pável began playing together in the late 1980s but had known each other since infancy. These were relatively good years in Cuba, a period of increasing possibilities for musicians. Neither artist had extensive formal training but were nurtured by an environment supportive of the arts.[37] Government-subsidized prices for food, housing, and other necessities meant that aspiring performers could dedicate long hours to creative work rather than seek full-time employment. Gema and Pável's first shows took place in *peñas* hosted by composer Teresita Fernández in Miramar (Raúl Martínez, pers. comm.) and in those of Marta Valdés in Vedado (Valdés 2004). They also collaborated with actors, painters, and others in multimedia "happenings" held almost nightly in the Casa del Joven Creador (House of the Young Artist), an old warehouse near the Havana docks that the UJC converted into a recreational space. As their reputation grew, they appeared

FIGURE 15.   Gema Corredera and Pável Urkiza performing a concert in the Artime Theater in Miami on November 13, 2004. Since leaving Cuba, the duo has maintained a small but devoted public there and has also toured in Europe and Latin America in addition to the United States. Photo by Lili Domínguez. Courtesy of Pável Urkiza.

regularly at state-sponsored youth events until their departure for Spain in the early 1990s. Among the strongest musical influences on the duo are Brazilian artists (Djavan, Caetano Veloso, Ivan Lins) and North American jazz performers (Billie Holiday, Thelonious Monk, the Manhattan Transfer).

Songs by Pável Urkiza and others interpreted by this duo are amazingly diverse.[38] Rhythms may be slow and relaxed or consist of driving and syncopated figures taken from Afro-Cuban folklore (*son*, rumba, African-derived religious song). Arrangements vary from stark a cappella voices to highly elaborated studio productions with string ensemble or jazz combo back tracks. Accompaniment patterns on the guitar, the most common instrument, are highly original, employing percussive strumming, pedals, and nonstandard inversions and chord sequences. Vertical harmonies tend to be extended, with unusual intervals emphasized between the voices of the singers: 5ths, flat 7ths, 9ths, and so forth. Vocal and instrumental improvisation is a prominent feature of most songs, as is African American–style melisma.

Gema and Pável's repertoire includes original work as well as compositions by fellow *trovadores,* adaptations of *vieja trova,* and arrangements of

EXAMPLE 8. Vocal excerpt from "Habana, devorando claridad" (Havana, Devouring Clarity) by Gema y Pável (1995).

international Latin standards by María Grever, Agustín Lara, or Antonio Carlos Jobim. In the same piece (e.g., "El bobo," The Fool), one might hear jazz set drumming, fragments of Hammond organ solos, vocal scatting, and excerpts from Beatles songs or the works of Silvio Rodríguez. The result is an almost bewilderingly intricate musical fabric. Example 8 provides a brief excerpt from one Gema y Pável composition that illustrates their creative vocal style and use of extended harmonies. The relative independence of the melodies is typical, with the female voice frequently creating its own countermelody. Accompaniment is provided by piano, bass, drum set, and cello.

Gema y Pável lyrics are personal, intimate, and subjective, a reaction against political slogans and rhetoric. Themes are varied, including love ("Longina"), adult misunderstanding of youthful innocence ("Aixa"), references to figures from Cuban history or folklore ("La caminadora," The Walking Woman), nostalgia, bittersweet memories of life in Cuba ("Domingo A.M.," Sunday A.M.; "Habana, devorando claridad," Havana, Devouring Clarity), self-doubt, depression, loneliness ("¿Hacia dónde?" Where to Go?), or events as simple and poignant as the disappearance of ice cream trucks ("Helado sobre ruedas," Ice Cream on Wheels) in Havana. Overall, the texts of these and other performers are of a surprisingly high caliber, a tribute to their cultural environment.

. . . . .

Nueva trova is more directly tied to the Cuban revolutionary experience than any other form of music. It represents an attempt to do something fresh and artistically vital and has created important space for musical experimentation through the years. Songs of the *trovadores* developed in a unique context, one reflecting the values of the socialist leadership and attempts to instill them in young people. The most successful examples of *nueva trova* composition demonstrate a high degree of creativity, poetics, stylistic synthesis, and political awareness. Drawing on diverse sources of inspiration, including music from the United States, Europe, and Latin America, they nevertheless represent an implicit critique of capitalist culture. Young composers attempt to avoid clichéd, formulaic song structures and to create music of high quality that documents the radical experiment of which they are (or were) a part. They consistently write pieces that do more than entertain, that engage the listener intellectually as well as emotionally. Above all, they strive to be true to themselves and to freely express their views on life, politics, and personal relations. Their songs continue to influence countless musicians: jazz performers (Pablo Menéndez, Arturo Sandoval), dance band leaders (Issac Delgado), *rumberos* (Yoruba Andabo), and others.

The spirit of freedom and rebellion surrounding *nueva trova* has inevitably resulted in conflicts with cultural officials. These conflicts were most severe in the late 1960s. *Trovadores* initially performed far from the media, but as their public grew, so too did interest in regulating their work. Most have experienced periods of censure and compromise. They do not emerge unscathed from every conflict but serve a valuable purpose by challenging the status quo. Young composers produce art that is intensely meaningful to local audiences. Humorously or seriously, *trova* contests boundaries of many kinds. It is precisely through engagement with unresolved aesthetic and social issues that it achieves its greatest relevance.

Since *nueva trova* began as a fusion of foreign and national styles, it is not surprising that the voices of young critics continue to find inspiration abroad. Beginning with the emergence of heavy metal groups (Venus, Zeus, and Metal Oscuro) in the 1980s and with Carlos Varela and Vicente Feliú in the 1990s, electrified rock has come to play an ever more prominent role in national music. More recently, rap too has influenced composers, especially Afro-Cubans. Countless new bands (Anónimo Consejo, Alto y Bajo, Irak) have signed recording contracts and are receiving widespread promotion (Sokol 2000a). *Nueva trova* no longer consists primarily of soloists with an acoustic guitar but is made up of individuals and ensembles that serve as Cuba's musical conscience.

Since the onset of economic crisis, *nueva trova* and even *novísima trova* have experienced a certain decline in popularity. The audience for socially conscious composition has always been circumscribed, appealing strongly to college-educated segments of the population. These days, dance repertoire and other more commercially viable genres represent the center of Cuban music making. Most performers within Cuba are directly involved in the tourist economy and are concerned with the appeal of their music to visitors as well as its sales potential abroad. They tend to write fewer songs oriented toward local listeners and concerns as a result. In retrospect, the period prior to 1989, despite its disadvantages, may have been more supportive of socially conscious art than the current one.

One unforeseen result of such changes is that the most consistent support for first-generation *trovadores* is now among audiences abroad rather than at home. For the politically conscious youth of the 1970s and 1980s who grew up in Latin America and Spain, the Cuban Revolution was a symbol of their aspirations; it demonstrated that grassroots activism could accomplish significant change. This public avidly listened to *trovadores*, performed their songs, and used them as a model to promote progressive musical activity within their own countries. Since most are unfamiliar with day-to-day realities in Cuba, the meanings of early *nueva trova* music remain largely the same for them today as it did when the songs were first written. Silvio Rodríguez, for example, performed in March of 1997 to an ecstatic crowd of thirty thousand in San Juan, Puerto Rico (Martínez Tabares 1997:6). Commentators noted that he, as well as Puerto Ricans Roy Brown, Andrés Jiménez, and others, evoked a powerful nationalist and anticolonialist response in listeners. Even in 1997, in a country that has consistently voted not to break ties with the United States, Silvio was able to briefly "rekindle . . . the spirit of the independence movement" (Correa 1997).

Frederick Starr suggests in his history of jazz in the Soviet Union that whenever government officials began to support particular genres of music (swing, bebop, etc.), it was a sign that they were no longer popular with the public. He further states that attempts to use music as a tool for ideological or political change were doomed there from the outset, that "the ideals of the October Revolution proved incapable of realization in popular music and culture generally unless backed by the use or threat of force" (Starr

1994:334). This commentary is provocative but seems to be contradicted in part by the history of *nueva trova*. It is true that the mass institutionalization of *trova* ultimately lead to greater regulation of its ideological content and its eventual declining popularity among many listeners. However, at the time the government initially endorsed it, the music represented a very popular form of expression and continued to be so for some time. I would argue further that the ideals of socialism as perceived by Cuban youth *have* been reflected in *nueva trova,* and very effectively. The problem is only that policy makers have not always accepted such views. *Trovadores* consistently support government positions they consider beneficial at the same time that they question others. Their songs reflect the attitudes of individuals who not only contemplate socialism in the abstract but have lived it as a reality their entire lives. It is hoped the insights of younger musicians will continue to affect cultural policy in a positive way and contribute to a more inclusive and dynamic socialist reality.

CHAPTER 6

Afro-Cuban Folklore in a Raceless Society

> The existence and character of a civilization are located in its cultural forms, and in their capacity to influence others. Cuban blacks have been fundamentally influential in both senses. On the one hand they created, through music, the nucleus of our national culture. On the other they have influenced the world with it, making Cuba famous, and leaving their mark on cultures abroad.
>
> ENRIQUE PATTERSON, "Cuba: Discursos sobre la identidad"

Throughout the Americas, the expressive forms of African descendants have proven central to the emergence of distinct regional and national identities. As slaves brought forcibly to the New World, they had no choice but to adapt to radically new social conditions, forms of labor, and language. While in some cases they perpetuated traditions brought with them across the Atlantic, it is not surprising that in their new environment Afro-Cubans were among the first to fashion a distinct cultural sensibility by fusing elements from their past with the practices of their colonial masters. Following abolitionist and independence movements in the nineteenth century, postcolonial leaders of all backgrounds learned (slowly) to embrace the culture of African descendants as symbols of local heritage. Nowhere is this more the case than in Cuba, where nationalist discourse since the late 1920s has described African-influenced music and dance as representative of everyone. Folkloric traditions of many sorts exist in Cuba but the most influential and widespread for centuries have been those of African origin. Perhaps for this reason the term "folklore" there is now synonymous with "Afro-Cuban folklore."[1]

Paradoxically, the colonial legacy also created strong bias against such expression, as discussed in chapter 1. Middle-class audiences, while arguably proud of their country's mixed ethnicity in the abstract, dismissed the country's African-derived traditions as primitive. Beginning in 1959, Castro's revolutionaries changed this dynamic for the better in a number of respects, creating more opportunities for folkloric ensembles and establishing centers for the study of Afro-Cuban heritage. Black working-class dance bands and singers of popular music achieved unprecedented levels of national exposure as part of the same trend. By the same token, biases inherited from earlier decades continued to affect cultural programming, especially related to noncommercial drumming. One might argue that Marxist philosophy itself also contributed to ambivalence toward folklore, at least in its traditional form. While one of the avowed aims of socialists has been the preservation of traditional music, such expression is often "ethnic, regional and conservative," traits at odds with the emergence of a united international proletariat (Silverman 1983:55).

This chapter provides an overview of traditional Afro-Cuban folkloric music since 1959. It foregrounds activity during the 1960s in which folk musicians flourished, focusing on Pedro Izquierdo, Enrique Bonne, and the Conjunto Folklórico Nacional as examples of well-known groups/artists. Later sections describe decreasing opportunities for such performance and then its resurgence. The chapter suggests that the public presentation of drumming in formal, staged contexts served for a time as a means of limiting its dissemination. Further, the ostensibly "raceless" vision of most of the revolutionary leadership limited the discussion of racial concerns. Discussion of Afro-Cuban religious music continues in chapter 7.[2]

THE CULTURAL LEGACY
OF THE REPUBLIC IN THE REVOLUTION

Any study of Afro-Cuban folklore and its place in revolutionary society must begin with an appreciation for controversies surrounding it before 1959. Afro-Cuban studies since its inception has been mired in racism and cultural misunderstanding of the worst sort. Writings of the Cuban Anthropological Society from the late nineteenth century, as one example, suggested that blacks and mulattos belonged to an inherently inferior race and questioned whether it was worth the trouble to educate them (León 1966:5–6). Members regularly exhumed black bodies from graveyards in order to support theories of racial superiority through the measurement of skulls and cranial cavities. The prominence of Afro-Cuban soldiers in the War of Independence (1895–98), together with the efforts of political leaders such as José Martí, Juan Gualberto Gómez, Antonio Maceo, and Rafael Serra, brought an end to openly racist discourse of this sort. Nevertheless, elite society remained decidedly anti-African, as manifested in attitudes toward culture. Newspapers such as *La Prensa* stated in the 1910s that the nation was doomed to failure as long as it tolerated, among other things, rumba and African-derived dances (Pappademos 2003:1). Many percussion instruments studied by scholars Jesús

Castellanos (1879–1912) and Fernando Ortiz (1881–1969) came from police stations, where they had been confiscated in campaigns to rid the island of "degenerate" cultural practices.[3] African labor had provided the economic foundation for the republic, but in the twentieth century Cubans went to considerable lengths to purge African elements from national expression (Carbonell 1961:12).

Middle-class Cubans even in the 1940s and 1950s considered Afro-Cuban folklore distasteful (Ortiz García 2003:701). Few ever went to see performances of rumba, *makuta,* or *yuka* drumming in working-class neighborhoods, let alone religious events. Indeed, many refused even to listen to works for chamber orchestra based loosely on Afro-Cuban music, such as those by Amadeo Roldán (Ardévol 1966:159, 199). Researchers who took an interest in Afro-Cuban arts did so in isolation from the public and largely at their own expense. Ortiz supported ongoing work through his law practice; Lydia Cabrera (1899–1991) eventually found a benefactress, María Teresa Rojas, who supported her (L. Menéndez 1996, interview). José Luciano Franco (1891–1988) wrote on Afro-Cuban history while employed as a journalist and city administrator. Rómulo Lachatañeré (1909–51) eventually immigrated to the United States in the 1940s because of his interest in pursuing research on Afro-Cuban culture and the difficulty of supporting himself while doing so in Cuba. With the exception of Lachatañeré, the study of Afro-Cuban culture remained in the hands of white Cubans. The black working class did not have the educational preparation or economic means to promote their own expressive forms. Black middle-class writers on the whole distanced themselves from stigmatized African-influenced culture and instead embraced European arts.

Few courses on Afro-Cuban history or culture could be taken at the University of Havana prior to 1959, and virtually none represented required courses. Ortiz offered intermittent summer seminars on Cuban ethnography beginning in 1943 that included material on Afro-Cuban subjects, however (Barnet 1983:132). Students in the first of these included composers Gilberto Valdés (1905–71) and Argeliers León (1918–91) as well as Isaac Barreal (1918–94), later a researcher in the revolution's Institute of Ethnology. Toward the end of the 1940s, León himself offered courses on Afro-Cuban music, as did others. Elective seminars of this sort continued into the 1950s but with chronically low enrollment (L. Menéndez 1996, interview). They had a limited impact because mainstream students considered them a waste of time, as they did history courses with an Afro-Cuban focus offered by José Luciano Franco.

As mentioned, very little Afro-Cuban drumming or song could be heard or seen in the mass media prior to 1959. This was symptomatic of racial barriers that pervaded all of Cuban society. Most citizens of color attended poorly funded public schools; a significant number never graduated high school, dropping out early in order to support themselves and their families. Afro-Cubans represented less than 10 percent of all university graduates in every field in the midcentury, despite constituting roughly one-third the total population (de la Fuente 1995:151). Those who managed to educate themselves and enter the professions received lower salaries than their white counterparts.

In the first months after 1959, the revolutionary leadership began to address these problems. New legislation in February 1959 mandated the desegregation of all neighborhoods, parks, hotels, cabarets, and beaches (Serviat 1986:164). Both Fidel Castro and Ernesto Guevara made strong statements against racism, especially as it affected access to employment. Beginning in January 1960, the Ministry of Labor began to oversee the hiring of state employees in order to ensure that positions were distributed fairly to blacks and whites (N. Fernández 2002). The government took possession of private homes abandoned by exiles and reassigned them to poorer families, frequently black or racially mixed. Changes instigated such as the lowering of utility rates and rental prices, the national literacy campaign, and the creation of free medical clinics benefited the Afro-Cuban population disproportionately in tangible ways. Over time, these policies contributed to a decline in racial inequality, as manifested in key social indicators such as life expectancy, infant mortality, and educational levels. As a result, working-class Afro-Cubans tended to be among the most enthusiastic supporters of the revolution.

Yet despite their beneficial effects, the new racial policies proved controversial. The desegregation of private clubs and recreational areas caused an outcry among white professionals, many of whom had no desire to mingle with Cubans of color. Perhaps realizing that he had underestimated the divisiveness of the issue, Castro backpedaled and avoided the subject. The campaign against racial inequality of 1959 and 1960 soon disappeared from the media and did not surface again for over twenty years. Few Afro-Cubans found positions in the new government, further limiting public discussion about race.[4] Revolutionaries clearly wished to improve the social conditions of the Afro-Cuban population but did not immediately cede its members any political authority. On the contrary, they forbade them from organizing interest groups based on race. The government allowed Afro-Cubans to express opinions as students or through professional groups, "but never as blacks, the social construct within which they were most vulnerable to discrimination" (Patterson 2000:22A).

The closing of the *sociedades de color* in 1962, while well intended, resulted in the loss of one of blacks' few spaces for socializing and independent discussion. *Sociedades* had been important not only as centers for recreational activity but also for musical learning. Most dance band musicians of the 1950s did not learn their art in conservatories but rather from family and friends in relatively informal venues such as these (Neustadt 2002:143). Societies of Spanish descendants as well as those of Jews and Arabs did not suffer the same fate, though their buildings and assets also came under state control (Patterson 1996:64). The Centro Gallego, for instance, was nationalized and known thereafter as the Sociedad de Amistad Cubana-Española.

Those interested in promoting greater awareness of racism found their efforts hampered as the result of the militarized state of the nation following the Bay of Pigs attack; for some time, officials equated the discussion of such problems with criticism of the revolution. They feared that assertions of racial difference might be used by enemies to divide the Cuban people and thus discouraged the study or projection of a distinct Afro-Cuban identity. Writers hoping to use revolutionary society as a vehicle for rethinking Cuba's history—to revisit the brutality of the slave trade, the importance of figures such as José Antonio Aponte, or the racial violence of 1912—thus found little opportunity to publish. Blacks and mulattos continued to find themselves at a "frank disadvantage" (Prieto 1996, interview) in many white-collar professions and facets of the entertainment industry such as radio, television, and acting. Those promoting Afro-Cuban folklore encountered similar limitations. Reynaldo Fernández Pavón suggests that the socialist government initially strove to create citizens who shed their individual differences and were converted into "a social entity for and with the socialist cause, a single undivided mass. . . . When the leadership was faced with expressions of ethnic identity among various groups manifest in folklore, they viewed them as something that needed to be eliminated or erased because they demonstrated difference and the leadership didn't know how to manage such difference" (March 9, 1998, interview).

AFRO-CUBAN ARTS IN THE EARLY 1960S

The revolutionary government has always recognized Afro-Cuban arts to be a repository of Cuba's unique character, a powerful populist symbol of the nation. It knows they are among "the most authentic creations of the masses" and have historically represented their interests, as spokespersons for the Afro-Cuban community themselves note (Martínez Furé 1979:259). For this reason, Afro-Cuban drumming has always received promotion through folk-lore troupes and recordings and has been the focus of some academic study. The government recognizes that support from the black community is cru-cial to the success of the revolution, and that valorization of its artistic forms contributes to that end. Castro went so far as to define Cubans as "an African Latin people" in 1976, becoming the first head of state in the hemisphere to make such a pronouncement (Casal 1979:24). Progressive individuals in charge of cultural affairs such as Ramiro Guerra, Argeliers León, and Odilio Urfé called for the study and promotion of Afro-Cuban folklore during the first months of the revolution (Orejuela Martínez 2004:53).

On the other hand, officials have also referred to Afro-Cuban folkloric drumming as *atrasada*, or "backward," primarily because of its associations with "primitive" West African societies and their "superstitious" beliefs. Composer Gonzalo Roig, interviewed by prominent newspapers in 1961, described traditional rumba as marginal, even barbaric, and having no place in "true" Cuban culture (as quoted in Orejuela Martínez 2004:127–28). Ernesto Guevara came out publicly against Afro-Cuban cultural or histor-ical study in 1963. When asked by students from abroad about the absence of textbooks in schools concerning Africa and its peoples, Guevara responded, "I see no more purpose in black people studying African history in Cuba than in my children studying Argentina. . . . Black people need to study Marxist-Leninism, not African history" (as quoted in Moore 1964:217–18). Carlos Moore concludes his documentation of the latter exchange with the following: "Did it ever cross Dr. Guevara's mind that . . . [a black Cuban], a product of a culture and a civilization which, from his earliest days in school has been *misrepresented, confused, distorted, and lied about,* does need the fullest and most precise knowledge of the African peoples, their culture and achievements, for his own *self-appreciation?*" (Moore 1964).

Despite these views, African-influenced music and culture became demon-strably more visible across the island during the early 1960s, owing in part to the large number of semiprofessional ensembles that emerged as part of the Amateurs' movement. Little information exists on the formation of such groups nationwide,[5] but Millet and Brea (1989:92–118) discuss representa-tive ensembles that appeared in the Santiago area. They include the Con-junto Folklórico de Oriente, founded in 1960 by Bertha Armiñán and Roberto Salazar; the Conjunto Folklórico Cutumba, established soon there-after by Roberto Sánchez; Los Tambores de Enrique Bonne, founded in 1960; the Cabildo Teatral Santiago, directed by Ramiro Herrero; the Conjunto Folklórico Abolengo, established in 1964 and specializing in Afro-Haitian folklore; and the Grupo Folklórico Guillermón Moncada, founded in 1967 by Walfrido Valerino. Similar groups from Havana date from the early 1960s, including Guaguancó Marítimo Portuario, created by stevedores, the majority of whom belonged to the same Abakuá society. This group changed its name in 1985 to Yoruba Andabo (Neris Gonález Bello, pers. comm.). Juanito García (2003, interview) affirms that although only a handful of folklore ensembles received support from the state, hundreds of *aficionado* groups came into existence.[6]

The presence of so many folklore groups contributed to a dramatic expansion of public drumming. The only groups prior to 1959 that achieved any level of recognition were the Conjunto Folklórico Antillano, a short-lived (1949–50) ensemble known for blending Afro-Cuban folkloric elements with modern dance, and the Guaguancó Matancero, founded in 1952, whose members eventually changed their name to the Muñequitos de Matanzas.[7] During the early years of the revolution, not even members of the Muñequitos received recognition as full-time professional artists. Yet television programs featured them to an unprecedented degree, such as a broadcast of rumba, *comparsa,* and Abakuá music and dance organized by Odilio Urfé on October 10, 1959 (Urfé 1982:165). *Tumba francesa* groups and Carabalí *cabildos* performed traditional songs and dances in Havana's theaters soon thereafter, something that would have been unheard of before the revolution (Orejuela Martínez 2004:126). Work undertaken at the Institute of Ethnology and Folklore, formed in 1961, also demonstrated a new level of commitment on the part of the government to valorize and promote Afro-Cuban arts. Miguel Barnet commented approvingly on the prominence of folklore in public venues in 1963.

> The Cuban public is getting accustomed to seeing manifestations of our musical folklore on theater stages. In times past, popular music was only heard in theaters of ill repute . . . now the most authentic, popular creations of our country have been brought to the best concert stages. . . . Efforts to valorize music that our people created over the centuries have culminated in the Festivals of Popular Culture . . . they take the *guaguancó* from the marginal neighborhoods, the *cocoyé* from the streets of Santiago, rescue Elena Burke from the nightclubs, and bring them all to the theater so that everyone can appreciate them. (As quoted in Orejuela Martínez 2004:141)

The Festivals of Popular Culture referred to by Barnet represented an important forum for the presentation of Afro-Cuban and other heritage. The first took place in August 1962 and included a wide variety of music: *changüí* dance music from Guantánamo, *punto* and *tonada* from Spanish-derived campesino traditions, *sucu-sucu* from the Isle of Pines, a Santiago carnival band, traditional rumba drumming and *coros de clave,* as well as dance music by the Conjunto Chappottín, Pacho Alonso, and others. A second, smaller festival of the same sort took place in August of 1963.

Carnival ensembles *(comparsas)* remained a strong presence across the island, yet state-controlled unions soon urged that they organize by work center rather than by city neighborhood. This seems to represent an attempt to regulate what was considered an unruly cultural manifestation and perhaps also to encourage members to identify across racial and neighborhood lines. Government warehouses represented virtually the only source of materials for costumes, instruments, parade floats, and so on, and thus officials had leverage to influence the theme songs and imagery adopted by participants as well. By 1963, the names of traditional *comparsas* appeared alongside new ones, such as "Musical Review of the Construction Workers' Union." Critics demonstrated ambivalent attitudes toward *comparsas.* Racially edged disdain blends with messages of anti-imperialism in this quote from *Bohemia.*

> Citizen President Dr. Osvaldo Dorticós Torrado has inaugurated the carnival event before the tribunal, lending with his presence a revolutionary dimension to the frivolous spectacle of more than five hundred men and women . . . responding to the ancestral call of jungle drums. . . . These individuals display combative exuberance that Cuba presents as a vivacious response to the insolent threat of aggression on the part of impotent and yet rapacious imperialism. (Sánchez Lalebret 1963:63)[8]

Older neighborhood *comparsas* never disappeared but received less recognition than their newly created counterparts for some time. Toward the end of the 1960s, leaders made the decision to move carnival in Havana to July 26 (carnival in Santiago has always been held at the end of July). This created more time for the spring sugar harvest, distanced the celebration from its Catholic origins, and added to the festive atmosphere surrounding the anniversary of Castro's attack on the Moncada garrison in Santiago. Since the late 1990s, the event has reverted to its original pre-Lenten dates.

ENRIQUE BONNE, PACHO ALONSO, AND PELLO EL AFROKÁN

The career of Enrique Alberto Bonne Castillo (b. 1926) illustrates the role that many Afro-Cuban performers played in promoting drumming traditions during the early revolution. Born on the outskirts of Santiago into a musical working-class family, Bonne studied classical piano with his mother and involved himself in folkloric events. His father composed *danzones* and played popular music in theaters when not cutting sugarcane (Bonne 1999, interview). By the 1950s, Bonne gained recognition as a composer himself, writing commercial jingles, chachachás, and theme songs for the Santiago carnival group La Placita. After the revolutionaries came to power, he worked in radio for a time, and then in 1960 organized about fifty *comparsa* musicians from the barrio of Los Hoyos into a group that became known as Enrique Bonne y sus Tambores. The instrumentation of the ensemble included twenty-seven drums of various kinds (conga drums in several sizes, *bombos*, or bass drums, *bocuses*, a regional drum from Santiago), three *chéqueres* (a Yoruba gourd percussion instrument), three brake shoes, two *cornetas chinas* (a Chinese double reed), a *catá*, or piece of hollowed wood struck with sticks, maracas, and singers (Ginori 1968:60–61). The group apparently represented the first state-supported experiment in revolutionary Cuba with a mass percussion ensemble.

Los Tambores debuted in the carnival celebrations of 1962, owing in part to the support of Lázaro Peña, a prominent Afro-Cuban politician who at that time directed the Cuban Workers Union (CTC). The group's repertoire featured a diversity of rhythms including *chachalokefún* (associated with sacred *batá* performance), *bembé* rhythms (also sacred), *comparsa* drumming patterns from Santiago and Havana, *rumba guaguancó*, and other hybrids of his own invention. None of the group's musicians read music, with the exception of the director, and so learned all arrangements by rote (Bonne 1999, interview). Bonne experimented in many ways with Los Tambores: by creating percussive accompaniment to traditional boleros ("Como el arrullo de palmas") or presenting dramatic poetry with Afro-Cuban themes ("La tragedia de saber") backed by drumming, the latter featuring Afro-Cuban actor Alden Knight. Los Tambores collaborated with famous stage personalities of the day, including Omara Portuondo, Rosita Fornés, even classical composers Rafael Somavilla and Adolfo Guzmán.

One is struck with the elaborate nature of Bonne's arrangements, which incorporated frequent breaks and timbral shifts and alternated between multiple rhythms within the same piece. He recognized a diversity of influences on his music, including Cuban folklore, traditional *trova*, dance music, even U.S. jazz. A great deal of prejudice existed against drumming within Cuba in the early 1960s; Bonne viewed his efforts as a way of changing such attitudes by presenting percussion in new ways and performing a wider variety of repertoire (Bonne 1999, interview). The Tambores continue to exist

EXAMPLE 9.   Enrique Bonne's *pilón* rhythm, as performed by José Luis Quintana (Quintana and Mauleón Santana 1996) and Yaroldi Abreu Robles (2003, interview).

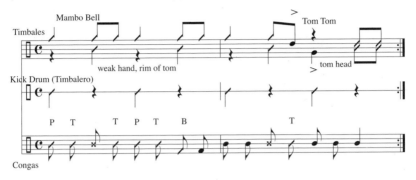

and to perform occasionally today, though funding from the state has been intermittent.

The most famous dance style popularized by Bonne is the *pilón* (literally "pestle"). This is the name of the largest *bombo* drum used in Santiago carnival celebrations. Traditionally, the *comparsa pilón* drum plays a characteristic two-measure rhythm in 4/4 time consisting of three pulses on strong beats followed by a sharp attack on the "and-of-four" of the second measure. It is similar to but distinct from Bonne's *pilón* rhythm for dance band, which also alternates straight beats with a syncopated accent but emphasizes the "and-of-two" and "3." Although carnival rhythms seem to have been the model for Bonne's *pilón,* he suggests that he also took inspiration from rural workers grinding up coffee beans (Bonne 1999, interview). Example 9 demonstrates how the sound of Bonne's *pilón* results from the intersecting patterns of the congas and timbales. The implicit clave pattern here is 2–3. In the conga sketch, as in an earlier example, P = palm, T = touch, and B = bass. Round note heads indicate open tones; "x" heads indicate slaps. Stems up on the timbales and conga lines indicate that the part should be played by the strong hand; stems down, with the weak hand.

Bonne first tried to popularize the *pilón* rhythm and dance in 1961 without much success.[9] It was only later through collaborations with singer Pacho Alonso (1928–82) that it became a national craze. Alonso, son of a Cuban mother and Puerto Rican father, also spent his childhood in the Santiago area. After studying to be a schoolteacher for a time in Havana, he returned to Santiago in 1951 and performed as vocalist in the orchestra of Mariano Mercerón. Beginning in 1957, Alonso recorded several popular songs written by Bonne, including "Que me digan Feo" with his first group, Pacho

FIGURE 16.   Pacho Alonso y sus Bocucos, popularizers of the *pilón* rhythm
invented by Enrique Bonne. The photo was taken in 1969 at the Habana Libre
hotel, formerly the Havana Hilton. Photo Archive, Ministry of Culture, Cuba.

Alonso y los Modernistas.[10] Bonne and Alonso slowly gained popularity together in subsequent years, the former as composer and the latter as interpreter (Martínez Rodríguez 1988:20). In 1962, Alonso formed Los Bocucos
(Fig. 16). This ensemble first brought the *pilón* to national attention, performing as of 1965 on national television, in cabarets, and in regional car-
nivals throughout the island. The *pilón* dance is a creation of Alonso's, also
based in part on motions associated with coffee grinding. It involves holding one's hands out in front of one's body as if around a pestle and rotat-
ing the hips. During early television appearances, Alonso filled the stage with
young, attractive women in miniskirts in order to teach the audience the
appropriate movements. In 1968, he reorganized his band yet again under
the name Los Pachucos. They continued to popularize new rhythms by
Bonne such as the *simalé* and *upa-upa,* touring France, Spain, Panama, and
the Soviet Union in addition to Cuba.

The career of Pedro Izquierdo (1933–2000), better known as Pello el
Afrokán, also underscores the prominence of black working-class artists after 1959. Izquierdo is significant as the percussionist to receive the widest
recognition during the early revolution. He was born in the predominantly
Afro-Cuban neighborhood of Jesús María, Havana, and collaborated on
drums with his father in the orchestra of Belisario López from an early age.

EXAMPLE 10. Rhythmic sketch of basic *mozambique* rhythms as performed by Kim Atkins (1996).

During the day he worked as a stevedore on the docks of Havana and occasionally as a furniture upholsterer (Piñeiro 1965:24). Izquierdo's family exposed him to a variety of folklore and instilled in him a sense of pride in his African ancestry. In statements after becoming a celebrity, he made a point of mentioning that he was an Abakuá and that his grandmother was a Makua (a Bantu group from Mozambique) and his grandfather a *curro,* or free black *ladino* from Spain. He chose the name *mozambique* for his new dance rhythm not because it had anything directly to do with that country, but because he wanted to emphasize his own African heritage and the contributions of Africa to Cuban culture more generally (Miller 2005:35). Many viewed the popularity of the genre in the mid-1960s as a clear statement of the government's support for African-influenced folklore. In a newspaper article from 1965 Izquierdo himself asserted, "Only now, within the revolution, has Cuba given the drum its rightful place."[11]

Example 10 provides a sketch of basic *mozambique* rhythms. The strong and weak hands used on the conga are indicated by stems up and down, as in previous examples. In the *bombo* transcriptions, a round note head indicates a strong open tone, while slash heads represent softer tones that are muted with the weak hand resting against the drumhead. All *bombo* strokes are played with a mallet.

Izquierdo began performing music for percussion ensemble as part of a construction workers' band in 1963 with more than one hundred other musicians but first achieved national recognition in the carnival of February 1964. His group and its music became an overnight sensation, playing across the island in almost every major city (Fig. 17). Band members consisted almost entirely of Afro-Cubans and performed on a wide variety of traditional percussion. Never before had a folklore troupe appeared so prominently in the national media. In part, the attention focused on Izquierdo was due to genuine interest about his music on the part of the public, his gifts as a showman, and the band's elaborate costumes. Victoria Eli Rodríguez links their prominence to the government's campaign against racism, reflecting the promotion of new cultural forms as part of that process (Perna 2001:36). The press saturation also seems to have been an attempt to cover the departure of many famous musicians during the same period as well as to focus attention on national styles of music rather than international influences such as rock (Vázquez 1988:5). Rock music, especially, had largely disappeared from the media as of 1964 (Orejuela Martínez 2004:180). Izquierdo caused such a stir with the *mozambique* that through 1967 he was asked to host a program on television called *Ritmos de Juventud*. His orchestra drew steady crowds to live performances in the Salón Mambí outside the Tropicana until the onset of the *ofensiva revolucionaria*. The group made frequent international tours in the mid-1960s, one of only a few permitted to do so.

Izquierdo's compositions influenced musicians in the New York area and in Puerto Rico (the Palmieri brothers, Ritchie Ray, Bobby Valentín, El Gran Combo) who recorded *mozambiques* from Cuba and of their own creation. The first foreign artist to adopt the genre was Eddie Palmieri, who recorded the LP *Mambo + Conga = Mozambique* in 1965. Palmieri later claimed to have invented the rhythm himself, apparently because he substantially altered and adapted it. However, Palmieri's recordings do strike the listener as derivative of Izquierdo's and of traditional *comparsa* rhythms. This is apparent in the timbales' "and-of-two" punch every other measure, similar to the *bombo* drum rhythm in the *mozambique*, and in the prominent bell patterns, much like those played on the *sartenes* (frying pans) in carnival bands. In a November 22, 2003, lecture at the Annenberg Center, Philadelphia, Palmieri mentioned that the release of the 1965 album created serious problems for himself and his orchestra. The Cuban government threatened to sue his record label, Tico, for having popularized the genre in the

FIGURE 17. Pedro Izquierdo, better known as Pello el Afrokán, featured here with his popular *mozambique* troupe and female dancer Daisy Monteavaro in 1969. Photo Archive, Ministry of Culture, Cuba.

United States without compensating its Cuban inventor. Members of the Cuban exile community also contacted Tico and made bomb threats, attempting to keep it from promoting music they associated with Castro. Understandably, Palmieri's enthusiasm for the new style soon waned.

As in the case of Bonne's *pilón*, the *mozambique* of Pedro Izquierdo represented an elaboration of traditional Afro-Cuban rhythms, incorporating them into a large dance ensemble. His initial group consisted of twelve conga drums tuned to four different pitches, two *bombos*, three bells, a *sartén*, five trombones, five trumpets, and accompanying female dancers. Thereafter, electric bass and piano were added. Izquierdo adapted rhythms into his *mozambique* drum battery from a diversity of sources, including carnival music, *rumba guaguancó*, *rumba columbia*, *rumba yambú*, and Abakuá drum and bell patterns (Piñeiro 1965:24). The dance step associated with the genre involved slow steps forward with both feet in alternation and a slight dip and turning motion to the side using the hips.

While secular, the *mozambique* melodies recorded by Izquierdo included notable influences from Yoruba and Iyesá sacred repertoire, some the most obvious that had ever been heard in popular song. On the release *Pello el Afrokan: Un sabor que canta*,[12] for instance, the band performs entire liturgical melodies from Santería with new secular lyrics. The melody of "La pillé" (I Saw Her), for instance, is actually a devotional song to Oyá, guardian of the cemetery; its lyrics in Yoruba, "Oya L'oya e adi-e adi-e oya," were transformed by the composer into "Mama Lola é, la pillé, la pillé mamá" (Mama Lola, hey, I saw her, woman).[13] Another example from the same recording is the song "Ara-ñakiña." It is a *son*-based piece, but the title comes from a phrase ("Bara ñakiñá, ñakiñá loro, bara ñakiñá") sung repeatedly by Santería practitioners when preparing to sacrifice a bird to the *orichas* (Michael Mason, pers. comm.). Another line, "Ogún cholo cholo," is also associated with ritual offerings. Other phrases mention prominent *santeros* of the period.

Fidel Castro is not known to take much personal interest in music, but a photo from April 13, 1965, in the newspaper *Hoy* shows him talking with Pedro Izquierdo. According to the accompanying story, Castro approached the bandleader and urged him to write a song that would help inspire volunteer workers to take part in the yearly sugar harvest. Izquierdo's resulting composition, based on "Arrímate pa' 'ca" (Come Over Here) by Juanito Márquez, was retitled "Bailando mozambique me voy a cortar caña" (Dancing *Mozambique* I'm Going to Cut Cane). It may have contributed to the government's labor efforts, but its humorous double entendre lyrics—"Ay, how tasty the cane is, honey . . . bring your cart over here"—contained other messages as well. Castro accompanied the group to its recording session at the CMQ television studios for this piece and is reported to have enthusiastically monitored Pello's efforts there (*Revolución*, April 12, 1965, pp. 1–2).

During the early years of his group's popularity, Izquierdo created significant controversy by inviting white women into his troupe as dancers and by interacting with them onstage. This was a period in which interracial marriages and even open interracial affairs were unacceptable to much of the population. Many disapproved of Pello's group for this reason, refused to go see him perform, and criticized him in the press. One of his white dancers, Daisy Monteavaro, was the inspiration of the famous *mozambique* "María caracoles." Its title referred to the fancy beehive hairstyle she adopted, with its many seashell-like curls.

As of 1968, Izquierdo had difficulty maintaining his former prominence. A faltering economy resulted in the closure of many performance spaces. Izquierdo also became a victim of the heavy promotion that state radio gave his music; listeners recall hearing his songs virtually every half-hour and eventually tiring of them (Perna 2001:27). The increasing popularity of *nueva trova* after 1973 also led to a decline in the *mozambique*. Yet in 1979, with the creation of the television show *Para bailar* under the direction of Eduardo

Cáceres Manso, the *mozambique* experienced a resurgence. This program helped disseminate a wide variety of folk music. Particular segments featured young people dancing *rumba guaguancó* and *mozambique* as well demonstrating international dance styles such as samba, flamenco, and merengue. The program's directors also invited local dancers who mixed *son*-style steps with those of the *rumba columbia* (Alexis Esquivel, pers. comm.).

GOVERNMENT-SPONSORED ENSEMBLES: THE EXAMPLE OF THE CFN

A number of folklore ensembles have achieved recognition internationally since 1959. By far the most famous is the Conjunto Folklórico Nacional (CFN), founded in May of 1962 in Havana by ethnographer Rogelio Martínez Furé and Mexican choreographer Rodolfo Reyes Cortés. In 1964, the CFN became the first state-funded artistic institution devoted exclusively to the performance of national folklore (Hagedorn 1995:225). It has always offered concerts in which songs from Santería ceremony might appear next to ballroom *contradanzas*, turn-of-the-century *coros de clave y guaguancó*, Spanish-derived *música guajira* traditions, Haitian-derived folklore from eastern Cuba, or carnival music. Nevertheless, its fundamental goals have been staging Afro-Cuban expression, which is too often hidden from public view, and educating the public on its beauty and complexity.

As mentioned, the early 1960s generated a tremendous sense of excitement in the Afro-Cuban community, leading many to conclude that they would no longer have to hide their culture or struggle vainly for artistic recognition (Hagedorn 2001:137). Founding members of the CFN began studying as an amateur group with this expectation. In early years they relied heavily on the expertise of master percussionists Trinidad Torregrosa (1893–1977) and Jesús Pérez (1925–85), dancer Nieves Fresneda (1900–80), and singer Lázaro Ros (1925–2005), among others (Martínez Furé 1982:4). Most participants were Afro-Cuban and had grown up surrounded by the traditions they hoped to bring to the stage, though they did eventually collaborate with professionals such as choreographer Ramiro Guerra. The CFN presented its first formal concert in the Teatro Mella in 1963. Shortly thereafter, ensemble members began to receive a small monthly stipend from the government (35–40 pesos a month) in recognition of their efforts. Toward the end of the decade, the CNC recognized them as full-time performers; salaries increased to approximately 170 pesos a month, allowing them to devote themselves more exclusively to their art.

The history of the CFN demonstrates ways in which the government has supported Afro-Cuban folklore but also provides evidence of the limits of such support. For years, this ensemble was the only one of its kind in the Havana area, a region with a population of millions.[14] After government support became available, salaries in the group remained relatively low relative to those of other full-time artists. It also received little airtime on television and few opportunities to record. CFN directors themselves recognize that the group's presentations generated little enthusiasm among much of the public, especially among white/Hispanic professionals. Their music continued to be viewed as a *cosa de negros,* expression that lacked "universal" relevance (Pedrito 1998, interview). In fact, few white Cubans watch their performances even today. Hagedorn (1995:242) mentions that "underneath the newly varnished layer of Revolutionary enthusiasm" for the CFN project "were several rougher layers of mistrust and wariness, as well as a hair-trigger readiness to lose faith in the endeavor."

State-supported ensembles were intended to valorize elements of traditional culture while simultaneously supporting ideological or educational initiatives. As in the case of the Soviet Bloc, a nationalist ideology supported musical genres and instruments as symbols of the nation while a socialist ideology demanded the presentation of those same genres in contexts suitable to the construction of new values (Rice 1994:229). Cultural advisors wished to "elevate" folk expression, professionalize it, and make it more intelligible for urban audiences. They often altered the structure and content of traditional genres for this reason. Advisors supported collaborations with conservatory-trained composers, musicians, and dancers and freely recombined rhythms, dance steps, and instruments in new ways. As one example, the ensemble Oru, consisting of several members of the CNF, performed their "Requiem for Che Guevara" in 1968, which involved the use of sacred Yoruba chants in an aleatoric avant-garde composition, composed and sung by Rogelio Martínez Furé (Martínez Furé 1994:35).[15]

Even in more traditional presentations, changes were made. Improvisation and spontaneity associated with community performance tended to disappear. Ritual songs that might be chosen at the moment and repeated or elaborated in sacred contexts would be selected ahead of time and presented in a particular order so that they could be choreographed more precisely (Prieto 1996, interview). Advisors added new musical or dramatic elements (Guerra 1991): vocal harmonies might be extended and sung more precisely in tune; lighting and costumes might be altered from one piece to the next; dances steps would be drilled until they could be flawlessly executed in unison; and so forth. The end result was an enjoyable and technically demanding but rather static spectacle that little resembled events in poorer black neighborhoods (Hagedorn 2001:122).

Some have criticized the circumscribed support for Afro-Cuban folklore and the changes instituted in its performance. Helio Orovio (interview, 1996), for instance, describes the CFN as a sort of "cultural reservation." He believes that the CNC intended the CFN to be the only significant outlet for many forms of traditional Afro-Cuban expression that it ultimately did not want to see perpetuated. Eugenio Matibag concurs, suggesting that the decidedly limited support of Afro-Cuban traditions in secularized, stylistically altered, and commodified form represented a "strategy of containment." "Folklorization serves to relegate a vital, lived cultural form to the category of the artistic and picturesque, thus neutralizing its ideological power" (1996:247). Perhaps the most virulent criticism of the staged folklore movement came during the early years of the revolution by Carlos Moore, who had recently chosen to leave Cuba. From his perspective, folklorization constituted nothing less than a subtle form of cultural "whitening" and "de-Africanization." His critique here discusses sacred practices but applies to all folklore.

> Dances and music which are part of the ceremonial *complex* of creeds and tenets of these adherents—considered, quite reasonably, as *sacred* . . . and bearing a functional meaning in their practices—are being *prostituted* and presented in theaters as "people's folklore." Why isn't the same applied to the sacred practices of the Judeo-Christian faiths? The subtle motives beneath this outrage are simple: a) to emasculate the faith, through a prostitution of its most cherished religious values and a demoralization of its followers as a result; b) to systematically destroy what are considered to be "pagan" and "savage" religious "cults" by means of "civilizing" them into a *palatable* "people's" folklore. (Moore 1964:220; italics in the original)

Sadly, the actions of CFN members often reinforced the negative attitudes toward black performers held by many administrators. Racial and class divisions led to frequent misunderstandings and conflicts. Percussionists in the ensemble had little experience with the exigencies of professional performance; they tended not to meet expectations, arriving late, refusing to rehearse at particular moments, or drinking on the job. Additionally, drummers had grown up in a culture of machismo and frequently refused to take orders from women. The group's first director, Marta Blanco, resigned as the result of conflicts with men in the troupe. In 1965, similar tensions led to a confrontation between one particularly violent individual, Miguel Valdés, and director María Teresa Linares (Hagedorn 1995:240) over salary issues. Valdés eventually brought a gun to a rehearsal and fired multiple shots, leaving Linares and other members of the troupe severely wounded. Cofounder Rodolfo Reyes resigned after the incident and returned to Mexico, throwing the group's leadership into disarray. CFN members, unused to the privileges afforded them while on tour abroad in the mid-1960s, also drank heavily, smoked marijuana, tore apart hotel rooms, and engaged in petty theft. Several defected while in Spain in the early 1970s, which resulted in much tighter controls being placed on all members and fewer opportunities for travel (Prieto 2001, interview).

In many respects, performers fortunate enough to perform in ensembles such as the CFN benefited professionally as well as economically. Felipe García Villamil recalled that as the result of involvement in a troupe in Matanzas he learned drumming styles from ethnic groups that he had heard but never attempted to play, such as *música arará* and *música iyesá* (Vélez 1996:90). However, members of the black religious community did not always consider public concerts appropriate. Villamil found himself physically threatened for performing Abakuá rhythms onstage, for instance (Vélez 1996:84). Older members usually expressed greater reservations about such presentations, while younger artists were more receptive to them. It took a decade or two before the idea of "universalized" or "folklorized" stage presentations became accepted as part of everyday life.

FOLKLORE IN HIGHER EDUCATION AND THE MEDIA

As might be expected, the relative indifference to Afro-Cuban folklore that existed before 1959 among music educators continued to manifest itself in revolutionary society. Many of the same individuals who had been directing music schools earlier continued to do so in the 1960s and 1970s and found little reason to alter their curricula. This attitude had less to do with racism in the typical sense than with ignorance, inflexibility, and the weight of established precedent. In Cuba, the United States, and elsewhere, attitudes toward marginal expression developed over the centuries have proven difficult to modify. Acosta (1983:23) notes that music education consistently demonstrates a "colonized optic" in which repertoire from Europe is viewed as inherently more sophisticated than its counterpart from the Americas. He distinguishes between typical "academic music history," with its tendency to focus exclusively on elite arts, and "real music history," which he suggests should be more inclusive and politically engaged. Even in revolutionary

Cuba, however, the creation of "real music history" or music education programs has proven difficult.

As mentioned, Afro-Cuban folklore and popular music remained almost totally excluded from curricula through the late 1970s. More recently, percussionists with special interest in Cuban rhythms have been able to spend two years studying them after completing three years' work with orchestral percussion (Pedrito 1998, interview). Students majoring in other instruments continue to learn little about folklore, however. Yet the status of folklore in music conservatories, however marginal, is more prominent than in universities, where Afro-Cuban subjects remain largely absent to the present day. The University of Havana, for example, has never formed an Afro-Cuban studies department or allowed students to specialize in such an area independently. Fields such as literature, philosophy, history, and art history include some courses that touch on Afro-Cuban themes, but the number of students allowed into such programs is quite small, perhaps twenty-five per subject per year; of these, only a fraction demonstrate interest in Afro-Cuban culture.

As of 1996, the university still offered only a single course devoted exclusively to Afro-Cuban culture: Lázara Menéndez's Estudios Afrocubanos, part of elective postgraduate seminars in literature; faculty members such as Enrique Sosa occasionally have offered additional elective courses (L. Menéndez 1996, interview).[16] Most instruction on Afro-Cuban subjects for the general student body comes in the form of poorly attended extracurricular lectures or noncredit summer seminars, just as was the case prior to 1959. In the 1960s and 1970s, Alejo Carpentier, Mirta Aguirre, Vicentica Antuña, and José Antonio Portuondo offered presentations of this sort. Others in recent decades have included Tomás Fernández Robaina, Jesús Guanche, Lázara Menéndez, and Guadalupe Ordaz.

The lack of attention to Afro-Cuban themes is symptomatic of a broader problem, namely, that all research in the humanities and social sciences has received meager support until recently. Anthropology never existed as a university program before 1959 and did not represent a priority to the socialist leadership in later years. The few students selected to pursue such study through the mid-1980s trained in Eastern Europe.[17] Initially, students found flexibility within the university to study Afro-Cuban subject matter on their own if they cared to. Later, work on history and culture was subject to greater regulation. Since 1970, entire departments, including psychology, philosophy, and sociology, have atrophied or disappeared for years at a time. To their credit, Cuban academics now recognize the deficiency of domestic social science programs (Hernández 2004) and are exploring options for addressing the situation.

Because of tepid support for research on Afro-Cuban subject matter, the work of authors from the prerevolutionary period—Fernando Ortiz, Lydia Cabrera, Pedro Deschamps Chapeaux, Rómulo Lachatañeré—has yet to be superseded in most respects by that of younger scholars. This is a serious deficiency in a country with a large Afro-Cuban population and one in which black history has never received much attention. Even older books have not always been available for purchase, either because their authors went into exile and had their work censored for a time (as in the case of Lydia Cabrera), because of the controversial topics they chose to address, or both. Authors from the revolutionary period have published valuable material on Afro-Cuban religion, music, and history. For the most part, however, their essays are rather introductory. Most avoid topics related to ongoing social problems.[18] Publications on black social history often experienced significant delays, as was the case with Tomás Fernández Robaina's *El negro en Cuba 1902–1958*. The author completed his book in 1980, ten years before it appeared. Publishers initially passed over it and released Pedro Serviat's *El negro en Cuba y su solución definitiva* instead, a book with less-rigorous content and one more conceptually in line with PCC pronouncements on race.

As a rule, Afro-Cuban folklore has not featured prominently on revolutionary radio or television. This imbalance has been improving, albeit slowly. Alberto Faya, a white Cuban professional, recalled that he had to fight tenaciously to get permission to include traditional rumba and related music on his weekly radio show *Son del Caimán*, which aired from 1979 to 1985 (1996, interview). Folklore groups have had difficulty recording their music as well. The CFN made one record in 1964, two years after they began performing, but were not able to do so again until 1975 (Martínez Furé 1982:27); additional discs have yet to appear. Yoruba Andabo, an excellent but less widely known group, rehearsed and performed for over twenty years before making their first album. Cristóbal Sosa, involved in Cuban radio for over twenty-five years, said of noncommercial drumming genres in 1996, "ni se oía, ni se oye" (they have neither been heard locally on the air in the past nor are they heard today) (interview). In recent times, however, this may have to do as much with the dynamics of the marketplace as with cultural bias.

GREATER OPPORTUNITIES FOR FOLKLORIC PERFORMANCE

Visitors to Cuba since the mid-1990s might be surprised to find large numbers of folkloric groups performing across the island, given the limitations on academic study and local dissemination described above. The past twenty years have unquestionably witnessed much greater opportunities for folk musicians in terms of performing, recording, and touring, as they have for virtually all musicians. Carlos Moore documents a gradual increase in cultural tolerance in this sense. He notes greater support for African and African American culture—though not necessarily in local Afro-Cuban forms—as early as the 1970s and describes this period as the "Africa decade" because of the frequent presence of black celebrities on the island. The change reflects broader political activities of the leadership and especially the involvement of the Cuban military in Africa. Castro himself demonstrated an interest in African culture, possibly for the first time, while visiting Guinea in 1972 (Moore 1988:293). That year marked the beginning of a stream of visitors to Cuba from the United States, West Africa, and the Caribbean, including the performance group Perú Negro, singers Harry Belafonte and Miriam Makeba, and the Dance Collective of Nigeria (Flores 1978:146). Activist Angela Davis created a sensation in Havana during a visit at approximately the same time, largely because of her large "Afro" hairstyle, considered inappropriate by some officials. Moore suggests that the presence of visitors who openly embraced African aesthetics, dress, and music had an electrifying effect on Cubans of color. Starved as they were for symbols of cultural identity, they closely followed the activities of each new arrival.

The 1980s are significant for having given rise to a number of new institutions within Cuba dedicated to the presentation of Afro-Cuban folklore and to increasing numbers of related publications. The year 1986 marked the beginning of what is now an ongoing celebration, the Wemilere Festival of Music and Dance of African Roots, based in Guanabacoa.[19] It attracts international as well as local participants and includes academic lectures, theater, and music events. In the same year, the Casa de Africa opened in the old colonial section of Havana. Designed as an ethnographic museum, a library resource, and a center for scholarly presentations related to African and African diaspora culture, the Casa contains a permanent display of musical instruments. Some were gifts given to Castro during his African travels; others represent items originally owned by Fernando Ortiz. The center coordinates its cultural activities with other institutions, including the University of Havana and the Ministry of the Exterior. It has become a locus of performance. Publications on Afro-Cuban themes appeared more frequently in the 1980s, most notably Tomás Fernández Robaina's impressive *Bibliografía de temas afrocubanos* (1985), based on work in the National Library. Afro-Cuban history books appeared as well, for instance Julio Angel Carreras's *Esclavitud, abolición, y racismo* (1985) and Pedro Serviat's *El problema*

FIGURE 18.   A performance of rumba in the Callejón
de Hamel by members of the group Yoruba Andabo and
others, 2000. Since the mid-1990s, folkloric drumming
and dance have become a frequent sight on Havana's
streets, and a popular attraction for locals and tourists.
Note the eclectic mix of congas, sacred *batás,* and decorated
cajón (resonant box) instruments. Photo by the author.

negro (1986), mentioned earlier. Tellingly, both focus on race relations prior
to 1959 and deny the existence of significant problems in later years.

Writings on Afro-Cuban culture from the 1980s by government spokespersons support folkloric traditions to a greater extent than in the late 1960s
or 1970s but continue to manifest ambivalence. Authors recognize, for instance, that "the values of African culture . . . were systematically discrim-
inated against" in colonial and republican Cuba and call for measures to re-
dress this legacy (Serviat 1986:150). Yet they also suggest that Afro-Cuban

culture was somehow stunted or debased in the colonial past and will never compare favorably with European forms. It is only "when the integrating factors of our nationality jell" into syncretic expression, argues one anonymous official quoted by Serviat (1986:150), that black music and dance will "acquire a substantial level of development."

Since the reorientation of Cuba's economy toward tourism and foreign investment in the 1990s, the study and performance of Afro-Cuban music has flourished as never before. This renaissance is the combined result of liberalized policies regarding the economics of music making discussed in chapter 8, demonstrated interest in such repertoire on the part of foreign visitors, and ongoing attempts on the part of the Afro-Cuban community to promote their own traditions. Havana is now replete with centers of Afro-Cuban folkloric performance, such as the Hurón Azul, the Callejón de Hamel (Fig. 18), and the patio of the Conjunto Folklórico; clubs and cabarets offer many similar presentations. Government agencies organize courses for those interested in coming to Cuba to study music and dance. Some of the first, known as FolkCuba Workshops, date from the 1980s. They involved the participation of percussionists Alberto Villareal, Mario Abreu, and other members of the Conjunto Folklórico Nacional (Hagedorn 1995:304). Many have developed since.

Folklore performers who had fallen into relative obscurity (Lázaro Ros, Merceditas Valdés) found their careers revived in the mid-1990s. Their repertoire has appeared on a host of new videos, CDs, and tapes for sale in government stores. Books by Fernando Ortiz, Rómulo Lachatañeré, and others that were out of print have been re-released. New publications on folklore, though not always of the highest quality, appear regularly.[20] Academic periodicals such as *Anales del Caribe, Catauro, Del Caribe* (based in Santiago), and *Temas* have devoted entire issues to Afro-Cuban themes on a range of topics.[21] Cuba hosts international conferences on Afro-Cuban culture in Matanzas, Havana, Santiago, and elsewhere. A host of new percussion ensembles have formed, including Afroamérica, Grupo Folklórico de Turarte, Grupo Oba-Ilú, and Raíces Profundas (Pedrito 1998, interview). Many have established professional contacts abroad and tour internationally on a regular basis. Dance bands that had never produced recordings with significant folkloric content suddenly began to do so; one example is the *Soy todo* album from 1999 by Los Van Van that includes ritual Abakuá language learned painstakingly by the group's leader, Juan Formell (Formell 2000:59).

To Cristóbal Sosa (interview, 1996), the prominence of African-derived folklore in the present represents a resurfacing of what has always been popular among the population rather than greater interest in the subject now. As in the 1960s, the boom of recent years is the result of individual efforts to promote forms overlooked or undersupported in past decades. Artists recognize that economic changes have made their expression more viable and strive to capitalize on the new possibilities. Working on street corners or developing stage presentations for tourist hotels, they generate income for themselves and establish vital professional contacts. On the negative side, the widespread commercialization of Afro-Cuban expression has led to a phenomenon that Rogelio Martínez Furé (1994:32) variously describes as "pseudo-folklorism," "autoexoticism," and *"jineterismo cultural."* Many who had never before demonstrated interest in Afro-Cuban subject matter now do so for financial gain. They often market local traditions in a superficial way or portray them as bizarre and unnatural. This might include stylized representations of Afro-Cuban religions, for instance, in which drooling, convulsing, or other behavior associated with possession is emphasized. Martínez Furé notes that folklore is "being converted into tourist merchandise" and calls for additional educational programs to ensure that Cubans themselves will achieve a more profound understanding of their own heritage.

·   ·   ·   ·   ·

Afro-Cubans as a whole have benefited from the revolutionary experiment in important ways. They, more than any other group, have experienced gains in educational and job opportunities and in access to social services. Cuba is a more integrated country than it used to be in the 1950s, with larger numbers of black professionals and civic leaders. One might add that it is more integrated than the United States, where most of the population lives in racially divided neighborhoods. By the same token, racial problems persist that are not always effectively addressed or even widely discussed. As one example, Alejandro de la Fuente and Laurence Glasco (1997) published a survey from the mid-1990s revealing that 58 percent of white Cubans considered blacks to be less intelligent, 69 percent believed they did not have the same "values" or "decency" as whites, and 68 percent were opposed to racial intermarriage. Many Cubans are unaware of present-day racism that manifests itself in such attitudes and in verbal terminology. This is partly the result of a political structure in which Cubans of color have had no independent voice. It also derives from a national discourse that emphasizes unity. Publications frequently suggest that socialist Cuba has become "a single indivisible entity" in cultural terms (e.g., Barnet 1983:152). With Cubanness defined in this way, it has been difficult for the population of color to assert its difference.

During the first seven or eight years of the revolution, performers in the black community created of hundreds of new amateur folklore ensembles. The same period witnessed the invention of new dance rhythms such as the *pilón* and *mozambique* and an unprecedented valorization of Afro-Cuban folkloric expression on the part of government-controlled institutions and media. This renaissance of drumming was part of a larger process of social transformation that did away with elite institutions and celebrated the arts of the masses. Festivals of National Culture organized by Odilio Urfé, the sponsorship of integrated dance events, the founding of the Conjunto Folklórico Nacional, and the educational efforts of Alejo Carpentier, Ramiro Guerra, Argeliers León, and others helped combat prejudice and make the public more receptive to Afro-Cuban folklore. Rogelio Martínez Furé recognized the symbolic importance of this process in describing the *mozambique* craze as "the definitive consecration of percussion" in Cuba and added that his nation, "free of social poisons, in full realization of its historic and cultural realities, now dances to rhythms played with bare hands on the drum" (as quoted in Orejuela Martínez 2004:179).

Beginning in the late 1960s, folklore groups found fewer opportunities to perform for large audiences. The actual substance of their performances came under greater scrutiny as well, especially that of professional groups. The state continued to promote their expression to an extent but strove to modify it. Through an active process of reinterpretation, of "discriminating inclusion and exclusion" (Williams 1977:123), administrators adapted public presentations of folklore so that they conformed to what they thought national culture should be. Artists who received the strongest support were not usually those who performed traditional folklore. On the contrary, they were highly trained professionals who had knowledge of folklore and incorporated elements of it into "high culture." The poetry of Nicolás Guillén has been extolled as an ideal for precisely this reason (e.g., Hart Dávalos 1988:39);[22] symphonic works such as Guido López Gavilán's "Camerata en guaguancó" fall into the same category.[23] Afro-Cuban drumming, and especially its religious manifestations discussed in the following chapter, were often derided as barbaric and replete with "antisocialist tendencies" resulting from ignorance and underdevelopment (Matibag 1996:227).

Drumming, song, and dance testify in certain ways to racial divisions that persist in Cuban society. Most folklore groups are still comprised of Afro-

Cuban performers rather than of an integrated membership, for instance. James Robbins notes that carnival groups in Santiago where he worked in the late 1980s remained divided into black and white ensembles. The black groups included San Augustín, La Conga de los Hoyos, Paso Franco, Heredia, and Guayabito. He describes another group, Textilera, as "a comparsa for whites" (Robbins 1990:310–12). The same divisions can be seen in the United States in the bifurcation between white rock and black soul and hip-hop.

The last twenty years have witnessed a growing appreciation for Afro-Cuban arts once again. The state has renewed efforts to document drumming traditions and has created additional performance spaces for them. Folkloric musicians find ways to promote their heritage locally and internationally as instrumentalists, teachers, and educators. Their music appeals to foreigners who support it through the purchase of recordings or music lessons. Many established educators in the humanities continue to express disinterest in African-derived music, however (L. Menéndez 1996, interview), and few institutions exist that promote its study. Ironically, more foreigners probably receive formal instruction in folkloric traditions through tourist workshops than Cubans themselves. Martínez Furé (1998: B57) blames the situation on "historical traumas and inferiority complexes." He suggests that the so-called New World has yet to come to terms with its cultural legacy and that as long as it does not accept the centrality of African heritage, it will continue to perpetuate long-standing biases.

The importance of Cuban folklore is precisely that it is not a static remnant from a bygone age but rather a dynamic mode of expression rooted in the everyday lives of the population, one that continues to develop. The creation of rhythms and dances through the years has been part of the black community's attempt to project their frequently deprecated culture into the mainstream. Recent experiments such as *songo, batum-batá,* and *batarumba* all constitute part of this trend. Folkloric performance served for decades as one of the few means Cubans of color had to promote markers of blackness in a context that did not allow for frank discussion of racial concerns. Its new prominence today, the broader celebration of Afro-Cuban heritage, and the emergence of global hybrid forms (Cuban rap, reggae) that link local issues of race with broader struggles ensure that folklore will continue to address important issues facing Cubans of color in the future.

CHAPTER 7

Ay, Dios Ampárame
Sacred Music and Revolution

> When the revolution triumphed and the study of the African roots
> of our culture began, many like me felt very happy, truly happy. But
> we soon noticed that something was lacking, or at least that what was
> being done represented only a single perspective. They were viewing
> our religions like something that was pure tradition, something that
> was in the process of dying out, something that would become part
> of history and memory over time. . . . The revolution helped bring the
> legends of our gods to the theater, studied our music and dances more
> earnestly. Something viewed as insignificant was seen at that time as
> important. But many had to keep their beliefs and their personal faith
> secret, their ideas, hide their religious necklaces.
>
> ENRIQUE HERNÁNDEZ ARMENTEROS, as quoted in
> Tomás Fernández Robaina, *Hablen paleros y santeros*

Those who study the arts as a pan-cultural phenomenon have long recognized the close ties between music and religious activity. Chanting and
singing are a prominent means of communication with the divine in nearly
every culture. Yet music and dance are more central to African-derived religions than most others, as ethnologist Roger Bastide noted years ago. The
orichas, or African deities, are said to love music so much that they rarely
resist the chance to visit worshippers personally when summoned by songs
and rhythms (Hagedorn 2001:75–76). Many have described the activities
surrounding Santería and related religions as a form of primarily musical
and choreographic, rather than verbal, liturgy. The most common vernacular name for events of this nature is *toque* or *tambor*, literally a musical/
rhythmic performance, or "drumming."

The repertoire associated with Afro-Cuban religions is extensive, consisting in many cases of intricate percussive sequences played in strict order,
mimetic body movement, interactive vocal and instrumental improvisation, and hundreds of responsorial songs with texts primarily in African languages. This rich heritage with contributions from many distinct ethnic
groups represents a powerful form of individual as well as group expression. It has served as the *fuente viva*, or living source—to use Miguel Bar-

net's term—that contributes to many innovations in commercial music making, much as black gospel has influenced popular song in the United States.
Afro-Cuban religions represent some of the most sophisticated and engaging manifestations of Cuban national culture.

The adoption of Marxist philosophy by Cuba's leadership in 1961 led to
tensions between the state and the people over religion. Ostensibly, the state's
position is neutral, involving neither attempts to "stimulate, support or aid
any religious group" nor to impede such activities (Ministerio de Educación
1971:201). Communist Party doctrine guarantees citizens the right to devote
themselves to any belief system as long as it does not incorporate antirevo-
lutionary ideology (Partido Comunista de Cuba 1978:101). Yet in practice, socialists intervened vigorously to suppress religious activity from the first years
of the revolution.[1] Tellingly, while in the 1950s a majority of Cubans described
themselves as Christian or participants in Afro-Cuban religions, by 1976 only
2 percent of the population openly professed such views (Cox 1987:24). Bias
against religion on the part of the state resulted in the disappearance of devotional activities from public view for decades. The leadership reacted to religion in ways similar to their counterparts in Eastern Europe (Verdery 1991b:
434; Rice 1994:171), monitoring the actions of believers even in private homes.

This chapter notes some specific ways that religious music, especially that
of Afro-Cuban groups, has been affected by socialist doctrine. It describes
negative attitudes toward religious repertoire in the 1950s, documenting the
repression of many forms of expression in subsequent decades and then the
movement toward increased tolerance. Finally, it describes the explosion in
religious music performance following the Fourth Party Congress in 1991.
Analysis suggests that party members believed religion itself to be misguided and unfounded, an impediment to social progress. Militant publications reserved their harshest criticism for Santería, Palo Monte, Espiritismo,
and Abakuá ritual, characterizing them as religions of the uneducated.

RELIGION AND MUSIC
IN THE PREREVOLUTIONARY PERIOD

The early twentieth century witnessed brutal campaigns to suppress African-
derived religions in the name of progress (Carbonell 1961). During most of
the early and mid-twentieth century, middle-class Cuban society did not refer to African-derived religions at all, but only to *brujería,* or witchcraft.
Ernesto Chávez Alvarez (1991) documents half a dozen cases between 1900
and the 1920s in which practitioners of Santería were falsely accused of

crimes associated with devotional events and imprisoned or even killed. Vélez's *Drumming for the Gods* (2000) describes the similarly antagonistic environment confronting believers in Matanzas during the 1940s and 1950s. The author notes that police inspector José Claro directed his force to persecute members of Afro-Cuban religions, confiscate their instruments, and jail them if they performed in ceremonies. Most members of middle-class society, though they had little firsthand exposure, considered African-derived religions savage (Carbonell 1961:108). Eugenio Matibag (1996:228) confirms that in the prevailing bourgeois opinion of the 1950s, Afro-Cuban religion and its associated culture represented "a stage of barbarity" that the republic would eventually outgrow.[2]

Little sacred drumming or accompanying song was recorded in Cuba before 1959, yet in popular music, references to Afro-Cuban religions appear constantly, because the working-class blacks who performed them dominated commercial performance. Songs with religious themes first gained popularity during the *afrocubanismo* period (Moore 1997). Pieces as European sounding as the Rodrigo Prats's bolero "Una rosa de Francia" include ritual greetings to Yemayá and Ifá in the Antonio Machín version from 1932. María Teresa Vera's recording of Ignacio Piñeiro's "En la alta sociedad" from 1925 is one of dozens to include Abakuá terminology—*obón*, or king; *iyamba*, or chief priest; *yuanza*, or ritual consultant; *eribó*, or sacred drum (Bolívar 1996, interview)—as does Piñeiro's "Lindo yambú" from 1934.[3]

This tendency became if anything even more marked in the 1940s and 1950s. Hermenegildo Cárdenas's "Un toque de bembé" represents an important and controversial composition because of its detailed description of ritual events and its extensive use of Yoruba terminology (Cristóbal Díaz Ayala, pers. comm.).[4] Arsenio Rodríguez included Kongo phrases in his *conjunto's* songs to such an extent that the uninitiated have difficulty understanding their meaning.[5] Benny Moré's first hit song in Cuba after returning from Mexico in the early 1950s was dedicated to Chola Anguenge, the equivalent of Ochún in the Palo pantheon; other pieces with overt religious references in his repertoire include "Mata siguaraya" and "Batanga #2" (Raul Fernandez, pers. comm.). Whites as well as blacks became famous composing and reinterpreting commercial tunes with lyrics and/or melodies taken from Afro-Cuban liturgy: Rita Montaner, Miguelito Valdés, Merceditas Valdés, Celina González and Reutilio Domínguez (Puerto Rican), Noro Morales, Facundo Rivero, Celia Cruz, and others. Many more were heavily involved in Santería or Palo in their personal lives, though they chose not to manifest their knowledge of religion as overtly, for example, as Ignacio Villa and Enrique Jorrín (Fernández Robaina 1994:71).

Afro-Cuban "religious pop" of the 1950s meant very different things to different social groups. For practitioners, the inclusion of African-derived terminology represented the only means by which they could publicly allude to their spiritual beliefs without risking harassment. For middle-class listeners unsympathetic to Santería, such references were in part unintelligible and in part tolerated as a means of referencing "colorful" elements of local tradition. The contradictions surrounding this repertoire cannot be stated strongly enough: while Cuban commercial music of the late Batista era constantly alluded to Afro-Cuban religions, much of the public remained largely (or totally) ignorant of the substance of ceremonies themselves, their traditional chants, drumming patterns, and dances, and the religious ideology that informed them. In fact, many Cubans know little about them today.

> In Cuba of the 1950s there was a very strong middle class consisting of bankers, telephone company employees, those in the electrical union, in commerce. Middle-class housewives listened avidly to radio soap operas and had the money to buy the products advertised on the air. As a result, their tastes dictated much of the programming. If you played them a traditional African chant, they wouldn't listen to it. On the contrary, they would revile it because they believed it was something evil. . . . They viewed it as obscurantism, backwards, something perpetuated by illiterate blacks. (Sosa 1996, interview)

Nowhere was Cuba's ongoing cultural war over Africanisms more aggressively negotiated than in the realm of music. At the same time that the José Claros of the 1950s continued to persecute practitioners of Afro-Cuban religions, performers made ever-bolder attempts to incorporate devotional songs into their recordings, and with fewer stylistic changes. The Panart *Santero* LP from approximately 1954 (Panart LD-2060), an important landmark in this sense, featured singing by Merceditas Valdés, Celia Cruz, Caridad Suárez, and *batá* drumming led by Jesús Pérez (Díaz Ayala 1981:238). Though arranged with four-part choral accompaniment and making other concessions to European aesthetics, the disc was one of the first to include sacred drumming sequences and Yoruba chants in their entirety. It featured *toques* (consecrated rhythms) and praise songs to Changó, Babalú Aye, Ochún, Obatalá, Elegguá, Ogún, and Ochosi, for instance, as well as *rezos* (nonmetrical praise songs over drumming) to Yemayá and Changó. At roughly the same time, commercial groups like the Sonora Matancera and Bebo Valdés experimented with the use of *batás* as part of secular dance compositions, elaborating on experimentation initiated by Gilberto Valdés in the 1930s (Acosta 2002:152). Radio stations CMBL (Radio Cadena Suaritos) and the Communist Party station Mil Diez played an important part in the dissemination of commercial recordings by featuring the artists mentioned above (Vélez 2000:80).

Despite the demonstrable repression of African-derived religions in the 1950s, practitioners not only perpetuated their beliefs in homes and communities but actively strove to organize themselves and make their voices heard on a national level. Every *casa de santo,* every *cabildo,* every Abakuá *plante* represented a grassroots institution affirming the place of African religions within Cuban society. Their members demonstrated the Afro-Cuban community's desire for religious self-determinism and helped create alternate histories and memories that contested official discourse. Initially, believers publicly espoused their ideology only in the realm of popular culture. Beginning in 1958, however, Afro-Cubans attempted to create social organizations that united *santeros* across the island. The first such group, convened by Arcadio Calvo in Guanabacoa, was referred to as "El Gran Ebbó" (García 2003, interview). Arcadio and other priests continued to meet subsequently but found their efforts complicated by the onset of the revolution.

THE NEW SOCIALIST GOVERNMENT AND RELIGION

A large number of practicing Protestants, Catholics, and Santería devotees joined in the struggle against Batista in the 1950s. This fact makes clear that the eventual positions adopted by the revolutionary leadership against religion represent a narrowing of policies that were initially more inclusive, or at least less well defined. Bishop Pérez Serantes of Santiago, a close friend of Castro, interceded to spare his life after the Moncada attack (Thomas 1971:1129). Father Guillermo Sardinas rose to the rank of *comandante* in the Rebel Army (Stubbs 1989:74). José Antonio Echeverría, prominent in the urban resistance, also participated in Catholic student organizations (Cardenal 1974:79). Notable Baptists in the fight against Batista included Frank País, Oscar Lucero, Marcelo Salado, Huber Matos, and Faustino Pérez (Pérez 1999:487).

Many of those involved in the insurrection also practiced African-derived religions. Perhaps the most prominent example is longtime union activist and Communist Party member Lázaro Peña, a *santero* and child of Obatalá (Vélez 1996: vol. 1, 95). René Vallejo, Fidel Castro's personal doctor, was a practicing *santero* as well as an *espiritista,* or spirit medium (Sosa 1996, interview). Granma survivor Juan Almeida, one of the few Afro-Cuban leaders of the Rebel Army, kept an altar devoted to Changó in his house until persuaded to remove it by members of the Central Committee (Montaner 1983:138). Celia Sánchez, Castro's personal secretary, frequently visited *babalaos* (Yoruba spiritual advisors) for guidance and support (Montaner 1983:138). Other *santeros* fought in the Sierra Maestra, seeing no contradiction between their religious views and the goals of the guerrillas (Fernández Robaina 1994:8–9, 20).

The new government's first conflicts with the religious community involved problems with Catholics. There are various reasons for this. Catholic institutions were hierarchical and centrally organized; their elders could thus make grand pronouncements on the part of multiple congregations and represented more of a potential political threat. Cardinal Manuel Arteaga of Havana, one of the church's most prominent spokesmen, had a close personal friendship with Batista and demonstrated only tepid support for rebel leaders from the outset (Castro and Betto 1987:177). Most priests came from Spain, at the time controlled by Franco, and tended to have right-wing political views (Cox 1987:24). A large percentage of the Directorio Estudiantil, an insurgent university organization, consisted of Catholics; this was one of the first groups that became a rival for Castro's authority when the members of the revolution came to power. Additionally, Catholics tended to be wealthier, middle-class professionals and elites (especially women) living in urban areas. This group had the least to gain from socialist reforms and was the first to become agitated by them. Professionals generally sent their children to private parochial schools and resented the nationalization of all such institutions in 1961. As a result of all these factors, Catholics became a thorn in the side of revolutionaries almost from the outset and biased the leadership against them.

With the nationalization of the media and the reorganization of unions and political groups under revolutionary control, the Catholic Church remained one of the few independent institutions left in Cuba after 1961. Though far from powerful, Catholic institutions soon became a refuge for oppositional movements, and Castro eventually decided to expel the majority of Spanish priests and nuns from the island (Kirk 1989:95). Church leaders believed to be antagonistic to the new leadership ended up in detention, under house arrest, or in prison, as in the case of the current archbishop of Havana, Jaime Lucas Ortega Alamino (Clark 1992:238; Vázquez Montalbán 1998:81). Popular song from 1961 documents the strong anti-Catholic sentiment in the country, as in this conga recorded by the Cuarteto Las D'Aida that included these lyrics: "Mom doesn't want me to go to church because the fascist priest will convert me into a terrorist. The priests should prepare their bags, they shouldn't mess with things in Cuba. Fidel, Fidel, now my Cuba is sovereign, you freed us from the thugs disguised in cassocks. . . . They should leave, leave, leave" (Orejuela Martínez 2004:124).[6]

The most immediate effect of the conflicts with Catholics on folk music involved the suppression of popular religious festivals. Cuba of the 1950s celebrated countless *fiestas patronales* (patron saint festivals), also associated with *verbenas* (secular parties that took place later the same evening), in almost every small town and city neighborhood, as well as others recognized nationally. The Centro de Investigación Juan Marinello has published research indicating that in the nineteenth century over three hundred such events took place each year (Centro de Investigación 1999:154–58). Among the more prominent festivals that survived into the early 1960s, in part because of their significance for Santería worshippers, included those dedicated to the Caridad del Cobre (September 8); San Juan (June 24); San José (March 18); San Lázaro (September 17); Santa Bárbara (December 4); the day of Nuestra Señora de la Candelaria (February 2); Kings' Day, or Epiphany (January 6); Altares de Cruz and Promesa celebrations (early May); carnival; and Christmas Eve *(Nochebuena)*. It is enlightening to compare present-day Cuba in this sense with neighboring Latin American countries such as the Dominican Republic, Mexico, or Puerto Rico: the latter still are known for a wealth of Catholic folk celebrations involving music and dance, while Cuba has virtually none except for events surrounding the days of San Lázaro and the Caridad. Sadly, few recordings of local religious folk songs among Catholics were made in the 1950s or during the early socialist period when they were still common. Much of the repertoire may be lost forever.

Musicologist María Teresa Linares (n.d.) produced one LP after the revolution that includes a few examples of religious music, however, including part of a celebration dedicated to the Altares de Cruz (Altars to the Cross). This event was recorded on May 2, 1960, in Bayamo, a city in eastern Cuba. According to Linares, individual families sponsored such festivities by creating altars in their living rooms consisting of nine tiers, each representing one day of the festival's duration (the entire period was known as a novena). They adorned the altar initially with a single cross and candelabras and each evening added new ornaments. Some days, members of the community would walk through the streets bearing the cross, passing the houses of members that had made donations for the event. In the evenings, participants gathered before the altar to sing songs. Afterward, they danced to secular music played by a small orchestra or organ grinder (Linares 2003, interview). Lyrics of the religious songs referred on occasion to the baby Jesus or the Virgin Mary but most often to the cross upon which Christ died.

According to Carolina Poncet (1961:10), Altares de Cruz events began with participants singing their thanks to the sponsors and to the Catholic saints associated with particular days of the novena. Following this, devotional singing commenced, consisting primarily of precomposed hymns but also of improvised melodies and verses.[7] Some Altares de Cruz songs came directly from Spain; others were composed later in Cuba. They were typically strophic and performed a capella, with simple harmonies in thirds or sixths. In the Linares recording, a soloist sings the first fifteen bars, after which other participants respond by repeating the same verse. The lyrics translate roughly as "Oh sacred wood, oh celestial cross / invincible shield, royal standard."[8]

Most celebrations of this sort ended about the time of the Bay of Pigs invasion. Thereafter, they never reappeared because the state chose not to allocate resources for them. To the new leadership, saints' festivals carried the taint of the discredited Catholic leadership and clashed in an ideological sense with their social goals. "It was understood that such events were something of the past, and that it was necessary to erase that past" (Orovio 2001, interview). Revolutionaries strove to create a new mentality among the population. They banned images of Santa Claus and the use of Christmas trees, both because of their religious associations and because they represented influences from the United States (Thomas 1971:1257). They began referring to the holy week prior to Easter as "Playa Girón week" and dedicating it to mass voluntary labor. In other cases they created new secular traditions to take the place of those that were no longer celebrated.[9] Musicians professing their Catholic faith experienced professional marginalization in the later 1960s and 1970s, for example, singer-songwriter Teresita Fernández (Elizundia Ramírez 2001:81–83).

ATTITUDES TOWARD AFRO-CUBAN RELIGIOUS MUSIC

The largely white, middle-class revolutionary leadership did not approve of African-derived religions, but they viewed them differently from Christian institutions. Perhaps most important, while they associated Catholicism with the rich and with a relatively small percentage of the population, they recognized Santería and related practices to be genuinely popular. African-derived religions played an important role in the lives of poorer people, especially blacks; these were precisely the individuals that leaders intended to help through their new social programs. Additionally, Afro-Cuban houses of worship had no strong authority on a national level that might pose a political threat. For these reasons, worshippers experienced few problems with the authorities during the early 1960s, very possibly less than they had in the 1950s.

Evidence suggests that Castro and his supporters made attempts to associate the new government with African religions in the minds of the public in order to increase their support. The colors red and black on the 26th of July movement's flag, for instance, are also associated with the Yoruba deity Elegguá. Just as Elegguá opens spiritual pathways, revolutionaries seem to have suggested with this symbol that the Moncada attack opened new political and social paths, and that African deities were directly involved in the process. On January 8, 1959, during one of Castro's first public speeches, someone arranged to have doves fly over his head and for one to land on his shoulder (Oppenheimer 1992:344). Since doves and the color white are associated with the *oricha* Obatalá, deity of creativity and wisdom, this had special significance as well.[10] Manipulation of religious imagery in this way brings to mind Haitian dictator François "Papa Doc" Duvalier and his government's use of Vodoun (Averill 1997:73). Castro's approach tended to be subtler, however, perhaps so as not to alienate the middle classes who disapproved of Santería.

The period extending from 1959 through the mid-1960s gave rise to a profusion of religious performance in folklore ensembles as well as "high" art compositions inspired by it (Fig. 19).[11] Oil paintings by René Portocarrero (1912–86), depicting *diablito* (African masked) dancers, and by Manuel Mendive (1944–), with Santería iconography, represent some of the most influential visual creations. Building on the work of Wifredo Lam and others, these individuals fused elements of folk religion with neoexpressionist techniques as a means of representing a modern nationalism.

Musical and choreographic works of a similar nature appeared as well in the newly created National Theater under the direction of Isabel Monal. Established in 1959, the National Theater played a central role in the cultural activities of the early revolution. It consisted of five departments devoted to modern classical music, modern dance, theater, choral activities, and folklore, respectively.[12] Of these, the departments of modern dance under Ramiro Guerra and folklore under Argeliers León made significant use of religious music. It should be noted that León, Guerra, and others had been involved in similar activities during the 1950s; León included fragments of ritual chants in his work "Akorín," for instance (Machover 1995:197), and the two collaborated in 1952 to produce a ballet sketch called *Toque* (Díaz Ayala 1981:313). Nevertheless, their new prominence as cultural leaders and the increasing numbers of presentations for which they were responsible are significant. Many events they organized after 1959 featured formally

FIGURE 19.   An amateur folklore ensemble, Isupo Irawó,
performing a mix of secular and sacred repertoire near
the National Theater in Havana, 1968. The use of *chéquere*
shakers and *batá* drums simultaneously is not traditional
and seems to be an innovation of these performers. Opportunities for the public performance of African-influenced
folklore increased substantially after the revolution.
Photo Archive, Ministry of Culture, Cuba.

trained white/Hispanic dancers performing together onstage with black
amateur dancers and folkloric drummers (Orejuela Martínez 2004:99). This
degree of integration in entertainment, and the strong the promotion of
working-class religious expression, had no precedent and is a tribute to the
efforts of the revolutionary government.

Many essayists in Cuba discuss the seminars organized by León on Afro-

Cuban religions in conjunction with his work in the National Theater. Though the seminars were of undeniably high quality, their scope and impact nevertheless have been exaggerated. The lectures began in October of 1960 and lasted through May of 1961 (León 1966:12). León hoped they would educate younger researchers and help combat the ignorance of Afro-Cuban religions that much of the public demonstrated (Hagedorn 2001:138–39). In part because of limited interest, and in part because acceptance into the classes required the personal invitation of León himself, only three to seven individuals attended any given class (Katherine Hagedorn, pers. comm.). Some of the most respected academics in the country offered presentations as part of the minicourse, however, including Léon himself, his wife, María Teresa Linares, ethnologists Isaac Barreal and Alberto Pedro Sr., historian Manuel Moreno Fraginals, and German anthropologist Peter Neumann. Though they lasted a short time, they did much to prepare future academics Miguel Barnet, Rogelio Martínez Furé, Eugenio Hernández, and others (Lapique Becali 1996, interview).

A review of program notes from the archives of the National Theater provides examples of the sorts of activities presented there under León's guidance. The earliest sketches seem to have involved the staging of *afrocubanismo* art music in conjunction with stylized dance choreographed by Ramiro Guerra. Amadeo Roldán's "Milagro de Anaquillé" (The Miracle of Anaquillé) and "La rembambaramba" (The Big Commotion) were presented in this way, featuring figures from nineteenth-century folklore: the *negro curro*, the *mulata del rumbo*, *diablito* dancers, and a *mayoral*, or plantation overseer, with his slaves. They received strong media promotion and played to full houses. Later events were more academically oriented. A concert entitled *Bembé* took place on May 5, 1960, with religious drumming by Jesús Pérez and singing by Lázaro Ros, among others. *Congos reales*, produced on November 18, 1961, under the guidance of León and Martínez Furé recreated nineteenth-century style *tango-congo* processional music from colonial *cabildos*. *Yimbula: Fiesta de Paleros* premiered on November 29, 1961. It included sacred music and dance of Bantu origin and recreated a Palo ceremony on stage. The accompanying program notes are impressive, describing in detail the fundamental beliefs of the religion, the instruments and rhythms used in worship, the sacred vestments employed, and the corresponding dances. Chants of ritual salutation to "open" the altar and to greet particular deities began the event and were followed by secular music and dance: a *baile de maní* and *toque de garabatos*.[13] Given the bias against Afro-Cuban culture on the part of many professionals, attendance at these events was probably limited.

INCREASING INTOLERANCE OF RELIGIOUS ACTIVITY

Beginning in the later 1960s, the climate of religious and artistic expression associated with the early revolution began to wane. In its schools and in official publications, the state advocated the renunciation of religion and the adoption of "scientific atheism."[14] Party documents recognized among the ideological goals of the country that of universally "overcoming" religious beliefs through scientific-materialist education (Partido Comunista de Cuba 1978:98).[15] Dedication to proving the fallacies of religion lasted through the late 1980s (Fernández Robaina, September 25, 1996, interview). Such efforts manifest themselves in multiple ways: in the realm of education, through training in work centers, and through interventions of a more personal level in homes and neighborhoods.

A few examples suffice to illustrate these policies. Beginning in the late 1960s, the government no longer allowed anyone professing a faith to be a member of the Communist Party, an affiliation extremely beneficial to one's educational opportunities and career. The same applied to membership in many trade unions (Fernández Robaina 1994:36). Educational centers barred members of religious groups from professions such as psychology, philosophy, and political science (Cardenal 1974:22, 142). Religion became taboo as a topic of academic investigation, even among many who did not profess a faith themselves.[16] Job application forms *(planillas de trabajo)* regularly asked applicants if they had religious beliefs and denied them prominent positions if they answered "yes."[17] By dressing in ceremonial white, shaving one's head for ritual purposes, or wearing a cross or sacred *collares* (necklaces), one also ran the risk of serious professional consequences. In terms of access to new housing, cars, appliances, and a host of related goods, the preference given to PCC members and atheist revolutionaries meant that religious beliefs could not be admitted openly.

Campaigns to inculcate negative views toward religion were especially aggressive toward the young. The state forbade the baptism of children or their initiation into Afro-Cuban religions, ordering the police to intervene and, in some cases, to forcibly remove them from ceremonies (Orejuela Martínez 1996, interview). In primary and secondary schools, instructors derided religious subject matter as worthless or backward (Esquivel, September 21, 1996, interview). Revolutionary summer camps sponsored by Communist youth organizations represented an important venue for the dissemination of such ideas as well. Adult practitioners were allowed to continue their religious involvement undisturbed in many cases, but the state intervened to stop young adults from doing so in order to ensure a gradual decline in the numbers of the faithful.

In addition to these impediments, other more vicious acts have been documented. They represent the actions of individuals and were not condoned by authorities. Overzealous militants hoping to prove their commitment to the revolution have harassed neighbors for keeping religious artifacts in their homes (Fontaine 1996, interview). On occasion, they have physically abused ministers or confiscated and burned bibles. This was especially common in Pentecostal churches in the interior of the island (Ismael Rodríguez, pers. comm.). In some cases, individuals took it upon themselves to tear down altars, throw *cazuelas* or *guerrero* statues (symbolic items associated with Santería) into the street, deface iconography or buildings, and destroy religious instruments.

Such attitudes help explain why research on religious folklore had stalled until recently. The year 1964 saw the publication of León's *Música folklórica cubana*, based on seminars at the National Theater. It is an important work but general in scope, intended only as an introduction to Cuban music, with an emphasis on African-derived repertoire. *Actas del Folklore*, the official journal of folklorists at the National Theater, published insightful articles on religious traditions beginning in January 1961, often written by Afro-Cubans themselves; unfortunately, it was discontinued the following year.[18] Articles of a similar nature appeared in *Etnología y Folklore* beginning in 1966 under the auspices of the Academy of Sciences, but that journal ceased publication in 1969. Issues during its first two years contain a number of essays on religious ritual, including an analysis of Abakuá ceremony by Rafael López Valdés (*Etnología y Folklore* 2 [July–December 1966]: 5–26) and of sacred Bantu/Palo vocabulary by Lydia González Huguet and Jean René Baudry (*Etnología y Folklore* 3 [January–June 1967]: 31–64). Afro-Cuban subjects appeared after 1968 but became more historical and secular. They revolved around social or demographic trends, often during the nineteenth century—for example, essays on abolition and its immediate social effects or on colonial maroon activity—and avoided religion.

Between approximately 1968 and the late 1970s, little of substance appeared in print or on LPs related to Afro-Cuban religious music, with the exception of a reprint of *Música folklórica cubana* under the title *Del canto y el tiempo* (León 1974). Publications that did allude to the subject expressed condescending attitudes toward the rituals or referred to the ways that revolutionary policy intended to hinder their perpetuation.[19] León and other progressive members of the academic community, despite their commitment to the revolution, met with growing resistance when attempting research on religious music. León himself seems to have lost his job in the Academy of Sciences over this issue (Lapique Becali 1996, interview). The entire careers of individuals interested in sacred ritual were ruined or stunted due to a general lack of support for the subject, as in the case of Teodoro Díaz Fabelo.[20]

Negative comments about Afro-Cuban religions in Communist Party documents fused multiple and often discrepant critiques into a single voice. Some derived from Marxist doctrine; others were based on thinly veiled racial prejudices. One of the most common justifications for the suppression of religion, of course, was the assertion that it represented a form of false consciousness (see, e.g., López 1978:11, 61). Publications frequently made reference to "the ludicrous beliefs of the enslaved" during colonial times and the fact that they constituted, among other things, a "false refuge for the oppressed, a sterile hope" (*Trabajo político: Boletín de organización del PCC-FAR* 2, no. 4 [December 1968]: 49).[21] Miguel Barnet described Afro-Cuban religions as a helmet donned by men living in inhuman conditions who would otherwise be unable to make sense of their fate (1983:143). However aesthetically engaging they believed religious folklore to be, critics ultimately denounced the beliefs surrounding it as an ideological fetter. Even in the mid-1980s, ethnologist Jesús Guanche described the principal motivations for the perpetuation of religion as "ignorance," "obscurantism," and "intellectual underdevelopment" (1983:450–51). He and others asserted that faith in the supernatural would eventually disappear altogether as a result of higher levels of education.[22] This belief, we now know, was unfounded.

The leadership argued for many years that Afro-Cuban religions derived from primitive modes of thought. They suggested that the views of *santeros* represented an "earlier stage" of mankind's development that had no place in revolutionary Cuba (Carbonell 1996, interview). Distinguished scholars, even from the Afro-Cuban community, described the belief system surrounding Santería as the "remainders of yesterday" (Deschamps Chapeaux in Matibag 1996:242).[23] Party militants derided Santería as less sophisticated than Christianity, based on crude symbols and mimetic rituals rather than on abstract ideas.[24] They attacked Abakuá and Palo ceremonies as misguided, confused, backward, uncultured, and submerged in myths of "antediluvian" origin.[25] Guanche (1983:400) characterized those involved in Santería as "limited in their physical and intellectual faculties," adding that when men and women manage "to transcend this phase of prehistory . . . they stop being the dependent subjects of supernatural beings created from ignorance and fear."[26] These views bear an eerie resemblance to racist commentary in work from the turn of the twentieth century.

Other, more extreme critiques of Afro-Cuban religion are found in some government publications from the late 1960s and 1970s. Representatives of the Ministry of Education, as part of their campaign against "delinquency," singled out Afro-Cuban religions as a central factor contributing to it (Ministerio de Educación 1971:202). Some characterized Santería as a "pathological" influence (McGarrity 1992:199) or accused religious elders of utilizing the faithful to organize criminal acts (*El Militante Comunista*, November 1968, pp. 24–25, 47). A surprising number of authors, such as Angel Bustamante (1969), suggested that belief in Afro-Cuban religion should be considered a symptom of mental disorder. This apparently represents a reaction to the complex phenomenon of spirit possession and trance. Contributors to *El Militante Comunista* described believers as "completely dominated by their neuroses" (January 1968, p. 45). Guanche, in his essay "Psychic Disorders" (Los trastornos psíquicos), also characterized Santería as a disease (1983:396) and believers as paranoids (pp. 397–99). "Syncretic beliefs, and particularly Santería . . . present symptomatic modalities that make the patient appear to be a real schizophrenic, along with manifesting hysterical, dissociative reactions" (p. 398).[27] He defines the term "schizophrenic" in a footnote as "a serious, morbid process characterized by mental incoherence and dissociative thought."[28] Not surprisingly, these authors call for the elimination of African-derived religions in the name of the well-being of society.

Many in the black community naturally opposed what they saw as a growing intolerance for their beliefs and traditional arts. It appeared as if Marxist doctrine was being used as an excuse to root out cultural practices that the white/Hispanic leadership did not approve of. Of course, blacks had few leaders of national stature within their own community and few options for public dissent. Figures who might have voiced such opinions—Juan René Betancourt, Walterio Carbonell, Rogelio Martínez Furé, Carlos Moore—had either been driven into exile, publicly humiliated, or otherwise silenced.

Nonetheless, most religious events continued much as they had during the capitalist era despite all this. Participants denied their involvement in order to get a job or obtain permission for studies at the university yet continued to worship. The revolution pressured them to adopt a hypocritical stance toward their faith in this sense (Fernández Robaina 1994:36) but did not end their participation. The fact that much Santería worship is conducted in private homes helped devotees hide their actions (Hagedorn 2001:115–16). Additionally, government authority was not always felt as strongly in marginal neighborhoods, where most Afro-Cuban religious activity took place, as in areas that were more integrated into the revolutionary power structure. In Pogolotti, Manglar, Atarés, Cerro, and elsewhere, PCC doctrine had less force because most residents had less to fear from censure.

AMBIVALENCE TOWARD SACRED MUSIC

With the hardening of government policy toward religion, presentations of religious folklore went into decline. The sorts of concerts promoted by Argeliers León during the early years of the revolution did not disappear overnight but became less frequent and lost their prominence in national planning. Religious folklore never disappeared from public view entirely, however. Many *aficionado* ensembles continued performing within their own communities, often as part of events scheduled in neighborhood *casas de cultura* or local festivals. Modern dancers based at the ENA incorporated sacred movements into their choreographies and performed with traditional drummers. After 1979, percussion students began to receive limited instruction on *batá* drums and other religious instruments.

It is difficult to interpret a government policy that supported the performance of religious folklore in particular settings and yet allowed few publications on African-derived traditions and suppressed the religions themselves. Tomás Fernández Robaina has explained this by suggesting that while officials believed Afro-Cuban religions to be undesirable, they nevertheless recognized that the music and dance associated with them had aesthetic value and thus chose to authorize their incorporation into some cultural presentations. The support of dances and drumming associated with Santería and Palo has not been, therefore, a statement in support of religion but instead of a secularized and thus "purified" national folklore. Socialist educators felt that folkloric elements—music, dance, instruments, and so forth—should be assimilated into educational programs while "divesting themselves of mystical elements" so that they did not "serve to maintain customs and practices alien to scientific truth" (Partido Comunista de Cuba 1982).[29] Similar policies have been documented in socialist Eastern Europe (e.g., Kundera 1992:47).

As of the mid-1960s, officials required celebrants to apply for a permit in order to hold a *toque de santo,* as had been the case during the prerevolutionary period; this could be acquired either through the newly created Bureau of Religion—part of the Ministry of the Interior—a police station, or one's local CDR (Matibag 1996:230). Applications involved submitting forms thirty days in advance with lists of all participants, information on how much money would be charged by the drummers, a photo of the person, if any, "making their saint," and an explanation of why they wanted to do so. Abakuá groups often suffered regulations of an even more intrusive nature: Helio Orovio (1996, interview) remembers that *plantes* (ritual events) became virtually impossible for years. Felipe García Villamil feared persecution in the 1970s even for making miniature replicas of Abakuá drums for sale as ornaments (Vélez n.d.: 88).

Authorities maintained strict limits on the quantity of religious music on the radio and television. To date, they have never created a program devoted to traditional religious song or drumming (Sosa 1996, interview). Through the late 1980s, EGREM bureaucrats strongly discouraged performers from including references to Santería in their compositions (Bolívar 1996, interview). Pieces written before the revolution such as "Veneración" and "Que viva Changó" disappeared from the airwaves.[30] Officials forbade the primary interpreter of the latter, Celina González, from singing the song even during live shows (Orovio 1996, interview). For decades they refused her permission to travel outside the country, apparently fearing that she would take royalty payments waiting for her in the United States and opt for exile (Bolívar, interview). Merceditas Valdés, who collaborated closely with Fernando Ortiz in the 1950s and who had likewise built her career performing the music of Santería, found herself unable to perform this repertoire publicly for decades as well.[31]

On occasion, the police forcibly confiscated musical instruments and other possessions of prominent spiritual leaders who died. Items owned by Arcadio, a famous *santero*, were taken from his family in this manner. Most of them eventually ended up in the Museum of Guanabacoa, where they remain to this day, though others have been stolen or lost (Fernández Robaina 1994:64). In other instances, the state banned Afro-Cuban celebrations outright, as in the case of an important annual ritual in Matanzas meant to spiritually prepare the community for the sugar harvest (Vinueza 1996, interview). Other isolated incidents have been documented as well. One especially tragic example is that of the temple of San Juan Bautista in Matanzas, one of the oldest centers of Afro-Cuban religion on the island. When the last of the older generation of worshippers who had sustained it died, youth from Havana entered the building and destroyed everything inside, including *tambores yuka*, *batás* from the nineteenth century, and sacred sculptures (Vinueza 1996, interview). Acts of this nature and the overall climate of religious intolerance led to the exodus of many believers during the Mariel crisis of 1980. Drummer Felipe García Villamil chose to leave at that time after being threatened with a four-year prison term for religious involvement if he stayed (Vélez n.d.: 95).

RECTIFICATION: GREATER TOLERANCE
FOR RELIGIOUS MUSIC

Tengo a una amiga alemana . . .
Que gusta buscar de raíces yorubas exóticas.
La necesidad la hizo Yemayá.
¿Quién iba a decirle a Cristóbal Colón
Que el mundo moderno estaría tan resguardado
por la mística de un mundo negro colonizado?

I have a German friend . . .
who likes to search for the roots of exotic Yoruba traditions.
Necessity made her become a child of Yemayá.
Who would have dreamed of telling Christopher Columbus
that modern society would be so protected
by the mysteries of a black, colonized world?

GERARDO ALFONSO, "Tetas africanas"

Beginning in the mid-1970s, intolerant attitudes toward religion and related music began to soften. The role played by the Catholic Church and by Liberation Theology in progressive movements within Central America had a positive impact in this sense. The actions of Oscar Romero in El Salvador and Camilo Torres in Colombia, especially, proved that belief in God was not inherently opposed to Marxism and could actually be a tool of insurgents (Cardenal 1974:102; Cox 1987:176). Cuba's involvement in Africa, beginning with Che Guevara's excursions in 1964 and ending with participation in the Angolan civil war in the 1970s and 1980s, also helped develop greater sensitivity on the part of the leadership to sub-Saharan culture. From the outset, contact with Africa stimulated new research and conferences in Cuba that included the participation of West African academics (see *Etnología y folklore*, no. 2 [July–December 1966], final pages, and no. 6 [July–December 1968], p. 106.). By the end of the 1970s, more than three hundred thousand Cubans had been active combatants in Africa, either in Angola or Ethiopia (Pérez-Stable 1993:176), and returned with a new appreciation for cultural forms that had long been stigmatized in the Caribbean (Oppenheimer 1992:341).

Early manifestations of change in the realm of music included the increased use of sacred instruments in secular repertoire. In the late 1960s, bands such as Irakere, Oru, and the Orquesta Elio Revé began experimenting with *batá* drums (Acosta 2002:152; Kirk and Padura Fuentes 2001:67). In 1976, the Afro-Cuban religious community itself reestablished an informal national organization of *babalaos* known as Ifá Ayer, Ifá Hoy, Ifá Mañana (García 2003, interview). In 1980, the government established the

Center for Investigation and Development of Cuban Music (CIDMUC) in Havana, a more dynamic agency than the previous Institute of Ethnology and Folklore. CIDMUC specialized for years in field recordings of predominantly Afro-Cuban sacred events and within a few years had released more recordings of them than had ever been attempted before. While commentary accompanying the LPs did not always valorize the religious practices they documented, the work of CIDMUC scholars nevertheless represented a seminal achievement.[32]

The slow liberalization of attitudes toward religion applied to Christians and practitioners of African religions alike (Cox 1987:25). In 1984, Castro met with the Reverend Jesse Jackson and publicly visited a Methodist church with him. In 1987, he permitted a series of interviews by the priest Frei Betto that resulted in the best-selling book *Fidel and Religion*. During conversations with Betto, Castro modified his earlier positions and attempted rapprochement with the Catholic Church. In June of 1987, the ICAP invited Alaiyeluwa Oba Okunade Sijuwade Olubuse II, the supreme representative of Yoruba religion in Nigeria, to Cuba for a five-day visit. Culture Minister Armando Hart, Castro himself, and other members of the Central Committee came to greet him personally (Matibag 1996:232). Members of the Afro-Cuban community noted that his presence meant a great deal to *santeros* but also that the subject of African religions continued to inspire controversy among the general public.

> There were many who didn't like [the coverage that African spirituality received]. They continued to view *Santería, Palo,* and *Abakuá* religions as a "black thing," something associated with degenerates, the superstitious, something to be rejected, forgotten. It was great that [Okunade] received attention in the press, the radio and television. But after the King left the subject of religion disappeared; nothing more was spoken or said about it. (Fernández Robaina 1994:90)

The increased tolerance also manifested itself in the realm of publications during the 1980s. In his 1983 book *La fuente viva*, Miguel Barnet devoted considerable attention to syncretic religions and described them, at least at times, as manifesting a "revolutionary" spirit and not merely misguided or delusional (e.g., p. 146). The following year the government released Argeliers León's 1964 musical study yet again. These books were followed by María Elena Vinueza's *Presencia arará en la música folclórica de Matanzas* (1988). The latter is typical of the 1980s in that, while well researched and doing much to valorize religious drumming and song, it simultaneously criticized the religions themselves.[33] Three years later, Letras

FIGURE 20.   The Conjunto Folklórico Nacional, Cuba's
best-known folklore troupe, performing in Havana, 1986.
Established during the first years of the revolution, it has
helped educate the public as to the diversity and complexity of African-influenced heritage in the Americas. Here a
dancer performs choreography associated with the *oricha*
Changó to *batá* accompaniment. Photo © David H. Brown,
all rights reserved.

Cubanas published Ramiro Guerra's *Teatralización del folklore y otros ensayos* (Guerra 1991). It is significant for having been published by a choreographer who worked closely with the National Folklore Troupe (Fig. 20).
The book includes useful information about African-influenced traditions
but sidesteps the question of whether the religions themselves constitute a
positive component of Cuban culture.

The conflicted nature of these studies have their corollary in popular song; one especially telling example is "Papá Eleguá" by Elio Revé (1930–97) and his *charanga*, composed in approximately 1984.[34] Revé, a black Cuban and member of the Communist Party, was one of many who kept his religious involvement hidden for some time in order to ingratiate himself to the establishment. In "Papá Eleguá," he simultaneously demonstrated his knowledge of Santería and Palo through the inclusion of ritual terminology—*Yalorddé* (a name for an incarnation of the goddess Ochún), *iré* (Yoruba for good, positive), *Kimbisa* (a specific form of Palo)—and suggested that religion in general was nothing but meaningless superstition. Despite this apparent attempt to make the song more acceptable through the inclusion of Marxist dogma, representatives of EGREM refused to record it for nearly a decade.

> La religión, la religión
> Es la concepción limitada de los hombres
> Los hombres, al verse imposibilitados
> ante los fenómenos que crean la naturaleza
> tuvieron que crear sus propios dioses . . .
>
> Religion, religion
> is a limited conception of mankind
> Men, unable to explain
> the phenomena created by nature
> Have had to create their own gods . . .
> (Revé 1993)

Noting the more-liberal attitudes in the 1980s, some musicians began experimenting aggressively with religious elements in their compositions. The group Síntesis, led by husband and wife Carlos and Ele Alfonso, stands out in this regard. It was one of the first to fuse entire ritual chants in African languages, often performed by singers from the religious community, with fusion rock accompaniment played on electric bass, guitar, synthesizer keyboard, and percussion. This tendency actually began in the late 1970s but gained momentum the following decade. According to Pablo Menéndez (pers. comm.), who played electric guitar in the group and studied with the Alonsos at the ENA, he and singer/keyboardist Lucía Huergo were the driving forces behind their interest in such music. Menéndez was attracted to Afro-Cuban repertoire as a teenager in the mid-1960s. He listened frequently to *batá* drummers in dance classes and attended folkloric events. In the 1970s, his work in the Grupo de Experimentación Sonora allowed for some experimentation with Afro-Cuban religious music, as did involvement in the jazz-fusion group Sonido Contemporáneo led by Nicolás Reinoso.[35] Menéndez joined Síntesis in 1978 and eventually managed to have Huergo invited in as well. She wrote one of the first pieces for them based on a sacred chant to Eleggúa, "Merewo timbo lowe."

Subsequent experiments led to close consultation with Afro-Cuban religious singer Lázaro Ros, the solicitation of his advice about appropriate vocal performance style, and in at least one case an invitation for him to sing with them. Síntesis became famous for their Afro-Cuban "religious rock" songs; their work was recorded on the albums *Ancestros* and *Ancestros II* (Alfonso et al. 1992, 1993), the first of which appeared nationally in 1987.[36] Lucía Huergo wrote most of the arrangements for the first LP. The repertoire is striking for the origins of many songs, often taken from obscure Dahomeyan (Arará) sources. Following the release of *Ancestros* and recognition that such expression would be condoned by state institutions, religion surfaced as a central theme in the songs of many bands.

The group Mezcla, founded by Pablo Menéndez, was also an early innovator in the fusion of religious melodies with rock, jazz, African dance music, and other influences. Menéndez formally established this group in 1985, surrounding himself with excellent musicians. These included trumpeter Roberto García (formerly of Afro-Cuba), trap drummer David Pimienta, *conguero* and *babalao* Octavio Rodríguez, bassist José Hermida, pianist Julián Gutiérrez, and keyboardist and arranger Lucía Huergo. Mezcla (literally "mixture") has experimented broadly since its inception, collaborating with exponents of Cuban rumba such as Los Muñequitos de Matanzas, *nueva trova* artists Silvio Rodríguez and Gerardo Alfonso, *timba* bands, and U.S. rockers Bonnie Raitt and Bruce Cockburn. The majority of the group now consists of Afro-Cuban performers. Beginning in the late 1980s, Mezcla collaborated with Lázaro Ros as well, creating hybrid compositions such as the one transcribed below (Ex. 11).

Menéndez attributes Mezcla's collaborations with Ros to a social gathering shortly after the release of *Ancestros* at which recordings by Malian singer Salif Keita were played. Noting admiration for this artist, Ros expressed interest in doing something similar with Mezcla based on traditional Yoruba music. Their subsequent release, which appeared on the Intuition label in 1992 as *Cantos*, attempted to create danceable pieces that nevertheless conformed closely to the traditional song and *tratado* structure of Santería devotional events. Octavio Rodríguez performed most of the lead *batá* drumming on the CD, aided by percussionists Pancho Quinto, John Santos, Sebastian Gagneux, and others. The excerpt transcribed in Example 11, from the song "Ikirí Adá," is based on a Yoruba chant. Its musical accom-

EXAMPLE 11.   A responsorial chant to Ogún, "Ile Logún Mo Iyó Lodé," as performed by Lázaro Ros and Mezcla in their fusion composition "Ikirí Adá" (Ros and Grupo Mezcla 1992).

paniment sounds like a cross between Nigerian juju music and Trinidadian *soca,* but with sacred vocals and *batá* added. The *batá* drums play a traditional *salida/Echú* rhythm accompanied by synthesizer, electric bass, piano, soprano saxophone, drum set, and other percussion. (In the example, "S" indicates a slap and "O" an open tone; *batá* notes above the center line are played on the smaller *chachá* drumhead, those below the line on the *enú,* or larger head.) In order to understand the extent of the song's transformation in the Mezcla arrangement, it is instructive to compare their version (Ros and Grupo Mezcla 1992) with a traditional version also sung by Ros on *Olorun 1* (Ros 1992).

In the years following the collapse of the Soviet Union, public devotion has reestablished itself in the lives of Cubans to a surprising extent. This religious "boom," as it is often described, brought virtually all facets of the sacred into view. The relaxation of state policies toward religion may have been a calculated move to assure continued support for socialism among believers during periods of severe food shortages (Esquivel, September 22,

1996, interview). Of course, all forms of religion, including Christianity, attracted more followers as life became difficult, as the future became uncertain, and as the state proved unable to effectively fulfill its role as provider. Adopting an overtly religious lifestyle also represented a way of manifesting one's dissatisfaction with past dogmatism. Natalia Bolívar (1996, interview) has described Cubans' enthusiastic involvement with religion in the 1990s in this way, as a rejection of twenty-five years of overzealous regulation of spiritual life. Similar trends in other postsocialist countries lend credence to her position.

Tolerance for religion in the 1990s may also result from the need to attract foreign investment and loans. Groups such as the EEC have consistently linked economic aid to improvements in human rights, including religious freedoms. Cuban officials additionally recognize the potential profits to be made both from the sale of music influenced by Santería and by folklore workshops in which foreigners pay to take drumming and dance classes. Foreign initiations into Yoruba religions have become an important form of tourism, generating considerable profits. Indeed, individual *santeros* and *babalaos* (including Enrique Hernández Armenteros, quoted at the beginning of this chapter) as well as the Ministry of Tourism now encourage visits by foreigners to "make their saint" on the island. Hernández Armenteros is recognized internationally as a *babalao* who caters to this sort of visitor (Katherine Hagedorn, pers. comm.).

About 1990, documentaries on Afro-Cuban religions began to appear with greater frequency on television, and recordings of music with religious themes received more representation on the radio. Officials granted spokesmen of the Catholic church access to the media on some religious holidays;[37] singer Celina González managed to record and distribute a new version of "Que viva Changó" for the first time in twenty years (Oppenheimer 1992:343). Also in 1990, the Union of Cuban Writers and Artists (UNEAC) published Natalia Bolívar's *Los orichas en Cuba,* the first book specifically discussing Santería in decades.[38] It appeared at roughly the same time as Lázara Menéndez's four-volume *Estudios afrocubanos* series (1988–90), which included significant religious content, Lino Neira's *Como suena un tambor abakuá* (1991), and Tomás Fernández Robaina's *Hablen paleros y santeros* (1994), which documents the experiences of believers in Afro-Cuban religions during the revolution.[39] This last work is especially noteworthy for including the comments of practitioners themselves.[40] Other books and videos continue to appear, primarily for the foreign market.[41]

The government helped establish a Yoruba Cultural Society in December of 1991. Dedicated to the conservation of Santería-related traditions, the

EXAMPLE 12. A devotional chant to the *oricha* Ochún incorporated into the introduction of Adalberto Álvarez's "¿Y qué tú quieres que te den?" (Álvarez 1999). A traditional version can be heard on Valdés 1992, and a translation of the Yoruba can be found in Mason 1992:337–38.

organization currently boasts five thousand members, over fifteen hundred of whom are spiritual leaders in their respective communities (García 2003, interview). Also in 1991 it became acceptable for initiates to walk in the streets wearing ritual vestments and necklaces. Perhaps most important, during the Fourth Party Congress of October 1991, the PCC began accepting believers as members of the party (see *CUBAInfo* 4, no. 8 [July 21, 1992], for more information). José Felipe Carneado, the chief of the Office of Religious Affairs (a working group of the Central Committee), is said to have spearheaded this policy change (Machado Ventura 1991); other advocates included historian Eusebio Leal and writer Cintio Vitier. Members of religious groups now freely identify themselves in public. For *santeros*, this state of affairs has no precedent in all of Cuban history. In 1993, a Catholic religious choir formed with the blessing of the government; it and other groups began recording sacred Christian music once again.

CDs of popular song with religious content continue to appear, similar to Síntesis's *Ancestros* or Elio Revé's "Papá Eleguá." Such pieces often combine lyrical descriptions of Santería ceremony, Yoruba terminology, or sacred melodies with a dance beat. One of the first *timba* songs to incorporate material of this nature was "¿Y qué tú quieres que te den?" by Adalberto Álvarez from 1991 (Álvarez 1999). It begins with a chant to Ochún, harmonized with arpeggiated chords and superimposed over sounds of water (Ex. 12). The religious community viewed Álvarez as daring at the time because of his decision to mention his spiritual godparents by name in the composition, openly acknowledging his personal involvement with Santería (Orovio 1996, interview).[42] "¿Y qué tú quieres que te den?" was a tremendous hit and inspired similar compositions by Dan Den, Los Van Van, Issac Delgado, and others.[43] Between 1992 and 1996, religion became more prevalent than virtually any other theme, effectively dominating dance music repertoire.[44] In many cases, bands that had never recorded songs with religious subject matter began to do so. CD anthologies appeared using religious references as central marketing ploy. A few years after the onset of this trend, traditional Afro-Cuban religious (and secular) folklore itself began to appear in increasing quantities.[45]

.   .   .   .

The Cuban Revolution had overtly moralist, one might even say quasi-religious, associations from the outset, involving a crusade on behalf of the downtrodden, forsaken, and exploited of society. On more than one occasion, Castro has described socialism as "brotherhood" (Cardenal 1974:329). Guevara similarly conceived of it as motivated by a spirit of love for others; a realization of the extent of poverty throughout Latin America provided the impetus for his initial involvement in revolutionary activity (Guevara 1965:53–54, 1973:26, 28). Through ongoing campaigns to build new schools and hospitals, provide work to the unemployed, foster adult literacy, retrain prostitutes, and provide universal health and retirement care, the goals of the leadership parallel those of established charities and religious institutions. Pianist Frank Fernández noted that one of the most central efforts of the Cuban Revolution has been to enrich the spiritual world of the public (Pola 1989:252). Discussion of love is a surprisingly common theme in revolutionary song (especially *nueva trova*), just as in religious repertoire.[46] Musicians such as Pedro Izquierdo likened Castro to "a materialized Jesus Christ" on various occasions because of his sacrifices and struggles on the part of poorer Cubans (e.g., Izquierdo 1990). Similar associations between religion and socialist thought have been noted in other countries.[47]

In light of their many common goals, it is striking that Cuban revolutionaries have been in such direct conflict with religious groups over the years. Conflicts with Christians surfaced early on, in part because of the close ties between the Catholicism and the social elite. Tensions with Afro-Cuban religious groups surfaced somewhat later, derived from long-standing prejudices in middle-class Cuban society against African-derived culture and aggravated further by Marxist philosophy. Most believers suffered some persecution through at least the late 1980s. Government spokespeople maintained that Afro-Cuban religion was on the decline and that the "deep well" represented by such confused beliefs was finally going dry (Barnet 1983:196).[48] There exists no official recognition of, let alone apology for, these attitudes and policies, resulting in the disappearance of religious music from public life for decades (Formell 1997:52).

Thankfully, conditions for worshippers and performers of religious music have improved dramatically. The ranks of Christian organizations have swelled, owing in part to political changes and in part to their support from aid groups abroad. Since 1997, Cubans have celebrated Christmas with the blessing of the government ("Cuba Readies for Pope Visit," *CUBAInfo* 10, no. 1 [January 8, 1998]: 7). State cultural institutions once again consider all religions "national heritage." Members of Afro-Cuban religious groups earn their living by performing and/or teaching ritual drumming, song, and dance to visitors. Others publish written works on Santería as independent scholars or sell ritual herbs and artifacts for ceremonies. Annual processions dedicated to the Caridad del Cobre and San Lázaro have developed massive followings involving tens of thousands of participants (Hagedorn 2002). Dance music with themes taken from Santería continues to be popular, with singers in bands such as Los Van Van often calling out ritual greetings to initiates while performing them (Lisa Knauer, pers. comm.). The pope's visit to Cuba in 1998 represents another important milestone in which a religious leader addressed the entire Cuban nation on live television for the first time in nearly forty years.

One might suggest, despite these changes, that religion and religious music derived from Africa remain controversial. On the one hand, the repertoire is accepted as a component of the nation's heritage. On the other, some members of the government continue to view popular religions as "false consciousness." Many middle-class Cubans, including academics in the humanities, remain surprisingly ignorant of the philosophies behind Santería. Religious performance ensembles still appear only rarely on television or the radio. Yoruba and Kongo chants have not been integrated into programs of study at national art schools in a consistent manner, and no specific institution exists where the tradition might be perpetuated and disseminated more widely.[49] Spokesmen of the Catholic Church in Cuba such as Jaime Ortega continue to belittle African-derived syncretic religions (Vázquez Montalbán 1998:554); the pope himself refused to meet with Afro-Cuban spiritual leaders during his visit.

However, we should not overemphasize the problems of present-day religious music, since the story of Afro-Cuban religions since the 1990s is largely a happy one. Despite all attempts on the part of particular individuals to suppress this heritage, before and after the revolution, practitioners have managed to perpetuate their beliefs and cultural forms. Religious music has resurfaced with a vengeance and is proving to be one of the most vital sources of inspiration among contemporary musicians of every sort. Performers in years past were forced to adopt a strategy similar to the *cimarronaje* described by Chuco Quintero in his work on salsa (1998): they found ways to camouflage their songs, rhythms, and dances as necessary within secular works so as to avoid confrontation with the authorities. It appears that this will no longer be necessary and that by adapting creatively to difficult circumstances, believers have both maintained their traditions and invigorated them with influences from other musical styles.

CHAPTER 8

Music and Ideological Crisis

> Balseros, Navidades, absolutismo,
> bautismos, testamentos, odio y ternura.
> Nadie sabe qué cosa es el comunismo . . .
> y eso puede ser pasto de la ventura.
>
> Rafters, Christmas celebrations, absolutism
> baptisms, final testaments, love and hate.
> No one knows what communism is anymore . . .
> and that could be fertile ground for hazards.
>
> SILVIO RODRÍGUEZ, "El reino de todavía"

Cuba at the turn of the millennium is undergoing a rapid series of changes that have affected almost every facet of society. In the space of only about fifteen years, the country has become less militantly socialist—in practice, if not discursively—and is more closely in contact with capitalist countries. Ideological slogans, once virtually the only messages seen in public spaces and on the radio, now compete with commercial advertisements. Job security is largely a thing of the past, with emphasis placed on competency and efficiency in the workplace. Cubans purchase many household products in foreign currency at international market prices, though they cannot easily afford them. Private business opportunities exist in addition to those offered through the state. Salaries and living standards vary much more than before, contributing to the emergence of class disparity. The country on the whole has changed more in the past ten years than in the previous thirty (Kirk and Padura Fuentes 2001:xxiv). Though the leadership may be slow to admit it, Cuba is gradually embracing a mixed capitalist economic system.

With such changes underway, one might ask whether the new millennium is the proper moment to write about Cuban socialism. During two recent trips to Havana, a few friends discouraged research for this project, suggesting that it wasn't. They felt the subject matter was still too controversial, that it could result in the denial of permission to visit the country in the future; perhaps most important, they considered the issues surrounding socialism and the arts passé. This final chapter recognizes that the Cuba of past decades often bears little resemblance to that of the present, and that many of its citizens are not terribly interested in socialist politics right now. They are more concerned with getting enough food on the table, securing a lucrative job, or in other ways adjusting their lifestyles to new circumstances.

Katherine Verdery notes in her work on Romania, however, that the essence of socialism is often perceived most clearly in the process of its transformation or decomposition (1991b: 420). My own experience confirms that debates about alterations in socialist policy often serve as a means of gauging the successes and failures of earlier decades. Indeed, in many cases it has been only through conversations about how life has changed recently that facets of socialism in the 1970s and 1980s have entered into the discussion at all. Some interviewees also feel freer to confront past problems since they no longer exist in the same form. In order to link this study to present-day realities, chapter 8 examines musical changes of the 1990s and beyond in greater detail. It provides background on the worst years of economic and social crisis and describes how the government has responded to them. It emphasizes the prominent role of music in the expansion of tourism. Finally, it details the legalistic reforms affecting the music industry and considers the compositions of performers who have lived through this period.

ECONOMIC AND SOCIAL CHANGES

With the collapse of the Soviet Union in 1989, Cuba gradually lost subsidies and trade agreements worth approximately $6 billion per year, as well as an additional $1.2 billion in Russian military aid (Frey 1997:3). This represented about 75 percent of its international business dealings. Without adequate energy supplies or manufactured goods, the island's highly dependent economy suffered a drop of over 40 percent in GNP the following year. The situation had dire effects in the first months of 1992, when for the first time in decades it received virtually no goods from its East Bloc trading partners.[1] Extended power blackouts, transportation crises, water rationing, and alarming shortages of food and basic domestic supplies were commonplace. This so-called special period of misery is no longer as severe, but the country's economy continues to falter. Lacking an industrial base that would allow for greater self-sufficiency and with little to sell on the international market, Cuba has been transformed overnight from one of the most affluent countries in Latin America to one of the poorest. The motivation for the mass exodus of rafters attempting to reach the United States in 1994 derives largely from these factors.

Economic woes of the early 1990s led in turn to the rise of acute social

problems. For several years, much of the population had no viable job option because their work centers were unable to function without adequate
electricity or raw materials. Epidemics of physical illness such as eye disease developed as the result of restricted diets or from the use of untreated
drinking water. Assaults and physical violence broke out frequently in what
was once the safest of nations. Individuals began stealing from one another
and from government-owned enterprises as a means of surviving within a
dysfunctional system. *Nueva trova* singer Pedro Luis Ferrer commented on
their desperation and loss of moral sensibilities in 1994 to journalists from
Spain.

> There's no gasoline, electricity, public transportation, medicine, food. . . .
> Now we realize that this humanistic project we've been defending
> required an economic foundation in order to develop that we don't have.
> It makes no sense to tell everyone that those living in capitalist coun-
> tries are thieves when ours is one of the societies with the most ram-
> pant theft in the world. We've even begun to lose the very concept of
> theft because need constantly forces us into it. If a Cuban tried to live
> on what the law allows him to have, he'd end up in the hospital. The
> result of all this is a society that is psychologically ill, with its members
> obliged to live their lives clandestinely or on the basis of illegal acts.
> (P.P. 1994:44)[2]

Recently, the state has managed to curtail the frequency of assaults. Theft
of state property has also diminished somewhat because of new security
measures, but theft from individuals remains a serious problem. In the past,
almost all Cubans owned the same domestic goods and had no reason to
steal. Now those who are needy live alongside others who are relatively rich,
creating friction and envy.

Leaders recognized the urgent need to bolster their country's economy.
As an initial step, they slashed military spending; over the course of the early
1990s, they cut enlisted forces by approximately half as well as spending on
armaments and other supplies.[3] They began borrowing heavily from international agencies and soliciting investment from foreign entrepreneurs.
These reforms have been supplemented from abroad. Money entering the
country from Cuban exiles increased exponentially as they realized the extent of their families' need. Monthly remittances now contribute well over
$800 million annually to the GNP through consumer purchases in govern-
ment stores (Monreal 1999:50).[4] Conservative leaders of the Miami community exhibit a certain hypocrisy toward the embargo in this respect.
Though officially unflinching in their desire to sever all economic ties with

the island—even to the extent of banning food and medical sales!—they readily break ranks in order to make sure that their own families lack for nothing. The result is an ineffectual, partial embargo in which the country suffers from a lack of investment and foreign contact but struggles along using capital provided by its political enemies.

One of the most radical economic shifts of late has been the legalization of foreign currency. Prior to the mid-1990s, Cuban shops were strictly divided into the few intended for tourists and diplomats that sold goods in U.S. dollars and others that sold selected items in pesos for the local population. Police generally refused Cubans access to dollar stores; in fact, the mere possession of foreign currency often resulted in jail sentences. In the 1990s, these prohibitions in combination with a near total lack of consumer goods led to the rapid expansion of the black market. Individuals clandestinely bought and sold everything the government could not provide in homes and on the street, often in dollars. In recognition of the need to convert such transactions into activity beneficial to the state, authorities legalized foreign currency in 1993. Cuba is now replete with dollar *bodegas* that sell a variety of basic domestic items.

Economic crisis had an adverse effect on the lives of many performers. In a country that experienced chronic shortages of supplies even before 1989, equipment for recording, amplification, transportation, and instruments themselves are rarely available now from the government. Music schools lack basic materials (instruments, valve oil, guitar strings, music paper, pencils) for their pupils; in many cases, students must supply their own. Established artists may live well, but those struggling to begin their careers face many obstacles, including fierce competition. Music represents a potential path to economic salvation open to nearly anyone. As a result, Cuba's cities have been inundated with amateur and semiprofessional performers. They play for tips, offer music or dance lessons, sell instruments or home recordings, and hope eventually to attract the attention of foreign entrepreneurs.

From the late 1960s through the early 1990s, the state served as the sole provider of employment in order to keep salaries balanced. Following the onset of economic crisis, however, the PCC authorized limited private employment in an effort to stimulate production. Interest in *cuenta propia* (individual rather than state-sponsored) employment remains high. The state maintains strict limits on the amount this activity, however, and since 1994 has taxed it so heavily that many aspiring entrepreneurs go out of business within a few months or years.

The adoption of capitalist-style business models has led to the proliferation of quasi-autonomous state corporations with greater responsibility for their respective bottom lines. One of the first was Cubanacan, created in 1987. It currently oversees about 40 percent of tourist hotels, restaurants, marinas, and charter and taxi services (Amuchastegui 2000:6–7). Cimex concentrates on the retail sale of consumer goods. Coptextel, S.A., is a high-tech enterprise selling appliances, hardware and software, and technical support to foreign businesses. These examples represent only the most visible of the approximately two hundred new government-owned enterprises, in addition to the more than four hundred foreign firms and joint capitalist ventures *(empresas mixtas)* now on the island.

Such economic trends have been ideologically taxing even for staunch supporters of the revolution. Those who sacrificed for decades to construct a better society based largely on Marxist principles now live in a radically different context. Policies are uncertain, and the promises of leaders for progressive change seem to be contradicted by recent actions. Castro denounces Yankee imperialism yet at the same time makes concessions to Spain's Sol Meliá Investments, Canada's Sherritt International, and countless other conglomerates. Cubans across the political spectrum don't know what to believe in or even how to describe the society around them. The result has been the emergence of a fundamental crisis of values (Fernández Robaina, September 1996, interview).

THE GROWTH OF TOURISM

At least as dramatic as the capitalization of the economy has been the rapid expansion of tourism. During most of the socialist period, the PCC discouraged contact with foreign visitors. Officials suggested that unnecessary interactions could compromise national security. They also believed tourists might spread unhealthy capitalist values or other ideologies that could hinder progress toward the Communist future. By all accounts, the tourist industry of the 1970s and 1980s was minimal and not terribly accommodating. The government charged little for hotel rooms but provided poor service and did nothing to promote visits. Few academic exchanges existed with capitalist countries either. Finnish musicologist Juhani Simila mentioned that when he arrived to take courses in the ENA in the early 1980s, the school's directors did not know what to do with him, as they had no established mechanism for accommodating foreigners. He experienced many personal difficulties as a result and eventually chose to leave.

By the early 1990s, tourism emerged as a strategy for economic survival.

Instead of discouraging visits from abroad, the government reversed policy and began encouraging them, even from the exile community. Anyone familiar with Cuba in earlier periods will be shocked at the degree of recent development in this sector. The José Martí International Airport expanded in the 1990s into a multiterminal structure three or four times its earlier size. The country now boasts eight additional facilities of similar caliber. Cubana Airlines no longer uses outmoded Soviet passenger planes but instead gleaming new aircraft of French construction. New clubs, bars, and restaurants open frequently. The government markets tourist packages abroad, luring potential visitors with slick, Western-style brochures and websites.

Tourism represents one of the fastest growing economic sectors, with Italians constituting the most-frequent visitors, followed by Canadians, Mexicans, Spaniards, and other Europeans (Lynn 1997:7). In 1997, 1.2 million tourists visited the island, generating $1.75 billion in gross earnings. That figure represents a 100 percent increase in revenues compared with three years earlier and a nearly 500 percent increase in the tourist presence compared with 1985. The numbers of tourists rose to 1.5 million in 1998, 1.77 million in 2000, and 1.9 million in 2003.[5] Government agencies have expanded major destinations beyond Havana, Santiago, and Varadero Beach with the opening of Club Med–style five-star resorts on Cayo Coco, Cayo Guillermo, and elsewhere (*CubaNews* 8, no. 9 [September 2000]: 6).[6]

The growing number of visitors has benefited entertainers, resulting in additional job opportunities. However, it has unpleasant consequences for the population as a whole. Havana and other cities are increasingly divided into foreign currency entertainment areas intended primarily for tourists and others for Cubans themselves. The best beaches, hotels, cabarets, and clubs once available to all are now "dollar zones." The result is a sort of musical apartheid system in which many concerts cannot be heard by the island's own residents simply because they cost too much. Such segregation first developed in the 1980s but has become much more marked over the past decade. Figure 21, a reproduction of tourist T-shirt designs, demonstrates the extent to which capitalist marketing and advertising have permeated the environment.

More populist entertainment venues in Havana (*casas de cultura*, the Hurón Azul café at the UNEAC, La Tropical, the patio of the Conjunto Folklórico Nacional Studios, matinee shows at the Casas de la Música in Centro Habana and Miramar) now charge foreigners entrance fees in dollars but also allow Cubans access in national currency. These are some of the only places in which Cubans and others can attend events together with relative ease. Their egalitarianism is appealing, and yet they too have been affected neg-

FIGURE 21.   Tourist T-shirt art from a dollar store in Habana Vieja, 2002. As part of its attempt to lure foreigners to the island, Cuba has radically refashioned its external image. Visitors are welcomed with open arms and the island described in promotional material as a haven of music, dance, and fiestas. Photos of Che Guevara now compete for shelf space in tourist stores with shirts sporting brand-name rum or cigar ads and dancing *mulatas*. Photo by the author.

atively. A tension often hangs in the air of smaller clubs that affects personal relations. Hustlers frequent them, hoping to sell cigars or rum stolen from government shops. Others arrive with the express intention of making a new foreign friend who might buy them drinks or invite them to a meal. Young women seek men willing to repay sex for money or gifts.[7] In general, it has become increasingly difficult as a foreigner to establish normal, relaxed personal relations with Cubans in the places that most encounter them.

Ariana Hernández-Reguant recently finished a study of a Cuban radio station, Radio Taíno, and its transition to commercial format in 1994. Her work is an excellent introduction in miniature to the sorts of changes taking place throughout the entertainment industry. The author describes the goals of the new Radio Taíno as presenting an image of normality to the capitalist world and entertaining tourists. As opposed to most stations, it did not broadcast political news and primarily featured dance music. This was the first station to fund itself through the sale of paid advertising since the early 1960s. Unexpectedly, Taíno's main audience turned out not to be foreigners but rather younger Cubans who were "tired of ideological battles" and "appreciated Radio Taíno's shallow tone" (2002:77). The history of the station provides a fascinating look at how government-appointed managers struggled to balance the interests of commercial patrons (foreign hotel owners, beer distributors, travel agents) and the ideological mandates of the Central Committee.

EXPANSION OF THE CUBAN MUSIC INDUSTRY

One of the ironies of the past ten years is that the onset of economic crisis has proven a blessing in disguise for the Cuban music industry in many respects. Sales of tapes and CDs abroad have expanded dramatically despite the ongoing trade embargo. In Tower Records and other U.S. stores, Cuban releases now constitute approximately one-quarter of all the Latin items in stock, where they had been virtually nonexistent before 1990. Such changes result in part from policy shifts on the island. Socialists are now genuinely interested in catering to the capitalist market; this had never been a concern before, let alone a priority. Increased music circulation also results from decisions by the U.S. Congress to ease the regulation of Cuban culture domestically. Surprisingly, such policies have received support from both the Right and Left of the U.S. political establishment.

In 1988, Representative Howard Berman (Democrat-CA) introduced an amendment to the Trading with the Enemy Act, the primary legislation dictating restrictions on commercial activity with Cuba. Eventually approved as part of the Omnibus Trade Bill of that year (sec. 2502 [P.L. 100–418]), it was designed as a means of facilitating an exchange of ideas between Cuba and the United States. The legislation, known as the Berman Amendment, exempted informational materials from the embargo and permitted the direct sale of books, artwork, film, and music between the two countries for the first time since the early 1960s. Subsection four reads in part: "The authority granted to the President . . . does not include the authority to regulate or prohibit, directly or indirectly, the importation from any country, or the exportation to any country, whether commercial or otherwise, of publications, films, posters, phonograph records, photographs, microfilm, microfiche, tapes, or other informational materials." Berman and his supporters paved the way for U.S. and other record labels to begin releasing Cuban music in the United States as well as for Cuban bands to perform there more easily.

At approximately the same time, Cuba began restructuring its music industry as part of a strategy to survive the collapse of the East Bloc. In 1989, it created an agency called Artex that permitted foreign record companies to purchase and reissue songs held in the vaults of the national label, EGREM (Cantor 1997:17). Artex had significant autonomy and began aggressively collecting royalties from abroad in addition to overseeing new recording contracts. The licensing of music continues to expand; Castro himself recognized the economic potential of the music industry in 1993 and encouraged its development (Perna 2001:79). More recently, the government has created various subdivisions of Artex, including BIS Music, spurred on by the explosion of interest in traditional repertoire created by the *Buena Vista Social Club* documentary.[8] Unable to compete with the tremendous investment capital of firms abroad or their lucrative advances, these agencies concentrate on licensing recordings from past years. Domestic recording has expanded recently but more through home productions of rap, reggae, and acoustic *trova* than through state initiatives.

In addition to the licensing of music from EGREM's archives, the government began staging high-profile trade expositions in Havana as a means of promoting the compositions of present-day artists. The first was the Feria del Disco Cubano, also known as Cubadisco, held in March of 1997 (Watrous 1997a: 34). Organizers scheduled a salsa marathon as part of the activities in which a series of dance groups played nonstop for days. This and subsequent events, which continue into the present, have resulted in additional trade agreements with foreign companies.[9] New music video production centers (RTV Commercial, facilities affiliated with the ICAIC, etc.) also exist that promote local music, largely for the tourist market.

Recognizing that Cuban labor costs are extremely low and that musicians and arrangers of high quality abound, the government has begun offering sound recording and production services to the international public. State-of-the-art facilities in Havana offer prices far below studios in London or New York. They include those of the EGREM itself in Centro Habana and of the ICRT (the national radio and television station) in Vedado (Perna 2001:82). Smaller studios exist under the direction of Pablo Milanés (Pablo Milanés Records), as part of his Foundation, and Silvio Rodríguez (Ojalá Studios in Miramar).[10] The former dates from 1992, the latter from 1996. Rodríguez also helped oversee the construction of Abdala Studios in 1998, a venture funded jointly by him and the Cuban government (Ned Sublette, pers. comm.). All have attracted a stream of international talent.

One unexpected result of the capitalization of music making is that recordings of exiled artists rarely heard on the island since the 1960s are more accessible. For years, Cubans listening to Osvaldo Farrés, Celia Cruz, Olga Guillot, Rolando Laserie, and others had to do so in their own homes behind closed doors; their music now appears on store shelves once again and on the street in pirated form. Releases by New York *salseros* are available as well, and in some cases even discs by devoutly anti-Communist Cuban Americans Gloria Estefan and Willie Chirino! Market forces seem to have broken down what Cubans refer to as the *autoblockade:* state policies that restricted the domestic circulation of certain products. Concern for sales has taken precedence over the ideological content of recordings in most cases.

The reintegration of Cuba into international trade networks has been a gradual process that began in earnest in the 1980s and continues to accelerate. As might be expected, the first labels to promote contemporary artists were European, such as Fonomusic in Spain and Messidor in Germany. Fonomusic began purchasing licenses and releasing previously recorded revolutionary music; their first LP was a reissue of Silvio Rodríguez's *Días y flores* in the late 1970s. Messidor took the even bolder step of producing new LPs, beginning in the 1980s with albums of Latin jazz artists Gonzalo Rubalcaba, Chucho Valdés, and Arturo Sandoval.[11] British World Circuit, specializing in African and African diaspora culture, established contacts on the island about 1990 (Reyes 2001, interview). Later arrivals included Peter Gabriel's Real World Records (1991); Corasón (Mexico, 1992); Artcolor (Colombia, 1993); Magic Music (Barcelona, 1994); Nubenegra (Madrid, 1994), and Eurotropical, a subsidiary of Santiago Auserón's Manzana label (Canary Islands, 1996). A comprehensive overview of the dozens of labels that signed trade agreements with Cuba in the 1990s is beyond the scope of this chapter but would have to include Caribe Productions, a subsidiary of EMI; the Paris-based Milan label, a subsidiary of BMG; Aro in Colombia; Changó Records; and Top Hit. Many early collaborators with the Cuban state, including Milan and Artcolor, have now terminated their contracts with EGREM (Ned Sublette, pers. comm.), but others continue to sign agreements.[12]

Within the United States, attempts to record and market Cuban artists have been more cautious. Barbara Dane may have been the first to produce an album of contemporary musicians on Paredon, a label devoted to the promotion of international protest song (Dane 1971). In 1978, René López rereleased LPs of dance music by contemporary Cuban musicians following the "Havana Jam" of 1978. In 1985, he also collaborated with Verna Gillis, Andrew Schloss, and others to release *Music of Cuba,* a noncommercial collection of folk repertoire produced with support from the Center for Cuban Studies in New York. Vitral Records produced seven recordings of Cuban music in the late 1980s, including discs by the Muñequitos de Matanzas, Los Papines, Pedro Izquierdo, the Conjunto Rumbavana, Irakere, and Los Van Van. These titles, along with the Los Van Van release *Songo* (Island Records, 1988) and the *¡Sabroso!* CD by Virgin Records/Earthworks (Vanren et al. 1989), were virtually the only revolution-era material available in the States before or concurrent with the passing of the Berman Amendment. Most of the

U.S. companies dodged restrictive embargo legislation by applying for subsidiary commercial licenses through British companies rather than dealing with Cuban nationals directly. A collaborative effort between American Ned Sublette and British David Byrne in 1991 resulted in the release *Dancing with the Enemy*. Though it appeared exclusively on the British label Luaka Bop, the CD received considerable promotion and distribution in the States and generated additional interest in Cuban performers.

One of the first North American labels to specialize in Cuban material in the post-Berman period was Qbadisc, founded in New York by Ned Sublette and Ben Socolov in 1990. Firms negotiating with the Cuban government more recently include the Miami-based Universal Music Group Latin America (UMG) and Peer International labels (Cantor 1998a: 21), Ralph Mercado's RMM Records in New York, and Ahí-Namá in Los Angeles, owned by Jimmy Maslon.[13] Demand for Cuban releases continues to grow, yet U.S. entrepreneurs typically act only as distributors of Cuban material rather than produce albums themselves because they are still prevented from doing so by law. They may apply for licenses to sell recordings made in Cuba but not contract musicians to make new albums. The Office of Foreign Assets Control (OFAC) accepts the licensing of existing artistic products as both a legitimate form of international trade and a means of supporting the free circulation of intellectual property but considers the contracting of Cuban artists on the island an unacceptably direct form of support of the socialist government (Jimmy Maslon, pers. comm.). Other U.S. labels serving as distributors of Cuban material include Alula Records, promoting releases by Nubenegra in Spain, and Rounder, which carries the Corason catalog from Mexico. Tepid interest even for the licensing of Cuban CDs is undoubtedly due to the shifting legal ground surrounding such arrangements. The possibility of an unexpected political event or new piece of legislation that might affect business makes all transactions risky.[14]

Even after licensing arrangements are finalized, legalistic snags develop between Cuban artists and North American businesses. In theory, for instance, Cuban performers may tour the United States following a new record release, but entrance visas have proven difficult to obtain. Additionally, concert promoters are not permitted to compensate Cubans adequately for their efforts and may only offer them a per diem allowance to cover basic expenses. Questions also remain about the enforceability of international copyright agreements given the ongoing refusal of U.S. courts to recognize the legitimacy of Cuba's government. Some Europeans and Latin Americans have taken advantage of this situation by selling bootleg copies of particular Cuban CDs in the United States. Others offer Cuban musicians exploitative contracts, knowing how desperate many of them are to promote their music internationally. Federico García of Caribe Productions notes that the embargo has created a situation in which thieves abound who ignore the rights of Cubans and their trading partners (Cantor 1998a: 24).[15]

LEGAL CHANGES IN MUSIC MAKING WITHIN CUBA

The trend toward allowing musicians to freely negotiate their job contracts abroad has been contentious. It began earlier than in other sectors of the economy, however, for the simple reason that musicians traveled more often. Contact with the capitalist world inevitably resulted in offers to record and perform, often at higher levels of compensation than they typically received at home. For years, the state forbade many artists from taking advantage of these invitations. In the 1980s, however, with the dissolution of the mono-lithic Centro de Contrataciones Artísticas and the founding of multiple music *empresas*, some contract flexibility developed (Acosta 2001, interview). Government agencies began offering special benefits to the most prominent performers in order to compensate them for their exceptional earning potential. The concessions solidified in the early 1990s into a more-or-less coherent policy applicable to everyone.

Before the depenalization of foreign currency in 1993, government agencies acted as the exclusive representative of artists abroad; they managed earnings and made agreements for the sale and distribution of music with little input from individuals. Officials maintained that since the state had paid for the musicians' education and provided for their needs at home, it had the right to appropriate their hard currency revenues and use them as they saw fit. To performers, this situation often seemed exploitative and was one motivation for artistic defection. Those who earned money unbeknownst to the government faced difficult alternatives. They could try to smuggle the money into Cuba, which if successful would allow them to spend it on the black market. This option involved the risk of detection and jailing. Alternately, they could declare the income to a customs agent and receive a percentage of it back in the form of vouchers to be redeemed in state-controlled dollar stores intended for diplomats and tourists.

Since depenalization, touring artists have achieved recognition as independent workers, a special sort of *cuentapropista*. The state no longer claims the right to all the income they earn abroad, only a percentage, typically between 10 and 50 percent.[16] Rates of taxation ostensibly vary as a function of services provided to groups by their unions while on the road (housing, meals, insurance, costumes, equipment transport, technical support). In the mid-1990s, as the details of the new system were being established, many musicians described it as unfair as well, complaining about low net earnings and the "bestial corruption" of many officials.[17] Now, for the most part, the taxation system functions more smoothly and continues to improve. Regulations of 1997 attached to Resolution 42 of the National Assembly have allowed musicians and composers to negotiate foreign contracts individually with little state intervention (Borges Suárez n.d.). They are authorized to join the Sociedad General de Autores y Editores de España (SGAE) or similar organizations and to receive royalties directly from them (Acosta 2001, interview). In the same year, the government invited Eduardo Batista, president of the SGAE, to establish a branch office in Havana (Watrous 1997a: 34).

The reestablishment of ties with the capitalist world has necessitated fundamental changes to domestic laws governing copyright. As discussed in chapter 2, the Cuban government had stopped honoring all international copyright agreements by 1967. Though it modified this position to an extent in the late 1970s, it made no attempt to shape its revised legislation to conform to international standards. This discouraged foreign companies from licensing and promoting Cuban music even if their home countries had favorable relations with the socialist state. Beginning in 1993, the government began to revise its intellectual property legislation again, and in 1997 it signed the international Berne Convention on copyright. This latter step, especially, opened the door for individuals to negotiate contracts with foreign companies and for non-U.S firms to trade more easily with Cuban institutions (Hernández-Reguant 2004b: 17).[18] It has resulted in many rags-to-riches stories, with artists collecting mammoth international royalty payments for the first time in decades.

The exponential growth of the music industry seems to have led to the exploitation of performers on an unprecedented scale. Though the extent of such activity is unknown, one anecdote from personal experience may help readers understand the dynamics of the process. Beginning in 1995, a former *nueva trova* artist, radio DJ, and friend of mine named Rodolfo de la Fuente began representing a group of clients who wanted the Ministry of Culture to pay them royalties collected from foreign agencies. The clients included relatives of deceased musicians Lorenzo Hierrezuelo, Sindo Garay, Félix Caignet, José Antonio Méndez, Ignacio Piñeiro, María Teresa Vera, and Enrique Jorrín. They and de la Fuente initially joined forces with a Spanish company, SEMSA, in order to force Peer International and others to compensate them. Over time, their focus shifted to the Cuban government's own copyright collection agency, ACDAM, and its director, Miguel Coma. According to de la Fuente and his wife, Yasmina, they learned that Coma had received substantial royalties from abroad in the name of these individuals, but instead of passing the money on to its rightful inheritors had been stealing it or at least diverting it. Such actions would have been easy to perpetrate against elderly clients unfamiliar with international finance.

Toward the end of the year 2000, de la Fuente learned that he himself had been accused by ACDAM of working illegally for SEMSA and receiving payments from them, a charge he denies. After a period of detention, the government charged him with "acts detrimental to economic activity and contractual agreements." His trial lasted approximately a year. Eventually the state found him guilty, despite letters of support written on his behalf by virtually all the clients he represented. De la Fuente began serving an eight-year term on January 6, 2003 (sentence no. 364–2002), and remains behind bars. According to his wife, he never received any compensation for the representation of his clients. Nothing ever appeared in Cuban newspapers about this sentence, though many journalists attended the proceedings, and nothing has come of de la Fuente's attempts to appeal his case. While one may dispute the claims of either ACDAM or de la Fuente, his plight makes clear the difficulty of negotiating artistic rights in this era of transition, especially with state institutions accustomed to unquestioned authority.

Artists who generate profits abroad may now lay claim to at least a portion of such income, but the state still pays most musicians working on the island in national currency. This is true regardless of who the public is for their shows and recordings or whether they generate sales in pesos or dollars (Castañeda 1997:12). The same is true of other creative workers: if they publish a book or deliver a lecture abroad, they must legally declare their hard currency income but can keep much of it for themselves. By contrast, if they are involved in the same activities at home through a government institution, they frequently earn relatively worthless Cuban pesos. This continues to be a source of contention, especially for individuals working in the tourist sector or generating items for sale in dollar stores. Lázaro Ros, for instance, has asserted that he failed to receive fair compensation for CDs and commercial videos contracted through state agencies (Hagedorn 1995:274). A perusal of contracts used by the Sindicato Nacional de Trabajadores de Cultura and the Consejo Nacional de Artes Escénicas suggests that attempts are being made to share a portion of hard currency profits with artists working within Cuba; similar plans are being debated in other fields. At least some musicians in high-profile tourist venues receive payment in dollars already.

So many popular musicians earn at least part of their salary in foreign currency relative to other sectors through tours and foreign contracts that they are rapidly becoming a sort of nouveau riche. Members of prominent dance bands are identifiable immediately because of their designer clothing, beautiful homes, new foreign cars, and so on. They have effectively stood the existing social order on its head by accruing more personal wealth than classical musicians, doctors, even some politicians and military personnel. Of course, discrepancies of this sort exist in the capitalist world as well—in fact, they derive from it—but they represent a new situation in Cuba and have created tensions. Heart surgeons do not take kindly to living in relative poverty while young singers and dancers with little formal education flaunt their opulence. Negative attitudes toward musicians often have racial overtones as well, given that most dance bands are comprised of Cubans of color. One white dentist I met at a lunch kiosk in 1996 discussed this subject with anyone who would listen. He angrily denounced the fact that so many *"negritos* banging on drums" were living better than he was as a white-collar professional. Though this was admittedly an isolated incident, experience suggests that his views are not unique.

Since those who work abroad tend to earn more than those at home, virtually all musicians attempt to travel. Getting permission to leave the country is a tedious process involving considerable bureaucracy, delays, and high fees in dollars. Cantor (1999:22) notes that the Ministry of Culture has such complex regulations and acts so capriciously at times that artists jokingly refer to it as the "Misterio de Cultura" (Mystery of Culture). Yet the years since 1995 have predictably witnessed record numbers of foreign tours. Over 3,500 of the country's roughly 11,600 state-sponsored music ensembles— nearly a third—spent time abroad in 1996 alone (Watrous 1997a: 34). By 1999, those numbers had apparently doubled, with groups abroad comprised mainly of musicians in the fields of salsa, *son*, and traditional music (Perna 2001:80). Los Van Van, the Charanga Habanera, Irakere, and other ensembles now spend the majority of the year on the road, performing only limited engagements within Cuba itself (Acosta n.d.: 5). Noteworthy musicologists have published abroad as well, also for economic reasons.[19] They earn significantly more from presses in Spain or Mexico and avoid waiting years to be accommodated by a domestic industry desperately short of supplies. Prominent researchers accept invitations to teach or live in foreign countries, consistently spending half the year or more away.

A high percentage of Cuba's musicians eventually decide to leave the country for good, opting for official or de facto exile. Saxophonist Paquito D'Rivera (1998:176), an exile himself, suggests that the government contributes to this trend by making travel difficult. Performers' frustrated desire for greater international contact, in combination with economic incentives, has converted living abroad into an obsession. The sheer number of artists who have decided to leave in recent years is startling. Examples include Gonzalo Rubalcaba, who lives in the Dominican Republic and in Fort Lauderdale; *nueva trova* singer Virulo, who lives in Mexico; trombonist Juan Pablo Torres, who left for Spain in 1992 and now resides in the United States; various members of the dance band Dan Den, who defected while in Colombia in 1993 (Orovio 1996, interview); the singer Albita, who moved first to Mexico and then Miami (Grau 1997); *nueva trova* artist Donato Poveda, also in Miami; saxophonists Carlos Averhoff (in Miami since 1997) and Yosvanny Terry, in New York; Alejandro Leyva of NG La Banda, who defected after a performance at New York's Lincoln Center in 1997 (*CUBAInfo 9*, no. 10 [July 31, 1997]: 9); Manolín, "El Médico de la Salsa," who defected in Atlanta, Georgia, in May 2001; Carlos Manuel, who defected through Mexico in June 2003; five dancers with the Ballet Nacional, who defected that same year (Madigan 2004); and forty-four members of the entertainment ensemble Havana Night Club, who defected in Las Vegas in November 2004.[20] Note that while some individuals publicly denounce the revolution and vow never to return, others keep a low profile, maintain ties, and return to the island with some frequency. Their reasons for defection are clearly more economic than political. Initially embarrassed by the trend and preoccupied that Cuba would lose its talent, the government now seems to have accepted the "musician drain." Policy makers understand that the country contains many aspiring performers and that someone always appears to take the place of those who leave (Leonardo Acosta, pers. comm.).

Another trend since the 1990s has been a gradual erosion of the *plantilla* system, with all of its advantages and disadvantages, and movement back to the pre-1968 situation in which artists worked as free agents. In reaction to performers' relatively high wages and their tendency to avoid working for the government, the government is gradually offering them fewer jobs and reducing their monthly peso salaries. Beginning in 1999, it gave some high-profile artists no salary at all (Cantor 1999:22). This change is a mixed blessing. It means that bands are freer to find their own jobs, work when they want to, and determine their own salaries but also that the safety net that existed for them is disappearing (Valdés Santandreu 2001, interview). Musicians increasingly succeed or fail based on their own efforts rather than those of their union.[21] The change also means that the government's role has been transformed from one of patron and social protector to mooch, much more like that of the IRS in the United States. Fees that bands pay to government agencies supposedly entitle them to promotional services, but in reality most of this burden too now falls on artists. One interesting development of late has been the Ministry of Culture's creation of a Foundation for Cultural Development intended to redirect earnings from commercial music to artistic enterprises that do not generate much foreign currency. These include the classical arts, experimental theater, and regional folklore (Cantor 1999:22).

COMPOSITIONS OF THE SPECIAL PERIOD

In the context of economic crisis, popular music has become an important vehicle for the expression of concerns about the country's future. The prominence of music as a revenue-generating art form has resulted in new opportunities for social critique. As mentioned, marketability and sales are now central factors determining whether a song will be recorded or disseminated rather than its ideological content (Acosta 1996, interview). Because of this, a wider variety of commercial genres has emerged, often with influences from abroad, and more subjects are discussed in song lyrics. Greater freedom of expression is also evident in "highbrow" publications such as *Temas* and *La Gaceta de Cuba* and in other media such as film.[22] The current minister of culture himself has spoken out against censorship, expressed interest in maintaining ties with artists in exile, and in other ways helped change the tone of cultural discourse (e.g., Díaz and del Pino 1996). The contradictions between socialist ideology and cultural realities of the present have been the subject of some discussion as well (e.g., Faya et al. 1996).

Various trends are evident in the lyrics of Cuban popular music today. As suggested, one has been to write songs that more directly address difficulties confronting the population. References to despair, isolation, feelings of insignificance, crime or violence, racial tensions, loss of hope, and loss of political direction are all common, especially in rock and *novísima trova*.[23] Gender relations are another topic that has surfaced, in reference to both male-female relations and homosexuality. Alan West-Durán (2004:21) has analyzed rap compositions, a major new movement, that include biting commentary on race relations, something he refers to as "choteo con conciencia." Hermanos de Causa, Los Paisanos, Obsesión, and many of the over five hundred similar groups that now exist demonstrate a high degree of racial consciousness (Fernandes 2003; West-Durán 2004:9), critiquing the ills confronting their society more directly than those of earlier generations. They freely fuse foreign musical influences with local rhythms and instruments. Another recent trend in composition has been the avoidance of political themes and an exclusive focus on lyrical songs with personal content. The performance of

boleros and arrangements of traditional *trova* and dance repertoire emphasizing subjective, emotional experiences can itself be viewed as significant, a
rejection of cultural policies that overprioritized politics.

The tendency of songwriters to express themselves in a potentially controversial manner has been matched by a public that frequently reads the
lyrics of pop culture as subversive or parodic, regardless of the composer's
intent. One example from 1996 is Adalberto Álvarez's "El baile del toca-toca"
(The Touch-Touch Dance), whose lyrics were understood by many to allude
to the financial "touching" associated with graft and illegal business deals.
Similarly, listeners adopted the phrase "prepare yourself for what's coming"
(Prepárate para lo que viene) from Manolín's 1995 song "Voy a mí" as a
tongue-in-cheek reference to Castro's autocratic style of leadership during
the special period. In some cases, popular songs of the past have also served
as vehicles of satire. The bolero "Y" by Mario de Jesús initially circulated in
the prerevolutionary period but acquired new significance in 1990s Havana.
Neighbors I knew sang a version whose lyrics demonstrated anxiety over the
lack of affordable food. A few lines suffice to convey the essence of the change.

ORIGINAL LYRICS

¿Y qué hiciste del amor que me juraste?
¿Y qué has hecho de los besos que te dí?
¿Y qué excusa puedes darme si faltaste
Y mataste la esperanza que hubo en mí?

And what have you done with the love you swore?
And what of the kisses I gave to you?
And what excuse can you give for your absence
And for crushing all the hope that I had?

MODIFIED LYRICS

¿Y qué hiciste de los pollos que ofreciste?
¿Y qué has hecho de la carne que había aquí?
¿Y qué excusa puedes darme de la leche?
Y me matas hoy de hambre porque sí.

What have you done with the chicken you offered?
And what of the red meat that used to be here?
And what excuse can you give for the lack of milk?
And you're starving me to death today, it's true.

Themes of consumerism have appeared in many songs. In some, especially
those of *nueva* and *novísima trova* artists, references to sales blend with sug-

FIGURE 22. Cover art from the Charanga Habanera CD
Pa' que se entere La Habana, 1996. The album was taken
off store shelves for a time, in part because of the controversial nature of some song lyrics such as "El temba"
that made reference to prostitution and that appeared to
glorify materialist values. Officials also considered the
image of a hundred-dollar bill on the jacket inappropriate.
Cosmopolitan Caribbean Music.

gestions that Cuba may be "selling out" conceptually or spiritually, losing
its moral compass. Those not involved in dance music are especially critical
in this sense, perhaps because they feel marginalized by the centrality of dance
repertoire in the new economy or because they view the spirit of *trova* as
antithetical to commercialization. Examples of songs that examine the implications of the dollar economy include "Paladar" by Silvio Rodríguez, an
introspective bolero on the *Domínguez* album, and Carlos Varela's "Tropicollage," a rock number that uses *son*-style piano *montunos* as a means of
iconically referencing the tourist trade. Dance pieces discussing consumerism
tend to present the theme with humor, as might be expected. The lyrics of
the Charanga Habanera's "La turística" discuss a lovely woman who ignores
men unless they can take her to expensive dollar locales. The state media actually banned the album it appeared on for a time, in part because its cover
art consisted largely of a U.S. hundred-dollar bill (Fig. 22). Van Van recorded

a similar song by Rodolfo Cárdenas, "Shopping Maniac" (Shopimaniaca; see Formell and Los Van Van 1997), in which a man bemoans the endless expenditures of his girlfriend in dollar stores.

Because of the large numbers of musicians in Cuba and the limited access to studios, many performers have never made recordings. Ironically, it is often only after they have left the country that young composers are able to record songs about their experiences at home. An anthology (Barbería et al. 1995) from Madrid, for instance, fittingly entitled *Habana oculta,* or Hidden Havana, consists of pieces by a loose collective of Cuban rock enthusiasts. This and subsequent releases epitomize the compositions of youth of the 1990s and beyond, as mentioned in chapter 5: they are eclectic and cosmopolitan, draw on R&B, *son,* pan–Latin American pop, and other sources of inspiration fused with traditional folkloric elements.[24] Despite living abroad, these artists have an avid public within Cuba that informally circulates copies of their recordings, and many return to the island on occasion to perform. Their popularity within Cuba demonstrates the extent to which "national music" is increasingly part of a larger international dialogue that includes the entire Cuban diaspora.

Younger musicians tend to use extended, jazz-influenced harmonies and complex rhythms. Ostinatos of various kinds feature prominently, a measure of African-derived aesthetic influences. Examples of the latter include the guitar accompaniment in "Guaguancó para Daniela" on *Habana oculta* and the four-measure vamp that serves as the basis for "Chachachá Cachybache" by Los Cachivache (Estrada and Carbonell 1994). Vocal and instrumental improvisation remains a central feature of many songs despite their elaboration in the studio. Composers create individualistic styles that demonstrate an aggressive postmodern amalgam. Comping patterns from Brazilian bossa nova in "Con tanta presión," reggae beats in "Paula," Santana-esque jazz-rock fusions with screaming electric guitar in "Enfermera," funk bass in "La cara de mi suerte," the straight-ahead R&B sound of "Quien pedirá," complete with Billy Preston–style organ fills, and adaptations of folkloric drumming genres for guitar in "La conga" represent only a fraction of the many sounds represented on the *Habana oculta* release. The group Angelitos Negros is also typical of recent performers, basing compositions in part on soul and African American gospel.

Lyrics on the *Habana oculta* album are sophisticated as well, testifying to the revolution's gains in the arts and education despite the fact that many pieces criticize aspects of the socialist experience. The excerpt below comes from "Ritmo sabroso" by José Luís Medina, one of the more politically edged pieces.

Está este ritmo sabroso
Me robaron la cartera y el carnet
Está este ritmo sabroso
Subieron las tarifas de nuevo este mes
Está este ritmo sabroso
Está la gente idiota inventando qué hacer
Está este ritmo sabroso
Violaron a una niña y no llegaba a diez

Está este ritmo sabroso
Está una suicida colgando de mí pared
Está este ritmo sabroso
Está un balsero despidiéndose otra vez

Está el poder ahogándose entre la verdad
Está la bolsa negra cerrando la llave
Está una madre llorando qué cocinar
Está un viejo borracho tirado en la calle
Está hablando en la tele quien tú sabes.

This rhythm is tasty
They stole my wallet and ID card
This rhythm is tasty
The utility prices went up again this month
This rhythm is tasty
All those idiotic people inventing things to do
This rhythm is tasty
They raped a girl not even ten years old

This rhythm is tasty
There's a suicide victim hanging from my wall
This rhythm is tasty
There's a rafter saying good-bye yet again

The authorities are drowning between truths
The black market is taking care of business
A mother is crying, nothing to cook
There's an old drunk strewn in the street
On TV "you-know-who" is talking.

Newer performers "signify" off traditional repertoire in fascinating ways, demonstrating a strong interest in songs of the past but altering them radically. In the case of groups such as Vocal Sampling (e.g., Baños et al. 1995) or Vocal LT (Díaz Laportilla 2000), this may involve adapting pre-revolutionary boleros, folkloric rumbas, or dance tunes for a cappella ensemble and imitating the sounds of percussion and melodic instruments with the mouth. The duo Cachivache takes inspiration from "Son de la

EXAMPLE 13. One of the traditional *charanga*-style *guajeos* incorporated as a looped sample into the Orishas' hip-hop composition "A lo cubano" (Nocchi et al. 2000).

loma" by Miguel Matamoros but transforms it into a slow modal composition. Orishas (Nocchi et al. 2000) creates fascinating blends of North American and Cuban material by sampling *guajeos* (dance ostinatos) from the prerevolutionary period and using them as the basis for rapped vocals (Ex. 13). Instinto, another rap ensemble comprised entirely of women, uses pieces from the 1930s such as the Guillén and Grenet composition "Quirino con su tres" as a means of reinforcing the importance of female performers generally and of Afro-Cuban religions in Cuban culture (West-Durán 2004:28–29).

·   ·   ·   ·   ·

Socialist Cuba has survived the breakup of the Soviet Union, but the transition to fiscal independence has not been easy. Under Soviet influence, the country produced primarily sugar, rum, and cigars, shipping them to the East Bloc in return for manufactured goods. The loss of its former trading partners has left Cuba's economy doubly crippled. Its lack of diversification means that the state can no longer provide items once imported from Eastern Europe. Its isolation in the "new world order" means that forming alternate trading ties has been problematic. As a result, the population has suffered under the U.S. embargo as never before. The government finds itself forced to borrow heavily from European and Asian lenders, raising the level of national debt to dangerous levels.[25] Hurricanes, droughts, and shortages of equipment and materials have combined to reduce earnings from sugar harvests.[26] These structural problems are difficult to overcome quickly, despite new revenue generated through tourism and foreign remittances.

Much of what socialism once stood for in Cuba—equality of income, sacrifice for the common good, the gradual creation of a more humane society—is now in question as the country adopts a mixed economic system. Faith in the revolutionary experiment has faded precisely because, with each passing day, its principles less directly reflect the experiences of the people. Political discourse and everyday reality tend ever more frequently to be at odds. In response, individuals concern themselves more with their own welfare and that of their immediate families, deprioritizing other issues. The revolution politicized life so completely and for so long that many Cubans have reacted by rejecting politics altogether. Those under forty, a majority of the population, express the least interest in socialist ideals. They have no direct experience with the capitalist past and take many of the positive changes of the revolution for granted. Rather than perceiving possibilities for the future under the current system, they recognize mostly limitations and difficulties.

Musicians have been at the forefront of recent economic transformations; because of their ties to the tourist sector and international trade, they have risen to unexpected prominence and are viewed as the embodiment of nascent capitalism (Hernández-Reguant 2004b: 3). Indeed, many dance musicians have generated controversy because of their pretentious lifestyles and the manner in which their compositions appear to celebrate consumerism. More broadly, current debates over artistic policy speak to the issues about how best to adapt socialism to new conditions since the collapse of the Soviet Union. The fact that the government has granted performers greater control over their intellectual property reflects both the country's increasing engagement with the capitalist world and the growing tension between individual and collective rights.

Leonardo Padura Fuentes (Kirk and Padura Fuentes 2001:181) characterizes cultural trends since the 1990s in terms of three primary factors: a general crisis of production in noncommercial sectors, certain increases in freedom of expression, and growing waves of exiles. In terms of music specifically, one might add to this list a heightened fascination with foreign culture and with the commercial potential of artistic expression, as well as the movement of music licensing, sales, and distribution out of the country. The music industry has expanded, but its growth has resulted largely from foreign rather than local government investment. Professional music recording, which had been firmly in national hands, is now increasingly controlled by entrepreneurs from Spain, France, Britain, and the United States. At present, Cuba has no facilities for making compact discs, for instance, and must outsource all such work (Cristóbal Díaz Ayala, pers. comm.).

Musicians have gained and lost in unexpected ways as part of the changes of the last fifteen years. Relative to others, those involved in popular genres have excelled. They are able to perform a wider range of styles, especially those from the United States, with at least the tacit approval of the government. They have greater freedom to critically address social concerns. Possibilities for travel have increased. The most successful performers have actually become a new elite class, capitalist-style superstars in the midst of a country struggling to remain socialist. Yet musicians have lost in certain respects as well. Lesser-known figures suffer the difficulties experienced by all Cubans since the early 1990s: lower standards of living, inadequate salaries, and housing and material shortages. Instruments and other equipment have become scarcer. A government that once supported a wide range of cultural activity regardless of its sales potential now bases decisions on more pragmatic factors. And the social safety net that guaranteed adequate health and retirement care for musicians is largely gone.

The quantity of live music and the number of clubs has increased, though most venues charge entrance fees in dollars. Class disparity is apparent, with wealthier Cubans patronizing music events and the less fortunate excluded. Smaller establishments are often associated with prostitution and other unsavory activities. While perhaps overstated, the following citation by Rafael Rojas draws provocative parallels between Cuba of the 1950s and the present: "In these difficult times we find the resurrection of the cabaret and carnival, of sensuality and hedonism, of the lascivious tourist and the nakedness of the native, of the whorehouse and the lottery. . . . Between the old Cuba and the new, a bridge is visible: the cadaver of the Revolution" (Rojas 1998:134).

None deny the radical changes in cultural production over the past decade, yet some representatives of the Ministry of Culture admit no contradiction between their present policies and those of the past. Alicia Perea, former director of the Instituto Cubano de la Música, has stated that socialism and Communism "are not at odds with commercialism" (Cantor 1997:18). She asserts that socialism signifies "justice in the distribution of riches" but emphasizes the need to generate riches in order to provide them to the public. Perea's views demonstrate a pragmatism that may well prove advantageous in the future. Nevertheless, many issues come to mind that merit further discussion. Is the current dominance of foreign record labels in the Cuban music industry inevitable? Is a revival of the domestic industry possible, and if so, how should it situate itself and its output vis-à-vis international firms? What is the role, if any, of socialist ideology in Cuban music compositions of the new millennium? And what of the countless critiques of capitalist music making that policy makers raised in PCC platform documents for years? How will the country avoid problems related to the influence of consumerism in years to come?

Political tensions with the United States continue to restrict the expansion of commerce, including that of artists. Carlos Varela (1994) succinctly paraphrased the views of nearly all Cubans on this aspect of North American foreign policy in "La política no cabe en la azucarera" with the repeated phrase "fuck your blockade." Far from furthering democracy and respect for human rights, such antagonism serves only to legitimize the socialist government's limitations on political activism and freedom of expression. By the same token, Cuba's government also makes capricious and short-sighted decisions. In the realm of culture, these include its unwillingness until recently to strongly support the projection of Cuban culture into the capitalist world through touring and licensing. Artists and musicians who had long wished to promote themselves could not do so until recently. The state has created additional career opportunities, but they have been driven largely by economic necessity rather than thoughtful consideration. A new set of comprehensive, socialist-friendly guidelines is needed that will allow for individual artistic agency and permit Cuba to remain a vital role in musical production, all the while safeguarding local genres and educational institutions from the negative influences of the marketplace.

Musical Politics
into the New Millennium

> Los maestros nunca enseñan la verdad
> ni los reyes, ni los Mesías,
> los ejércitos no tienen la verdad
> ni las leyes, ni la astrología.
> La verdad de la verdad
> es que nunca es una,
> ni la mía, ni la de él, ni la tuya . . .
>
> Teachers never teach the truth,
> nor do kings or messiahs.
> Armies don't spread the truth,
> nor do laws or astrology.
> The truth about truth
> is that there is never a single version,
> not mine, not his, not yours . . .
>
> CARLOS VARELA, "25 mil mentiras
> sobre la verdad"

It is difficult to foresee a resolution to long-standing tensions between Cuba and the United States in this period of escalating political rhetoric and extremism. Politicians in Washington and Havana show little willingness to compromise. On the contrary, they have converted ideological intransigence into a virtue; their pronouncements have become "mirrors of intolerance" (Rojas 1998:131). Hostility toward Cuba on the part of recent U.S. administrations contradicts their ostensible goal of fostering understanding, dialogue, and political reconciliation. This is especially inappropriate given Cuba's massive troop reductions in recent years and the State Department's own conclusion that it is neither involved in international terrorism nor represents a significant threat (*CUBAInfo* 10, no. 7 [May 21, 1998]: 3). Embargo policy continues to affect access to food and medicine within Cuba, contributing to suffering, illness, and premature death. U.S. leaders seem bent on *imposing* a particular sort of social and political structure on Cuba rather than promoting true pluralism. Cuban American congressman Lincoln Díaz-Balart called in March 2004 for renewed attempts to assassinate Castro and to infiltrate spies into the island disguised as tourists (Sublette 2004:6). He and others overlook the obvious fact that a peaceful transition to democracy cannot develop in a "fortress under siege" (Hernández 2003:20).

With respect to cultural exchange, the position of the U.S. government has also become more extreme. The 1990s witnessed expanding cultural ties under President Clinton; by the end of the decade, tens of thousands of Americans traveled to Cuba every year to take part in art exhibitions, film festivals, music and dance classes, and academic seminars. U.S. scholars conducted work on the island with relative ease and often brought along student groups. Cuban academics and musicians also visited the United States in relatively large numbers, though embargo legislation prohibited them from receiving honoraria in many cases. Even in the mid-1990s, however, the Treasury Department denied visitation visas to many Cuban performers. In some instances, they provided no justification for such decisions. In others, they withheld permission because they believed applicants had unnecessarily close ties with the Cuban government or because their artistic excellence might "cast a favorable light on Cuba's Marxist system" (*CUBAInfo* 10, no. 5 [April 1998]: 4–5)! It is a sorry state of affairs when the U.S. government feels it cannot allow Cuban musicians into the country because they play too well.

Since September 11, 2001, the Office of Foreign Assets Control has restricted travel between Cuba and the United States even more forcefully on the grounds of national security. Its representatives note that Cuba remains (most believe erroneously) on the list of nations that sponsor terrorism. As a result, universities and nonprofit organizations that had sent groups to learn about music, dance, and cultural history in many cases can no longer renew their licenses.[1] The idea that music and the arts might be beneficial for all parties and help foster political détente has disappeared from U.S. foreign policy. Procedures currently required to invite Cuban performers into the United States are so complex, expensive, and time consuming that they have effectively put an end to all such visits.[2] By contrast, artists from Iran, Algeria, Morocco, and other Middle Eastern countries continue to perform in the United States with relative ease; apparently the State Department considers them less of a threat. Cuba may be the only country in the world to be treated in this extreme fashion.

> [Virtually] no Cuban music group has been allowed to enter the United States to perform since November 2003. The United States is systematically denying visas outright, across the board, to all performing artists who live in Cuba. This is ostensibly . . . done on grounds of national security, but the motivation is transparently political. In the process, the right of Americans to hear the music of Cuba's artists and exchange

information with them [has been deemed] insignificant. Cuban artists who have lost performing dates in the U.S. in these last months . . . [include the] Orquesta Aragón, Omara Portuondo, Ibrahim Ferrer, Los Van Van, Jesús "Chucho" Valdés, Los Muñequitos de Matanzas, Maraca y Otra Visión, Carlos Varela, and many more. There are two underlying legal assumptions behind this: (1) that Cuba is a "state-sponsor of terrorism," and (2) that all Cuban artists are "employees or agents of the Cuban government or are members of the Communist party." The first is a complete fabrication; the second is highly questionable as an assertion of fact and is in any case irrelevant to issues of artistic freedom in the United States. (Sublette 2004:4)[3]

Angel Romero, founder of Alula Records, believes that key figures in the State Department are using the veil of heightened national security to promote the agenda of the Cuban American, anti-Castro lobby. He notes that Roger Noriega, current assistant secretary of state for western hemisphere affairs, wrote recently to a group called the Cuban Liberty Council and assured them that "Castro's cash cows will not be grazing through the United States under this administration" (Pfeiffenberger 2004:51). In 2003, both houses of Congress voted to lift the U.S. ban on travel to Cuba, yet the Republican congressional leadership stripped the provision from legislation headed to the White House at the last minute. As of July 2004, executive orders from President Bush have further tightened the parameters of the embargo, forbidding Cubans in the United States from visiting the island more than once every three years and reducing the amount of financial support they may send to family members. These measures have generated significant protest among moderate exiles. They have also prompted Castro to begin taxing remittances heavily before they are distributed to the population, resulting in less economic support for private citizens.

For its part, the Cuban government's sense of insecurity in the face of North American belligerence has increased since the collapse of the Soviet Union; this has not furthered the cause of political freedom. Cuba remains a one-party state whose leadership has never seriously entertained the notion of sharing power with any other group. Most progressive, reform-minded opposition figures are harassed or jailed and eventually forced into exile, as has been the case for decades. Castro arguably acts in what he considers the best interests of the people but in the end makes imperious pronouncements in essentially the same manner that he criticizes in other leaders. Political discussion on the island is severely limited. Mass exoduses since 1994 suggest that the government has lost support among much of the population; individuals who cannot vote for a new commander in chief are instead voting against him with their feet.[4] Benítez-Rojo's "repeating island" has become a reality around the globe, with miniature Cuban communities forming and perpetuating themselves in their own demographic archipelago. It remains to be seen whether a transition to a more democratic Cuba is possible from within that will safeguard the sovereignty of the nation and its liberal social and cultural policies.

Antagonisms between Havana and Washington, D.C., are exacerbated by Miami's community leaders; indeed, Miami's political lobby appears to be the real force behind many of Washington's pronouncements. Businesspeople and wealthier individuals who left the island in the 1960s have every incentive to avoid rapprochement with revolutionaries. If the United States formally recognizes the socialist government and normalizes relations, Cubans in exile will find it virtually impossible to sue for their lost property through the American courts. As one might expect, they are eager to reclaim assets and use every means at their disposal to oppose reconciliation. Anti-socialist discourse in Miami that centers around the need for democratic reforms in Cuba may thus derive more from financial than political motivations. One might add that many Cuban American leaders continue to escalate tensions through their support of violence. A *New York Times* article directly linked the Cuban American National Foundation (CANF) to terrorist activities perpetrated by the Movement of Revolutionary Recovery, to cite one example from 1998 (Ann Louise Bordach and Larry Rohter, "A Bomber's Tale: Taking Aim at Castro," *New York Times,* July 12, 1998, p. 1). Recent years have witnessed an attenuation of ties to terrorists, especially since Mas Canosa's death in 1997, but more conservative factions still support such activity (Townsend 2001). To the extent that the U.S. government tolerates violence linked to the exile community, it damages its own credibility in the eyes of Latin America and the world.

In contrast to Cuba itself, Miami has produced few music figures of national or international stature; a number of star performers live there, but most have settled in the area after making a name for themselves elsewhere (Díaz Ayala 2003b:406). Miami has become a center of commerce and of recording and distributing music but not of artistic effervescence, with a few notable exceptions. On the contrary, some characterize it as culturally impoverished and overly materialistic. Those Cuban Americans who have distinguished themselves as performers occasionally use their popularity as a platform for political critique, as might be expected. Willie Chirino represents the most prominent example, with compositions such as "Memorandum para un tirano," "Nuestro día," "Viva la libertad," and "La jinetera." Local radio stations in Miami also demonstrate an anti-Cuba bias, from Radio

Martí (aired and transmitted primarily to Cuban nationals) to local talk shows and music on WQBA (La Cubanísima, 1140 AM), WXDJ (El Zol, 95.7 FM), and WRTO (Salsa, 98.3 FM). The latter features the duo Los Mikimbín, which writes parodies of songs from Havana.[5] The primary artistic mark Miami has left on the Latin music establishment is the development of the "Miami sound" in the 1980s, a blend of *son* and salsa with rock, funk, and rhythms from the French and British Caribbean. Its primary exponents are Willie Chirino and the Miami Sound Machine.

The Cuban American leadership has attempted to isolate Cuba culturally as well as politically. In the 1980s, they blacklisted artists who visited the island such as Rubén Blades and Oscar de León (Manuel 1987:169). They have also barred Latin Americans visiting Cuba from participation in Miami's Calle Ocho Festival. Such was the case with Brazilian singer Denise de Kalafe in 1989;[6] Puerto Rican Andy Montañez received similar treatment in the 1990s for hugging Silvio Rodríguez in public (Correa 1997). Cuban American leaders throughout the United States have used their economic clout to discourage entrepreneurs and even universities from contracting Cuban musicians. They have also used bomb threats, and in some cases actual bombings, in order to scare club owners for the same purpose. Achy Obejas 1996:19 provides information on incidents of this nature in 1990s Chicago involving the local Cuban American Chamber of Commerce. Asked how he characterized the antagonistic international context in 1998, Chucho Valdés said that planning U.S. tours in the face of Cuban American opposition was "like an Alfred Hitchcock movie. It's pure suspense—da-da-da-dum. You either have to laugh or cry" (Cantor 1998b: 14).

Of course, the intimidation of Cuban musicians has been most severe in Miami. Many CANF leaders consider any musician living on the island a Castro supporter who should be blacklisted. To Ned Sublette, a key strategy of the Cuban American Right has been to control the image of socialist Cuba in this country, "which means restricting Americans' ability to have direct contact with . . . its musicians" (Sublette 2004:10). Performers who have suffered harassment in Miami, aside from those mentioned above, include jazz pianist Gonzalo Rubalcaba and aging *vedette* Rosita Fornés (Obejas 1996). The case of Fornés is especially tragic, given that she chose to stay in Cuba following the revolution but faced many professional difficulties there. After decades of obscurity, she received an invitation to perform in Miami's Centro Vasco in July of 1996 but canceled after unknown assailants firebombed the club in the middle of the night.[7] In 1999, Los Van Van changed their Miami performance venue as well after the city's mayor, Joe Carollo, pressured the James L. Knight Center into canceling their contract.

The concert eventually took place in the Miami Arena on October 11, despite a picket line of angry demonstrators, only because organizer Debbie Ohanian and the ACLU threatened to sue the city on First Amendment grounds if it stood in the way (see www.salsapower.com/concerts/vvcontroversy .htm).

Through the late 1990s, Miami radio stations could not play music by Cuban nationals without risking repercussions. Reuters news service reported in 1997 that WRTO, known at the time as La Nueva Tropical, attempted in March to become the first local station to play *timba*, featuring music by Issac Delgado, Manolín, and others. Station director Zummy Oro reported strong interest in the repertoire on the part of younger listeners, especially those recently arrived from Cuba and other Latin American countries. According to the report, "anti-Castro Spanish-language radio stations immediately went on the offensive." Callers phoned in to denounce the move. Some described the airing of such music as a plot devised by Castro to divide the exile community. Advertisers cancelled their sponsorship. On Monday, March 24, the station had to be evacuated because of a bomb threat; it turned out to be a hoax, but owners chose to stop broadcasting songs by Cuban nationals for some time thereafter. Manager Luis Díaz Albertini noted the absurdity of the event in its aftermath. "This is the United States and a democracy, but apparently some people in Miami don't feel like that. What happened [here] is what happens every day in Cuba. That's the irony."[8]

Later the same year, controversy arose in Miami over a conference organized by a European-owned agency known as MIDEM. Based in Cannes, France, MIDEM brings together representatives from all facets of the music business world. During the day, its annual conferences include panels devoted to licensing, copyright, distribution, sales trends, and other topics. Later, participants attend marathon musical performances, choosing between multiple stages and venues. In 1997, MIDEM representatives decided to create a new event called MIDEM-Americas devoted exclusively to music from North and South America. They selected Miami as the ideal site for this meeting because of the city's key position between the Spanish- and English-speaking Americas and because of the many music producers and distributors in the area (Díaz Ayala 1999). MIDEM-Americas took place in Miami in 1997, 1998, and 1999 before being suspended. Unfortunately, those organizing the conference had little understanding of local politics in Miami or the historical importance of Cubans in the development of the Latin music industry. Ignoring older performers and executives living in the area, they chose instead to invite many Cubans from the island to participate. As the latter had recently signed contracts with European distributors and copyright agencies, they held more interest for conference organizers.

As we have seen, CANF representatives invariably use their influence to discourage performances by Cuban nationals within the United States. During the first MIDEM event, their opposition, in combination with legal difficulties surrounding the processing of visas, resulted in the cancellation of all such acts. In the following year, however, MIDEM organizers managed to include appearances by Compay Segundo, Chucho Valdés, Omara Portuondo, and others. This resulted in angry protests by exiles, despite the fact that Cuban exiles (Albita, Paquito D'Rivera, etc.) had also been invited to perform. The third and final year, organizers avoided such antagonism by focusing more exclusively on North American music and on genres from the French and British Caribbean (Díaz Ayala 1999).

The decision to suspend MIDEM-Americas events after 1999 seems to have resulted from the protests of Cuban Americans. Many Miami residents expressed satisfaction with the decision even though it resulted in the loss of tens of millions of dollars in expected annual revenues for local merchants. When Peggy McKinley, a member of the Dade County business community, suggested that the policy of ostracizing Cuban performers be changed so that Miami could continue to attract MIDEM to the area, CANF spokesperson Ninoska Pérez and others excoriated her and marginalized her from subsequent decisions on Miami's city council (*CUBAInfo* 9, no. 3 [October 2, 1997]: 11). This controversial action led to the publication of numerous editorials in south Florida newspapers, including one by singer Gloria Estefan. To her credit, Estefan called for the depoliticization of Miami's cultural policy and denounced what she considered the unfair treatment of McKinley by CANF. For this she, too, was denounced, despite her family's impeccable anti-Castro credentials (her father worked prior to the revolution as a bodyguard for Fulgencio Batista). Estefan's letter included the following:

> Let me state clearly that I am staunchly anti-communist. I would not support any system of government that infringes on the rights of people, especially the right to freedom of expression. That is why I feel compelled to express my dismay at the expulsion of Peggi McKinley . . . simply for stating her opinion. As a Cuban American, I am embarrassed that non-Cubans might think that we are all narrow of mind. I cannot imagine how we could explain to the people of Cuba, who have suffered so much oppression, that the very freedoms that they so desperately desire and deserve are being annihilated in their name. (*Miami Herald*, August 31, 1997, p. L03)

Over time, the increasingly large sums of money generated from the international sale, broadcasting, and staging of Cuban music have led to an environment of greater tolerance, even in Miami. In May 1998, Issac Delgado made history by staging the first concert of *timba* there (Perna 2001:95). Various factions protested vigorously, to be sure, but the show attracted a sizeable audience. Since then, NG La Banda, Los Van Van, and others have played in Miami, alongside recent defectors such as Manolín. Whereas in the mid-1990s Miami residents had few means of listening to modern Cuban artists, much of their music now appears on local radio play lists. Music stores along the Calle Ocho stock releases by *nueva trova* singers and Cuban rappers and rockers, even when the recordings appear on the Cuban state label EGREM and must be purchased directly from it through a third country. Latin dance bands in Miami and elsewhere are beginning to incorporate stylistic influences from Cuban *timba* as well.

Nowhere are such changes more evident than in discourse surrounding the Latin Grammy awards of 2001. Cities with large Latino populations typically lobby to have the event held in their area owing to the revenues and publicity it generates. Miami represented an exception until recently, however, since hosting the Latin Grammys usually entailed inviting Cuban nationals. Beginning in February 2001, Mas Canosa's son Jorge Mas Santos broke with conservative ranks within the CANF and, together with mayor Alex Penelas, encouraged the Grammy committee to consider Miami as a host site (Rosenberg 2001:1B). Horacio García, Elpidio Núñez, Diego Suárez, and other old-guard CANF members protested Jorge Mas's position openly in local newspapers; some of them even staged public resignations from the organization. As many as three conservative Cuban American groups—CANF, Brothers to the Rescue, and the Democracia Movement—all planned concurrent street demonstrations against the Grammys, had they been held in Miami (Viglucci 2001). Committee chair Michael Greene eventually rejected the proposed Miami site in favor of Los Angeles.[9]

Jorge Mas Santos contends that his decision to support the hosting of the Grammys was appropriate. "The majority of the community [supported] the Latin Grammys coming here. We made great strides trying to dispel the stereotype of Miami as intolerant and disrespectful of the rights of others" (Viglucci 2001:1B). Some believe that the Elián González controversy of 2000 may have contributed to the spirit of tolerance now espoused by Jorge Mas and others. Miami's unwavering position against Elián's repatriation struck many in the United States as extreme, leading to a decrease in support for Cuban Americans' broader political agenda. This in turn increased concern on the part of the CANF for revising its national image and made its leadership more willing to compromise on issues related to freedom of expression. In the end, the Latin Grammys finally came to Miami in 2003. But just as the exile community appeared to have accepted the idea that Cuban nationals would take part, the Bush administration denied visas to all of them. Artists failing to appear for this reason included Grammy nominees Juan Formell, Muñequitos de Matanzas director Diosdado Ramos, singer Ibrahim Ferrer, and classical conductor Zenaida Romeu (Sokol 2003).

Despite the difficulties faced daily by Cubans on the island—the ongoing U.S. embargo, food and material shortages, momentous economic difficulties—musical performance has survived and flourished in recent years. At present, approximately 13,000 professional musicians live in Cuba, more than 1 for every 900 citizens (Perna 2001:84). This represents an astounding increase of approximately 50 percent over levels that existed in the 1980s when the country's economy was stronger (Giro 1986:9). Cristóbal Díaz Ayala (2003b: 401) suggests that the current numbers are much higher than in other Latin American countries. By way of comparison, he mentions that Cali, Colombia, during the height of its salsa craze in the 1980s could only boast 1 professional musician for every 2,850 inhabitants. Even the American Federation of Musicians Local 802, representing all of New York City's roughly 9 million inhabitants, has only about 10,000 members (Sublette 2004a:8). Alberto Faya characterizes the last ten years as "one of the most musically fecund moments for our country (Faya et al. 1996:74), while John Kirk and Leonardo Padura Fuentes (2001:185) similarly describe Cuba as experiencing "a period of special creative effervescence. . . . We . . . need to recognize that today many people in the cultural sector are expressing themselves with greater depth within the space of 'conditional freedom' that they have been winning." Waldo Leyva adds that recent artistic efforts demonstrate "a new sort of introspection, a turning inwards and also abroad" that has made Cuban culture "more complex" and "more transcendent" (Hernández 2002:74).

Under Minister Abel Prieto, campaigns of cultural enrichment continue in an attempt to compensate for the island's material shortages. The government uses funds from commercial music sales to fund noncommercial initiatives. In 2001, it opened fifteen new institutes across the island to train art instructors in dance, theater, and music. According to a recent broadcast on Radio Habana Cuba, more than 2,300 individuals have already graduated from them, and more than 25,000 youth take part in the arts instruction they help support.[10] Media executives have created television shows such as *University for All* that feature programming on subjects ranging from foreign languages and art to history, comparative religion, and geography (Barthélémy 2001). These efforts demonstrate the state's commitment to education and the arts. Cuba continues to be a focal point of music making, with state support for international festivals of jazz, pan-Caribbean, and electro-acoustic music. They represent an amazing achievement in a country where most citizens lack the money to purchase toilet paper, hand soap, and toothpaste. By the same token, recent years have witnessed declines in book production and in university enrollment. The former problem derives from shortages of paper, the latter from the disillusionment of a younger generation that fails to see education as the road to success in the context of the new tourist-oriented economy (Barthélémy 2001).

One reason that music making in Cuba continues to be so prominent is because performing and listening to it is a decidedly enjoyable experience, and enjoyable experiences have been in short supply. Music serves a crucial role as a vehicle for laughter and relaxation, a means of forgetting about the problems of everyday life for a time or at least making light of them. As Quintero Rivera has noted (1998:13), the study of Caribbean music necessarily involves reflection on the happiness that it has brought the world and not merely the difficult contexts in which it emerges. Perhaps I have not emphasized enough the pleasure that Cuban music holds for its fans, myself included. Cubans on the whole are tremendously gifted dancers, singers, and musicians and have an amazing capacity for transcending difficulties. Within our larger discussion of bomb threats, terrorism, and political squabbles, we must keep in mind that one of music's roles is to provide badly needed relief from such concerns.

Socialist states, and especially those founded in developing countries, face tremendous obstacles. Despite the best of intentions and even without the aggressive interference from the United States to which Cuba has been subjected, they often fail to create more utopian societies. Their intense regulation or elimination of private enterprise stifles individual initiative. Their goal of voluntary participation in grandiose social projects often transforms itself over time into hierarchical authoritarianism in which the masses have little voice. Yet even those who fault revolutionary Cuba in these and other ways generally admit that something unique has happened there. The Cuban Revolution was not superficial or partial but rather involved a fundamental reorientation of society. The new government successfully challenged the United States' economic penetration and neoimperialist maneuverings in a decisive fashion, becoming the first Latin American country to do so (Dumont 1970:244). Dissident Elizardo Sánchez believes that Castro, for all of his faults, has proven himself one of the most intelligent and charismatic politicians of the twentieth century and a true social reformer (Balaban et al. 1998:17). By struggling to address social inequality, hunger, poverty, illiteracy, and exploitation, the revolutionary leadership has drawn attention to problems that capitalist liberal democracies have not adequately resolved (Verdery 1996:4).

Critics of Cuba emphasize that the government rarely permits discussion of the failings of state socialism or mentions other political and economic alternatives. While they make a valid point, these authors often overlook the fact that the failings of capitalism often fail to appear in the United States media. The late twentieth and early twenty-first centuries have given rise to what McLaren and Pinkney-Pastrana (2001:208) describe as a "corporate priesthood" dominating world markets. Large businesses based primarily in the United States and Europe control enormous assets and have converted the Nike "swoosh" and the golden arches into more common and more powerful symbols than the flags of entire countries. Recent documentaries such as *The Corporation* describe the rapacious tactics many businesses employ, their frequently exploitative labor practices (especially in developing countries), their disregard at various times for public safety, the extent to which their actions may degrade the environment, and the difficulty of holding them legally accountable for such actions.[11] Commentary by W. E. B. DuBois from the 1950s about the dominance of business interests in the United States still applies today.

> This Administration is dominated and directed by wealth and for the accumulation of wealth. It runs smoothly like a well-organized industry and should do so because industry runs it for the benefit of industry. Corporate wealth profits as never before in our history. We turn over the national resources to private profit and have few funds left for education, health, or housing. . . . We let men take wealth which is not theirs; if the seizure is "legal" we call it high profits. . . . We want money in vast amounts, no matter how we get it. So we have it, and what then? (DuBois 2002: n.p.)

Though an undeniably successful economic system, there is a moral emptiness associated with much modern capitalism, especially in the United States. As in Marx's time, one is struck with the disparity between the abundance made possible by mass production and the marginalization of millions from the American dream. And it is amazing to note the widespread indifference to such disparities. I myself have been working for some time in the Philadelphia area, a region where social inequalities are marked. It shames me to live in the wealthiest country in the world and yet to work at a university surrounded by a ghetto that stretches for miles in all directions. Philadelphia is a city plagued by dysfunctional public schools, crime, a crumbling infrastructure, drug problems, and high indexes of murder, rape, and other violence. By contrast, suburbs only ten or fifteen miles away boast some of the best public schools and highest property values in the Northeast. One might expect indifference to this situation in a developing country, but not in the United States. With more attention devoted to such problems, we could do much to eliminate them.

I confess that I do not support many policies of the current Cuban government. The Ministry of Culture and related institutions have hampered my attempts to conduct research over the past eight years more than they have facilitated them. I have had books confiscated, handwritten notes to myself pored over in airports by overzealous customs officials, research visas and requests for interviews denied, and basic statistical information on Cuban music making withheld gratuitously, to mention only a few problems. By the same token, I continue to believe that U.S. policy toward Cuba is unjust and counterproductive. More important, it seems hypocritical to attack Cuban domestic or foreign policy without also recognizing the injustice of policies championed in Washington, D.C. Castro is a dictator who has made decisions with extremely unpleasant consequences for the Cuban people in many cases. But the current U.S. administration appears to care little for social justice and has displayed both a frightening degree of arrogance in international affairs and a willingness to resort to violence prematurely. As a result, it has lost much of the moral high ground it may have had from which to criticize Cuba.

In the final analysis, the significance of the Cuban Revolution lies in its concern for national sovereignty and for the physical and spiritual well-being of the disenfranchised. Its one-party politics is largely discredited, yet its fundamental principles challenge other nations to share wealth more equally and to provide additional educational and artistic opportunities to their citizens. Moreover, many of the leadership's socialist-derived critiques of the international community remain applicable. Capitalism is a flawed system that often exploits at the same time it creates economic opportunity. And the issue is not only that it creates inequality but that the material goods and services it generates have come to hold too predominant a position in the mindset of those influenced by it (Dupré 1983:282). Marxism's critique of materialism and concern for working people carries a powerful message in this sense.

Much of the art from Cuba embodies such values, demonstrating a love of humanity, a concern for the common welfare, and a desire to improve society. And many of its performers' achievements derive from opportunities created on the basis of such values. The revolution deserves ongoing recognition for this, for reminding us of our obligations to one another and for attempting to enrich the human experience through support of the arts. Of course, Cuban revolutionary culture also merits recognition because it transcends socialist rhetoric. As the expression of individuals from many different backgrounds, it maintains a connection to personal concerns that political discourse often lacks. Performers are able to react to changing circumstances quickly with new songs and styles of music that underscore the complexities of their lives. Now more than ever, the arts represent a quasi-independent realm of commentary in dialogue with the state. These creations, representing varied reactions to a unique environment, help provide an insightful and nuanced view of the revolutionary experience.

Appendix

Publications on Music from Revolutionary Cuba

Although not exhaustive, the following list represents a fair sampling of the existing works (books and articles at least forty pages long) about Cuban music that were published in Cuba or written by Cubans living on the island between 1960 and the present. It also includes some reeditions of material published before 1959 that cultural leaders chose to make available again. The publications are grouped by decade to reveal the exponential increase in musicological research over time. (For works cited in the notes, please refer to the separate bibliography on pages 317–39.)

1960s

Ardévol, José. 1966. *Música y revolución*. Havana: UNEAC.
———. 1969. *Introducción a Cuba: La música*. Havana: Instituto del Libro.
Carpentier, Alejo. [1946] 1961. *La música en Cuba*. Havana: Editorial Letras Cubanas.
Castillo Faílde, Osvaldo. 1964. *Miguel Faílde: Creador musical del danzón*. Havana: Oficina del Historiador de la Ciudad.
Hallorans, A. O. [1882] 1963. *Guarachas cubanas: Curiosa recopilación desde las más antiguas hasta las más modernas*. Havana: no publisher.
Hernández Balaguer, Pablo. 1961. *Catálogo de música de los archivos de la Catedral de Santiago de Cuba y del Museo Bacardí*. Havana: Biblioteca Nacional José Martí.
———. 1964. *Breve historia de la música cubana*. Havana: Editora del Consejo Nacional de Universidades, Universidad de Oriente.
Lapique Becali, Zoila. 1963. *Catalogación y clasificación de la música cubana*. Havana: Biblioteca Nacional José Martí.
León, Argeliers. 1964. *Música folklórica cubana*. Havana: Biblioteca Nacional José Martí.
Ortiz, Fernando. [1950] 1965. *La africanía de la música folklórica de Cuba*. Havana: Universidad Central de las Villas.

Rodríguez Domínguez, Ezequiel. 1967. *Iconografía del danzón.* Havana: Consejo Nacional de Cultura.

Vázquez Millares, Ángel. 1964. *Carnaval de La Habana: Desarrollo histórico.* Havana: Biblioteca Nacional José Martí.

———. 1966. *Iconografía de la trova: Creadores e intérpretes.*

1970S

Aguirre, Mirta. 1975. *La lírica castellana hasta los siglos de oro: Sus orígenes al siglo XVI.* Havana: Editorial Arte y Literatura.

Alarco, Rosa. 1979. *Alfonso de Silva.* Havana: Casa de las Américas.

Biblioteca Nacional José Martí. 1972. *Bibliografía de música latinoamericana: Integrada con fichas del catálogo formado por la Biblioteca Nacional "José Martí," la Biblioteca Central "Rubén Martínez Villena" de la Universidad de La Habana y la Biblioteca "José Antonio Echeverría" de la Casa de las Américas.* Havana: Biblioteca Nacional José Martí.

Cañizares, Dulcila. 1978. *Gonzalo Roig.* Havana: Editorial Letras Cubanas.

Carpentier, Alejo. [1946] 1979. *La música en Cuba.* Havana: Editorial Letras Cubanas.

———. 1975. *América latina en su música.* Havana: UNESCO.

Chao Carbonero, Graciela. 1979a. *Bailes yorubas en Cuba: Guía de estudio.* Havana: Editorial Pueblo y Educación.

———. 1979b. *Folklore cubano I, II, III, IV: Guía de estudio.* Havana: Editorial Pueblo y Educación.

Feijóo, Samuel. 1975. *Signos 17: Música de Cuba.* December. Santa Clara: Consejo Nacional de Cultura.

Fernández, María Antonia. 1974. *Bailes populares cubanos.* Buenos Aires: Gráfica Devoto.

García Caturla, Alejandro. 1978. *Correspondencia.* Havana: Editorial Letras Cubanas.

Giro, Radamés, and Mario Romeu. 1974. *Himno nacional cubano.* Havana: Editorial Pueblo y Educación.

Gómez, Zoila. 1977. *Amadeo Roldán.* Havana: Editorial Arte y Literatura.

Henríquez, Antonieta. 1978. *Adiestramiento musical.* Havana: Editorial Orbe.

Lapique Becali, Zoila. 1979. *Música colonial cubana, tomo 1 (1812–1902).* Havana: Editorial Letras Cubanas.

León, Argeliers. [1964] 1974. *Del canto y el tiempo.* Havana: Editorial Letras Cubanas.

Linares, María Teresa. 1970. *La música popular.* Havana: Instituto del Libro.

———. 1974. *La música y el pueblo.* Havana: Editorial Pueblo y Educación.

Martín, Edgardo. 1971. *Panorama histórica de la música cubana.* Havana: Cuadernos CEU, Universidad de la Habana.

Rodríguez Domínguez, Ezequiel. 1978. *Trío Matamoros: Treinta y cinco años de música popular.* Havana: Editorial Arte y Literatura.

Sánchez, Marucha. 1979. *Memoria de la Orquesta Filarmónica de La Habana, 1924–1959.* Havana: Editorial Orbe.

Vázquez Rodríguez, Rosa Elena. 1979. *La práctica musical de la población negra en Perú: La danza de los negritos de El Carmen.* Havana: Casa de las Américas.

1980s

Acosta, Leonardo. 1982. *Música y descolonización.* Mexico City: Presencia Latinoamericana.

———. 1983. *Del tambor al sintetizador.* Havana: Editorial Letras Cubanas.

Acosta, Leonardo, and Jorge Gómez. 1981. *Canciones de la nueva trova.* Havana: Editorial Letras Cubanas.

Alén, Olavo. 1986. *La música de las sociedades de tumba francesa en Cuba.* Havana: Casa de las Américas.

Alén Pérez, Alberto. 1986. *Diagnosticar la musicalidad.* Havana: Casa de las Américas.

Barnet, Miguel. 1983. *La fuente viva.* Havana: Editorial Letras Cubanas.

Brouwer, Leo. 1989. *La música, lo cubano y la innovación.* Havana: Editorial Letras Cubanas.

Carpentier, Alejo. [1946] 1988. *La música en Cuba.* Havana: Editorial Letras Cubanas.

———. 1980. *Ese músico que llevo adentro.* 3 vols. Havana: Editorial Letras Cubanas.

Casanova Oliva, Ana Victoria. 1988. *Problemática organológica cubana: Crítica a la sistemática de los instrumentos musicales.* Havana: Casa de las Américas.

———. 1989. *Ciego de Ávila: Identidad musical cubana y caribeña.* Havana: CIDMUC.

Contreras, Félix. 1989. *Porque tiene filin.* Santiago de Cuba: Editorial Oriente.

Editorial Orbe. 1981. *Cancionero Orbe: Éxitos nacionales e internacionales.* Havana: Editorial Orbe.

Eli Rodríguez, Victoria. 1989. *Haciendo música cubana.* Havana: Editorial Pueblo y Educación.

Esquenazi Pérez, Martha. 1980. *Atlas de las expresiones de nuestra música popular tradicional: Quinquenio 1980–85.* Havana: no publisher.

Feijoó, Samuel. 1986. *El son cubano: Poesía general.* Havana: Editorial Letras Cubanas.

Fernández Valdés, Olga. 1984. *A pura guitarra y tambor.* Santiago de Cuba: Editorial Oriente.

Giro, Radamés. 1986. *Leo Brouwer y la guitarra en Cuba.* Havana: Editorial Letras Cubanas.

Gloria, Antolitia. 1984. *Cuba: Dos siglos de música.* Havana: Editorial Letras Cubanas.

Gómez, Zoila. 1986. *La actividad presupuestada y autofinanciada en la música cubana.* Havana: no publisher.

Gramatges, Harold. 1983. *Presencia de la revolución en la música cubana*. Havana: Editorial Letras Cubanas.

Guanche, Jesús. 1983. *Procesos etnoculturales de Cuba*. Havana: Editorial Letras Cubanas.

Hernández, Erena. 1986. *La música en persona*. Havana: Editorial Letras Cubanas.

Hernández Balaguer, Pablo. 1986. *El más antiguo documento de la música cubana y otros ensayos*. Havana: Editorial Letras Cubanas.

Ignaza, Diana. 1982. *El estudio del arte negro en Fernando Ortiz*. Havana: Instituto del Libro.

Isidrón del Valle, Aldo. 1982. *Dos estilos y un cantar: El Indio Naborí y Chanito Isidrón*. Havana: Arte y Letras.

Lamerán, Sara. 1982. *El vestuario y su importancia en la danza*. Havana: Editorial Pueblo y Educación.

León, Argeliers. [1964] 1984. *Del canto y el tiempo*. Havana: Editorial Letras Cubanas.

Linares, María Teresa. [1974] 1985. *La música y el pueblo*. Havana: Editorial Pueblo y Educación.

López, Oscar Luis. 1981. *La radio en Cuba: Estudio de su desarrollo en la sociedad neocolonial*. Havana: Editorial Letras Cubanas.

———. 1982. *Luis Casas Romero*. Havana: UNEAC.

Martínez, Orlando. 1989. *Ernesto Lecuona*. Havana: UNEAC.

Martínez-Malo, Aldo. 1988. *Del bardo que te canta*. Havana: Editorial Letras Cubanas.

Mateo Palmer, Margarita. 1988. *Rita la única*. Havana: Editorial Abril.

Millet, José, and Rafael Brea. 1989. *Grupos folklóricos de Santiago de Cuba*. Santiago de Cuba: Editorial Oriente.

Ministerio de Cultura, ed. 1981. *IV jornada de música contemporanea: En homenaje al XX aniversario de la Campaña de Alfabetización*. Havana: Ministerio de Cultura.

———. 1982. *La cultura en Cuba socialista*. Havana: Editorial Arte y Letras.

———. 1984. *Banda Nacional de Conciertos: 85 aniversario, 1899–1984; apuntes históricos, agrupación nacional de conciertos*. Havana: Ministry of Culture.

Muguercia, Alberto. 1985. *Algo de la trova en Santiago*. Serie Nuestros Autores, no. 3. Havana: Biblioteca Nacional José Martí.

Ordaz Caballero, Guadalupe. 1982. *Música en América: Orientaciones metodológicas*. Havana: Universidad de La Habana.

Orovio, Helio. 1981. *Diccionario de la música cubana: Biográfico y técnico*. Havana: Editorial Letras Cubanas.

Ortiz, Fernando. [1935] 1984. *La clave xilofónica de la música cubana: Ensayo etnográfico*. Havana: Editorial Letras Cubanas.

———. [1951] 1981. *Los bailes y el teatro de los negros en el folklore de Cuba*. Havana: Editorial Letras Cubanas.

Palacios García, Eliseo. 1987. *Catálogo de música popular cubana*. Havana: Editorial Pueblo y Educación.

Pérez Fernández, Rolando Antonio. 1986. *La binarización de los ritmos ternarios africanos en la América Latina.* Havana: Casa de las Américas.

Pérez Rodríguez, Nancy. 1982. *El cabildo carabalí isuama.* Santiago de Cuba: Editorial Oriente.

———. 1988. *El carnaval santiaguero.* 2 vols. Santiago de Cuba: Editorial Oriente.

Pola, José A. 1989. *Entrevistas: Temas relacionados con la cultura.* Havana: Pablo de la Torriente.

Puebla, Carlos. 1984. *Hablar por hablar.* Havana: UNEAC.

Ramírez, Serafín. [1891] 1983. *La Habana artística: Apuntes para una historia.* Havana: Editorial Letras Cubanas.

Ramos Blanco, Georgina. 1989. *Fundamentos teóricos de la música.* Havana: Literatura Musical Pedagógica.

Rodríguez Musso, Osvaldo. 1986. *La nueva canción chilena.* Havana: Casa de las Américas.

Sánchez de Fuentes, Eduardo. [1923] 1984. *El folk-lor en la música cubana.* Havana: Imprenta "El Siglo XX."

Suco Campos, Idalberto. 1982. *La música en el complejo cultural del walagallo en Nicaragua.* Havana: Casa de las Américas.

Toledo, Armando. 1981. *Presencia y vigencia de Brindis de Salas.* Havana: Editorial Letras Cubanas.

Valdés, Carmen. 1984. *La música que nos rodea.* Havana: Editorial Arte y Literatura.

Valdés Cantero, Alicia. 1986a. *La distribución de la población de músicos y su planificación territorial.* Havana: CIDMUC.

———. 1986b. *El músico en Cuba: Ubicación social y situación laboral en el período 1939–1946.* Havana: Editorial Pueblo y Educación.

———. 1987. *Un estudio sociodemográfico: La Orquesta Sinfónica Nacional.* Havana: Ministerio de Cultura.

———. 1988a. *Diagnóstico del Coro Nacional.* Havana: Ministerio de Cultura.

———. 1988b. *Formell en tres tiempos (1965–1988).* Havana: Ministerio de Cultura.

———. 1989. *Viajera del tiempo: Marta Valdés.* Havana: Ediciones Unión.

Valdés Pérez, Dinorah. 1982. *Historia y apreciación de la música y el teatro.* Havana: Editorial Pueblo y Educación.

Valencia Chacón, Américo. 1982. *El siku altiplano.* Havana: Casa de las Américas.

Vinueza, María Elena. 1987. *Estudios musicológicos, provincia Matanzas.* Havana: CIDMUC.

———. 1988. *Presencia arará en la música folclórica de Matanzas.* Havana: Editorial Letras Cubanas.

1990s

Acosta, Leonardo. 1991. *Elige tú que canto yo.* Havana: Editorial Letras Cubanas.

Aguilar Cabelo, Juan Carlos, and Alberto Fernández Miranda. 1996. *Tropicana de Cuba.* Havana: Visual América.

Alén, Olavo. 1995. *De lo afrocubano a la salsa: Géneros musicales de Cuba*. Havana: Ediciones Artex.

Armas Rigal, Nieves. 1991. *Los bailes de las sociedades de tumba francesa*. Havana: Editorial Pueblo y Educación.

Batista Meneses, Alberto, et al. 1992. *Música cubana: Panfletos*. Havana: Instituto Cubano del Libro.

Bernal Echemendía, Eduardo. 1994. *Resonancia de la trova espirituana*. Santi Spiritus, Cuba: Ediciones Luminaria.

———. 1999. *Razones de la ciudad que canta*. Santi Spiritus, Cuba: Ediciones Luminaria.

Bode Hernández, Germán. 1997. *Décimas rescatadas del aire y del olvido: Estudio y selección de 140 décimas cubanas improvisadas (1940–1944)*. Havana: Fundación Fernando Ortiz.

Cañizares, Dulcila. 1992. *La trova tradicional cubana*. Havana: Editorial Letras Cubanas.

———. 1993. *La música sacra en Cuba*. Havana: Editorial Letras Cubanas.

———. 1999. *Gonzalo Roig: Hombre y creador*. Havana: Editorial Letras Cubanas.

Carpentier, Alejo. 1994. *Temas de la lira y el bongó*. Havana: Editorial Letras Cubanas.

Casademunt, Tomàs. 1995. *Son de Cuba*. Barcelona: Focal Ediciones.

Castellanos, Ernesto Juan. 1997. *Los Beatles en Cuba: Un viaje mágico y misterioso*. Havana: Ediciones Unión.

Castro Aniyar, Daniel. 1995. *El entendimiento: Historia y significación de la música indígena del Lago Maracaibo*. Havana: Casa de las Américas.

Causas, Víctor, and Luis Nogueras. 1993. *Silvio: Que levante la mano la guitarra*. Havana: Editorial Letras Cubanas.

Centro de Investigación Juan Marinello. 1999. *Cultura tradicional cubana*. Havana: Centro de Antropología.

Contreras, Félix. 1999. *La música cubana: Una cuestión personal*. Havana: Ediciones Unión.

de León, Carmela. 1990. *Sindo Garay: Memorias de un trovador*. Havana: Editorial Letras Cubanas.

Depestre, Leonardo. 1990. *Cuatro músicos de una villa*. Havana: Editorial Letras Cubanas.

Díaz Pérez, Clara. 1993. *Silvio Rodríguez*. Havana: Editorial Letras Cubanas.

———. 1994a. *Pablo Milanés: Con luz propia*. Nafarroa-Navarra, Spain: Txalaparta.

———. 1994b. *Sobre la guitarra, la voz: Una historia de la nueva trova cubana*. Havana: Editorial Letras Cubanas.

———. 1995a. *De Cuba, soy hijo: Correspondencia cruzada de Gonzalo Roig*. Havana: Editorial Letras Cubanas.

———. 1995b. *Silvio Rodríguez: Hay quien precisa*. Madrid: Música Mundana.

Eli Rodríguez, Victoria, et al. 1997. *Instrumentos de la música folklórica-popular de Cuba*. 2 vols. Havana: Editorial de Ciencias Sociales (CIDMUC).

Escudero Suástegui, Miriam. 1998. *El archivo de música de la iglesia habanera de La Merced: Estudio y catálogo.* Havana: Casa de las Américas.

Fajardo, Ramón. 1993. *Rita Montaner.* Havana: Editorial Letras Cubanas.

Garriga, Silvana, ed. 1999. *Mamá, yo quiero saber. . . : Entrevistas a músicos cubanos.* Havana: Editorial Letras Cubanas.

Giro, Radamés. 1990. *Heitor Villa-Lobos: Una sensibilidad americana.* Havana: UNEAC.

―――. 1992. *Nicolás Guillén en la música cubana.* Havana: Editorial Letras Cubanas.

―――. 1993. *El mambo.* Havana: Editorial Letras Cubanas.

―――. 1997. *Visión panorámica de la guitarra en Cuba.* Havana: Editorial Letras Cubanas.

―――. 1998. *El filin: César Portillo de la Luz.* Madrid: Fundación Autor.

―――, ed. 1996. *Panorama de la música popular cubana.* Havana: Editorial Letras Cubanas.

Giro, Radamés, and Harold Gramatges. 1997. *Presencia de la revolución en la música cubana.* Havana: Editorial Letras Cubanas.

Gómez Cairo, Jesús. 1995. *El arte musical de Ernesto Lecuona.* Madrid: SGAE.

Gómez García, Zoila, and Victoria Eli Rodríguez. 1995. *Música latinoamericana y caribeña.* Havana: Editorial Pueblo y Educación.

Henríquez, Antonieta. 1998. *Alejandro García Caturla.* Havana: Ediciones Unión.

Lam, Rafael. 1997. *Tropicana: Un paraiso bajo las estrellas.* Havana: Editorial José Martí.

Linares Savio, María Teresa. 1997. *Décimas rescatadas del aire y del olvido: Estudio y selección de 140 décimas cubanas improvisadas (1940–1944).* Havana: Fundación Fernándo Ortiz.

―――. 1999. *El punto cubano.* Santiago de Cuba: Editorial Oriente.

Linares Savio, María Teresa, and Faustino Núñez. 1998. *La música entre Cuba y España.* Madrid: Fundación Autor.

Londoño Fernández, María Eugenia. 1993. *La música en la comunidad indígena Ebera-Chamí de Cristianía.* Havana: Casa de las Américas.

Loyola Fernández, José. 1992. *Boleros de oro: Cancionero.* Havana: UNEAC.

―――. 1996. *En ritmo de bolero: El bolero en la música bailable cubana.* Río Piedras, Puerto Rico: Ediciones Huracán.

Martín, Tamara. 1991. *Música coral.* Havana: Editorial Pueblo y Educación.

Martínez, Mayra. 1993. *Cubanos en la música.* Havana: Editorial Letras Cubanas.

Melián, Ramón, and Georgina Arango. 1990. *Música, revolución y dependencia.* Havana: Casa de las Américas.

Melis Gras, Hilda. 1991. *Acerca de la literatura pianística cubana del siglo XIX.* Havana: Editorial Pueblo y Educación.

Milanés, Pablo. 1992. *Canciones.* Havana: Editorial PM.

Milanés, Pablo, and Mario Benedetti. 1995. *Yolanda y otras canciones.* Buenos Aires: Espasa Calpe.

Millet, José. 1997. *Barrio, comparsa y carnaval santiaguero.* Santiago: Casa del Caribe.

Moreno, Dennis. 1994. *Un tambor arará*. Havana: Editorial de Ciencias Sociales.

Neira Betancourt, Lino A. 1991. *Como suena un tambor abakuá*. Havana: Editorial Pueblo y Educación.

Ojeda, Miguelito, ed. 1998. *Bola de Nieve: Selección de textos, anexos y notas.* Havana: Editorial Letras Cubanas.

Orovio, Helio. 1992a. *Diccionario de la música cubana: Biográfico y técnico.* 2nd ed. Havana: Editorial Letras Cubanas.

———. 1992b. *300 boleros de oro: Antología de obras cubanas.* Maracay, Venezuela: Pomaire/Fuentes.

———. 1994. *El son, la guaracha, y la salsa.* Santiago: Editorial Oriente.

Ortiz, Fernando. [1920] 1993. *Los cabildos y la fiesta afrocubanos del Día de Reyes.* Havana: Editorial de Ciencias Sociales.

———. [1951] 1993. *Los bailes y el teatro de los negros en el folklore de Cuba.* Havana: Editorial Letras Cubanas.

———. [1955] 1994. *Los instrumentos de la música afrocubana.* Havana: Editorial Letras Cubanas.

———. 1993. *La africanía de la música folklórica de Cuba.* Havana: Editorial Letras Cubanas.

Parera, Celida. 1990. *Pro-Arte Musical y su divulgación cultural en Cuba, 1918–1967.* New York: Sendas Nuevas Ediciones.

Rodríguez, Silvio. 1996. *Canciones del mar.* Madrid: Ojalá S.L.

Rodríguez, Silvio, and Miguel Russo. 1996. *Ángel para un final.* Buenos Aires: R. Cedeño.

Sánchez Oliva, Iraida, and Santiago Moreaux Jardines. 1999. *Guantanamera.* Havana: Editorial José Martí.

Sánchez Ortega, Paula. 1992. *Algunas consideraciones acerca de la educación musical en Cuba.* Havana: Editorial Pueblo y Educación.

Simón, Pedro. 1995. *La danza en Ernesto Lecuona.* Havana: Ediciones "Cuba en el Ballet."

Tello, Aurelio. 1999. *Cancionero musical de Gaspar Fernandes.* Havana: Casa de las Américas.

2000 TO THE PRESENT

Acosta, Leonardo. 2000. *Descarga cubana: El jazz en Cuba 1900–1950.* Havana: Ediciones Unión.

———. 2002. *Descarga número dos: El jazz en Cuba 1950–2000.* Havana: Ediciones Unión.

Almeida León, Ismael. 2003. *Polo: Cantor de la montaña.* Pinar del Río, Cuba: Ediciones Vitral.

Alonso Grau, Alpidio. 2002. *Otros alzan las cabezas: Cancionero de la joven trova santaclareña.* Santa Clara: Ediciones de Sed de Belleza.

Balbuena, Bárbara. 2003. *El casino y la salsa en Cuba.* Havana: Editorial Letras Cubanas.

Bernal Echemendía, Eduardo. 2001. *Diccionario de la trova espirituana*. Santi Spiritus, Cuba: Ediciones Luminaria.

Betancourt Molina, Lino. 2000. *Compay Segundo*. Havana: Editorial José Martí.

Brouwer, Leo. 2004. *Gajes del oficio*. Havana: Editorial Letras Cubanas.

Calzadilla Núñez, Julia. 2002. *Trío Hermanas Lago*. Havana: Editorial Letras Cubanas.

Carpentier, Alejo. [1946] 2004. *La música en Cuba*. Havana: Editorial Letras Cubanas.

———. 2003. *La cultura en Cuba y en el mundo*. Havana: Editorial Letras Cubanas. [Previously unprinted lectures delivered by Carpentier on Radio Habana Cuba, 1964–66.]

Castellanos, Ernesto Juan. 2000. *El Sgto. Pimienta vino a Cuba en un submarino amarillo*. Havana: Editorial Letras Cubanas.

———. 2005. *John Lennon en La Habana: With a Little Help from My Friends*. Havana: Ediciones Unión.

Cedeño Pineda, Reinaldo, and Michel Damián Suárez. 2001. *Son de la loma: Los dioses de la música cantan en Santiago de Cuba*. Havana: Editora Musical de Cuba.

Contreras, Félix. 2002. *Yo conocí a Benny Moré*. Havana: Ediciones Unión.

Domínguez Benejam, Yarelis. 2000. *Caminos de la musicología cubana*. Havana: Editorial Letras Cubanas.

Elizundia Ramírez, Alicia. 2001. *Yo soy una maestra que canta*. Havana: Ediciones Unión.

Esquenazi Pérez, Martha. 2001. *Del areíto y otros sones*. Havana: Editorial Letras Cubanas.

Giro, Radamés. 2001. *El filin de César Portillo de la Luz*. Havana: Ediciones Unión.

González, Elcida. 2000. *Cancionero de la trova cubana*. Havana: Andante.

González, Juan Pablo. 2003. *Historia social de la música popular en Chile, 1890–1950*. Havana: Casa de las Américas.

Henríquez, Antonieta, and José Piñeiro Díaz. 2001. *Amadeo Roldán: Testimonios*. Havana: Editorial Letras Cubanas.

Hernández, Zenovio. 2001. *La música en Holguín*. Holguín, Cuba: Ediciones Holguín.

López, Ariel, and Enrique Ramos. 2000. *Diez jutges a tempo: Mirada a la nova cançó, acercamiento a la nueva trova*. Matanzas: Ediciones Vigía.

Manduley López, Humberto. 2001. *El rock en Cuba*. Havana: Atril.

Marrero, Gaspar. 2001. *La Orquesta Aragón*. Havana: José Martí.

Martí, José, and Carmen Suárez León. 2001. *Músicos, poetas y pintores*. Havana: CEDISAC y Centro de Estudios Martianos.

Maury, Omar Felipe. 2000. *De la mágica cubanía: Charangas de Bejucal*. Havana: Ediciones Unión.

Oramas Oliva, Oscar. 2002. *El alma del cubano: Su música*. Havana: Ediciones Prensa Latina.

———. 2004. *Miel de la vida: El bolero*. Buenos Aires: Ediciones Vinciguerra.

Peñalver Hernández, Ivón. 2003. *Eduardo Rosillo: Alma de la música popular cubana*. Havana: Ediciones Guajira.

Ramos, Enrique, and Letitia Hernández Benítez. 2000. *Danzones: Antología de músicos matanceros contemporaneos*. Matanzas: Ediciones Vigía.

Sánchez León, Miguel. 2001. *Esa huella olvidada: El Teatro Nacional de Cuba (1959–1961)*. Havana: Editorial Letras Cubanas.

Santos Gracia, Caridad, and Nieves Armas Rigal. 2002. *Danzas populares tradicionales cubanas*. Havana: Centro de Investigación Juan Marinello.

Valdés Cantero, Alicia. 2000. *Nosotros y el bolero*. Havana: Editorial Letras Cubanas.

Valenzuela Arce, José Manuel. 2001. *Jefe de jefes: Corridos y narcocultura en México*. Havana: Casa de las Américas.

Notes

1. Revolutionary leaders felt that the Centro de Estudios sobre las Américas (CEA) had established links of an unnecessarily intimate nature with capitalist countries and that the relationships had ideologically tainted the work of Cubans themselves. The majority of Raúl Castro's commentary has been published in *Revista Encuentro de la Cultura Cubana* 1 (Summer 1996): 18–24. One of those who lost a job in the CEA was Rafael Hernández, an insightful scholar who now directs the influential journal *Temas*.

2. Weiss (1985:120), for instance, apparently bases her discussion of education and cultural policy entirely on the pronouncements of Armando Hart, former minister of culture.

3. Domínguez 1978:474 mentions the difficulty of obtaining candid answers from Cuban interviewees as well.

4. The full citations are as follows: "From the *canción protesta* to the *nueva trova*, 1965–85," *International Journal of Qualitative Studies in Education* 14, no. 2 (2001): 177–200; "*Sones* and Socialism: Dance Music in Cuba, 1959–99," in *Situating Salsa: Global Markets and Local Meanings in Latin Popular Music*, ed. Gage Averill and Lise Waxer (New York: Routledge, 2002), pp. 51–74; "*'Revolución con pachanga'*?: Debates over the Place of Fun in the Dance Music of Socialist Cuba," *Canadian Journal of Latin American and Caribbean Studies* 26, no. 52 (2002): 151–77; "Transformations in Cuban *nueva trova*, 1965–95," *Ethnomusicology* 47, no. 1 (Winter 2003): 1–41; "Revolution and Religion: Yoruba Sacred Music in Socialist Cuba," in *The Yoruba Diaspora in the Atlantic World*, ed. Toyin Falola and Matt D. Childs (Bloomington: Indiana University Press, 2004), pp. 260–90.

The original Spanish for the epigraph reads, "Nuestra más alta aspiración ha estado relacionada con promover los vínculos entre el movimiento artístico e intelectual y el desarrollo político, social y moral del país. Es decir, rechazar la concepción estrecha de un arte y una cultura como algo añadido o superpuesto a la vida social, y situarlos en el lugar que les corresponde en la construcción del socialismo" (Dávalos 1988:52).

1. The term "Afro-Cuban" continues to be polemical because it is not used frequently by Cubans themselves and because to some it appears to create a distinction between "Cubans" (implicitly white/Hispanic Cubans) and "Cubans of color." I employ "Afro-Cuban" throughout this book for lack of a better term to refer to the black community, those who perceive themselves as black or racially mixed. This is the approach adopted by prominent Cuban writers including Fernando Ortiz and Rogelio Martínez Furé (Hernández and Coatsworth 2001:67).

2. The first official organization to which Cubans typically belong is the Unión de Pioneros de Cuba (UPC), the Union of Cuban Pioneers. The UPC organizes extracurricular activities for children as young as four or five years old. Other government organizations intended for adolescents and students include the FEEM (Federación de Estudiantes de Enseñanza Media), intended for junior high school and high school students, and the FEU (Federación de Estudiantes Universitarios), for those in the university. See Domínguez 1978:279 for further discussion of these groups. The national organization linking all unions and trade organizations is the CTC (Central de Trabajadores Cubanos), the Union of Cuban Workers. Virtually every sort of manual and professional labor is associated with its own government-controlled union. Examples of organizations that link those of similar ethnic backgrounds or interests include the Federation of Cuban Women (Federación de Mujeres Cubanas) and state organizations created for descendants of Chinese, Arab, and Jewish immigrants. Local community groups, established on every city block of most urban areas, are referred to as Comités de Defensa de la Revolución (CDRs), Committees in Defense of the Revolution. They might be considered a socialist version of town-watch organizations.

3. Rafael Hernández's book *Looking at Cuba* (2003) includes insightful commentary on the concept of civil society and its relation to Cuban socialism. Among other things, Hernández notes that discourse from the Right tends to present the state and civil society as opposites, assuming (1) that civil society is an ideologically neutral facet of the capitalist world, and (2) that nongovernmental groups in control of much of civil society invariably have the best interests of the common people in mind. He contests both points, arguing that civil society reinforces hierarchies of power and authority and that nongovernmental groups do not necessarily make democratic decisions.

4. Much of the legislation giving rise to these institutions was published during the first years of the revolution by the Editorial Lex in their *Folletos de Divulgación Legislativa* series. Information on the establishment of the ICAIC is found in law no. 169, *Leyes del Gobierno Provisional de la Revolución* 5:144–52. Legislation pertaining to the Ballet Nacional and Orquesta Sinfónica Nacional appear in cuaderno 20, pp. 69 and 75; the creation of ICAP is mandated in cuaderno 27, p. 45.

5. Despite the best intentions of the government to deemphasize material incentives, it was in fact forced to reintroduce many of them in the 1970s. Items offered to workers thereafter included new refrigerators, washing machines, and cars. This policy shift attempted to stimulate productivity, which reached dangerous lows during the first half of that decade (Cristóbal Díaz Ayala, pers. comm.).

6. Typical slogans of various periods include "Socialism or Death," "We Will Be Victorious," "Join In," "Our Battlefield Covers the Whole World," "Make Man's Life Perfect," When a Communist Is Born Difficulties Die," "The Sugar Harvest Needs You," "The Welfare of the Many Is Preferable to the Luxury of the Few," and so on. Many of these are mentioned in Cardenal 1974. From a capitalist perspective, the slogans often seem heavy-handed, yet they contain more food for thought than the mindless advertising jingles permeating the capitalist world, such as "Tonight Let It Be Lowenbrau" or "Put a Tiger in Your Tank."

In the context of ongoing economic difficulties and widespread doubt about the value of Cuban socialism today, however, socialist slogans probably attest more to the difficulty of building consensus around Marxist principles than the actual views of the people. I am reminded of Gramsci's observation that discourses of political unity appear most often in nation-states that are the weakest and most fragmented.

7. Castro's original reads, "Valoramos las creaciones culturales y artísticas en función de la utilidad para el pueblo, en función de lo que aporten al hombre, en función de lo que aporten a la reivindicación, a la liberación del hombre" (as quoted in Leal 1982:242).

8. Solomon (1973) describes the social realism movement in this way: "At the root of the Zhdanovist aesthetic is the economic determinist theory of direct superstructural reflection of society: the art of the bourgeois world reflects bourgeois economic decadence; the art of socialist society must mirror socialist reality" (p. 237).

9. The *ofensiva* formally began in the spring of 1968, but the radicalization of government policies had been escalating for some time. Jorge Domínguez discusses manifestations of social realism under the leadership of the National Culture Advisory beginning in the early 1960s (Domínguez 1978:393). See also Ardévol 1966:194.

10. Zemtosovsky (2002) comments on his experiences as a musicologist in socialist Russia. He emphasizes the importance of distinguishing between the rich legacy of Marxist thought on the one hand and the achievements and mistakes of socialists through the years. He notes that censorship is in no way inherent to Marxism and that authors in the Soviet Union and elsewhere, even at the worst of times, found ways to express their oppositional points of view.

11. Castro's well-known "Within the Revolution everything, against the Revolution nothing" comes from the "Words to the Intellectuals" speech (Castro 1961). This phrase is similar to Mao's "Let a hundred flowers blossom, let a hundred schools of thought contend" (Mao 1977:134).

12. In fact, Castro's comments from "Words to the Intellectuals" continue to generate controversy. Issue no. 4 of the *Gaceta de Cuba* from 2001 (July–August) contains a series of retrospective essays on this speech, the context in which it was given, and its repercussions (e.g., Fernández Retamar 2001; Otero 2001).

13. For those interested in further reading on this topic, critiques of capitalist music making published in Cuba include Acosta 1982, 1983; Aharonián 1990; Ardévol 1966:97–100; Barnet 1983:43–52; Díaz Pérez 1994:8–17; Faya et al. 1996; and León 1985. Of these, Acosta's and Faya's analyses are the most penetrating.

14. As many are aware, Solzhenitsyn did live for a time in the United States after being exiled from the Soviet Union in 1974. He continued publishing; readers will have to decide for themselves whether his works had the impact he intended or whether they were marginalized by the capitalist marketplace. His son, Ignat, has chosen a musical career, incidentally. He continues to perform classical music to critical acclaim in the United States.

15. César Portillo de la Luz and Rosendo Ruiz Jr. (1959a–f) jointly published a series of six essays on the financial exploitation of Cuban artists by United States recording companies.

16. Compare Acosta's "pseudopopular" with the term "latunes" used in much the same way by Gustavo Pérez Firmat (1994:88, 95). María Teresa Linares also comments on this phenomenon in Díaz Pérez 1994:66–67.

17. Cristóbal Díaz Ayala disputes this view. He notes that although the North American presence in television programming was strong, Cubans themselves were not mere passive receptors of foreign culture. On the contrary, they produced and exported TV soap operas as well as music to other countries. Though noting that certain stations featured North American music, even exclusively, Díaz Ayala does not believe that Cuban music was marginalized. "When I aired my first radio program in 1947 (I was 18 years old), *Twilight Time*, there was one station (among dozens), CMOX, that transmitted in English all the time, and an additional three or so programs of American music on other stations, on other days and times. The rest of the stations all played popular or classical music from Cuba, Latin America, or Spain. American music was consumed by the elite classes . . . it never threatened local production. By the 1950s, RCA Victor had lost its hegemony in Cuba" (pers. comm.).

18. The original Spanish reads, "Las creaciones de la nación opresora son presentadas como realizaciones de validez universal, sirviendo además, para medir las producciones del país explotado; estas últimas serán más o menos apreciadas en la medida en que se aproximen o no a los modelos establecidos. Las que divergen de esos modelos son subestimadas y consideradas simples productos inferiores. A lo que aspira la clase dominante es a que el país oprimido llegue a creer que la lengua, las costumbres, las modas, las artes del opresor son fatalmente superiores a las suyas y que, en consecuencia, renuncia a su propio ser, se entregue a la imitación y se aisle de las fuerzas que puedan apoyar su liberación. Con ello no sólo se empobrece, sino que espiritual y materialmente queda a merced del enemigo" (Partido Comunista de Cuba 1977:91).

19. Castro's original Spanish reads, "Eso es lo que queremos de las futuras generaciones, que sepan ser consecuentes." This inscription appears over the door of the provincial headquarters of the Unión de Jóvenes Comunistas in Habana Vieja.

CHAPTER 1

1. Examples abound; studies related to society in general include Serviat 1986, Cirules 1999, and Pino Santos 2001; those focusing on the arts include León [1964] 1984, Giro 1986:5–6, and López Segrera 1989. The journal *Temas* has devoted entire issues to the 1950s in recent years (e.g., nos. 24–25, January–June 2001) that present a more nuanced evaluation than earlier publications.

2. Additional statistics on the mass media are available in Salwen 1994.

3. In fact, U.S. troops did invade Cuba on two more occasions (Moore 1997:29). At one point in 1906, the troops returned for three more years.

4. See, for instance, the insightful analysis in José Alvarez Díaz 1963:781–83 related to education reform and fiscal policy during Batista's presidency.

5. Masdeu 1953 includes visual documentation of rural poverty in Cuba in the 1950s.

6. Many historians believe that the percentage of Cuba's racially mixed population relative to its white/Hispanic population was significantly higher; Walterio Carbonell, for instance, believes it was greater than 50 percent (Moore 1988:359). The conservative figure cited in the text comes from national census data that reflects how the population self-identified in racial terms (de la Fuente 1995).

7. Cubans of virtually all races and classes began to emigrate in search of better employment opportunities. Between 1946 and 1954, approximately thirty-five thousand left for the United States (Pino Santos 2001:122–23).

8. For information on the Pro-Arte Musical Society, see Parera 1990.

9. Sánchez 1979 contains extensive information on the Havana Philharmonic. Havana actually boasted a second symphony orchestra for a brief time between 1922 and 1924 conducted by Gonzalo Roig.

10. Ardévol describes much of the public as adamantly opposed to listening to the sorts of music that his chamber group presented, such as works by himself, Bartók, or García Caturla. Some listeners came armed with whistles, pots and pans, or other items that they could beat on and thus disrupt the concerts. In at least one instance, fistfights are said to have broken out between these individuals and supporters of twentieth-century repertoire (Ardévol 1966:114).

11. See García 2003:203, Roldán Viñas 1954:724–30, and de Posada 1954:731–41 for further information on black social clubs in Havana of the 1940s and 1950s.

12. The first commercial recording of traditional folkloric rumba and *comparsa* music took place in 1955, under the supervision of Odilio Urfé. The resulting LP was entitled *Festival in Havana: Folk Music of Cuba*. Cristóbal Díaz

Ayala (pers. comm.) notes that the first folkloric *guaguancó* to get popular through jukebox recordings at roughly the same time was "El vive bien" by the *conjunto* of Alberto Zayas, based in Guanabacoa. This recording and the consumer interest that it generated led to the national promotion of the Grupo Guaguancó Matancero, later known as the Muñequitos de Matanzas.

13. Guillermo Portabales's repertoire is described in precisely this way by *Bohemia* magazine ("Guillermo Portabales: No quiso cantarle a la tiranía," 52, no. 14 [April 3, 1960]: 107).

14. See Collazo 1987, Díaz Ayala 1981, and Rosell 1992 for listings of prominent figures in the midcentury entertainment industry.

15. See Acosta 2002 for a more exhaustive listing of the many clubs and cabarets of the 1950s.

16. Acosta, Espí, and Orovio 1999 includes a map of Havana providing the locations of major cabarets.

17. Referring to a *charanga* in the previous century seems to have been a demeaning way of describing a small, makeshift group comprised of whatever instruments were at hand; the term *bunga* was used in much the same way. Over time, the negative connotations have been lost. Díaz Ayala 2003a discusses *charanga* history at greater length.

18. Given the multifaceted meanings of the term "mambo," perhaps it is best to reproduce Ortiz's original comments in translation here: "Kongo priests or witches . . . refer to their liturgical songs as *mambo*. This term comes from *mambu* in the Kongo language. *Mambu* is the plural form of *diambu*, and so African descendants in Cuba who say *mambos*, employing the plural declension in Castillian Spanish, commit an unnecessary redundancy. *Mambu* has various meanings including 'matters,' 'words,' 'conversations,' 'discussions,' 'messages,' 'stipulations,' etc., all alluding to the manner of ritually addressing supernatural creatures through song" (1965:235).

19. Acosta 2000:164 discusses the controversy generated by Arsenio Rodríguez when he published comments claiming to have invented the mambo in *Bohemia* magazine. Rodríguez's original statements can be found in Cubillas 1952.

20. See www.laventure.net/tourist/prez_bio.htm for biographical information on Dámaso Pérez Prado.

21. For an example of Pérez Prado's arrangements and piano solos, listen to the first four tracks on the CD *Memories of Cuba: Orquesta Casino de la Playa (1937–1944)*, 1991. Track one, "Llora," includes a harmonically experimental piano solo followed by mambo-like sections at about 2:45".

22. The involvement of individuals in entertainment and music industries in these organizations has never been fully documented, but seems to have been extensive. Thomas 1971:945 mentions one case of an RCA Victor employee arrested for suspicion of planting explosives. *Bohemia* describes the death of a CMQ worker involved in resistance to Batista as well ("Los artistas con la guardia en alto," June 18, 1961, p. 4). This makes sense, as many of the workers at CMQ in the 1950s had come from Mil Diez, a Communist radio station closed by Carlos Prío in the 1940s.

CHAPTER 2

The original Spanish for the epigraph reads, "Tengo el convencimiento de que hemos emprendido un camino que nos llevará muy lejos; de que no habrá pasos atrás, por primera vez en nuestra historia, en la conquista de nuestra completa soberanía; de que la 'dignidad plena del hombre' será una realidad entre nosotros; de que serán posibles, convertidos en hermosas presencias, muchos de los sueños que hemos alimentado cálida y agónicamente en el hondón de nuestro ser; de que al trabajo de los intelectuales y artistas se le abren posibilidades que nunca antes han existido aquí" (Ardévol 1966:75–76).

1. Díaz Ayala 1981:268, Orejuela Martínez 2004:49, and *Bohemia* 51, no. 5 (February 1, 1959): 158, contain more complete listings of songs inspired by the end of the Batista dictatorship. Recent recorded collections of early revolutionary songs include Loyola Fernández 1996 and Rupérez 2000.

2. Pedro Sosa also filled the position of voice and maracas for a time (Rodríguez 1961:76).

3. Some have suggested that Carlos Puebla was an opportunist. They argue that during the 1950s he wrote pieces in favor of Batista's policies and only after 1959 became an ardent supporter of the revolution.

4. The February 8, 1959, issue of *Bohemia* (51, no. 6: 156) discusses some of the damage done to casinos and the fact that money was stolen.

5. In Spanish the quote reads: "El régimen derrocado . . . con el fin de desviar la atención pública acerca de sus actividades ilícitas, fomentó hasta límites insospechados el juego de azar en todas sus manifestaciones, convirtiendo a la República en un verdadero garito, centro del hampa internacional" (*Leyes del Gobierno Provisionales de la Revolución,* cuaderno 3, February 11, 1959, p. 76).

6. References to the ban on jukeboxes are found in *Bohemia* 51, no. 7 (February 18, 1959): 2; no. 8 (February 22): 154; and no. 9 (March 1): 140. See also *Revolución,* February 17, 1959, p. 5. In the February 22 article from *Bohemia,* Gema Records owner Guillermo Álvarez Guedes criticized the prohibition, noting that sales to jukebox companies represented 95 percent of all retail trade by his company.

7. *Show,* in its April 1959 issue, p. 33, describes the cabaret La Gruta's attempts to raise money for the agrarian reform campaign, as one example.

8. Orejuela Martínez (2004:46, 128) provides additional details about the gaming prohibitions. She documents how authorities reauthorized gaming in deluxe casinos for a short time in order to placate the establishments' owners. Yet they placed so many restrictions on the sorts of games permitted and the guests who could take part in them that the practice became unprofitable. Castro closed the last of the casinos on September 28, 1961, along with the last remaining dance academy, the Galiano Sport Club.

9. The legislation creating the National Institute of Tourist Industries appears in the *Gaceta Oficial* from November 23, 1959, p. 26502, law no. 636. See also *Bohemia* 52, no. 3 (January 17, 1960): 108.

10. *Bohemia* 54, no. 9 (August 3, 1962): n.p. (archives, Cristóbal Díaz Ayala),

describes one altercation between club managers and bureaucrats involving Humberto Anido, stage manager of the Salón Rojo.

11. Information about the Workers' Palace can be found in *Show* 6, no. 3 (May 1959): 32. The theater, previously known as the Teatro CTC, was located near Belascoaín and Carlos III. Union groups constructed it before 1959, and thus its "inauguration" was more symbolic than substantive.

12. The article "Ritmo oriental: Tambores en La Habana" (Castillo 1962) describes one national tour involving a large group from Los Hoyos, Santiago. It consisted of fifty drummers under the direction of Enrique Bonne. Institutions sponsoring the group's presentations in Havana included the ORI (Integrated Revolutionary Organizations), JUCEI (the national economic planning board), and CTC (the Confederation of Cuban Workers).

13. Portabales's return is discussed in "Guillermo Portabales: No quiso cantarle a la tiranía," *Bohemia* 52, no. 13 (March 27, 1960): 107. Information on the other artists comes from personal communications with Cristóbal Díaz Ayala and Joaquín Ordoqui.

14. JUCEI stands for Juntas de Coordinación, Ejecución e Inspección (Coordination, Execution, and Inspection Groups). The juntas were modeled after the *soviets* of East Bloc nations.

15. One unsigned article discussing the disappearance of jazz from the media appears in *Bohemia* 55, no. 11 (March 15, 1963): 62. See also the account of Robert Williams's difficulties in broadcasting jazz on Cuban radio (Tyson 1999:293).

16. *Revolución* contains two unsigned articles on the *filin* controversy (April 8, 1963, p. 5) entitled "'Adiós felicidad.' Ela O'Farrill hace aclaraciones" and "Iniciado el fórum sobre el 'Feeling.'"

17. The original Spanish reads, "No puede ocultarse que con anterioridad al triunfo de la Revolución, el disfrute de las altas manifestaciones del arte era sólo patrimonio de una privilegiada minoría que, organizada en instituciones exclusivas, vedaba el acceso a los espectáculos que patrocinaba a los sectores de escasos recursos económicos, que constituyen las grandes mayorías de nuestra población" (*Decreto* 2905, *Leyes del Gobierno Provisional de la Revolución*, December 31, 1960, pp. 182–84).

18. Considerable antagonism continued to exist between Cuban nationals and exiles in league with the CIA and the mafia from 1961 through the mid-1970s (Hinckle and Turner 1981).

19. Díaz Ayala 1981 contains a more complete listing of entertainers who opted for exile: pp. 267, 348.

20. The January 1961 issue of *Bohemia* (53, no. 1:28), discusses the impact of urban reform laws on Olga Guillot. D'Rivera 1998:68 briefly mentions the circumstances surrounding the confiscation of Ernesto Lecuona's *finca* La Comparsa while he was away on business in the United States.

21. Those leaving Los Trovadores del Cayo included pianist and arranger Javier Vázquez, trumpet player Mario Chong, and lead singer Domingo Vargas. The director, Alfonsín Quintana, had no desire to continue playing after losing so many of his musicians.

22. Blacklisting is not merely a phenomenon associated with the early revolution. In 1981, as one example, party representatives chose to exclude all references to Cubans living abroad in Helio Orovio's *Diccionario de la música cubana*. Entries on exiles only appeared in the second edition from 1992. The two-volume *Diccionario de la literatura cubana* (1980–84) also lacks entries on Cubans in exile.

23. The laws regulating travel can be found in the *Leyes del Gobierno Provisional de la Revolución*, July 11, 1960, law no. 418 (cuaderno 22), p. 256, and September 29, 1960, law no. 442 (cuaderno 25), p. 27.

24. An ensemble of this nature that included the Orquesta Aragón, Pedro Izquierdo, Los Zafiros, Elena Burke, and others toured East Berlin, Warsaw, and Moscow in 1965, for instance, before visiting Paris and returning home. See *Bohemia* 57, no. 52 (December 24, 1965): 62.

25. Joaquín Ordoqui (pers. comm.) remembers that the financial changes in the early years of the revolution occurred in various stages. Beginning in 1960 or 1961, the government began issuing new currency. The change attempted to render useless bills from the Batista era that had been taken out of national banks in mass quantities by exiles or those contemplating exile. Only later in the decade did the government restrict Cubans' access to other currency.

26. The armed forces grew from thirty-nine thousand in 1959 to well over two hundred fifty thousand active soldiers by the early 1960s, with hundreds of thousands of active reserves (Schroeder 1982:522).

27. The exile community managed to reestablish some Cuban labels in Miami and New York in the early 1960s, but they never attained the same levels of success that they had before 1959.

28. See *Leyes del Gobierno Provisional de la Revolución*, August 8, 1960, law no. 860 (cuaderno 23), p. 9, for the legislation creating the Instituto Cubano de Derechos Musicales. Orejuela Martínez 2004:106 describes the charges leveled against Lecuona and Roig, which were apparently justified.

29. Commentary in *Bohemia* from January 7, 1962 (51, no. 1: 89), discusses one of the earliest competitions sponsored by the ORI (Integrated Revolutionary Organizations), a political entity that eventually became the Partido Comunista de Cuba.

30. Ley del Derecho de Autor, *Gaceta Oficial de la República de Cuba*, December 30, 1977, pp. 757–62. My thanks to Ariana Hernández-Reguant (2004a: 15) for providing these references.

CHAPTER 3

1. Writings that avoid commentary critical of the revolution include *Cultural Policy in Cuba* (Otero and Hinojosa 1972) and *La cultura en Cuba socialista* (Ministerio de Cultura 1982). Leonardo Acosta's *Del tambor al sintetizador* (1983) and José Pola's *Entrevistas* (1989) contain some of the only essays available before the mid-1990s that considered how to improve domestic cultural institutions.

2. Books such as Domínguez 1978, Lewis, Lewis, and Rigdon 1977a and b, Mesa-Lago 1979, Mesa-Lago and Arenas de Mesa et al. 2000, and Stubbs 1989 provide a good initial overview of processes of change in revolutionary Cuba.

3. The ORI consisted of three previously autonomous groups: the Partido Socialista Popular, with its newspaper *Hoy;* the 26th of July movement, with its newspaper *Revolución;* and the Directorio Revolucionario, with its newspaper *Combate.* As of 1965, only the PCC remained, with its newspaper *Granma.*

4. One should note that the emphasis in higher education has shifted away from critical inquiry and toward the dissemination of practical technical skills of various kinds. The University of Havana is no longer a center of debate but remains an excellent place to learn engineering, receive medical training, and so forth.

5. Consult the appendix for a full listing of publications on music that have appeared since 1959.

6. The Teatro Nacional is located near what was earlier known as the Plaza de la República and is now called the Plaza de la Revolución. Construction of the theater actually began during the Batista years but was still unfinished when he fled the country (Cristóbal Díaz Ayala, pers. comm.).

7. See Acosta 1983:142 for a more complete listing of music documentaries.

8. Juan Marinello, 1898–1977. Lawyer, political activist, and leftist intellectual. He participated in the famous "Protesta de los 13" of 1923, becoming a nationally recognized leader. Marinello served brief prison terms under Machado and Batista for his political activism. In the early 1960s, he became involved in curricular reform at the University of Havana. He remained active in political and literary circles until his death.

Carlos Rafael Rodríguez, 1913–97. Rafael Rodríguez's training and background are similar to those of Marinello's in many respects. He fought against the Machado regime in the early 1930s and later served as mayor of Cienfuegos. In 1939, he graduated with a law degree from the University of Havana. Heavily involved in literary and cultural movements from an early age, Rafael Rodríguez collaborated with other well-known figures such as poet Nicolás Guillén, essayist José Antonio Portuondo, and journalist Angel Augier. He remained an important figure in Cuban letters until his death.

Vicentina Antuña, 1902–92. A professional educator with degrees in education and the humanities, Antuña was born in Güines. In the 1930s, she studied Latin at Columbia University in New York and after returning home offered classes at the Universidad Popular José Martí. Beginning in 1936, she worked as a board member of the Lyceum, an association dedicated to women's education. After serving as a member of the CNC for many years and as its president from 1959 to 61, she became president of the Cuban delegation of UNESCO. She was closely involved with the Classics and Literature Departments at the University of Havana in the 1960s and 1970s.

Little information is available on Edith García Buchaca, apparently because she is considered to have turned against the revolution and has had little official support in recent decades. She married prominent Communist Carlos Rafael Rodríguez in the 1930s but later divorced him and married Joaquín Ordoqui Mesa in the early 1960s, a figure in the hierarchy of the Cuban army and the PSP. García Buchaca continues to live in Cuba, though her second husband also ran afoul of the present leadership.

9. Founded in 1961, the Union of Cuban Artists and Writers (UNEAC) is subdivided into various artistic areas, including literature, plastic arts, film, and music. It continues to serve as a channel by which artists give voice to their ideas and express them to the government (Robbins 1990:134) and vice versa. The creation of the UNEAC was intended to bring intellectuals together as a unified political force. According to Antón Arrufat, the decision to establish it came after "loose cannons," such as those involved in *Lunes de Revolución*, began to create controversy. Following the state Soviet model, "it was necessary to unite all forces in a single institution and then hire . . . someone with prestige to direct it. In the Cuban case, that person was Nicolás Guillén" (Kirk and Padura Fuentes 2001:28). A youth branch of the UNEAC, known as the Brigada Hermanos Saíz (BHS), was founded in 1962 for persons under the age of thirty (Robbins 1990:137). The association took its name from two brothers, Luis Rodolfo and Sergio Enrique Saíz Montes de Oca. They joined the Revolutionary Directorate in the mid-1950s and were killed by Batista. With the support of the Unión de Jóvenes Comunistas, the BHS expanded its activities in the late 1970s across the island (Pola 1989:318).

10. Leonardo Acosta (pers. comm.) notes that, in terms of policy, Muzio and Otero deferred to the opinions of José Llanusa, then minister of education.

11. Pita Rodríguez 1965 contains information on the vocal quintet Los Guamá and Conjunto de mozambique; a November 26, 1965, issue of *Bohemia* mentions the Vocal Ensemble of the Syndicate of Public Administration and the Theater Group of the Gastronomic Union.

12. Ignaza and Pola 1975 contains some information on the Amateurs' movement in the 1970s. Díaz Rosell (1989) comments on an amateur event in the late 1980s.

13. Robbins 1990:520, for instance, notes that as of the late 1980s the government had recognized only two professional *agrupaciones folklóricas* in all of Matanzas province.

14. Carretero 1990 includes details on the history of one such school, the Escuela Gerardo Delgado Guanche in Guanabacoa, directed by Jesús Hernández Villapol.

15. Robbins 1991 provides a good introduction to the complex workings of labor organization in the Cuban music industry.

16. JUCEPLAN refers to the Junta Central de Planificación (Central Planning Board).

17. The first director of the national music museum was María Antonieta Henríquez. Employees of the museum relate that their extensive collections of sheet music and recordings came in part from the homes of wealthier Cuban families who chose to abandon the country, as well as from personal donations and music holdings in the National Library.

18. Ardévol 1966:221 provides an extensive list of many foreign artists who worked and performed in Cuba during the 1960s.

19. Guillermoprieto 2004 includes interesting data on the ENA's architecture (p. 268). She notes that while Porro's designs had full support initially, some began to criticize them as too sensual and individualistic. In 1965, Castro himself denounced the ENA's design as "egocentric" and called for a more standardized model of construction based on Soviet prefabricated proletarian architecture. In 1966, Porro left the country, largely as the result of these criticisms.

20. Flores 1978 mentions that enrollment in the ENA's 1976–77 academic year reached 228. This is presumably typical of the early 1970s as well. After the ISA opened in 1977, however, combined enrollment increased to 404 (p. 68).

21. Seguin (1997) discusses this in an interview with Chucho Valdés, who notes the exceptional quality of graduates from the ENA and ISA such as César López, Orlando Valle, Jorge Reyes, Gonzalo Rubalcaba, and others who now perform jazz and popular music.

22. Castro's commentary came in a speech delivered on October 6, 2001, commemorating the twenty-fifth anniversary of the bombing of a Cuban passenger airline off the coast of Barbados. Thanks to Ned Sublette for bringing the speech to my attention. Even if the figures are exaggerated (I have been unable to confirm them), his point is well taken.

23. For information regarding the U.S. government's attempts to assassinate Castro, see commentary in the Church report (U.S. Congress 1976:2–6), *CUBAInfo* 9, no. 9 (July 1997): 3, and Hinckle and Turner 1981:20.

24. While visiting Miami for a conference, I found the local media covering a trial of Eduardo Díaz Betancourt and others in Havana. This was my first introduction to the ongoing armed conflicts between Cuba and the exile community. Information about the incident can be found at the following website: www.miami.com/mld/miamiherald/5616317.htm.

See www.poptel.org.uk/cuba-solidarity/CubaSi-Autumn/Bombs4.html for information regarding the bombing of Cuban tourist hotels in 1997.

25. A substantial amount has been written already about the *quinquenio gris.* Rojas 1998:158 provides a good summary of events surrounding the trial and imprisonment of writer Heberto Padilla, for instance, as well as the climate of fear associated with the Congreso Nacional de Educación y Cultura in 1971. Related events include the closing of the journal *Pensamiento Crítico,* the disappearance of the University of Havana's Department of Philosophy in 1973, and the suspension of many other cultural publications (*Naranja Dulce, El Caimán Barbudo, Credo*). I discuss the *quinquenio* in various essays but have chosen not to duplicate this earlier work. See Domínguez 1978, Mesa-Lago 1979, and *Temas* 1, no. 1 (Summer 1996), for further information.

CHAPTER 4

1. Orejuela Martínez 2004 provides an excellent description of year-to-year musical activities during this period.

2. The original Spanish reads, "Estamos de acuerdo en que los espectáculos de entretenimiento no están especialmente destinados a mejorar el campo ideológico, ni a educar, ni a instruir. En cierto sentido, funcionan como una válvula de escape, como un paréntesis de diversión superficial, y así debe ser. Ahora bien, si además de ser un pasatiempo a flor de piel fomentan la chabacanería, el mal gusto, lo procaz, el sensualismo barato, la indefinición sexual, es evidente que pueden ser un importante factor negativo, un modo de difundir hábitos y preferencias que, aunque no lo parezca a primera vista, conspiran abiertamente contra los fines revolucionarios, ya que, lo que se gana en ciertos conocimientos por el trabajo educacional, se pierde, con creces, en lo más profundo del modo de ser, de sentir, o sea en lo ideológico" (Ardévol 1966:135–36).

3. Interestingly, Alfredo Muñoz-Unsain is said to have enjoyed cabaret performances himself and attended them frequently in the mid-1960s; it remains unclear what led him to write this essay. Frederick Starr has observed similar moralizing discourses in the Soviet Union. He notes that jazz gained popularity among the public precisely because it was associated with sensuality and diversion, yet the Communist Party tended to view jazz lovers' "passion for amusement" as an impediment to the goals of the nation (Starr 1994:10–11).

4. *Granma* is the name of the boat used by Castro and his followers to sail from Mexico to eastern Cuba to begin their insurrection.

A fair sampling of music with political or socially conscious lyrics has been collected on the CD anthology *Música y revolución* (Loyola Fernández et al. 1996).

5. Both "De Kabinda a Kunene un solo pueblo" and "El son de Nicaragua" have been released on the Earthworks anthology *¡Sabroso! Havana Hits* (Vanrenen et al. 1989).

6. As an aside, we should recognize that music institutions in the United States commit, if anything, worse abuses of this kind and that they still turn a blind eye to a majority of national traditions (Wicks 1998). To date, there are few schools in the United States where one can major in the study of local popular or traditional music.

7. Following Van Van, other ensembles to emerge include Irakere (1973), Sierra Maestra (1976), and Son 14 (1978).

8. Izquierdo's career and the development of his influential *mozambique* rhythm are discussed in chapter 6.

9. The creation of *songo* is often attributed to Van Van's first *timbalero*, Blas Egües, who first performed it in 1969. It seems likely, however, that the rhythm developed as the result of years of experimentation by numerous percussionists. In any event, Changuito adapted and elaborated Egües's version of *songo* a year later when he joined Van Van so that it became much more virtuosic. He also added a characteristic kick drum beat on the and-of-two and and-of-four.

10. Thanks to Yaroldy Abreu Robles for help with this transcription.

11. "One Mint Julep" was known in Cuba as "Pastilla de menta." Orejuela Martínez 2004:15 notes that OCMM copycat groups formed at approximately the same time in Santiago, Las Villas, and Matanzas.

12. The refrain of "El coco," *rompe el coco,* or "break the coconut," is a slang expression for realizing a sexual desire. The title "Moja el pan" (Wet the Bread) is a sexual double entendre as well.

13. This information regarding government officials and their views about jazz appears in an NPR tribute to Valdés that aired in August 2001. During the segment, Arturo Sandoval stated that the OCMM could not use cymbals for years because they were too closely associated with music from the United States. This forced members to replace the ride cymbal with bells and other Cuban percussion. In the long run, the prohibitions may have helped them develop their unique sound.

14. D'Rivera's autobiography includes an amusing account of the Havana shows in the Mella Theater, which were controversial because of the large numbers of North Americans included in the program. In order to avoid any chance of public unrest or conflict, party representatives decided to fill up much of the theater with a group of old sugarcane workers who were being honored for fifty years of service. As might be expected, the cane cutters demonstrated little interest in jazz, and many true jazz enthusiasts could not get in because all tickets had been presold to them. D'Rivera recalls, "During Stan Getz's set I climbed up to the balcony and sat next to an old farmer who exclaimed 'Oh shit, when will this end! [¡Ay, coño, cuándo se acabará todo esto!] At his side another snored as if to accompany the acoustic bass solo of Ron McClure, with his straw hat over his face" (1989:211).

15. "Menéame la cuna" by Ñico Saquito (1993) and recorded by the Fania All Stars (Rodríguez 1996) represents one example of the appropriation of traditional Cuban repertoire by New York *salseros* without recognition. See also Hierrezuelo and Hierrezuelo 1993 for an example of the Los Compadres tune "Llanto de cocodrilo" later covered by Ray Barreto (1973) in essentially the same manner.

16. José Antonio Méndez's composition "Decídete mi amor," as one example, is attributed to Edgardo Donato on a recording by Héctor Lavoe (1999) from the 1970s and retitled "Déjala que siga."

17. Consider the use of *bomba* percussion rhythms in the title track of Ray Barreto's *Ritmo en el corazón* release (Barreto and Cruz 1988) or in Rubén Blades's "Pablo Pueblo" (1992).

18. Perna (2001:126–27) notes that NG's Rodolfo Argudín Justiz helped develop this new keyboard style using innovative *montuno* patterns in the 1980s.

19. Thanks to Elio Villafranca for help with the transcription of the Delgado example.

20. Perna (2001:115) notes that many Afro-Cuban couples remain on the side of the dance floor during the verse of *timba* songs and only begin dancing during the *montuno,* a practice reminiscent of folkloric rumba. Hernández-Reguant (2004a:33) states that most *timba* choreography developed in La Tropical, an outdoor dance venue associated primarily with the Afro-Cuban community.

21. "Mi estrella" by David Calzado (1994) is filled with Afro-Cuban street slang, for example. It refers to Donna Summer and Whitney Houston one moment and then quotes the melody to the Niño Rivera chachachá "El jamaiquino."

"La turística," on the same album, is an example of ultramodern *timba* and yet quotes Ignacio Piñeiro's "Tres lindas cubanas" from the 1920s.

Vincenzo Perna has written an excellent dissertation (2001) and book (2005) that treat the subject of *timba* music in detail and include extended musical transcriptions.

22. Thanks to Elio Villafranca, Elizabeth Sayre, and Orlando Fiol for help with this transcription.

23. A round table discussion chaired by Alberto Faya expresses many music critics' views regarding *timba* lyrics (Faya et al. 1996). See also Hernández 2002:70.

24. Literally "riders," *jinetero/a* is the term used in Cuba to describe individuals who make their living off foreigners, by selling them black market items, by making friends and asking for "gifts," or through prostitution.

25. Cuban interviewees often describe songs such as "El temba" as *bajada de frecuencia* (literally, "lowered in frequency"), or rarely played, rather than totally banned.

26. The lyrics to "Green Mango" include the line, "Hey green mango, since you're so ripe when are you going to fall?"

CHAPTER 5

1. *Trova* in Cuba, derived from *trovador,* or "troubadour," is the term used to refer to the national repertory of traditional song. *Nueva trova* has been used since the early 1970s to refer to songs based in part on older styles but written during the socialist period. One of the most comprehensive articles written about the early history of this music in English is Rina Benmayor's "La 'Nueva Trova': New Cuban Song" (1981).

2. For information on *nova música popular brasileira,* see Carrasco Pirard 1982:600; Díaz Pérez 1994:113–15 provides an overview of protest song movements in Mexico, Venezuela, and Puerto Rico, while Díaz Ayala 1981:302 discusses artists Raimón and Joan Manuel Serrat from northern Spain.

3. The *teatro vernáculo,* or comic theater, was essentially a form of vaudeville entertainment influenced by Spanish theatrical traditions as well as by U.S. minstrelsy. Short *sainetes,* or one-act plays, alternated onstage with song and dance routines, recitation of poetry, and the like. Numerous *sainetes* made parodic reference to contemporary political events. This tradition continued well into the 1930s; examples from the Teatro Alhambra include *El ciclón* (1906), alluding to the events of the August Revolution, and *La isla de los cotorros* (1923), about attempts by U.S. authorities to annex the Isle of Pines.

4. *Son guajiro* is a rural dance music form from eastern Cuba and towns in the interior of the island. It is slower in tempo than many other *son* styles, and its lyrics most often discuss the beauty of the countryside or incorporate other nationalist imagery.

5. *Copla* and *décima* refer to four- and ten-line poetic forms used in Cuban *música guajira* or Spanish-derived country music and in other genres.

6. Nicola's "Para una imaginaria María del Carmen" can be heard on Costales and Pinelli 1993, and Rodríguez's "Oleo de mujer con sombrero" is found on Rodríguez 1991.

7. The Alejandro "Virulo" García composition is available on the release *La historia de Cuba* (García and Grupo Moncada n.d.). Benmayor 1981:16–17 includes a detailed summary of the varied stylistic characteristics in *nueva trova* of the 1980s as described by musicologist Danilo Orozco. These include elaborations of past genres such as *filin*, elaborations and transformations of folkloric styles such as *rumba guaguancó*, the use of jazz and rock influences and new electrified instruments, and so forth.

8. José Martí was a Cuban revolutionary hero, leader of the War of Independence against Spain, and is considered one of the most important poets and essayists of the Spanish language in the nineteenth century. He died fighting Spanish troops 1898.

Considered Cuba's national poet, Nicolás Guillén (1902–89), an Afro-Cuban, is most famous for his work of the 1930s. He was one of the first to incorporate serious racial themes and issues as well as black working-class slang into published poetry.

César Vallejo is a Peruvian poet (1892–1938) of mixed Indian and European descent known for writing about human suffering and the fate of the poor.

A Chilean, Pablo Neruda is one of the most widely celebrated Latin American poets of all time and winner of the Nobel Prize for Literature in 1971. His open support of socialist issues is evident in later works such as *Tercera residencia* from 1947 and *Canto general* from 1950.

9. Specific examples of political *nueva trova* lyrics include "El programa del Moncada" and "Girón: La victoria" by Sara González and "A Lázaro Peña" by Martín Rojas. Lyrics to both can be found in Acosta and Gómez 1981.

10. The original Spanish reads, "Un fenómeno surgido entre las generaciones más jóvenes . . . una ruptura deliberada con la producción inmediatamente anterior y una cierta 'vuelta a las raíces' combinada con aires renovadores; y por último . . . una toma de conciencia política y social" (Acosta and Gómez 1981:6).

11. Although this analysis focuses on music, younger Cubans left their mark in many artistic fields of the 1960s, including film, dance, and literature. Examples include the films of Sara Gómez, dance choreographies for the Conjunto Folklórico Nacional by Rogelio Martínez Furé, and novels by Miguel Barnet.

12. In the 1980s, Pablo Milanés produced a series of albums entitled *Años* with Luis Peña and others that featured works from eastern Cuba of the 1910s and 1920s. These recordings include essentially the same material that has made such a splash in conjunction with the Buena Vista Social Club.

13. Tragically, Haydée Santamaría committed suicide in 1980. Apparently the Mariel crisis of that year and the realization that large percentages of the population did not support the revolution she had sacrificed so dearly for caused her terrible grief (Patterson 2000, interview).

The Festivals of Popular Song were discontinued after a few years because officials felt that rock and other styles from capitalist countries had become too popular among participants—they considered this music ideologically incompatible with the revolution. The festivals later reappeared in the 1980s (Reynaldo Fernández, pers. comm.).

14. Ariana Hernández-Reguant (pers. comm.) notes that through the mid-1970s the Instituto Cubano de Radio y Televisión was known only as the ICR, the final "R" standing for "Radiofusión."

15. Jorge Serguera Riveri trained as a lawyer and in literature and later fought under Raúl Castro in the Sierra Maestra. During the early years of the revolution, he served as a prosecutor of war criminals and then as judge advocate of the army. Subsequently he became military commander in Matanzas province, Cuban ambassador to Algeria, and finally director of radio and television in the late 1960s (Thomas 1971:1255).

16. The police did not force anyone to go to a *granja*. Instead, they requested that individuals remain there for an unspecified period with the understanding that if they did so they could eventually come back and continue life as before. If they chose not to go, however, they lost their job and professional affiliations. An aside: friends have remarked jokingly to me that Cuba is the only country in which dirt "cleans" you. The implication is that physical labor has the ability to wipe away the perceived stains on one's ideological record.

17. Elizundia Ramírez 2001:77–83 contains insightful commentary on what it was like to be a performer in Cuba during the gray period.

18. Fears of invasion were lessened by agreements reached between the United States and the Soviet Union in the wake of the missile crisis. Additionally, the size and resources of the Cuban military grew considerably after 1959, creating a strong deterrent.

19. No specific dates are available for Pablo Milanés's arrest. In fact, given the countless books written about this artist, it is dumbfounding to realize that very few even mention that he served prison time. Francisco Morín's *Por amor al arte* (1998:316–18) contains some anecdotal information, however. The 1966 date was provided by Clara Díaz Pérez (1996, interview), who suggested that his jailing may have involved accusations of drug use. Leonardo Acosta (1996, interview) believes that it resulted from personal problems with military leaders similar to those experienced by Silvio Rodríguez a short time later. Quintín Pino Machado commanded the UMAP facility where Milanés was held.

Unidades Militares para la Ayuda a la Producción (UMAP), or Military Units to Aid in Production, were essentially detention camps that subjected inmates to harsh living conditions in rural areas and required them to perform labor for the duration of their sentences. The UMAPs existed for only a short time, from about 1965 to 1968; inmates consisted primarily of homosexuals, religious figures, and political dissidents. Major international outcry over the existence of the UMAPs and letters of protest by renowned socialists such as Jean-Paul Sartre eventually led to their disbanding.

20. Silvio Rodríguez's compositions from this period include "Debo partirme en dos," in which one finds references to conflicts with the authorities as well as to censorship; "Ojalá," another challenge to the leadership, said to

have been directed at an officer associated with Silvio's military service or possibly Castro himself; the more openly autobiographical "Playa Girón" exhorting members of the crew to write their own histories rather than accept those imposed upon them; and "Resumen de noticias," a declaration of principles intended for friends and enemies alike. These song lyrics and others have been published in Rodríguez 1996. Cao 1992 includes discussion on this topic as well.

21. Gerardo Alfonso (2000) mentions that the government refused to allow him to appear on television singing his hit song of 1987, "Yo te quería María." This may have been because Alfonso wore Rastafarian-style dreadlocks, considered inappropriate.

22. Díaz Pérez 1994:200 provides a list of the documentaries and films featuring incidental music composed by the Grupo de Experimentación Sonora. See Brouwer 1989:48–51 for details about their musical objectives, and Dane 1971 for examples of the songs they recorded.

23. Pablo Milanés wrote his first compositions with overtly politicized lyrics, such as "Yo he visto la sangre de un niño brotar" (I Saw the Blood of a Child Spilled), after the international Encuentro de la Canción Protesta in 1967 (Díaz Pérez 1996, interview). He appears to have been influenced heavily by compositions from abroad.

24. Gerardo Alfonso refers to this "audition" process at the beginning of a CD he recorded live in the Casa de las Américas (Alfonso 2000).

25. *Te doy una canción* stayed on the air through 1985 (Acosta 1983:121).

26. Bureaucrats are said to have taken issue with the suggestion that life could ever be "worth nothing" in a progressive socialist society such as Cuba, though Milanés's lyrics do not directly imply that.

27. According to Cao (1992:22), the first time Castro himself formally received Silvio Rodríguez and Pablo Milanés at the airport was after their tour of Latin America in 1985.

28. Examples of songs about housing shortages and censorship include Noel Nicola's "A Small Housing Problem," mentioned by Ernesto Cardenal (1974:154–55), and "Reza el cartel allí" (Dane 1971) and Pablo Milanés's "Pobre el cantor," in addition to the Silvio Rodríguez songs "Resumen de noticias" and "Ojalá." It is difficult to fully document the extent of the trend because most artists never recorded their most controversial songs.

29. The Helms-Burton legislation, passed in 1996 with the support of Republican Jesse Helms and other senior congressmen, represented an intensification of the Cuban trade embargo. It allowed punitive actions to be brought against businesses in third countries that occupied property owned by U.S. businesses prior to 1959.

30. I base this conclusion about target audiences on the fact that potentially controversial songs by Rodríguez ("Paladar," "Reino de todavía") from his *Domínguez* release (Rodríguez 1996) are sold abroad and in dollar stores within Cuba but are largely unknown to the Cuban public. Similar works by Carlos

Varela (e.g., "Cuchilla en la acera") are likewise unfamiliar to domestic audiences. This may be because of government policy, because his songs appeared on foreign record labels, or both.

31. Thanks to Lucia Binotti and Raúl and Remigio Fernández for help with the translation of the excerpt of the lyrics from "Mariposa."

32. Lyric excerpt, "El abuelo Paco," modern *guaracha* composition (Ferrer 1994). The disc has been signed to the Ceyba label and is now available for purchase through distributors such as Museodeldisco.com.

33. Canek now lives in Oaxaca, Mexico, where he works as a freelance graphic artist.

34. Ramón Fernández Larrea now lives in Spain.

35. The prominence of Varela's group has diminished since about 1996, owing largely to the departure of musical director and pianist Elio Villafranca to the United States. Villafranca now lives in the New York area.

36. According to Vilar (1998:25), Varela's first opportunity to record came as the result of a tour in the Canary Islands organized by the Brigada Hermanos Saiz. Subsequent albums have either been recorded in Madrid or Caracas, the result of foreign initiative rather than that of the Cuban government. It is likely that Varela now prefers to record abroad since foreign contracts pay much better than those made with Cuban labels. One live album, *Carlos Varela en vivo*, did appear on the Cuban label Artex in 1993, though it is unclear whether Varela made the decision to release it there or whether he receives royalties.

37. Gema studied voice for several years, completing a degree in classical guitar and musicology at the ENA and ISA, respectively. While fairly rigorous, her training in music does not have a direct application to most of the music that she recorded as a *novísima trova* artist. Pável learned guitar on his own, but later as a semiprofessional performer took some classes in harmony and music theory (Corredera 2001, interview).

38. For a representative sampling of Gema y Pável's work, listen to Urkiza and Corredera 1995 and 1996 on the Nubenegra label, distributed by Intuition in the United States. They have released two additional albums since then, *Síntomas de fe* (1999) and *Arte bembé* (2004). See also www.gemaypavel.net/.

CHAPTER 6

1. I employ "folklore" to describe music and dance traditionally performed within particular community groups by and for themselves. Usually, its performers are amateurs who play and sing without the expectation of financial gain and who learn their art in informal settings. Of course, folklore may be presented to broader audiences through the media or onstage, and thus becomes part of "popular" or "commercial" entertainment. In socialist Cuba, the status of folklore vis-à-vis particular communities has become somewhat ambiguous owing to its promotion by state agencies.

2. It is difficult to distinguish between secular and sacred folklore in the Afro-

Cuban community. I made the somewhat artificial separation here only in order to divide the material into chapter-length segments.

3. These same percussion instruments are now on view in the revolution's National Music Museum in Old Havana.

4. During the first decades of the revolution, the only prominent Afro-Cubans in the government were Commander Juan Almeida, a veteran of the guerrilla struggle with Castro in the Sierra Maestra, and Lázaro Peña, a labor activist and former member of the PSP.

5. Vélez 1996: vol. 1, 79 includes information about one folklore ensemble from Matanzas called Emikeké that began performing in approximately 1970. It received support from the CNC and performed actively until its leader went into exile during the Mariel crisis. Other groups that received at least some financing during the same period include the Grupo Folklórico Universitario and Conjunto Afro-Cuba in Havana, the Grupo de Tambores Sikamarié in Guanabacoa, and a few of the Santiago-based groups mentioned in chapter 6 such as the Conjunto Folklórico, Cutumba, and the Tambores of Enrique Bonne (Ministerio de Cultura 1982:76; Gramatges 1982:145; Orejuela Martínez 2004:192).

6. Support from the state here refers to salaries for members. The groups he cites are the Conjunto Folklórico Nacional, the Conjunto Folklórico de Oriente, and the Muñequitos de Matanzas. All three troupes resulted from grassroots initiatives but achieved professional status by 1968. Robbins (1990:520) notes that as of the late 1980s, the government had recognized only two professional *agrupaciones folklóricas* in all of Matanzas province.

7. The Muñequitos de Matanzas are especially important for having made some of the first recordings of traditional rumba on the Panart label beginning in 1953.

8. The original Spanish reads, "Frente a la tribuna que inauguró el ciudadano Presidente, doctor Osvaldo Dorticós Torrado, dándole con su presencia dimensión revolucionaria al frívolo espectáculo de más de quinientos hombres y mujeres . . . respondiendo al llamado ancestral de los selváticos tambores. . . . Alegría combatiente que Cuba opone como viva respuesta a las insolentes amenazas de agresión del imperialismo impotente y rapaz" (Sánchez Lalebret 1963:63).

9. Bonne's first pieces in *pilón* rhythm are said to have been "El bajo cun-cun" and "Baila José Ramón" (Ginori 1968:60–61).

10. Initial members of Pacho Alonso y los Modernistas included Manuel Couto Pavón on piano, Modesto Balvuena on bass, Manuel Cobas "Quenque" on congas, Miguel A. Albear Manzano on timbales, Raúl Bosque Grillo, Epifanio Rabell Selva, and Pedro J. Crespo Pérez y Oreste Suárez on trumpet, as well as vocalists Ibrahím Ferrer and Carlos Querol. Juanito Márquez arranged the first two *pilón* hits recorded by Alonso and Bonne (Raul Fernandez, pers. comm.).

11. *Hoy*, April 15, 1965, no page. Much of this information about Izquierdo comes from unreferenced newspaper clippings in the Museo Nacional de la Música.

12. *Pello el Afrokan: Un sabor que canta*, originally an Areíto/EGREM recording, has been re-released by Vitral Records on their compact disc VCD-4122.

13. Mason 1992:328 includes a translation of most of this phrase from the praise song to Oyá, and Altmann 1998:200 contains a notated version of the melody that he entitles "Mama Loya E." The musical transformation on Izquierdo's album brings to mind similar phenomena in the United States, for instance, Ray Charles's use of the spiritual "This Little Light of Mine" as the basis for his R&B hit "This Little Girl of Mine."

14. The only similar group that received state funding was the Grupo de Danza Contemporánea, a modern classical troupe that incorporated stylized Afro-Cuban dance steps into some of their choreographies.

15. The core of Oru consisted of director Sergio Vitier, Rogelio Martínez Furé, Jesús Pérez, and Carlos Aldama. This ensemble formed in the mid-1960s and continued to perform as an experimental offshoot of the CFN through 1986.

16. Enrique Sosa passed away in the 1990s.

17. Examples of Cuban anthropologists and ethnomusicologists trained in the East Bloc include Olavo Alén, Victoria Eli Rodríguez, Jesús Gómez Cairo, and Lourdes Serrano. Around 1990 an "anthropology group" was created as part of the philosophy faculty to facilitate masters-level study options. As of the time of my initial inquiries in 1996 they had not yet been realized, but apparently in the new millennium the beginnings of a masters program in anthropology now exists. It is based at the University of Havana, with guidance from the independently staffed Centro de Antropología (L. Menéndez 1996, interview).

18. Prominent publications from the 1960s, 1970s, and 1980s on Afro-Cuban subjects include essays and books by Argeliers León (e.g., 1969, 1982), Miguel Barnet's *El cimarrón* (1969) and *La fuente viva* (1983), José Luciano Franco's *Ensayos históricos* (1974), and Rogelio Martínez Furé's *Diálogos imaginarios* (1979). Martínez Furé's book is especially useful in linking Cuban cultural traditions to African antecedents and to the larger circum-Caribbean region. Barnet's writings are also important. *La fuente viva,* for instance, is the first study to include essays on the history of Cuban folklore studies. For years, however, these individuals and a handful of others were the only ones publishing on Afro-Cuban topics. In the mid-1990s, the Centro Juan Marinello, Fundación Fernando Ortiz, and Centro de Antropología have emerged as new sources of information on Afro-Cuban culture.

19. The Wemilere Festival of Music and Dance of African Roots is organized by the Casa de Cultura "Rita Montaner" on Máximo Gómez St. no. 59.

20. Examples of less-than-rigorous folklore publications apparently intended for the tourist market include Andreu Alonso 1992 and Fernández de Juan et al. 1996. More rigorous works from the same period have been written by Tato Quiñones, José Millet, and others.

21. See *Anales del Caribe,* nos. 14/15, 16–18, and 19/20, for examples of issues of an academic periodical devoted to Afro-Cuban themes.

22. Though an overview of Guillén's poetry and its use by musicians is beyond the scope of this essay, readers should be aware that many performers have taken inspiration from it. Writers of popular song from the 1930s such as Eliseo Grenet first set Guillén's poems to music; classical composers Amadeo Roldán

and Alejandro García Caturla soon followed suit. *Nueva trova* star Pablo Milanés has created lovely pieces in the same tradition ("De qué callada manera," "Tú no sabe inglé"). New York *salseros* Willie Colón and Hector Lavoe recorded a dance piece entitled "Sóngoro cosongo" after the Guillén publication of the same name, while David Calzado's "El temba" makes repeated reference to the poem "Tengo." Cuban rap groups have recorded versions of Guillén's poetry as well: Cuarta Imagen ("La muralla"), Hermanos de Causa ("Tengo"), Instinto ("Kirino"), and so forth. Though Guillén is generally recognized as a "high culture" figure, many recent adaptations of his poetry are decidedly populist.

23. Guido López Gavilán's "Camerata en guaguancó" uses a nineteenth-century rumba melody as the basis for a chamber orchestra composition. It can be found on the Camerata Romeu's CD *La bella cubana* (1996).

CHAPTER 7

1. Hagedorn (2002:46) notes that Cuba's current penal code criminalizes the "abuse of freedom of religion," which may involve opposing revolutionary educational initiatives, failing to join the military, or showing irreverence for the nation or its leaders.

2. Ironically, Batista himself was a practitioner of Santería, as was his brother Panchín. However, he took pains to hide the fact and did little to protect believers from the police (Cristóbal Díaz Ayala, pers. comm.). Though Batista was more supportive of Santería during the 1940s and 1950s than the socialist leaders that later forced him from power, Villamil's testimony suggests that the president's personal views did not prevent widespread persecution.

3. Natalia Bolívar (pers. comm.) notes that terms appearing in "Lindo yambú" include *iborere*, the greeting for Ifá, and *akolona silaguao*, corresponding to Yemayá. For additional information on the recording of "En la alta sociedad," see Calderón 1986:52–53. African-derived terminology in "Lindo yambú" as interpreted by Bolívar includes *masa como indilisamba* (run, mulatto), *masamba me lo sambuye* (corn that we ritually offer), *gamba* (sun), and *jubilanga* (in drunkenness and joy). A reissue of "Lindo yambú" is available on Piñeiro 1992.

4. Cristóbal Díaz Ayala (pers. comm.) notes that "Un toque de bembé" was first recorded on the Puchito label, MLP-595, in the 1940s. Ivor Miller's work on Abakuá terminology contains a great deal of additional information on African-derived terminology in early *son* recordings from the 1930s (Miller 2000).

5. Though religious references were prominent in Arsenio Rodríguez's recordings throughout his career, the culmination of these references comes on the album *Quindembo* from 1964, in which Kongo terminology blends with Santería chants performed instrumentally on the *tres* (David García, pers. comm.).

6. The original Spanish lyrics to this conga read: "Mamá no quiere que yo

vaya a la iglesia, porque el cura falangista me convierte en terrorista. A los curas falangistas que preparen sus maletas, que las cosas de mi Cuba, no las enreden, ni se metan. Fidel, Fidel, ya mi Cuba está soberana, nos libraste de los esbirros, disfrazados, disfrazados con sotana. . . . Que se vayan, que se vayan, que se vayan" (Orejuela Martínez 2004:124).

7. For a description of a similar Sacred Cross tradition celebrated in the town of Jiguaní in the early twentieth century, see Tarín Blanco 1961.

8. Linares notes that the Cuban version of the lyrics to "Altares de cruz" differ somewhat from the way it is sung in Spain. The complete text sung by the group she recorded is (soloist) "Osa cruz madero, o Cruz celestial, escudo invencible de santo arterial"; (chorus) "Osa cruz madero, madero de yeso, donde Jesús Cristo descansó sus huesos." The original Spanish version begins, "O sacro madero, o cruz celestial real."

9. Millet and Brea 1989:93–94 mentions many of these new secular tradi-tions, including the Noches Culturales de la Calle Heredia, the Semana de la Cultura, the Tívoli Festival, the Festival of the Pregón, and the Caribbean Cul-ture Festival (all in Santiago), the Festival of Popular Arts in Ciego de Avila, and the Jornada Cucalambeana in Las Tunas.

10. Some suggest that Castro is an initiate of Santería and claim to have at-tended ceremonies with him, though this remains unsubstantiated.

11. The large numbers of Afro-Cuban performers appearing from 1959 through the mid-1960s may have resulted in part from attempts to diversify the Cuban economy during the early years of the revolution. Many religious drummers, singers, and dancers were involved in sugar production; as these jobs became more difficult to secure, they searched for other employment (Vélez 2000:69).

12. Hagedorn (2001:137) notes that all departments of the National Theater eventually played an even more significant role in national culture. The de-partment of art music, led by composer Carlos Fariñas, developed into the Na-tional Symphony Orchestra. The department of modern dance became an in-dependent modern performance ensemble. The choir, under Serafín Pro, was transformed eventually into the National Polyphonic Chorus, while Léon's folk-lore group bifurcated into the Institute of Ethnology and Folklore (a research center) and the National Folklore Troupe, or Conjunto Folklórico Nacional (ded-icated to performance).

13. For more detailed information on the history of the National Theater, see Sánchez León 2001. Orejuela Martínez (2004:100) notes the strong im-pression that such theatrical events made on Jean-Paul Sartre during his visits to Cuba.

14. See *El Militante Comunista*, January 1968, p. 43, for one example of the promotion of scientific atheism.

15. The original Spanish quote reads, "La superación paulatina de las creen-cias religiosas, mediante la propaganda científica materialista y la elevación del nivel cultural de los trabajadores" (Partido Comunista de Cuba 1978:98).

16. The limits on academic investigation of religion appear to be due in part to the creation of a separate Centro de Investigaciones Socio-Religiosas, staffed by PCC members. Individuals at this center were the only ones authorized to pursue such matters.

17. A picture of a typical *planilla* can be found in Clark 1992. Cristóbal Sosa (interview, 1996) notes that, as an unwritten rule, the directors of virtually all work centers tended to be party militants. These individuals took a hard line against believers that in many cases exceeded guidelines they received from the PCC.

18. Examples of work published by Afro-Cuban authors in *Actas del folklore* include reprints of Rómulo Lachatañeré's (1909–51) work on slave ethnicity in the nineteenth century (March 1961); studies of *cabildos de nación* by poet Marcelino Arozarena in the same issue; and Elisa Tamanes's "Antecedentes históricos de las tumbas francesas" (September 1961). Alberto Pedro Sr. is another important Afro-Cuban author represented in the journal.

19. See, for instance, "La expansión del 'espiritismo de Cordón'" by Armando Andrés Bermúdez in *Etnología y Folklore* 5 (January–June 1968): 5–32. It is typical of the period in its negative attitudes toward religion. López Valdés 1966 expresses many of the same opinions.

20. Teodoro Díaz Fabelo, who began his work as an assistant of Fernando Ortiz, found himself marginalized during what would have been the most productive years of his professional life. His only significant works published in Cuba are *Lengua de santeros* from 1956—a book that he paid to have printed—and *Olórun*, which appeared in 1960 with the help of León at the National Theater. Díaz Fabelo's frustration over the lack of support for his work eventually led to his defection to Venezuela (L. Menéndez 1996, interview), where he died in the 1970s. His unpublished manuscripts, many of which are available at the National Library, include "Análisis y evaluación cultural de las letras del Diloggún" (1967), "Los caracoles" (1967), "Introducción al estudio de las culturas afrocubanas: El poblamiento" (1969), and "Cómo se tira y lee el coco" (1969). Other works were printed by UNESCO but never became well known on the island: *Diccionario de yerbas y palos rituales, medicinales y el alimenticios en el uso por los afrocubanos* (1969), *La escritura de los Abakuá* (1971), *Diccionario de la cultura conga residual en Cuba*, 2 vols. (1972), and *Los negros cimarrones de Cuba* (1974).

21. The original Spanish reads, "Las creencias disparatadas de los esclavizados; ellas constituían para los oprimidos un falso refugio, una esperanza estéril, opio elemental y aguardiente para anestesiar los sufrimientos y escapar mentalmente de la situación real" (*Trabajo político: Boletín de organización del PCC-FAR* 2, no. 4 [December 1968]: 49). The article is signed "EMC." For a similar example from the 1970s, see the introduction to *Estudio de un babalao* (López 1978), written by Mirta Aguirre.

22. López Valdés 1966 also contains critiques of religion. Fernández Robaina 1994:48 includes similar commentary, even by former practitioners. During the

early years of the revolution, many decided to bring all of their *canastilleros, soperas,* and other ritual items to museums or to break them as gestures of solidarity with the government.

23. Deschamps Chapeaux was Afro-Cuban. A number of black and mulatto scholars derided African-derived religions in their publications at times either out of genuine conviction or because they felt compelled to conform to the views of the leadership.

24. Consider the following unsigned quote from *El Militante Comunista,* October 1968, p. 85, that belittles Afro-Cuban religions: "Una religión es primitiva cuando no ha llegado ni siquiera a elaborar abstracciones, sino que trabaja directamente con objetos y sujetos. Ahí tenemos un ejemplo: secreciones de los ojos de un ave de vista penetrante para aumentar la clarividencia de los ojos humanos. A nosotros el asunto nos revuelve el estómago, mas para una mentalidad primitiva tiene lógica." [A religion is primitive when it has not even managed to elaborate abstractions, but instead works directly with objects and subjects. Here is an example: secretions from the eyes of a bird with sharp sight used to increase vision in human eyes. To us the idea turns the stomach, but to the primitive mind it appears logical.]

25. Reference to Kongo/Palo religion can be found in an unsigned article from *El Militante Comunista,* November 1968, pp. 24–25. The article on Abakuá groups is entitled "La sociedad secreta Abakuá," p. 44. Elsewhere, a writer for *El Militante Comunista* described all Afro-Cuban religions as "sumamente arcaicas," or totally archaic (December 1968, p. 39).

26. The original Spanish reads, "El creyente [de Santería] queda limitado en sus facultades físicas e intelectuales. . . . Cuando el hombre logre superar esta etapa de la prehistoria universal de la sociedad, dejará de ser un sujeto dependiente de entidades sobrenaturales que por miedo e ignorancia creó, y se convertirá en un hombre realmente libre, dueño de sus actos y capaz de transformar la naturaleza, la sociedad y su pensamiento a plenitud, para transformarse a sí mismo" (Guanche 1983:400).

27. The original Spanish reads, "Las creencias sincréticas, particularmente la Santería . . . presentan modalidades sintomáticas que hacen parecer al paciente como *esquizofrénico* real, junto con *reacciones disociativas histéricas*" (Guanche 1983:398; italics in the original).

28. The original Spanish reads, "Proceso morboso grave caracterizado por la incoherencia mental y la disgregación del pensamiento" (Guanche 1983:398).

29. The original statement from the Cuban Communist Party reads, "Los valores culturales folklóricos—música, danza, instrumentos musicales, etc.—que aportan las etnias representadas en estos grupos, deben asimilarse, depurándolos de elementos místicos, de manera que la utilización de sus esencias no sirva al mantenimiento de costumbres y criterios ajenos a la verdad científica." This quote came from a document in the Instituto de Lingüística in Havana, Cuba. No page number is available.

30. "Veneración" is the famous piece that begins, "Y si vas al Cobre quiero

que me traigas una Virgencita de la Caridad." It was written by Rafael Cueto and his wife, Naomia Matos.

31. Merceditas Valdés's first opportunity to record religious music in the socialist period came in the late 1980s with the release of *Aché I, II,* and *III.*

32. The best known of CIDMUC's field recordings is its nine-volume *Antología de la música afrocubana.* The set includes examples of *bembé* music, Dahomeyan-derived Arará ceremony, *batá* drumming, *música iyesá,* and other sacred styles. Many of the recordings from which these LPs were taken date from the 1970s but did not become commercially available until the following decade. Cristóbal Díaz Ayala (pers. comm.) notes that volume 1 first appeared in Mexico in 1980 on the label Nueva Cultura Latinoamericana in collaboration with the Cuban Academy of Sciences.

33. On p. 51, María Elena Vinueza 1988 describes Dahomeyan beliefs as "obscurantism" resulting from a lack of formal education. On p. 55, it refers to the Arará community as if it were a relic of the past and emphasizes that the goal of Marxism is to eradicate religion.

34. Cristóbal Sosa notes that Elio Revé wrote the piece in 1984, though it first appeared commercially in 1993.

35. Nicolás Reinoso, a black Cuban and Santería initiate, now lives in Uruguay.

36. Thanks to Ned Sublette for providing the 1987 date for the first national appearance of Síntesis's Afro-Cuban "religious rock" album *Ancestros.* He notes that an earlier incarnation of the Síntesis band, named Tema IV, made a record a few years before *Ancestros* that included a few of the same pieces. The release of *Ancestros,* however, represented the most definitive moment of its popularization.

37. Documents from Radio Habana Cuba (RHC), as one example, indicate that on March 31, 1991, a program dedicated to the celebration of Holy Week aired on that station. Speakers included Raúl Suárez Ramos, president of the Ecumenical Council of Cuba, Rev. Arnarldo Mirando, president of the Nazarene Church, and Joel Ajo, bishop of the Methodist Church. Note that RHC is a shortwave station intended primarily for listeners abroad.

38. *Los orichas en Cuba* represented a condensed reproduction of writings on the *orichas* from the prerevolutionary years. Nevertheless, the fact that it appeared at all is significant.

39. Neira's *Como suena un tambor abakuá* (1991) is rather odd. Its initial pages reproduce information from Fernando Ortiz's studies of Abakuá ritual, and particularly on the role of the *bonkó-enchemiyá* drum. He devotes the remainder of the study to mathematical analyses of the sine wave produced by the same instrument.

40. Fernández Robaina relates that *Hablen paleros y santeros* initially appeared in a limited-edition pamphlet from 1984 called "Los santeros." The government allowed it to appear because it did not advocate the perpetuation of Afro-Cuban religions explicitly and especially because one of the *santeros* interviewed mentions questioning his beliefs.

41. Examples of more recently published works on Afro-Cuban religions in-

clude Bolívar 1994 and de Lahaye Guerra and Zardoya Loureda 1994, as well as Gloria Rolando's video *Un eterno presente: Oggún* and many others.

42. Adalberto Álvarez mentions his *madrina* in "¿Y qué tú quieres que te den?", for instance, giving her public name (Rosa Zayas) as well as her religious name (Oché Elogüe).

43. Example of subsequent dance pieces inspired by Afro-Cuban religions include "Maferefú Obatalá" and "La reina de Ifé" by Pachito Alonso y su Kini Kini, "Viejo Lázaro" by Dan Den, "Babalú Ayé" by Kiki Korona, "Santa palabra" by NG La Banda, and "Soy todo," "Hierbero, ven," and "Ay, dios ampárame" by Los Van Van. The Caribe Productions CD *Despójate* from 1994 contains many of these songs.

44. Since 1998, the subject of religion has been less prominent. The topic began to be overused and the market for such material saturated. Recordings of traditional religious drumming and song continue to be made in increasing numbers, however.

45. Traditional song and drumming recordings that have appeared since the mid-1990s include Lázaro Ros's *Olorun 1* (Ros 1992); *Ito Iban Echu* by the Muñequitos de Matanzas (Muñequitos de Matanzas 1996); and Justo Pelladito's *Cuba. Afroamérica: Chants et rythmes afrocubaines* (Pelladito et al. 1997).

46. *Nueva trova* songs with texts about brotherly love include "Cuba va" by the Grupo de Experimentación Sonora (Dane 1971), "Su nombre es pueblo" by Eduardo Ramos (1998), and "Acerca del amor" by Silvio Rodríguez (lyrics in Rodríguez et al. 1996).

47. Consider the following commentary by Milan Kundera about Czechoslovakia in the 1950s (Kundera 1992:224–25): "It was an era of great collective faith. A man who kept in step with this era experienced feelings that were akin to religious ones; he renounced his ego, his person, his private life in favor of something higher, something suprapersonal. True, the Marxist teachings were purely secular in origin, but the significance assigned them was similar to the significance of the Gospel and the biblical commandments. They have created a range of ideas that are untouchable and therefore, in our terminology, sacred."

48. Barnet's exact comment, in this case discussing African-derived religions, is as follows: "En Cuba se ha hecho evidente que cultos como la Santería han ido perdiendo su preeminencia desde los primeros años del triunfo de la revolución. La nueva sociedad . . . crea incentivos de vida que permiten ampliar las perspectivas humanas, irá prescindiendo cada vez más de estas estructuras religiosas. . . . Las divinidades ocuparán en un tiempo futuro, ya próximo, el lugar que ocupan hoy las del panteón griego o romano. Serán figuras de leyenda. . . . El pozo de las religiones africanas en Cuba . . . se irá secando cada vez más" (1983:196).

49. Lázaro Ros himself along with his manager discussed the difficulty of teaching and broadly disseminating Afro-Cuban religious music with me in 1996. They had lobbied repeatedly for the creation of compilations of sacred chants and their inclusion in music curricula without success.

CHAPTER 8

1. Many of the events related to the onset of economic crisis were summarized in statements made by Vice President Carlos Lage to the Fifth Party Congress. See *CUBAInfo* 9, no. 14 (October 22, 1997): 4–5.

2. The original Spanish reads, "Se acaba el gas, la electricidad, el transporte público, los medicamentos, los alimentos. . . . Ahora nos damos cuenta de que ese proyecto humanista que nosotros hemos defendido requería de un fundamento económico para desarrollarse del que hemos carecido. Crearle a toda la gente la visión de que quien vive del capitalismo es un ladrón no tiene ningún sentido cuando la nuestra es una de las sociedades del mundo donde más se roba. . . . Incluso hemos llegado a perder la noción del robo porque es la misma necesidad la que nos empuja a él. Si un cubano se propone vivir con lo establecido por la ley lo tienen que ingresar. El resultado es una sociedad que se enferma psicológicamente obligada a diseñar su propia vida de forma clandestina o sobre la base de un proyecto de delito" (P.P. 1994:44).

3. For information on the cutting of enlisted forces, see *CUBAInfo* 10, no. 5 (April 9, 1998): 1. Cuba's military strength has fallen from a peak of one hundred thirty thousand troops in the late 1980s to half of that as of 1998.

4. Apparently the value of remittances reached $800 million in 1996 but has dropped somewhat since then (Lynn 1997:7). Even now, however, Monreal (1999) notes that the amount of foreign cash sent to Cuba each year is a sum several times higher than the total salaries paid by the state to employees over the same period. It is still unclear whether new Bush legislation from July 2004 will effectively curb the flow of remittances.

5. Information on tourism in the 1980s comes from Stubbs 1989:138. She mentions that only 96,600 tourists visited Cuba in 1978. Palmié (2003:12) states that 340,000 came in 1990 and 750,000 in 1995, essentially doubling in the space of five years. The figures for 1997, 1998, 2000, and 2003 are from *CUBAInfo* 10, no. 1 (January 8, 1998): 6; Cantor 1999:17; *CubaNews* 9, no. 3 [March 2001]: 1; and *Cuba Facts*, no. 14 (June 2005; http://ctp.iccas.miami.edu/cubafacts.asp).

6. See www.1click2cuba.com/menu.html for links to web pages containing information on Cayo Coco, Cayo Guillermo, and elsewhere.

7. Prostitution in Cuba since the 1990s has received significant scholarly attention. It is a pertinent topic to this study because much of it occurs in the context of music events and because Cuba has become known in certain circles as a destination for "sex tourism." Nevertheless, Cuban prostitution is difficult to generalize about. Not all women (or men) have a hardened, mercenary attitude toward their prospective clients, demanding specific cash payments. Some are honestly interested in making a foreign friend. Others may wish to fall in love with and marry a foreigner in order to leave the country. "Prostitutes," therefore, reflect a wide gamut of expectations. An additional complication is that attitudes toward sexuality are not always as conservative in Cuba as in many parts of Latin America.

8. BIS Music, established in 1994, specializes in older recordings of artists who either lived outside of Cuba as of 1959 or left the country shortly thereafter (Cristóbal Díaz Ayala, pers. comm.).

9. See www.cubadisco.soycubano.com/indexi.htm for additional details on the Cubadisco events of 2002, 2003, and 2004. They seem to have taken place every year since 1997. Some have centered around particular themes, such as the Feria del Disco 2001, dedicated to collaborations between Cuban and Brazilian artists.

10. The Pablo Milanés Foundation in Vedado closed in 1995 due to conflicts with other state agencies but reopened as a scaled-down enterprise approximately a year later.

11. Of course, other labels have existed since the 1960s devoted to the re-release of prerevolutionary material (Harlequin, Tumbao, Cubanacán, etc.). In many cases, these individuals have no official contact with the Cuban government but instead negotiate license agreements with the international companies that originally recorded the prerevolutionary LPs or treat the recordings as public domain.

12. See Díaz Ayala 2003b: 420–32 for additional commentary on the licensing of Cuban music abroad.

13. Jimmy Maslon (pers. comm.) relates that he began working with Cuban musicians in 1994. His first releases included titles by Bamboleo and Manolín "El Médico," the latter under license from Caribe Productions.

14. Ned Sublette (pers. comm.), for instance, notes that Ry Cooder was fined $25,000 by the Treasury Department merely for visiting Cuba to make the Buena Vista Social Club CDs; if he had funded the production himself he would be considered a felon and probably would be serving jail time.

15. One should recognize that the Cuban government also takes advantage of such ambiguity by showing pirated movies from the United States on television and in movie theaters.

16. Cantor 1997:24 describes the amount of taxed income as approximately 10–15 percent of the total earned, but the documents I have seen suggest that it can be considerably higher. Watrous 1997a: 34 and Robinson 2004:171 maintain it may be as much as 50 percent, with an additional 20 percent of gross income deducted in many state-owned clubs to pay the workers there. Contracts governing these agreements are not easy to access and are not always consistent from agency to agency.

17. Consider the comments of bassist Rafael Almazán, quoted in D'Rivera 1998:54: "Estos 'convenios de trabajo' son unos mecanismos de extorsión que el gobierno cubano aplica a su gente para sacar dólares. Mis compromisos eran: costearme los boletos de avión, alojamiento, manutención, mis bienes de trabajo, un representante artístico, el vestuario, etc., por lo cual la EGREM recibiría mi salario mensual en dólares en Cuba. Tuvieras trabajo o no." By this Almazán apparently means that EGREM required the equivalent of his normal Cuban salary in pesos to be paid to it in dollars as a prerequisite for travel authorization.

18. Hernández-Reguant 2004b:16–18 refers readers to various pieces of leg-

islation for further information on copyright. These include Decreto-ley 141 (*Gaceta Oficial*, September 8, 1993); Decreto-ley 144 (*Gaceta Oficial*, November 19, 1993), Decreto-ley 145 (*Gaceta Oficial*, November 17, 1993); Resolution 61/1993 (*Gaceta Oficial*, November 4, 1993); and Resolution 42/1997 (*Gaceta Oficial*, July 2, 1997).

19. Examples of works by musicologists published abroad include the anthology *Panorama de la música popular cubana* (Giro 1995) released in Colombia, Clara Díaz Pérez's *Silvio Rodríguez: Hay quien precisa* (1995), and the collaboration *La música entre Cuba y España* by María Teresa Linares and Faustino Núñez (1998).

20. Information on the mass defection is also in Madigan 2004. Díaz Ayala 2003b:404 contains a more complete listing of exiled artists.

21. Eugene Robinson 2004:91–94 and 181–85 contains an interesting account of one group, Ébano, and its attempts to establish and maintain an orchestra during the 1990s.

22. *Temas,* especially, has developed into a lively academic journal that regularly publishes discussions about previously taboo subjects (the new waves of exiles, the future of Marxist thought, domestic race relations, censorship). Adding to its attractiveness is the fact that it solicits contributions from many international scholars (Noam Chomsky, Jorge Duany, Louis Pérez, Marifeli Pérez-Stable) as well as Cuban nationals. One article on music that demonstrates the journal's spirit of intellectual openness is "La música popular como espejo social" (Hernández 2002).

Diane Soles has written a fascinating account of the creation and screening of *Alicia en el pueblo de maravillas*, a film from the early 1990s directed by Daniel Díaz Torres. Her work demonstrates both the greater freedom of artists to create controversial works and the continuing artistic restraints to which they remain subject. Soles notes that because of its criticism of bureaucracy, *Alicia* "prompted the Cuban Communist Party to mobilize hundreds of [party] members to fill Havana theaters and deride the film." After only four days, party members removed it from theaters (Soles 1997:1). The leadership of the ICAIC successfully weathered the outcry from conservatives, however, and has shown the film repeatedly in film festivals since that time.

23. Hernández 2002:66 contains references to specific songs and albums on which such pieces appear.

24. See also *Habana abierta* (1997) and *Habana abierta: 24 horas* (1999) on the Ariola label, produced by Gema Corredera and Pável Urkiza. Susan Thomas (pers. comm.) mentions that many of the same individuals appear on all these CDs and that the name change of the collective only reflects legal disputes between Nubenegra and BMI.

25. Estimates suggest that the total foreign debt as of 1999 surpasses $11 billion, and that 76 percent of the interest payments are in arrears (*CubaNews* 9, no. 2 [February 2001]: 4).

26. The 1997–98 harvest of 3.2 million tons of sugar represented a fifty-year low (*CUBAInfo* 10, no. 13 [October 1, 1998]: 9–10).

CONCLUSION

1. For information on recent Treasury Department actions regarding travel restrictions, see www.treas.gov/offices/eotffc/ofac/.

2. Bill Martínez has compiled a list of procedures required to invite Cuban performers into the United States in Sublette 2004. They involve review by the Immigration Service, the State Department, the Department of Homeland Security, the FBI, and the CIA. All procedures must be accompanied by a $1000.00 per person "premium processing fee." Of late, even those who apply well in advance of their proposed trip and complete all necessary requirements have been unsuccessful in their petitions. Martínez describes the current situation as a bureaucratic nightmare. "Files get lost. One agency isn't sure what another is doing. A name check problem for one artist can jeopardize the entire group tour" (p. 15).

3. The defection of dancers and musicians from Las Vegas in November 2004 suggests that at least some artists may receive visas once again. This group's case may also represent a singular exception, however; its visas were granted largely through insider connections in Washington and the political skill of ex-CANF member and lobbyist Dennis Hays (Ned Sublette, pers. comm.).

4. Approximately 30,000 Cubans left the island in 1994 on rafts, and 25,000 a year continue to leave through the lottery system that developed in direct response to the rafter crisis. Most of these are young, well-educated individuals who would otherwise be making significant contributions to their country. The number of Cubans who attempt to leave by entering the lottery pool increased from 189,000 in the first year of its existence to well over 500,000 by 1998; demand continues to rise (Duany 2004). Applications for marriages to foreigners, another exit strategy, have similarly skyrocketed since the early 1990s (Hernández-Reguant 2004a:35).

5. One piece recorded by the duo Los Mikimbín is a spoof of the Manolín hit "La bola." The chorus, instead of using the text "arriba de la bola" (on top of the ball), substituted "Arriba de una goma" (on top of an inner tube), making allusions to the rafter crisis of 1994. Thanks to Lara Greene for this reference.

6. In Denise de Kalafe's case, a Dade County jury eventually forced festival organizers to offer de Kalafe a cash settlement in compensation (Obejas 1996).

7. Rosita Fornés's show eventually took place in the Jackie Gleason Theater on August 30, 1996. See http://cuban-exile.com/doc_276–300/doc0281.html.

8. For further details on the bomb threat, consult the article "Cuban Music Yanked," *Miami Herald*, March 27, 1997, p. 30A.

9. See *Miami Herald*, August 21, 2001, pp. 1A and 6B, for more information on the 2001 Latin Grammys. The event, initially scheduled for September 11, 2001, was postponed because of the al-Qaeda terrorist attacks in New York and Washington. A low-key, untelevised awards ceremony took place instead on October 30.

10. This information regarding new institutes devoted to arts education for youth comes from Cristóbal Sosa, an employee at the station who copied data

from a program hosted by Joaquín G. Santana called *Estampas de Cuba* that aired on September 17, 2004. It additionally notes that nearly fifty schools across the island are devoted to elementary and midlevel arts education.

11. *The Corporation* is a Canadian film by Mark Achbar, Jennifer Abbott, and Joel Bakan based on the book *The Corporation: The Pathological Pursuit of Profit and Power* by Joel Bakan (New York: Free Press, 2004).

Glossary

ICAIC	Instituto Cubano de Artes e Industrias Cinematográficas: Cuban Institute of Cinema Arts and Industries
ICAP	Instituto Cubano de Amistad con los Pueblos: Cuban Institute of Friendship with Nations
ICRT	Instituto Cubano de Radio y Televisión: Cuban Institute of Radio and Television
IEF	Instituto de Etnología y Folklore: Institute of Ethnology and Folklore
INIT	Instituto Nacional de la Industria Turística: National Institute of Tourist Industries
ISA	Instituto Superior de Arte: Superior Art Institute
JUCEI	Juntas de Coordinación, Ejecución e Inspección: Coordination, Execution, and Inspection Groups
JUCEPLAN	Junta Central de Planificación: Central Economic Planning Board
MININT	Ministry of the Interior
MNT	Movimiento de la Nueva Trova: *Nueva trova* movement
OCMM	Orquesta Cubana de Música Moderna: Cuban Orchestra of Modern Music
ORI	Organizaciones Revolucionarias Integradas: Integrated Revolutionary Organizations
PCC	Partido Comunista de Cuba: Cuban Communist Party
PSP	Partido Socialista del Pueblo: People's Socialist Party
UJC	Unión de Jóvenes Comunistas: Young Communists' Union
UMAP	Unidades Militares para la Ayuda a la Producción: Military Units to Aid in Production
UNEAC	Unión Nacional de Escritores y Artistas Cubanos: National Union of Cuban Writers and Artists
UPC	Unión de Pioneros de Cuba: Union of Cuban Pioneers

TERMS

Abakuá (*also* Ñáñigo).   A name for men of predominantly Afro-Cuban origin who belong to secret societies of African origin (from the Cameroon area). These brotherhoods perform sacred and secular rituals involving music on unique percussion instruments.

academias de baile.   Literally, "dance academies." Recreational institutions associated with dance, musical entertainment, and often prostitution. Popular in Cuba through the 1950s, they were eventually closed by the revolutionary government.

aficionado. Amateur. A musical *aficionado* refers to someone involved in the Amateurs' movement or in a nonprofessional ensemble.

afrocubanismo. A movement of the late 1920s and 1930s that attempted to valorize many forms of Afro-Cuban cultural expression. It was similar in many respects to the Harlem Renaissance in the United States.

Amateurs' movement. A utopian attempt, based on Marx's writings, to directly involve as many people as possible in the arts. Some of its most visible manifestations included neighborhood mural projects and the formation of theater and dance troupes, choruses, and amateur music ensembles. The initiative began in 1960 and reached a peak in about 1965, though it persisted for decades.

Arará. People or cultural forms of Dahomeyan origin.

babalao. A male priest of the Yoruba *oricha* Ifá. *Babalaos* are consulted for spiritual guidance and for help resolving personal problems.

baile de maní. Literally, "peanut dance." One of many African-influenced dance forms common to Cuba of the late nineteenth century and a precursor to the present-day *rumba columbia.* The *baile de maní* was performed to the sound of *yuka* drums by one man surrounded by others in the center of a circle. It involved belligerent gestures and blows imposed by the central figure on the others, who defended themselves while continuing to dance.

batá drums. Two-headed, hourglass-shaped drums of Yoruba origin that are used in Santería ceremony. They are performed in sets of three and are considered sacred; they execute some of the most complex and virtuosic rhythms in all of Cuban music. During the first half of the twentieth century, performers hid *batá* drums from the public to avoid persecution. Gradually, secular versions of the *batás* have developed and have been incorporated into popular music.

bembé. A semiformal religious event of Yoruba origin involving music and dance. Percussion instruments used in a *bembé* tend to be secular, such as normal conga drums and bells. The term can also be used in a general sense to mean "party" or "dance."

bocú (pl. *bocuses*). *Bocú* in Kongo terminology means "drum." The term is used in eastern Cuba to refer to long, slightly conical single-headed drums used in carnival celebrations.

bodega. A corner grocery store.

bomba section. See **masacote.**

bombo. Bass drum. This instrument was first used in European military regiments in the nineteenth century. Since then its performance style has been modified and musicians have incorporated it into carnival bands.

bunga. A somewhat condescending term used to describe an impromptu or ad hoc musical group.

cabildos. Afro-Cuban social groups that proliferated in the nineteenth century. With the permission of colonial authorities, slaves and free blacks from virtually every West African ethnic group represented in Cuba formed these organizations as a means of helping each other adapt to their new environment. *Cabildos* served as an important means of perpetuating African cultural practices in Cuba. A handful survived into the late twentieth century.

canto. Literally, "chant" or "song." In Cuban dance music, the *canto* refers to the initial strophic verse section of a *son* composition. See also *son* and *montuno.*

Carabalí. An adjective used to describe people or institutions originating in the Calabar region of Africa, in present-day Cameroon.

casas de cultura. Neighborhood cultural centers created by the socialist government beginning in the 1970s. They still exist today, offering children introductory music education classes in many cases and sponsoring a diversity of other activities.

casa de santo. Literally, "house of the saints." Sites of worship in Afro-Cuban religions, usually the private home of a spiritual leader.

cáscara. Literally, "shell." In musical performance, the *cáscara* pattern refers to rhythms performed with sticks on the external shell of a drum such as a conga or timbal.

catá. A circular wooden percussion instrument beaten with sticks. The *catá* is used in Haitian-derived *tumba francesa* repertoire in eastern Cuba.

chachá. "Butt" in Yoruba. The smaller of the two heads on a *batá* drum.

chachachá. A form of Cuban dance music that gained popularity in the early 1950s. It adopted the instrumentation of *charanga francesa* dance bands but included rhythms taken from the *son.*

changüí. A rural form of dance music similar to the *son* that is performed in eastern Cuba.

charanga (or *charanga francesa*). In the nineteenth century, *charanga* was a term similar to *bunga* that referred to small, informal musical groups. In the twentieth century, *charanga* or *charanga francesa* came to denote dance orchestras consisting of piano, acoustic bass, timbales, *güiro*, flute, and violins. They performed *danzones* for many years and later the chachachá and *son* as well.

chéquere. An African-derived musical instrument consisting of a dried gourd around which a net with seeds, nuts, or beads has been fastened. The net is pulled or manipulated over the gourd, creating percussive sounds. The gourd itself can also be struck on the bottom, which produces a clear, resonant tone.

cinquillo. The *cinquillo* is one of the most widespread rhythms in the circum-Caribbean area. The simplest form of the *cinquillo* consists, as its name suggests, of a five-beat pattern in the following configuration:

The *danzón* is probably the musical form most closely associated with the *cinquillo* that is still performed in Cuba today. *Danzón clave* (*see* clave) consists of a *cinquillo* or similar pattern followed by four quarter notes. The entire phrase is usually performed on the timbales using a series of open and closed tones on the head to create timbral variety.

clave.   The concept of clave in Cuban music refers to the use of a constantly repeating rhythmic figure, usually two measures in length, that serves as the structural basis for the rest of the composition's rhythms and melodies. Clave rhythms may be played on the claves (wooden sticks) themselves, or on wood blocks, the timbales, bells, or other objects. Distinct clave patterns exist for the *son*, rumba, *danzón*, Yoruba-derived religious music, and other genres.

cocoyé.   Song and dance repertoire of Dahomeyan origin that made its way to Cuba by means of Haitian immigration in the late eighteenth century. Also, a particular song popular in 1840s Santiago de Cuba known as "El cocoyé."

columbia.   See rumba.

comparsa.   Afro-Cuban carnival band. *Comparsas* today derive from similar groups organized by *cabildos* in the nineteenth century that performed on Epiphany, January 6. In more recent years, *comparsas* have been organized by the residents of particular neighborhoods or by work center. Each ensemble consists of approximately thirty members and includes drummers, horn players, singers, and dancers.

conjunto (or *conjunto de son*).   The name for dance bands playing *son*-based repertoire; they first became popular in the 1940s. Arsenio Rodríguez was a seminal figure in the development of *conjunto* instrumentation. It expanded upon the earlier format of the 1930s (trumpet, guitar, *tres*, bongo, maracas, clave, bass) by adding an additional trumpet or two and conga drums as well as piano.

cordón de La Habana.   Havana cordon. An agricultural initiative of the late 1960s, it proposed to ring the city with coffee plants that could be used domestically and for export.

corneta china.   An Asian double-reed instrument introduced by Chinese immigrants and now a typical part of most carnival bands in Santiago de Cuba.

coros de clave.   Afro-Cuban musical ensembles common in the early twentieth century that contributed to the development of the modern *son*. Frequently, singers accompanied themselves on instruments such as the *viola* (a small bass or banjo without strings, used as a percussion instrument), guitar, clave, harp, and jug bass.

cuentapropista.   A self-employed worker. This sort of employment option is relatively new in socialist Cuba, having been prohibited in 1968. It was authorized once again in the mid-1990s as part of broader economic reforms.

danzón. An instrumental dance genre that developed in Matanzas during the late nineteenth century in black middle-class social clubs. *Danzones* are in duple meter and are danced by couples. The repertoire is instrumental and features flute and violin melodies.

danzón cantado. Danzón compositions featuring vocalists. This variant first became popular in the 1920s.

danzón de nuevo ritmo. Literally, "*danzón* in a new rhythm." First performed by the orchestra of Antonio Arcaño in the late 1930s, this *danzón* variant incorporated the conga drums and featured syncopated melodic figures and a final *montuno*-like improvisational section taken from the *son.*

danzonete. A *danzón* variant similar to the *danzón de nuevo ritmo* but less syncopated and without the conga drum. It served primarily as a vehicle for featuring singers.

diablitos. Literally, "little devils." Masked Afro-Cuban dancers whose costumes represent ancestor spirits. *Diablitos* first paraded through the streets of Cuba in the early nineteenth century as part of Christmas celebrations.

empresas. Literally, "enterprises." While the term may be used in reference to businesses of all sorts, Cuban musicians use it most often to refer to management and contracting agencies that coordinate domestic musical performance. The music *empresas* were established in the 1980s.

enú. "Mouth" in Yoruba. The larger of the two heads on a *batá* drum.

escuelas del campo. Literally, "countryside schools." The so-called schools are actually work brigades consisting of student groups. They spend time in rural areas at particular moments in order to help with agricultural care or harvests.

Espiritismo. A form of spiritual practice involving communication with deceased members of the community. Derived from the writings of Alain Kardec, it first attracted adherents in the nineteenth century and has since blended with African-derived conceptions of religious worship and spirit possession.

espiritista. A practitioner of Espiritismo.

filin (also feeling). A style of music that developed in 1950s. Sung by one or two vocalists with guitar accompaniment, it fuses elements taken from jazz (especially extended harmonies) with the traditional Cuban bolero. Vocal lines tend to incorporate considerable rubato, while the guitar keeps a somewhat more constant pulse.

guaguancó (rumba guaguancó). See rumba.

guajeo. One of the terms for the repetitive, syncopated melodies and rhythms used as the basis for improvisation in Cuban dance music.

güiro. A scraped percussion instrument made out of a dried gourd.

Iyesá. A form of Yoruba-derived religious expression in Cuba associated with specific drum rhythms and songs.

jinetero/a. Literally, "rider." A term for Cuban hustlers who make a living off tourists. This may involve selling them things (rum, tobacco) or providing services, including sexual services. *Jineterismo* is the practice of being a *jinetero*.

ladino (also *negro curro*). A term applied to Cuban emigrants of African ancestry who came directly from Spain, not as slaves but as free men and women. *Ladinos* spoke a unique form of Andalusian Spanish and wore characteristic, fancy clothing.

makuta. A form of Kongo-derived music and dance employing two single-headed drums. It is associated primarily with the area surrounding the city of Trinidad and is danced only by men.

mambí (pl. *mambises*). A revolutionary soldier in the war against Spain at the turn of the twentieth century.

mambo. Originally a Kongo term meaning "conversation" or "message." Among mid-twentieth-century musicians it has two common usages. The first refers to a *montuno*-like interlude within a composition, during which one or more syncopated melodic riffs is repeated many times by string players and/or horns. The second, related, meaning refers to a distinct musical genre for Cuban dance band based exclusively on the cyclical *montuno* concept. This second meaning has gained the most recognition internationally, in large part because of the success of recordings by bandleader Dámaso Pérez Prado beginning in 1949.

marímbula. An instrument of African origin found in Cuba and other parts of Latin America, often referred to as "thumb piano" in English. The *marímbula* consists of a wooden box with a sound hole cut out of one side; strips of metal are attached near this hole and are plucked or struck with the fingers. In Cuba the box is usually large, serving as a seat for the musician playing it, and functions as a bass instrument in various ensembles.

masacote (also *bombo*). The "breakdown" section in modern *timba* dance music. It consists of a transitional moment in which the piano and horns drop out and percussion becomes the primary focus of interest. The electric bass stops playing its *tumbao* but may add slaps or long, sliding pitches to the *masacote*.

montuno. Literally, "pertaining to the mountains or the countryside." The term refers to the final section of a *son* composition characterized by a cyclic, African-derived formal structure. It often features prominent improvisation and call-response interaction between a chorus and lead vocalist or instrumental soloist. See also **canto** and **son**.

mulatas del rumbo. Literally, "mulatto women of the street." Free women of mixed racial background associated with colonial Cuba. They were generally characterized in literature from the period as ostentatious and promiscuous.

música arará.   See Arará.

música iyesá.   See Iyesá.

negro curro.   Literally, "free black." See *ladino.*

nueva trova.   Literally, "new song." Known initially as protest song, this genre of Cuban music developed in the 1960s. It was performed primarily by teenagers who were attracted to international rock and popular music. They blended such influences with local musical styles and also lyrical themes reflecting their experiences in a revolutionary society.

orichas.   Yoruba deities associated with Santería worship. The *orichas* are complex spiritual forces that have multiple associations with natural phenomena, characteristics of human personality, and philosophical or life principles. In many cases, their names and characteristics derive from historical figures in West Africa who were later deified.

palero.   A practitioner of Palo Monte.

Palo (*or* Palo Monte).   A term used to refer to various forms of religion of Kongo-Bantu origin in Cuba including Biyumba and Kimbisa. Palo Monte ceremonies use percussion instruments, song, and dance as a means of communication with divinities.

pilón.   Literally, "pestle." The *pilón* is most commonly recognized as a rhythm and dance music genre developed by Enrique Bonne and popularized by Pacho Alonso in the early 1960s.

plante.   One of the names for a group or society of Abakuá initiates or one of their ceremonies.

plantilla musician.   A full-time, professional musician who is an employee of the Cuban government and whose performances are coordinated through an *empresa.*

pregón (pl. *pregones*).   A short, songlike chant used by street vendors to sell products. Since the early twentieth century, *pregones* have been used as the inspiration for longer, more formal musical compositions as well.

punto.   A generic term used to describe various kinds of Spanish-derived "country music" in Cuba. It is often written in triple meter and features prominent use of string instruments.

rezo.   Literally, "prayer." In Santería ceremony, *rezos* are sacred songs that are sung in a metrically free fashion over accompanying drum rhythms, usually on the *batás.*

rumba.   A heavily African-influenced form of secular entertainment unique to Cuba. Traditional rumba is a complex and highly improvisatory form involving performance on various percussion instruments, song, and dance. It developed in the mid-nineteenth century in the provinces of Havana and Matanzas. Many subgenres and regional variants exist, including *rumba yambú* (an older form with mimetic choreography that is often used to tell humorous stories), *rumba columbia* (a fast variant in 6/8 danced only by men), and *rumba guaguancó* (a flirtatious couple dance).

salsa.   A commercial label initially used to describe Latin dance music from New York in the late 1960s and 1970s. It combines elements of Cuban *son* with Puerto Rican musical forms and others.

salsero.   A salsa performer, dancer, or enthusiast.

Santería.   Various syncretic religious practices fusing West African and Catholic elements. Properly speaking, Santería refers only to Yoruba-influenced worship. Music and dance play a prominent role in all ceremonies.

santero.   A practitioner of Santería; an initiate.

sartén (pl. *sartenes*).   Frying pans used as musical instruments in *comparsa* bands during carnival season. Musicians fasten two or more of them to a frame and strike them with sticks or spoons.

septeto.   Septet. A seven-person musical group associated with performance of the traditional *son*. *Septetos* first became popular in the 1920s.

sociedades (de recreo).   Literally, recreational societies. Private social clubs that existed throughout Cuba before 1959. Before they were closed by the revolutionary authorities in the early 1960s, they constituted one of the most popular venues for dance music.

son (pl. *sones*).   A genre of dance music created by Afro-Cuban performers in eastern Cuba toward the end of the nineteenth century. In form and instrumentation, *son* demonstrates the fusion of African and European elements. It has become a powerful symbol of Afro-Hispanic cultural fusion and Cuban nationalism. See also **canto** and **montuno.**

soneos (also *inspiraciones*).   Improvised melodies and lyrics sung by a lead vocalist. They typically appear in the *montuno* section of dance music in alternation with a choral response.

sucu-sucu.   A subgenre of *son* that developed on the Isle of Pines in the late nineteenth century.

tango-congo.   Literally, "Kongo slave dance." A term used in the colonial period to describe the music, dance, and rhythmic patterns employed by slaves in street processions. In the twentieth century, a stylized rhythm of the same name became popular as a means of referencing Afro-Cuban heritage in commercial songs.

timba.   Modern Cuban dance music. *Timba* combines influences from traditional Cuban *son* and foreign genres such as jazz, funk, and rap.

timbal (pl. timbales).   A percussion instrument, also called the *paila,* or kettle. It consists of one or two round, metal, single-headed drums, often mounted on a frame. The timbales' origins are in European military bands, but Afro-Cuban performers developed a unique performance style on the instrument at the turn of the twentieth century that has strongly influenced popular music. It is played with sticks both on the side of the drum and on the head.

timbalero. A performer on the timbales.

timbero. A *timba* performer, dancer, or enthusiast.

tonada. Strophic vocal repertoire derived from Spain, often accompanied by the guitar or other string instruments.

toque (de santo). Literally, "playing for the saints." Afro-Cuban religious events that revolve around sacred drumming, song, and dance.

tratado. Literally, "treatment." A series of ritual songs and/or rhythms performed in a specific sequence as a form of worship in Santería ceremony. *Tratados.* are typically dedicated to a specific *oricha.*

tresero. A performer on the *tres,* a small, steel-stringed, guitarlike instrument.

trova (also *vieja trova*). Traditional Cuban song, usually romantic in nature and performed by two singers with guitar accompaniment. It first became popular in eastern Cuba among black and mulatto shopkeepers at the turn of the twentieth century. *Trova* can also be used to refer to *nueva trova.*

trovador (pl. *trovadores*). Literally, "troubador." A performer of *vieja* or *nueva trova.*

tumba francesa. Literally, "French drum." Music and dance associated with *cabildos* and mutual aid societies established by Afro-Haitian immigrants in the early nineteenth century. *Tumba francesa* repertoire uses unique instruments, songs, and choreography.

tumbao. A basic rhythmic and/or melodic pattern repeated frequently on particular dance instruments such as the conga drum, bass, or piano. See *guajeo.*

verbena. Popular, all-day celebrations associated with the patron saint festivals of the Catholic church. *Verbenas* hosted numerous musical events before their gradual disappearance in the 1960s.

yambú. See rumba.

yuka drums. A three-drum set and accompanying musical repertoire of Kongo origin. It is found primarily in rural areas. *Yuka* drumming is secular and developed out of slave traditions in the mid-nineteenth century.

zarzuela. In Cuba, a form of light opera with local and/or nationalist themes, often taken from nineteenth-century novels.

Works Cited

BOOKS, ARTICLES, AND WEBSITES

Acosta, Leonardo. N.d. "El ambiente musical en La Habana de hoy." Unpublished manuscript.
———. 1982. *Música y descolonización.* Mexico City: Presencia Latinoamericana, S.A.
———. 1983. *Del tambor al sintetizador.* Havana: Editorial Letras Cubanas.
———. 1991. *Elige tú que canto yo.* Havana: Editorial Letras Cubanas.
———. 1995a. "¿Ha envejecido la nueva trova?" *El Nuevo Día,* October 15, pp. 20–21.
———. 1995b. "La nueva trova: ¿Un movimiento masivo?" In *Panorama de la música popular cubana,* edited by Radamés Giro, pp. 375–83. Cali: Editorial de la Universidad del Valle.
———. 1997. "¿Terminó la polémica sobre la salsa?" *Música cubana* 0:26–29.
———. 1998. "El capítulo que faltaba: unos años después." In *Del tamburo al sintetizzatore: La musica cubana e afrocubana,* edited by Leonardo Acosta, 2:171–87. Bolsena: Massari Editore.
———. 2000a. *Descarga cubana: El jazz en Cuba 1900–1950.* Havana: Ediciones Unión.
———. 2000b. "La diaspora musical cubana en Estados Unidos." *Encuentro de la cultura cubana* 15:96–99.
———. 2002. *Descarga cubana: El jazz en Cuba 1950–2000.* Havana: Ediciones Unión.
———. 2003. *Cubano Be Cubano Bop.* Washington, D.C.: Smithsonian Books.
Acosta, Leonardo, and Jorge Gómez. 1981. *Canciones de la nueva trova.* Havana: Editorial Letras Cubanas.
Acosta, Leonardo, René Espí, and Helio Orovio. 1999. *Fiesta Havana 1940–1960: L'âge d'or de la musique cubaine.* Paris: Editions Vade Retro.
Adorno, Theodor. 1992. *Introduction to the Sociology of Music.* Translated by E. B. Ashton. New York: Seabury Press.
Aguilar, Luis E. 1989. "From Immutable Proclamations to Unintended Consequences: Marxism-Leninism and the Cuban Government, 1959–1986." In *Cuban Communism,* edited by Irving Louis Horowitz, 7th ed., pp. 166–86. New Brunswick, NJ: Transaction Publishers.
Aharonián, Coriún. 1990. "Música, revolución y dependencia en América Latina." *Música* 118 (January–April): 3–26.
Alberto, Eliseo. 1996. "Los años grises." *Revista Encuentro de la Cultura Cubana* 1, no. 1 (Summer): 33–41.
Altmann, Thomas. 1998. *Cantos lucumí a los orichas.* New York: Descarga.
Alvarez Díaz, José R., ed. 1963. *Un estudio sobre Cuba.* Miami: University of Miami Press.
Amuchastegui, Domingo. 2000. "Cuban Conglomerates Setting the Pace for Island's Business." *Cuba News* 8, no. 8 (August): 6–7.

Andreu Alonso, Guillermo. 1992. *Los arará en Cuba: Florentina, la princesa dahomeyana.* Havana: Editorial José Martí.

Anonymous. 1968. "La sociedad secreta abakuá." *El militante comunista* (August), pp. 36–45.

Ardévol, José. 1966. *Música y revolución.* Havana: UNEAC.

Arias, Salvador. 1982. "Literatura cubana (1959–1978)." In *La cultura en Cuba socialista,* edited by Ministerio de la Cultura, pp. 7–34. Havana: Editorial Letras Cubanas.

Arozarena, Marcelino. 1961. "Los cabildos de nación ante el registro de la propiedad." *Actas del folklore* 1, no. 3 (March): 13–22.

Arrufat, Antón. 2001. "Pequeña profesión de fe." *Encuentro de la cultura cubana* 20 (Spring): 5–7.

Averill, Gage. 1997. *A Day for the Hunter, a Day for the Prey: Popular Music and Power in Haiti.* Chicago: University of Chicago Press.

Balaban, John, et al. 1998. "Image Isn't Everything." *Miami Herald Sunday Magazine,* March 1, pp. 10–13, 16–20.

Barnet, Miguel. 1966. *Biografía de un cimarrón.* Havana: Instituto de Etnología y Folklore.

———. 1983. *La fuente viva.* Havana: Editorial Letras Cubanas.

Barthélémy, Françoise. 2001. "An Island Poor in Everything but Culture." *Le Monde diplomatique,* September 2001. Available at http://mondediplo.com/2001/09/05cuba.

Belmonte, Adriana. 1974. "Grupo Irakere: Un ritmo con raíces populares." *Revolución y cultura* 24 (August): 68–72.

Benítez-Rojo, Antonio. 1990. "Comments on Georgina Dopico Black's 'The Limits of Expression: Intellectual Freedom in Postrevolutionary Cuba.'" *Cuban Studies* 20:171–74.

Benjamin, Jules B. 1990. *The United States and the Origins of the Cuban Revolution.* Princeton, NJ: Princeton University Press.

Benmayor, Rina. 1981. "La 'Nueva Trova': New Cuban Song." *Latin American Music Review* 2, no. 1 (Spring): 11–44.

Berg, Mette Louise. 1999. "Localising Cubanness: Place Making and Social Exclusion in Old Havana." Masters thesis, Institut for Antropologi, Denmark.

Bermúdez, Armando Andrés. 1968. "La expansión del 'espiritismo de Cordón.'" *Etnología y Folklore* 5 (January–June): 5–32.

Betancourt, Juan René. 1959a. "La cuestión racial." *Revolución,* January 17, p. 4.

———. 1959b. "Fidel Castro y la integración nacional." *Bohemia* 51, no. 7 (February 15): 66, 122–23.

———. 1959c. *El negro, ciudadano del futuro.* Havana: Cárdenas y Cía.

Boggs, Vernon, ed. 1992. *Salsiology: Afro-Cuban Music and the Evolution of Salsa in New York City.* New York: Greenwood Press.

Bolívar, Natalia. 1990. *Los oricha en Cuba.* Havana: Editorial de Ciencias Sociales.

———. 1994. *Opolopo Owo.* Havana: Editorial de Ciencias Sociales.

Booth, David. 1976. "Cuba, Color and the Revolution." *Science and Society* 11, no. 2:129–72.

Borges Suárez, Liset. N.d. "La protección del Derecho de Autor y su papel en la promoción literaria, musical y la creatividad artística." Unpublished manuscript, Centro Nacional de Derecho de Autor.

Brenner, Phillip, et al., eds. 1989. *The Cuba Reader: The Making of a Revolutionary Society.* New York: Grove Press.

Brouwer, Leo. 1989. *La música, lo cubano y la innovación.* Havana: Editorial Letras Cubanas.

Buchanan, Donna A. 1991. "The Bulgarian Folk Orchestra: Cultural Performance, Symbol, and the Construction of National Identity in Socialist Bulgaria." PhD diss., University of Texas, Austin.

———. 1995. "Metaphors of Truth: The Politics of Music Professionalism in Bulgarian Folk Orchestras." *Ethnomusicology* 39, no. 3 (Fall): 381–416.

Bulit, Ilse. 1972. "Después de diez años de trabajo." *Juventud Rebelde,* December 13, n.p. (archives, Museo Nacional de la Música).

Burckhardt Qureshi, Regula. 2002. *Music and Marx: Ideas, Practice, Politics.* New York: Routledge.

Burton, Julianne. 1982. "Folk Music, Circuses, Variety Shows and Other Endangered Species: A Conversation with Julio García Espinosa on the Preservation of Popular Culture in Cuba." *Studies in Latin American Culture,* 216–24.

Bustamante, José Angel. 1969. "Influencia de algunos factores culturales en nuestros cuadros psiquiátricos." *Etnología y folklore* 7 (January–June): 75–84.

Caballero, Rufo. 2001. "La excusa: Semiosis, ideología y montaje en *Buena Vista Social Club.*" *Temas* 27 (October–December): 133–40.

Cabrera Infante, Guillermo. 1983. *Tres tristes tigres.* Barcelona: Editorial Seix Barral.

Calderón González, Jorge. 1986. *María Teresa Vera.* Havana: Editorial Letras Cubanas.

Calero Martín, José, et al., eds. 1929. *Cuba musical: Album-resumen ilustrado de la historia y de la actual situación del arte en Cuba.* Havana: Imprenta Molina y Cía.

Calvet, Robinson. 1990. "Pello, con acero vivo." *Trabajadores,* February 22, pp. 8–9.

Cancio Isla, Wilfredo. 2000. "Pide asilo en Miami un destacado profesor universitario cubano." *Miami Herald,* June 5, p. 12A. See also www.cubanet.org/CNews/y00/jun00/0501.htm

Cañizares, Dulcila. 1999. *Gonzalo Roig: Hombre y creador.* Havana: Editorial Letras Cubanas.

Cantor, Judy. 1997. "Bring on the Cubans!" *Miami New Times,* June 19–25, pp. 15–33.

———. 1998a. "Isla de la música." *Miami New Times,* May 28–June 3, pp. 21–23, 25–31.

———. 1998b. "The Politics of Music." *Miami New Times,* September 17–23, pp. 13–25.

———. 1999. "A Portrait of the Artist as a Communist Bureaucrat." *Miami New Times,* June 24–30, pp. 17–34.

Cao, Juan Manuel. 1992. "Silvio Rodríguez: ¿Será o no será?" *Guángara* 13:20–23.

Carbó, Elsie. 1990. "El festivalismo no ayuda al artista." *Juventud Rebelde,* February 12, n.p. (archives, Museo Nacional de la Música, Havana).

Carbonell, Walterio. 1961. *Crítica: Cómo surgió la cultura nacional.* Havana: published by author.

Cardenal, Ernesto. 1974. *In Cuba.* Translated by D. Walsh. New York: New Directions.

Carrasco Pirard, Eduardo. 1982. "The *nueva canción* in Latin America." *International Social Science Journal* 34, no. 4:599–623.

Carreras, Julio Angel. 1985. *Esclavitud, abolición, y racismo.* Havana: Editorial de Ciencias Sociales.

Carretero, Nuria. 1990. "Experiencias de una escuela de música para adultos." *Tribuna,* May 6, n.p. (archives, Museo Nacional de la Música).

Casademunt, Tomàs. 1995. *Son de Cuba.* Barcelona: Focal Ediciones.

Casal, Lourdes. 1979. "Race Relations in Contemporary Cuba." In *The Position of Blacks in Brazilian and Cuban Society,* by Anani Dzidzienyo and Lourdes Casal, Minority Rights Group Report no. 7, pp. 11–27. London: Minority Rights Group.

Castañeda, Mireya. 1997. "Musical Confrontation." *Granma International,* April 9, p. 12.

Castellanos, Isabel. 1983. *Elegua quiere tambó: Cosmovisión religiosa afrocubana en las canciones populares.* Cali: Departamento de Publicaciones, Universidad del Valle.

Castillo, A. 1962. "Ritmo oriental: Tambores en La Habana." *Bohemia,* March 2, n.p. (archives, Cristóbal Díaz Ayala).

Castillo Faílde, Osvaldo. 1964. *Miguel Faílde: Creador musical del danzón.* Havana: Oficina del Historiador de la Ciudad.

Castro, Fidel. 1961. *Palabras a los intelectuales.* Havana: Ediciones del Consejo Nacional de Cultura.

———. 1968. *History Will Absolve Me: The Moncada Trial Defence Speech, Santiago de Cuba, October 16th, 1953.* London: Johnathan Cape.

Castro, Fidel, and Frei Betto. 1987. *Fidel and Religion.* New York: Simon and Schuster.

Castro, Raúl. 1996. "Fragmento del informe del Buró Político presentado por Raúl Castro." *Revista encuentro de la cultura cubana* 1, no.1 (Spring): 18–24.

Catholic Bishops of Cuba. 1993. "El amor todo lo espera: Mensaje de la conferencia de obispos de Cuba." Unpublished manuscript distributed by the Catholic Church within Cuba.

Centro de Investigación Juan Marinello. 1999. *Cultura tradicional cubana.* Havana: Centro de Antropología.

César, Antonieta. 1996. "Cálido equinoccio." *Trabajadores,* September 13, p. 10.

Chávez Alvarez, Ernesto. 1991. *El crimen de la niña Cecilia: La brujería en Cuba como fenómeno social (1902–25).* Havana: Editorial de Ciencias Sociales.

Chijona, Gerardo. 1982. "El cine cubano: Hecho cultural de la revolución." In *La cultura en Cuba socialista,* edited by Ministerio de Cultura, pp. 215–29. Havana: Editorial Arte y Letras.

Cirules, Enrique. 1999. *El imperio de La Habana.* Havana: Editorial Letras Cubanas.

Clark, Juan. 1992. *Cuba: Mito y realidad.* Miami: Saeta Ediciones.

Clytus, John, and Jane Rieker. 1970. *Black Man in Red Cuba.* Coral Gables, FL: University of Miami Press.

Collazo, Bobby. 1987. *La última noche que pasé contigo: 40 años de farándula cubana.* San Juan, Puerto Rico: Editorial Cubanacán.

Contreras, Félix. 1988. "Enrique Bonne: Cuando el refrán es de bailar, no vale refrán malo." *Bohemia* 36 (September 2): 41–44.

———. 1989. *Porque tiene filin.* Santiago de Cuba: Editorial Oriente.

Correa, Armando. 1997. "Silvio Rodríguez canta en Puerto Rico entre aplausos y protestas." *Nuevo Herald,* March 8.

Corzo, Cynthia. 1972. "Boricuas de Miami suspenden su protesta en fiesta de Calle Ocho." *Nuevo Herald,* March 8.

Cox, Harvey. 1987. Introduction to *Fidel and Religion.* New York: Simon and Schuster.

Cuadra, Angel. 1987. "La trova cubana del exilio." *Diario de las Américas,* October 10, pp. 5A, 11A.

Cubillas, Vicente. 1952. "Habla Arsenio Rodríguez." *Bohemia* 44, no. 49 (December 7): 24–25.

Daniel, Yvonne P. 1991. "Changing Values in Cuban Rumba, a Lower-Class Black Dance Appropriated by the Cuban Revolution." *Dance Research Journal* 23, no. 2 (Fall): 1–10.

———. 1995. *Rumba: Dance and Social Change in Contemporary Cuba.* Bloomington: Indiana University Press.

———. 1996. "Tourism Dance Performances: Authenticity and Creativity." *Annals of Tourism Research* 23, no. 4:780–97.

de Aragón, Uva. 2002. "En el centenario de la República de Cuba." Unpublished manuscript.

de Juan, Adelaida. 1982. "Las artes plásticas en Cuba socialista." In *La cultura en Cuba socialista,* edited by Ministerio de Culturas, pp. 35–62. Havana: Editorial Letras Cubanas.

de la Fuente, Alejandro. 1995. "Race and Inequality in Cuba, 1899–1981." *Journal of Contemporary History* 30, no. 1 (January): 131–68.

———. 2001. *A Nation for All: Race, Inequality, and Politics in Twentieth-Century Cuba.* Chapel Hill: University of North Carolina Press.

de la Fuente, Alejandro, and Lawrence Glasco. 1997. "Are Blacks 'Getting Out of Control'? Racial Attitudes, Revolution, and Political Transition in Cuba." In *Toward a New Cuba? Legacies of a Revolution,* edited by Miguel A. Centeno and Mauricio Font, 53–71. Boulder, CO: Lynn Rienner Publishers.

De Lahaye Guerra, Rosa María, and Rubén Zardoya Loureda. 1994. *Yemayá a través de sus mitos.* Havana: Editorial de Ciencias Sociales.

de la Hoz, Pedro. 2000. "¿Qué tiene Van Van?" *Granma,* July 28, p. 6.

de la Vega, Aurelio. 2001. "Nacionalismo y universalismo." *Encuentro de la cultura cubana* 20 (Spring): 49–56.

de León, Carmela. 1990. *Sindo Garay: Memorias de un trovador.* Havana: Editorial Letras Cubanas.

Depestre, Leonardo. 1990. *Cuatro músicos de una villa.* Havana: Editorial Letras Cubanas.

de Posada, Luis. 1954. "Clubes sociales y deportivos." In *Libro de Cuba, una enciclopedia ilustrada,* edited by Juan Joaquín Otero et al., 731–41. Havana: Publicaciones Unidas.

Deschamps Chapeaux, Pedro. 1971. *El negro en la economía habanera del siglo XIX.* Havana: UNEAC.

Díaz, Elisabet, and Amado del Pino. 1996. "Oficialismo o herejía? Entrevista a Abel Prieto." *Revolución y cultura* 1–2, pp. 4–9.

Díaz Ayala, Cristóbal. 1981. *Música cubana del areíto a la nueva trova.* Miami: Ediciones Universal.

———. 1998. *Cuando salí de la Habana, 1898–1998: Cien años de música cubana por el mundo.* San Juan, Puerto Rico: Fundación Musicalia.

———. 1999. "¿Midem o Midas?" Unpublished manuscript.

———. 2000. "Intercambios, diásporas, fusiones." *Encuentro de la cultura cubana* 15 (Winter): 86–95.

———. 2002a. "Buscando la melodía: La música popular cubana de 1902 a 1959." *Encuentro de la cultura cubana* 24 (Spring): 79–96.

———. 2002b. "La música cubana como producto exportable." Paper presented at the Cuban Research Institute conference, Florida International University, Miami, March 6.

———. 2003a. "La invencible charanga." *Encuentro de la cultura cubana* 26/27 (Fall/Winter): 295–308.

———. 2003b. *Música cubana del areyto al rap cubano.* 4th ed. San Juan, Puerto Rico: Fundación Musicalia.

Díaz Fabelo, Teodoro. 1956. *Lengua de santeros.* Havana.

———. 1960. *Olórun.* Havana: Teatro Nacional.

———. 1967a. "Análisis y evaluación cultural de las letras del Diloggún." Unpublished manuscript, Biblioteca Nacional José Martí.

———. 1967b. "Los caracoles." Unpublished manuscript, Biblioteca Nacional José Martí.

———. 1969a. *Diccionario de yerbas y palos rituales, medicinales y el alimenticios en el uso por los afrocubanos.* Paris: UNESCO Library.

———. 1969b. "Introducción al estudio de las culturas afrocubanas." Unpublished manuscript, Biblioteca Nacional José Martí.

———. 1969c. "El poblamiento." Unpublished manuscript, Biblioteca Nacional José Martí.

———. 1971. *La escritura de los abakuá.* Paris: UNESCO Library.

———. 1972. *Diccionario de la cultura conga residual en Cuba.* 2 vols. Paris: UNESCO Library.

———. 1974. *Los negros cimarrones de Cuba.* Paris: UNESCO Library.

Díaz Pérez, Clara. 1994. *Sobre la guitarra, la voz: Una historia de la nueva trova cubana.* Havana: Editorial Letras Cubanas.

———. 1995. *Silvio Rodríguez: Hay quien precisa.* Madrid: Música Mundana.

Díaz Rosell, Raimundo. 1989. "Hay que seguir trabajando." *Bastión,* December 19, n.p. (archives, Museo Nacional de la Música, Havana).

Diehl, Kiehla. 1992. "Tempered Steel: The Steel Drum as a Site for Social, Political, and Aesthetic Negotiation in Trinidad." Master's thesis, University of Texas, Austin.

Domínguez, Jorge I. 1978. *Cuba: Order and Revolution.* Cambridge, MA: Belknap Press of Harvard University Press.

Domínguez Benejam, Yarelis. 2000. *Caminos de la musicología cubana.* Havana: Editorial Letras Cubanas.

Douglas, María Eulalia. 1999. "Stages in the Thematic Development of the Cuban Cinema." *CUBA Update* 19, no. 1 (October–December): 12–52.

Drake, Dawn. 2000. "Timba: The 'New' Salsa from Cuba." Unpublished manuscript.

Draper, Theodore. 1965. *Castroism: Theory and Practice.* New York: Frederick A. Praeger.

D'Rivera, Paquito. 1998. *Mi vida saxual.* San Juan, Puerto Rico: Editorial Plaza Mayor.

Duany, Jorge. 2004. "Más allá de las balsas." *El Nuevo Día,* September 9, p. 89.

Duarte Oropesa, José. 1993. *Historiología cubana: Desde 1959 hasta 1980.* Miami: Ediciones Universal.

DuBois, W. E. B. 2002. "I Won't Vote." Reprint of an October 20, 1956, article in *The Nation*, posted February 7 at www.thenation.com.

Dumont, René. 1970. *Cuba ¿es socialista?* Translated by Mariela Álvarez. Caracas: Editorial Arte.

Dupré, Louis. 1983. *Marx's Social Critique of Culture*. New Haven: Yale University Press.

Eckstein, Susan Eva. 1994. *Back from the Future: Cuba under Castro*. Princeton, NJ: Princeton University Press.

Elizundia Ramírez, Alicia. 2001. *Yo soy una maestra que canta*. Havana: Ediciones Unión.

Evora, José Antonio. 1996. "Cien por ciento cubano." *Éxito* (Miami), January 24, pp. 44–45.

———. 2000. "Frank Delgado: La trova que habla por sí misma." *Nuevo Herald*, September 7.

Fagen, Richard R. 1969. *The Transformation of Political Culture in Cuba*. Stanford, CA: Stanford University Press.

Fagg, John Edwin. 1965. *Cuba, Haiti, and the Dominican Republic*. Englewood Cliffs, NJ: Prentice-Hall.

Fanon, Frantz. 1967. *Black Skin, White Masks: The Experiences of a Black Man in a White World*. New York: Grove Press.

Faya, Alberto. 1995. "Nueva trova y cultura de la rebeldía." In *Panorama de la música popular cubana*, edited by Radamés Giro, pp. 385–96. Cali: Editorial de la Universidad del Valle.

Faya, Alberto, et al. 1996. "Controversia. La música y el mercado." *Temas* 66 (April–June): 74–85.

Fehér, Ferenc, Agnes Heller, and György Márkus, eds. 1983. *Dictatorship over Needs: An Analysis of Soviet Societies*. New York: Basil Blackwell.

Feijoó, Samuel. 1961. "La expresión social de los trovadores cubanos." *Bohemia*, April 2, pp. 22–23, 108.

———. 1986. *El son cubano: Poesía general*. Havana: Editorial Letras Cubanas.

Feld, Steven. 1988. "Notes on World Beat." *Public Culture Bulletin* 1, no. 1 (Fall): 31–37.

———. 1992. "From Schizophonia to Schismogenesis." Unpublished manuscript.

Feliú, Vicente. 1997. "Algunas reflexiones sobre la canción." *Música cubana* 0:9–10.

Fernandes, Sujatha. 2003. "Fear of a Black Nation: Local Rappers, Transnational Crossings, and State Power in Contemporary Cuba." *Anthropological Quarterly* 76, no. 4 (Fall): 575–608.

Fernandez, Nadine. 1996. "Race, Romance, and Revolution: The Cultural Politics of Interracial Encounters in Cuba." PhD diss., University of California, Berkeley.

———. 2002. "What's Love Got to Do with It? Despair, Hope, and the Anthropology of Interracial Couples in Cuba." Unpublished manuscript.

Fernández de Juan, Adelaida, et al. 1996. *Cuentos africanos*. Havana: Editorial de Ciencias Sociales.

Fernández Retamar, Roberto. 2001. "Cuarenta años después." *La Gaceta de Cuba* 4 (July–August): 47–53.

Fernández Robaina, Tomás. 1983. *Recuerdos secretos de dos mujeres públicas*. Havana: Editorial Letras Cubanas.

———. 1985. *Bibliografía de temas afrocubanos*. Havana: Biblioteca Nacional José Martí.

———. 1990. *El negro en Cuba 1902–1958: Apuntes para la historia de la lucha contra la discriminación racial*. Havana: Editorial de Ciencias Sociales.

———. 1994. *Hablen paleros y santeros*. Havana: Editorial de Ciencias Sociales.

———. 1997a. "La cultura y la historia afrocubana valorada por Juan René Betancourt, Gustavo Urrutia y Fernando Ortiz, entre otros." Unpublished manuscript.

———. 1997b. "Fresa y chocolate: El homosexualismo en la Cuba de hoy. Invitación para el debate." Unpublished manuscript.

Fiske, John. 1989. *Understanding Popular Culture*. Cambridge, MA: Unwin Hyman.

Fitzgerald, Frank T. 1994. *The Cuban Revolution in Crisis: From Managing Socialism to Managing Survival*. New York: Monthly Review Press.

Flores, Bernardo, ed. 1978. *Perfiles culturales: Cuba 1977*. Havana: Editorial Orbe.

Formell, Juan. 1997. "Embajador de la música bailable." *Newsweek en Español*, January 22, p. 52.

―――. 2000. "Ganamos la pelea." *Bohemia* 92, no. 6 (March 10): 58–59.

Fornet, Ambrosio, et al. 2001. "Buena Vista Social Club y la cultura musical cubana." *Temas* 22–23 (July–December): 163–79.

Franco, José Luciano. 1974. *Ensayos históricos.* Havana: Editorial de Ciencias Sociales.

Franqui, Carlos. 2001. *Camilo Cienfuegos.* Barcelona: Editorial Planeta.

Frederick, Laurie Aleen. N.d. "The Contestation of Cuba's Public Sphere in National Theater and the Transformation from Teatro Bufo to Teatro Nuevo." Hewlitt Foundation Working Paper Series. Chicago: University of Chicago, Center for Latin American Studies.

Frey, Louis, Jr. 1997. "Report by the Delegation of the U.S. Association of Former Members of Congress Visit to Cuba, December 9–14, 1996." Washington, D.C.: United States Association of Former Members of Congress.

Gaceta Oficial de la República de Cuba. 1902–. Havana: [n.p.].

Gal, Susan. 1991. "Bartók's Funeral: Representations of Europe in Hungarian Political Rhetoric." *American Ethnologist* 18, no. 3 (August): 440–58.

García, David F. 2003. "Arsenio Rodríguez: A Black Cuban Musician in the Dance Milieus of Havana, New York City, and Los Angeles." PhD diss., City University of New York.

García, Luis Manuel. 1996. "Crónica de la inocencia perdida: La cuentística cubana contemporánea." *Revista encuentro de la cultura cubana* 1, no. 1 (Spring): 121–27.

García, Mariana, ed. 1980. *Diccionario de la literatura cubana.* 2 vols. Havana: Editorial Letras Cubanas.

García Joya, Mario, and María Haya. 1985. *La Diane Havanaise, ou La rumba s'appelle Chano.* Havana: José Martí Editions.

García Meralla, Emir. 2001. "Abuelos, timba y otros asuntos." *La Gaceta de Cuba* 2 (March–April): 40–43.

Gilroy, Paul. 1993. *The Black Atlantic: Modernity and Double Consciousness.* Cambridge, MA: Harvard University Press.

Ginori, Pedraza. 1968. "Lo más santiaguero que pueda imaginarse." *Cuba* 7, no. 6 (June): 57–61.

Giovan, Tria, and Marilú Menéndez. 1996. *Cuba: The Elusive Island.* New York: Harry N. Abrams.

Giro, Radamés, ed. 1986. *La enseñanza artística en Cuba.* Havana: Editorial Letras Cubanas.

―――, ed. 1995. *Panorama de la música popular cubana.* Cali: Editorial de la Universidad del Valle.

Godfried, Eugène. 2000. "Buena Vista Social Club: Critics, Self-Criticism, and the Survival of the Cuban Son." Posted in November at www.afrocubaweb.com/eugenegodfried/buenavistacritics.htm.

Goldenberg, Boris. 1965. *The Cuban Revolution and Latin America.* New York: Frederick A. Praeger.

Goldman, Emma. 1934. *Living My Life.* New York: Knopf.

Golendorf, Pierre. 1977. *7 años en Cuba: 38 meses en las prisiones de Fidel Castro.* Barcelona: Plaza & Janes.

Gómez, Zoila. 1977. *Amadeo Roldán.* Havana: Editorial Arte y Literatura.

González, Reynaldo. 1983. *Contradanzas y latigazos.* Havana: Editorial Letras Cubanas.

González Bello, Neris, and Liliana Casanella. 2002. "La timba cubana: Un intergénero contemporáneo." *Clave* 4, no. 1:2–9.

González García, Agustín. 2001. "Loving the Music of the Enemy: How American Popular Music Changed Cuban Youth in Castro's Cuba." Unpublished manuscript.

González Huguet, Lydia, and Jean René Baudry. 1967. "Voces 'bantu' en el vocabulario 'palero.'" *Etnología y Folklore* 3 (January–June): 31–64.

González Manet, Enrique. 1962. "Transforma la revolución las costumbres del cubano." *Bohemia*, May 11, pp. 16–18, 97.

―――. 1964. "La naciente ciudad mágica de Cubanacán." *El mundo*, November 25, pp. 1–2.

González Portal, Elsida. 2003. "Cantar con Pablo, contar con él." Posted in November at www.lajiribilla.cu/2003/n095_03/095_01.html.

González Ruisánchez, Luis. 2001. "Salsa de Cuba: A que me mantengo, va, a que me mantengo." *Encuentro de la cultura cubana* 20 (Spring): 97–101.

Goodwin, Andrew, and Joe Gore. 1990. "World Beat and the Cultural Imperialism Debate." *Socialist Review* 90, no. 3:64–80.

Gramatges, Harold. 1982. "La música culta." In *La cultura en Cuba socialista*, edited by Ministerio de Cultura, 124–50. Havana: Editorial Letras Cubanas.

——. 1983. *Presencia de la revolución en la música cubana*. Havana: Editorial Letras Cubanas.

——. 1997. "El Conservatorio Municipal de La Habana: Un histórico ejemplo definidor." *Música cubana* 0:34–37.

Grau, Adriane. 1997. "Albito mostra que Cuba não é só salsa." *Folha ilustrada* (São Paulo), November 15, p. 10.

Groth, Carl-Johan. 1996. "Conclusiones y recomendaciones del informe sobre la situación de los derechos humanos en Cuba." Partial reprinting of United Nations findings. *Revista encuentro de la cultura cubana* 1, no. 1 (Spring): 16–17.

Guanche, Jesús. 1983. *Procesos etnoculturales de Cuba*. Havana: Editorial Letras Cubanas.

Guerra, Ramiro. 1991. *Teatralización del folklore y otros ensayos*. Havana: Editorial Letras Cubanas.

——. 1999. *Coordenadas danzarias*. Havana: Ediciones Unión.

Guevara, Ernesto "Che". 1965. *El socialismo y el hombre en Cuba*. Havana: Ediciones R.

——. 1973. *La revolución latinoamericana*. Rosario, Argentina: Editorial Encuadre.

Guillén, Nicolás. 1967. *Tengo*. Montevideo, Uruguay: Editorial El Siglo Ilustrado.

Guillermoprieto, Alma. 2004. *Dancing with Cuba: A Memoir of the Revolution*. New York: Pantheon Books.

Gurza, Agustín. 2003. "Big Band, a Very Big Life." *Los Angeles Times*, December 30, pp. E1, E8.

Hagedorn, Katherine J. 1995. "Anatomía del proceso folklórico: The 'Folkloricization' of Afro-Cuban Religious Performance in Cuba." PhD diss., Brown University.

——. 2001. *Divine Utterances: The Performance of Afro-Cuban Santería*. Washington, D.C.: Smithsonian Institution Press.

——. 2002. "Long Day's Journey to Rincón: From Suffering to Resistance in the Procession of San Lázaro / Babalú Ayé." *British Journal of Ethnomusicology* 11, no. 1:43–69.

Haraszti, Miklós. 1987. *The Velvet Prison: Artists under State Socialism*. Translated by Katalin Landesmann and Stephen Landesmann. New York: New Republic.

Hart Dávalos, Armando. 1988. *Adelante el arte*. Havana: Editorial Letras Cubanas.

Hernández, Rafael. 2003. *Looking at Cuba: Essays on Culture and Civil Society*. Gainesville: University Press of Florida.

——, ed. 2002. "La música popular como espejo social." *Temas* 29 (April–June): 61–80.

——, ed. 1997. "Las ciencias sociales en la cultura cubana contemporanea." *Temas* 9 (January–March): 68–86.

Hernández, Rafael, and John Coatsworth, eds. 2001. *Culturas encontradas: Cuba y los Estados Unidos*. Havana: Centro Juan Marinello; Cambridge, MA: David Rockefeller Center for Latin American Studies.

Hernández-Reguant, Ariana. 2000. "The Nostalgia of *Buena Vista Social Club:* Cuban Music and 'World Marketing.'" Paper presented at the conference Musical Intersections, Toronto, Canada, November.

——. 2002. "Radio Taíno and the Globalization of the Cuban Culture Industries." PhD diss., University of Chicago.

——. 2004a. "Blackness with a Cuban Beat." *NACLA Report on the Americas* 38, no. 2 (September–October): 31–36.

——. 2004b. "Copyrighting Che: Art and Authorship under Cuban Late Socialism." *Public Culture* 16, no. 1:1–29.

——. 2004c. "Radio in Cuba." In *Encyclopedia of Radio*, edited by Christopher Sterling, 428–32. New York: Fitzroy Dearborn Publishers.

Herrera Echavarría, Pedro. 1982. "Ramón y Coralia: Compañeros en el arte y en la vida." *Tribuna de La Habana*, November 11, n.p. (archives, Instituto Cubano de Radio y Televisión).

———. 1986. "Ramón Veloz: Unas notas como recuerdo." *Juventud Rebelde*, August 18, p. 5.

Hinckle, Warren, and William W. Turner. 1981. *The Fish Is Red: The Story of the Secret War against Castro*. New York: Harper and Row.

Hobsbawm, Eric. 1987. *The Age of Empire, 1875–1914*. New York: Random House.

Horowitz, Irving Louis, ed. 1989. *Cuban Communism*. 7th ed. New Brunswick, NJ: Transaction Publishers.

———. 2001. "Marxismo y revolución." *Nuevo Herald*, May 5, n.p. (archives, Cristóbal Díaz Ayala).

Ignaza, Alcides, and Juan Antonio Pola. 1975. "Movimiento nacional de aficionados." *Bohemia* 67, no. 9 (February 28): 11–13.

Isidrón del Valle, Aldo. 1982. *Dos estilos y un cantar: El Indio Naborí y Chanito Isidrón*. Havana: Arte y Letras.

Iznaga, Diana. 1986. Prólogo to *Los negros curros*, by Fernando Ortiz, vii–xxiii. Havana: Editorial de Ciencias Sociales.

Izquierdo, Pedro. 1990. "Detrás de la música, mi música, esta música." *Trabajadores*, April 4, n.p. (archives, Instituto Cubano de Radio y Televisión).

Kirk, John M. 1989. *Between God and Party: Religion and Politics in Revolutionary Cuba*. Tampa: University of South Florida Press.

Kirk, John, and Leonardo Padura Fuentes. 2001. *Culture and the Cuban Revolution: Conversations in Havana*. Gainesville: University Press of Florida.

Konrád, George, and Ivan Szelényi. 1979. *The Intellectuals on the Road to Class Power: A Sociological Study of the Role of the Intelligentsia in Socialism*. Translated by Andrew Arato and Richard E. Allen. New York: Harcourt Brace Jovanovich.

Kundera, Milan. 1992. *The Joke*. New York: Harper Collins Perennial.

Lachatañeré, Romulo. 1961a. "Nota histórica sobre los lucumís." *Actas del folklore* 1, no. 2 (February): 3–18.

———. 1961b. "Tipos étnicos africanos que concurrieron en la amalgama cubana." *Actas del folklore* 1, no. 3 (March): 5–12.

———. 1961c. "Las creencias religiosas de los afrocubanos y la falsa aplicación del término brujería." *Actas del folklore* 1, no. 5 (May): 11–16.

Lafargue, Paul. 1907. *The Right to Be Lazy and Other Studies*. Translated by Charles H. Kerr. Chicago: Charles H. Kerr and Co.

Lam, Rafael. 1989. "Pónle el cuño con La Aragón." *Tribuna*, October 8, n.p. (archives, Instituto Cubano de Artes e Industrias Cinematográficas).

———. 1999. *Tropicana: A Paradise under the Stars*. Havana: Editorial José Martí.

Lapique Becali, Zoila. 1979. *Música colonial cubana, tomo 1 (1812–1902)*. Havana: Editorial Letras Cubanas.

Lazarte Fundora, Solange. 1961. "La puya y el perejil." *Actas del folklore* 1, no. 2 (February): 23–25.

Leal, Rine. 1982. "Hacia una dramaturgia del socialismo." In *La cultura en Cuba socialista*, edited by Ministerio de Cultura, 230–53. Havana: Editorial Arte y Letras.

Lenin, Vladimir Ilich. 1966. *Lenin Reader*. Edited by Stefan T. Possony. Chicago: Henry Regnery Company.

León, Argeliers. 1964. *Música folklórica cubana*. Havana: Ediciones del Departamento de Música de la Biblioteca Nacional José Martí.

———. 1966. "El instituto de etnología y folklore de la academia de ciencias de Cuba." *Etnología y Folklore* 1:5–16.

———. 1969. "Música popular de origen africano en América Latina." *América indígena: Órgano oficial del Instituto Indigenista Interamericano* 29, no. 3:627–64.

———. 1982. "El folklore: Su estudio y recuperación." In *La cultura en Cuba socialista,* edited by Ministerio de Cultura, 182–93. Havana: Editorial Arte y Letras.

———. 1984. *Del canto y el tiempo.* Havana: Editorial Letras Cubanas.

———. 1985. "La música como mercancía." In *Musicología en Latinoamérica,* edited by Zoila Gómez García, 406–29. Havana: Editorial Arte y Literatura.

Le Riverend, Ada Rosa, ed. 1984. *Diccionario de la literatura Cuba.* 2 vols. Havana: Editorial Letras Cubanas.

Levin, Theodore. 1996. *The Hundred Thousand Fools of God: Musical Travels in Central Asia (and Queens, New York).* Bloomington: Indiana University Press.

———. 2002. "Making Marxist-Lenninist Music in Uzbekistan." In *Music and Marx: Ideas, Practice, Politics,* edited by Regula Burckhardt Qureshi, 190–203. New York: Routledge.

Lewis, Oscar, Ruth M. Lewis, and Susan M. Rigdon. 1977a. *Four Men. Living the Revolution: An Oral History of Contemporary Cuba.* Urbana: University of Illinois Press.

———. 1977b. *Four Women. Living the Revolution: An Oral History of Contemporary Cuba.* Urbana: University of Illinois Press.

Leyes del Gobierno Provisional de le Revolución. 1959–60. Havana: Editorial Lex.

Lifshitz, Mikhail. 1938. *The Philosophy of Art of Karl Marx.* Translated by Ralph B. Winn. New York: Critics Group.

Linares, María Teresa. 1979. *La música y el pueblo.* Havana: Editorial Pueblo y Educación.

———. 1982. "La música campesina, la infantil y las ediciones musicales en Cuba socialista." In *La cultura en Cuba socialista,* edited by Ministerio de Cultura, 174–81. Havana: Editorial Arte y Letras.

Linares, María Teresa, and Faustino Núñez. 1998. *La música entre Cuba y España.* Madrid: Fundación Autor.

Llenera, Mario. 1978. *The Unsuspected Revolution: The Birth and Rise of Castroism.* Ithaca, NY: Cornell University Press.

López, Leovigildo. 1961. "Las firmas de los santos." *Actas del folklore* 1, no. 5 (May): 17–24.

López, Lourdes. 1978. *Estudio de un babalao.* Havana: Universidad de La Habana.

López, Oscar Luis. 1981. *La radio en Cuba: Estudio de su desarrollo en la sociedad neocolonial.* Havana: Editorial Letras Cubanas.

López Segrera, Francisco. 1989. *Cuba: Cultura y sociedad.* Havana: Editorial Letras Cubanas.

López Valdés, Rafael. 1966. "La sociedad secreta 'Abakuá' en un grupo de obreros portuarios." *Etnología y Folklore* 2 (July–December): 5–26.

Lorenzo, Alejandro. 1998. "Montes-Huidobro, Matías." *Nuevo Herald,* April 5, p. 3F.

Lumsden, Ian. 1996. *Machos, Maricones and Gays: Cuba and Homosexuality.* Philadelphia: Temple University Press.

Machado Ventura, José R. 1991. "Comenzaron deliberaciones por la consideración del Proyecto de Resolución sobre los Estatutos del Partido." *Granma,* October 13, n.p.

Machover, Jacobo. 1995. *La Habana 1952–1961: El final de un mundo, el principio de una ilusión.* Madrid: Alianza Editorial.

Madigan, Nick. 2004. "Members of Cuban Troupe Say They Will Seek Asylum." *New York Times,* November 15, p. 15.

Malcomson, Scott L. 1994. "Socialism or Death?" *New York Times Magazine,* September 25, pp. 44–49.

Manduley López, Humberto. 1997. "Rock in Cuba: History of a Wayward Son." *South Atlantic Quarterly* 96, no. 1 (Winter): 135–42.

———. 2001. *El rock en Cuba.* Havana and Bogotá: Atril Ediciones Musicales.

Manuel, Peter. 1987. "Marxism, Nationalism and Popular Music in Revolutionary Cuba." *Popular Music* 6, no. 2 (May): 161–78.

———. 1988. *Popular Musics of the Non-Western World: An Introductory Survey.* New York: Oxford University Press.

———. 1991. "Salsa and the Music Industry: Corporate Control or Grassroots Expression."

In *Essays on Cuban Music: North American and Cuban Perspectives,* edited by Peter Manuel, 157–81. Lanham, MD: University Press of America.

Manuel, Peter, Kenneth Bilby, and Michael Largey. 1995. *Caribbean Currents: Caribbean Music from Rumba to Reggae.* Philadelphia: Temple University Press.

Mao Tse-tung. 1977. *Mao Tse-tung on Literature and Art.* Beijing: Foreign Language Press.

Mariátegui, José Carlos. 1967. *El artista y la época.* Lima: Empresa Editora Amaute.

Martínez, Mayra A. 1987. "La palabra en el canto." *Revolución y Cultura* 4 (April): 13–19.

———. 1995. "Por la vereda con Tito Gómez." *Revolución y Cultura* 1–2 (January–February): 4–8.

Martínez, Orlando. 1989. *Ernesto Lecuona.* Havana: Ediciones Unión.

Martínez Fernández, Luis, et al., eds. 2003. *Encyclopedia of Cuba: People, History, Culture.* 2 vols. Westport, CT: Greenwood Press.

Martínez Furé, Rogelio. 1961a. "Los collares." *Actas del folklore* 1, no. 3 (March): 23–24.

———. 1961b. "El bando azul." *Actas del folklore* 1, no. 7 (July): 21–23.

———. 1979. *Diálogos imaginarios.* Havana: Editorial Arte y Literatura.

———. 1982. "Conjunto folkórico de Cuba: XX aniversario (1962–1982), apuntos cronológicos." Havana: Ministerio de Cultura.

———. 1994. "Modas y modos: Pseudofolklorismo y folklor." Interview by Evangelina Chio. *Revolución y Cultura* 5 (September–October): 32–35.

———. 1998. "No caímos con el último aguacero." *Bohemia* 90, no. 9 (April 24): B56–58.

Martínez Heredia, Fernando. 1999. *En el horno de los noventa.* Buenos Aires: Ediciones Barbarroja.

———. 2001. *El corrimiento hacia el rojo.* Havana: Editorial Letras Cubanas.

Martínez-Malo, Aldo. 1988. *Rita la única.* Havana: Editorial Abril.

Martínez Rodríguez, Raúl. 1988. "Pacho Alonso." *Revolución y Cultura* 10 (October): 20–26.

Martínez Tabares, Vivian. 1997. "Impresionante acogida a Silvio en Puerto Rico." *Granma,* March 12, p. 6.

Martins Villaça, Mariana. 2002. "Música cubana com sotaque brasileiro: entrecruzamentos culturais nos anos sessenta." Paper presented at the Latin American meeting of the International Association for the Study of Popular Music, Mexico City, April.

Marx, Karl, and Friedrich Engels. 1978. *The Marx-Engels Reader.* Edited by Robert C. Tucker. New York: W. W. Norton.

Masdeu, Jesús. 1953. "Arrojadas al hambre diez mil familias." *Bohemia* 45, no. 15 (April 12): 36–38.

Mason, John. 1992. *Orin Orisa: Songs for Selected Heads.* New York: Yoruba Theological Archministry.

Matibag, Eugenio. 1996. *Afro-Cuban Religious Experience: Cultural Reflections in Narrative.* Gainesville: University Press of Florida.

McGarrity, Gayle L. 1992. "Race, Culture, and Social Change in Contemporary Cuba." In *Cuba in Transition: Crisis and Transformation,* edited by Sandor Halebsky and John M. Kirk, 193–206. Boulder, CO: Westview Press.

McLaren, Peter, and Jill Pinkney-Pastrana. 2001. "Cuba, *Yanquización* and the Cult of Elián González: A View from the 'Enlightened' States." *International Journal of Qualitative Studies in Education* 14, no. 2 (April): 201–20.

Medin, Tzvi. 1990. *Cuba: The Shaping of Revolutionary Consciousness.* Translated by Martha Grenzback. Boulder, CO: Lynne Rienner Publishers.

Meintjes, Louise. 1990. "Paul Simon's *Graceland,* South Africa, and the Mediation of Musical Meaning." *Ethnomusicology* 34, no. 1 (Winter): 37–73.

Menéndez, Lázara. 1998–90. *Estudios afrocubanas: Selección de lecturas.* 4 vols. Havana: Editorial Félix Varela.

Merullo, Roland. 2002. "America's Secret Culture." *The Chronicle of Higher Education,* March 1, pp. B7–B9.

Mesa-Lago, Carmelo. 1979. *Dialéctica de la revolución cubana: Del idealismo carismático al pragmatismo institucionalista*. Madrid: Bibliotecta Cubana Contemporánea.

———. 1989. "The Cuban Economy in the 1980s: The Return of Ideology." In *Cuban Communism*, edited by Irving Louis Horowitz, 7th ed., 187–226. New Brunswick, NJ: Transaction Publishers.

Mesa-Lago, Carmelo, Alberto Arenas de Mesa, et al. 2000. *Market, Socialist, and Mixed Economies: Comparative Policy and Performance: Chile, Cuba, and Costa Rica*. Baltimore: Johns Hopkins University Press.

Miller, Ivor. 2000. "A Secret Society Goes Public: The Relationship between Abakuá and Cuban Popular Culture." *African Studies Review* 43, no. 1 (April): 161–88.

———. 2005. "Cuban Abakuá Chants: Examining New Evidence for the African Diaspora." *African Studies Review* 48, no. 1 (April): 23–58.

Millet, José, and Rafael Brea. 1989. *Grupos folklóricos de Santiago de Cuba*. Santiago de Cuba: Editorial Oriente.

Ministerio de Cultura, ed. 1982. *La cultura en Cuba socialista*. Havana: Editorial Arte y Letras.

Ministerio de Educación. 1971. *Memorias: Congreso nacional de educación y cultura*. Havana: Ministerio de Educación.

Mola Fernández, Claudia. N.d. "Programa, Casa de Africa." Unpublished pamphlet from the Casa de Africa.

Monreal, Pedro. 1999. "Las remesas familiares en la economía cubana." *Encuentro* 14 (Fall): 49–62.

Montaner, Carlos Alberto. 1983. *Fidel Castro y la revolución cubana*. Barcelona: Plaza y Janes.

———. 2001. "El testamento de Fidel Castro." *Nuevo Herald*, May 20, n.p. (archives, Cristóbal Díaz Ayala).

Montaner, Gina. 1999. "Así que pasen 40 años." *Nuevo Herald*, January 11, n.p. (archives, Cristóbal Díaz Ayala).

Moore, Carlos. 1964. "Cuba: The Untold Story." *Présence Africaine: Cultural Review of the Negro World* (English edition) 24, no. 52:177–229.

———. 1988. *Castro, the Blacks, and Africa*. Los Angeles: Center for Afro-American Studies, UCLA.

Moore, Robin. 1994. "Representations of Afrocuban Expressive Culture in the Writings of Fernando Ortiz." *Latin American Music Review* 15, no. 1 (Spring/Summer): 32–54.

———. 1997. *Nationalizing Blackness: Afrocubanismo and Artistic Revolution in Havana, 1920–1940*. Pittsburgh: University of Pittsburgh Press.

Morejón, Nancy. 1970. "Cantos africanos de Cuba." *Revista de la Biblioteca Nacional José Martí* 12, no. 2 (May–August): 173–75.

Moreno, Dennis. 1994. *Un tambor arará*. Havana: Editorial de Ciencias Sociales.

Morín, Francisco. 1998. *Por amor al arte: Memorias de un teatrista cubano 1940–1970*. Miami: Ediciones Universal.

Morris, Nancy. 1986. "'Canto porque es necesario cantar': The New Song Movement in Chile, 1973–83." *Latin American Research Review* 21, no. 2 (Summer): 111–36.

Mouffe, Chantal. 1979. "Hegemony and Ideology in Gramsci." In *Gramsci and Marxist Theory*, edited by Chantal Mouffe, 168–204. London: Routledge and Kegan Paul.

Mûjal-León, Eusebio. 1989. "Higher Education and the Institutionalized Regime." In *Cuban Communism*, edited by Irving Louis Horowitz, 7th ed., 407–28. New Brunswick, NJ: Transaction Publishers.

Muñoz-Unsain, Alfredo. 1967. "El cabaret, ¿también cultura?" *Bohemia* 59, no. 5 (February 3): 34.

Navarro, Noel. 1964. "Una escuela de enseñanza musical." *Revolución*, July 15, p. 8.

Neira Betancourt, Lino A. 1991. *Como suena un tambor abakuá*. Havana: Editorial Pueblo y Educación.

Neustadt, Robert. 2002. "Buena Vista Social Club versus La Charanga Habanera: The Politics of Rhythm." *Journal of Popular Music Studies* 14, no. 2:139–62.

Nichols, John Spicer. 1984. "A Communication Perspective on Radio Martí." *Cuban Studies* 14, no. 2 (Summer): 35–46.

Nicola, Noel. [1975] 1995. "¿Porqué nueva trova?" In *Panorama de la música popular cubana*, edited by Radamés Giro, 365–73. Cali: Editorial de la Universidad del Valle.

Niurka, Norma. 1996. "Pedro Luís Ferrer: Trovador de duro carapacho." *Nuevo Herald*, January 12, n.p.

Noble, Patrick. 2001. "Timba." Undergraduate honors thesis, Harvard College.

Obejas, Achy. 1996. "Cultural Exchange: To Cuban Exiles, Music Can Be Revolutionary." *Chicago Tribune*, November 17, pp. 7, 18–19.

Oficina Nacional de los Censos, Demográfico y Electoral. 1953. *Censos de población, viviendas y electoral, enero 28 de 1953*. Havana: Tribunal Superior Electoral.

Ojito, Mirta. 1987. "Nada más efectivo que una canción." *Miami Herald*, January 11, n.p. (archives, Cristóbal Díaz Ayala).

Olson, Laura J. 1994. *Performing Russia: Folk Revival and Russian Identity*. New York: RoutledgeCurzon.

Oppenheimer, Andrés. 1992. *Castro's Final Hour: The Secret Story behind the Coming Downfall of Communist Cuba*. New York: Simon and Schuster.

Orejuela Martínez, Adriana. 2004. *El son no se fue de Cuba: Claves para una historia 1959–1973*. Bogotá: Ediciones Arte Sociedad y Cultura.

Orovio, Helio. 1981. *Diccionario de la música cubana: Biográfico y técnico*. Havana: Editorial Letras Cubanas.

———. 1992. *Diccionario de la música cubana: Biográfico y técnico*. 2nd ed. Havana: Editorial Letras Cubanas.

Ortiz, Fernando. 1965. *La africanía de la música folklórica de Cuba*. Havana: Editora Universitaria.

———. 1981. *Los bailes y el teatro de los negros en el folklore de Cuba*. 2nd ed. Havana: Editorial Letras Cubanas.

Ortiz García, Carmen. 2003. "Cultura popular y construcción nacional: La institucionalización de los estudios de folklore en Cuba." *Revista de Indias* 63, no. 229:695–736.

Otero, Lisandro. 2001. "Cuando se abrieron las ventanas a la imaginación." *La Gaceta de Cuba* 4 (July–August): 52–55.

Otero, Lisandro, and Francisco Martínez Hinojosa. 1972. *Cultural Policy in Cuba*. Paris: UNESCO Library.

Pacini Hernandez, Deborah, and Reebee Garofalo. 2000. "Hip Hop in Havana: Rap, Race, and National Identity in Contemporary Cuba." *Journal of Popular Music Studies* 11–12:18–47.

Padilla, Heberto, and Luis Suardíaz. 1967. *Cuban Poetry, 1959–66*. Havana: Editorial Arte y Letras.

Palmié, Stephan. 2003. "Fascinans or Tremendum? Permutations of the State, the Body, and the Divine in Late Twentieth-Century Havana." *New West Indian Guide* 78, nos. 3–4: 229–68

Pappademos, Melina. 2003. "Black Consciousness and Black Societies, 1900–1915." Unpublished paper presented at the Latin American Studies Association meeting in Dallas, Texas, on March 29.

Parera, Celida. 1990. *Pro-Arte musical y su divulgación cultural en Cuba, 1918–1967*. New York: Sendas Nuevas Ediciones.

Partido Comunista de Cuba. 1976. *Tesis y resoluciones: Primer Congreso del Partido Comunista de Cuba*. Havana: Departamento de Orientación Revolucionaria del Comité Central del Partido Comunista de Cuba.

———. 1977. *Política cultural de la revolución*. Havana: Editorial de Ciencias Sociales.

———. 1978. *Plataforma programática del Partido Comunista de Cuba: Tesis y resolución.* Havana: Editorial de Ciencias Sociales.

———. 1982. *Selección de documentos del I y II Congresos del Partido Comunista de Cuba.* Havana: Editora Política.

Partido Comunista de Cuba, Fuerzas Armadas Revolucionarias. 1967. *Trabajo político: Boletín de organización del PCC-FAR.* Havana: Imprenta de la dirección política MINFAR.

Patterson, Enrique. N.d. "The Role of Race in Cuba–United States Relations." Unpublished manuscript.

———. 1996. "Cuba: Discursos sobre la identidad." *Revista Encuentro de la Cultura Cubana* 2 (Fall): 49–67.

———. 1998. "Nacionalismo vs. anexionismo." *Nuevo Herald,* June 15, p. 10A.

———. 1999a. "¿Revolución eterna?" *Nuevo Herald,* January 11, p. 11A.

———. 1999b. "¿Cuándo levantan el otro embargo?" *Nuevo Herald,* January 16, p. 10A.

———. 2000. "Nuevos rumbos de la revolución." *Nuevo Herald,* August 16, p. 22A.

Pavón Tamayo, Roberto. 1965. "Ritmos cubanos con fuerza de megatones." *Verde Olivio,* June 6, pp. 42–44.

Peláez, Rosa Elvira. 1986. "Cantar desde la sensibilidad como premisa." *Bohemia* 78, no. 4 (January): 3–7.

———. 1988. "Los Van Van: Al asalto de la tercera generación." *Granma,* August 8, p. 5.

Pérez, Jorge Ignacio. 1993. "La música en las academias, fusión culto-popular." *Granma,* July 3, p. 9.

Pérez, Lizandro. 1999. "¿Ha cambiado el exilio de Miami en 40 años?" *Nuevo Herald,* January 17, p. 25A.

Pérez, Luis A. 1988. *Cuba: Between Reform and Revolution.* New York: Oxford University Press.

———. 1999. *On Becoming Cuban: Identity, Nationality, and Culture.* Chapel Hill: University of North Carolina Press.

Pérez del Río, Hilda. 1961. "El minuet de sala." *Actas del folklore* 1, no. 3 (March): pp. 3–4.

Pérez Firmat, Gustavo. 1994. *Life on the Hyphen: The Cuban-American Way.* Austin: University of Texas Press.

Pérez-Stable, Marifeli. 1993. *The Cuban Revolution: Origins, Course, and Legacy.* New York: Oxford University Press.

Perna, Vincenzo A. 2001 "Timba: The Sound of the Cuban Crisis. Black Dance Music in Havana during the Período Especial." PhD diss., University of London.

———. 2005. *Timba: The Sound of the Cuban Crisis.* Burlington, VT: Ashgate.

Pfeiffenberger, Sylvia. 2004. "World Stage without the World: How Homeland Security Is Affecting Your Eardrums—and America's Cultural IQ." *Independent: The Triangle's Weekly,* September 15, pp. 50–51.

Pineda, Cedeño, and Michel Damián Suárez. 2000. "Reynaldo Hierrezuelo, el rey de la osadía." *Juventud Rebelde,* August 1, p. 8.

Piñeiro, Abelardo. 1965. "Ton, qui, pa." *Cuba Internacional* 4, no. 37 (May): 24–25.

Piñeiro, Jorge Alberto. 1989. "Conmigo o sin mí, ahí están los humoristas." *Juventud Rebelde,* October 11, n.p. (archives, Instituto Cubano de Radio y Televisión).

Pino Santos, Oscar. 2001. *Los años 50: En una Cuba que algunos añoran, otros no quieren ni recordar y lo más desconocen.* Havana: Instituto Cubano del Libro.

Pita Rodríguez, Francisco. 1965. "Más de dos mil aficionados actúan en el Teatro 'Mella.'" *Bohemia* 57, no. 48 (November 26): 55–57.

Pola, José A. 1989. *Entrevistas: Temas relacionados con la cultura.* Havana: Editorial Pablo de la Torriente.

Poncet, Carolina. 1961. "Los altares de cruz." *Actas de folklore* 1, no. 8 (August): 7–11.

Portell Vila, Herminio. 1953. "Barrio suburbano." *Bohemia* 45, no. 11 (March): 46–47, 114.

Portillo de la Luz, César, and Rosendo Ruiz Jr. 1959a. "La tragedia del compositor cubano." *Bohemia* 51, no. 44 (November 1): 52, 92.

———. 1959b. "La tragedia del compositor cubano (II)." *Bohemia* 51, no. 45 (November 8): 50, 104.

———. 1959c. "La tragedia del compositor cubano (III)." *Bohemia* 51, no. 46 (November 15): 50, 100–101.

———. 1959d. "La tragedia del compositor cubano (IV)." *Bohemia* 51, no. 47 (November 22): 50, 91.

———. 1959e. "La tragedia del compositor cubano (V)." *Bohemia* 51, no. 49 (December 6): 54, 113.

———. 1959f. "La tragedia del compositor cubano (VI)." *Bohemia* 51, no. 50 (December 13): 48, 93.

Portuondo, Alfredo Nieves. 1989. "Desde Etiopía: Festival en el desierto." *Bastión,* May 28, n.p. (archives, Museo Nacional de la Música, Havana).

"P.P." [staff writer]. 1994. "La voz de la calle: Pedro Luís Ferrer." *Ajo blanco* 69 (December): 42–44.

Puebla, Carlos. 1984. *Hablar por hablar.* Havana: UNEAC.

Quintero Rivera, Ángel "Chuco". 1998. *Salsa, sabor y control: Sociología de la música tropical.* Mexico City: Siglo XXI.

Radelat, Ana. 1997. "Pentagon Documents Detail Kennedy-Era Dirty Tricks Campaign against Cuba." *CUBAInfo* 9, no. 19 (December 11): 2–3.

Ramos, Jorge. 1999. "El periodista que dobló a Fidel." *Nuevo Herald,* November 17, p. 19A.

Rego, Oscar F. 1982. "Como un combinado." *Bohemia* 74, no. 3 (January 15): 8–11.

Reid, John. 1978. "The Rise and Decline of the Ariel-Caliban Antithesis in Spanish America." *The Americas* 34, no. 3 (January): 345–55.

Rice, Timothy. 1994. *May It Fill Your Soul: Experiencing Bulgarian Music.* Chicago: University of Chicago Press.

Ripoll, Carlos. 1989. "Writers and Artists in Today's Cuba." In *Cuban Communism,* edited by Irving Louis Horowitz, 7th ed., 499–513. New Brunswick, NJ: Transaction Publishers.

Rivas Rodríguez, Jorge. 1989. "Virulo en serio." *Trabajadores,* April 19, n.p. (archives, Instituto Cubano de Radio y Televisión).

Rivero García, José. 1977. "La poesía y un trovador." *El Caimán Barbudo* 110 (January): 6–7.

———. 1990. "Vigencia y empeños del movimiento aficionado." *Trabajadores,* May 21, n.p. (archives, Museo Nacional de la Música, Havana).

———. 2000. "El exilio tiene servida la mesa." *Nuevo Herald,* July 3, n.p. (archives, Cristóbal Díaz Ayala).

Robbins, James Lawrence. 1990. "Making Popular Music in Cuba: A Study of the Cuban Institutions of Musical Production and the Musical Life of Santiago de Cuba." PhD diss., University of Illinois, Urbana-Champaign.

———. 1991. "Institutions, Incentives, and Evaluations in Cuban Music-Making." In *Essays on Cuban Music: North American and Cuban Perspectives,* edited by Peter Manuel, 215–48. Landham, MD: University Press of America.

Robinson, Eugene. 2004. *Last Dance in Havana: The Final Days of Fidel and the Start of the New Cuban Revolution.* New York: Free Press.

Roca, Sergio G. 1989. "State Enterprises in Cuba under the New System of Planning and Management." In *Cuban Communism,* edited by Irving Louis Horowitz, 7th ed., 295–318. New Brunswick, NJ: Transaction Publishers.

Rodríguez, Javier. 1961. "Unos minutos con Carlos Puebla." *Bohemia* 40 (October 1): 75–77.

Rodríguez, Silvio. 1996. *Canciones del mar.* Madrid: Ojalá S.L.

Rodríguez Domínguez, Ezequiel. 1978. *Trío Matamoros: Treinta y cinco años de música popular.* Havana: Editorial Arte y Literatura.

Rodríguez Núñez, Víctor. 1981. "Toda canción es política." *Caimán barbudo* 160 (April): 8–9.

Rojas, Rafael. 1998. *El arte de la espera: Notas al margen de la política cubana.* Madrid: Editorial Colibrí.

———. 2001. "El castrismo mundial." *Nuevo Herald,* May 11, n.p. (archives, Cristóbal Díaz Ayala).

Roldán Viñas, Miguel. 1954. "Las sociedades españolas: Sólidos pilares de nuestra nacionalidad." In *Libro de Cuba, una enciclopedia ilustrada,* edited by Juan Joaquín Otero et al., 724–30. Havana: Publicaciones Unidas.

Román, Marcelino. 1961. "El criterio sociológico en la investigación folkórica." *Actas de folklore* 1, no. 9 (September): 3–6.

Román, Reinaldo. 2002. "The Routes of Cuban Spiritism: Disciplining Man-Gods in Town and Country." Paper presented at the Cuban Research Institute conference, Florida International University, Miami, March.

Rosell, Rosendo. 1992. *Vida y milagros de la farándula de Cuba.* 2 vols. Miami: Ediciones Universales.

Rosenberg, Carl. 2001. "Lobbying for Latin Grammys Challenged." *Miami Herald,* March 6, p. 1B.

Rosendahl, Mona. 1997. *Inside the Revolution: Everyday Life in Socialist Cuba.* Ithaca, NY: Cornell University Press.

Rubio, Vladia, Katiuska Blanco, and Roger Ricardo Luis 1990. "Sin esperar al año 2000." *Granma,* June 17, n.p.

Ruiz, Ramón Eduardo. 1968. *Cuba: The Making of a Revolution.* New York: W. W. Norton.

Ruiz Ruiz, Orlando. 1990. "Ritmo 83, una vocación más allá de las dificultades." *El Habanero,* July 10, n.p. (archives, Museo Nacional de la Música, Havana).

Salado, Minerva. 1985. "Cara a cara con Juan." *Cuba Internacional* 2:70–72.

Salazar, Adolfo. 1938. "La obra musical de Alejandro García Caturla." *Revista cubana* 11, no. 31 (January–March): 5–43.

Salwen, Michael. 1994. *Radio and Television in Cuba: The Pre-Castro Era.* Ames: Iowa State University Press.

Sanabria, Izzy. 1992. "Visions and Views of Salsa Promoter Izzy 'Mr. Salsa' Sanabria: Popularizing Music." In *Salsiology: Afro-Cuban Music and the Evolution of Salsa in New York City,* edited by Vernon Boggs, 187–93. New York: Greenwood Press.

Sánchez, Marucha. 1979. *Memoria de la Orquesta Filharmónica de La Habana, 1924–1959.* Havana: Editorial Orbe.

Sánchez Cabrera, Maruja. 1997. *Orquesta Filharmónica de La Habana: Memoria 1924–1959.* Havana: Editorial Orbe.

Sánchez Lalebret, Rafael. 1962. "Festival de música popular cubana." *Bohemia,* September 14, n.p. (archives, Cristóbal Díaz Ayala).

———. 1963. "Carnavales con alegría combatiente: La revista musical de los obreros de las construcciones." *Bohemia* 55, no. 12 (March 22): 63–65.

Sánchez León, Miguel. 2001. *Esa huella olvidada: El Teatro Nacional de Cuba (1959–1961).* Havana: Editorial Letras Cubanas.

Santamaría, Haydée. 1980. *Moncada.* Translated by Robert Taber. Secaucus, NJ: Lyle Stuart.

Santos, John. 2002. "Jazz Latino: America's Music." Lecture, January 31, Temple University, Philadelphia.

Sauri Olivia, Alberto. 1990. "La revolución me encontró con las tripas sin estrenar." *El Habanero,* January 14, p. 4.

Schroeder, Susan. 1982. *Cuba: A Handbook of Historical Statistics.* Boston: G. K. Hall and Co.

Schwartz, Lawrence H. 1973. *Marxism and Culture: The CPUSA and Aesthetics in the 1930s.* Port Washington, NY: Kennikat Press.

Schwartz, Rosalie. 1997. *Pleasure Island: Tourism and Temptation in Cuba.* Lincoln: University of Nebraska Press.

Scruggs, T. M. 1994. "The Nicaraguan baile de la marimba and the Empowerment of Identity." PhD diss., University of Texas, Austin.

———. 1998. "Nicaraguan State Cultural Initiative and 'the Unseen Made Manifest.'" Unpublished manuscript.

Seguin, Yvonne. 1997. "Cuban Jazz Conversations." Unpublished manuscript.

Serguera Riveri, Jorge "Papito". 1997. *Caminos del Che: Datos inéditos de su vida.* Mexico City: Plaza y Valdés.

Serviat, Pedro. 1986. *El problema negro en Cuba y su solución definitiva.* Havana: Editora Política.

Siegel, Paul. 1992. Introduction to *Art and Revolution: Writings on Literature, Politics, and Culture,* by Leon Trotsky, pp. 7–26. New York: Pathfinder.

Silverman, Carol. 1983. "The Politics of Folklore in Bulgaria." *Anthropological Quarterly* 56, no. 2 (April): 55–61.

Smith, Wayne. 1987. *The Closest of Enemies: A Personal and Diplomatic Account of U.S.-Cuban Relations since 1957.* New York: W. W. Norton.

———. 1997. "Controversy over the Center for the Study of the Americas Resurfaces." *CUBAInfo* 9, no. 2 (October 2): 12.

Sokol, Brett. 2000a. "Los raperos de La Habana: Hip-hop Culture Puts Down Roots in Cuba." *Miami New Times,* July 13–19, p. 25.

———. 2000b. "Hip-hop and Socialism: In Cuba the Revolution Will Be Rhymed." *Miami New Times,* July 20–26, pp. 19, 21.

———. 2003. "No Cuban, No Problem." *Miami New Times,* September 11, pp. 20–22.

Soles, Diane. 1997. "She Who Laughs With, Laughs Best: Bakhtin, Alice in Wondertown, and Revolutionary Panic in Cuba, 1991." Unpublished manuscript.

Solomon, Maynard, ed. 1973. *Marxism and Art: Essays Classic and Contemporary.* New York: Alfred A. Knopf.

Starr, S. Frederick. 1994. *Red and Hot: The Fate of Jazz in the Soviet Union.* 2nd ed. New York: Limelight Editions.

Stearn, Jess. 1956. "Las Vegas se vuelve hacia los trópicos: La Habana paraíso de jugadores." *Bohemia* 48, no. 12 (March 18): 38, 96–97.

Stubbs, Jean. 1989. *Cuba: The Test of Time.* London: Latin American Bureau (Research and Action) Limited.

Suardíaz, Luis. 1989. "Pierde Cuba una gloria de la música popular." *Granma,* July 7, n.p. (archives, Instituto Cubano de Radio y Televisión).

Sublette, Ned. 2004. *Cuba and Its Music: From the First Drums to the Mambo.* Chicago: Chicago Review.

Sublette, Ned, et al. 2004. "The Missing Cuban Musicians." Unpublished manuscript.

Suchlicki, Jaime. 1988. *Historical Dictionary of Cuba.* Metuchen, NJ: Scarecrow Press.

Tamanes, Elisa. 1961. "Antecedentes históricos de las tumbas francesas." *Actas del folklore* 1, no. 9 (September): 7–14.

Tarín Blanco, Lydia. 1961. "Las fiestas de la Cruz de Mayo." *Actas de folklore* 1, no. 1 (January): 17–19.

Thomas, Hugh. 1971. *Cuba: The Pursuit of Freedom.* New York: Harper and Row.

Torres, Dora Ileana. 1982. "El fenómeno de la salsa y lo nuestro latinoamericano y caribeño." Unpublished manuscript.

———. 1995. "Del danzón cantado al chachachá." In *Panorama de la música popular cubana,* edited by Radamés Giro, 193–218. Cali: Editorial Universidad del Valle.

Townsend, Rosa. 2001. "El anticastrismo radical de Miami cambia su imagen y apuesta por la moderación." *El País,* July 24, p. 5.

Triff, Soren. 2001. "'Bipartición' social." *Nuevo Herald,* July 6, n.p. (archives, Cristóbal Díaz Ayala).

Trotsky, Leon. 1992. *Art and Revolution: Essays on Literature, Politics, and Culture.* New York: Pathfinder Books.

Tyson, Timothy B. 1999. *Radio Free Dixie: Robert F. Williams and the Roots of Black Power.* Chapel Hill: University of North Carolina Press.

Unión de Escritores y Artistas Cubanos. 1998. "La creación de la música cubana." Unpublished manuscript (archives, Centro de Desarrollo e Investigación de la Música Cubana).

Urfé, Odilio. 1982. "La música folklórica, popular y del teatro cubano." In *La cultura en Cuba socialista*, edited by Ministerio de Cultura, 151–73. Havana: Editorial Arte y Letras.

U.S. Congress. Senate. 1976. *The Investigation of the Assassination of President John F. Kennedy: Performance of the Intelligence Agencies.* Book 5 of *Final Report of the Select Committee to Study Governmental Operations with Respect to Intelligence Activities.* 94th Congress, 2nd sess. S. Rep. 94–755 ("Church report").

Valdés, Marta. 2004. "Gema y Pável." In the liner notes to *Art bembé.* Conspiradores CD lcd33. Madrid: Peer Music.

Valdés Cantero, Alicia. 1986. *El músico en Cuba: Ubicación social y situación laboral en el período 1939–1946.* Havana: Editorial Pueblo y Educación.

Valladares, Armando. 1986. *Against All Hope.* Translated by Andrew Hurley. New York: Ballantine Books.

Vázquez, Omar. 1987. "En los 70 del cantor de la revolución cubana, Carlos Puebla." *Granma Revista Semanal,* September 20, n.p. (archives, Instituto Cubano de Radio y Televisión).

———. 1998. "Pacho Alonso y la vigencia de un estilo." *Granma,* August 23, n.p. (archives, Instituto Cubano de Artes e Industrias Cinematográficas).

———. 1988. "El mozambique de Pello el Afrokan: 25 años de una aventura musical." *Granma,* July 22, p. 5.

Vázquez Millares, Angel. 1966. *La trova cubana (iconografía).* Havana: Ediciones de la Coordinación Provincial Habana del Consejo Nacional de Cultura.

Vázquez Montalbán, Manuel. 1998. *Y dios entró en La Habana.* Madrid: Aguilar.

Vélez, María Teresa. N.d. "Drumming for the Gods: The Life and Times of Felipe García Villamil." Unpublished manuscript.

———. 1996. "The Trade of an Afrocuban Religious Drummer: Felipe García Villamil." 2 vols. PhD diss., Wesleyan University.

———. 2000. *Drumming for the Gods: The Life and Times of Felipe García Villamil, Santero, Palero y Abakuá.* Philadelphia: Temple University Press.

Verdery, Katherine. 1991a. *National Ideology under Socialism: Identity and Cultural Politics in Ceausescu's Romania.* Berkeley: University of California Press.

———. 1991b. "Theorizing Socialism: A Prologue to the 'Transition.'" *American Ethnologist* 18, no. 3 (August): 419–39.

———. 1996. *What Was Socialism and What Comes Next?* Princeton, NJ: Princeton University Press.

Viglucci, Andres. 2001. "Grammy Flap Exposes Split among Exiles." *Miami Herald,* September 2, p. 1B.

Vilar, Juan "Pin". 1998. *Carlos Varela.* Madrid: Fundación Autor.

Vinueza, María Elena. 1988. *Presencia arará en la música folclórica de Matanzas.* Havana: Editorial Letras Cubanas.

Wallis, Roger, and Krister Malm. 1984. *Big Sounds from Small Peoples: The Music Industry in Small Countries.* New York: Pendragon.

Watrous, Peter. 1997a. "A Hip-Swaying State-Sponsored Export." *New York Times,* March 23, p. 34.

———. 1997b. "A Song Sails Forth from Cuba." *New York Times,* August 21, p. C11.

Weiss, Judith A. 1985. "The Emergence of Popular Culture." In *Cuba: Twenty-Five Years of Revolution, 1959–1984,* edited by Sandor Halebsky and John M. Kirk, 117–33. New York: Praeger.

West-Durán, Alan. 2004. "Rap's Diasporic Dialogues: Cuba's Redefinition of Blackness." *Journal of Popular Music Studies* 16, no. 1:4–39.

Wicks, Sammie Ann. 1998. "America's Popular Music Tradition as 'Canon-Fodder.'" *Popular Music and Society* 22, no. 1 (Spring): 55–89.

Williams, Raymond. 1977. *Marxism and Literature*. New York: Oxford University Press.

Zaldívar, Rudel. 1983. "Cómo y cuándo compuso Carlos Puebla la canción 'Hasta siempre.'" *Tribuna*, December 12, p. 3.

Zeitlin, Marilyn A., ed. 1999. *Contemporary Art from Cuba: Irony and Survival on the Utopian Island*. New York: Delano Greenidge Editions.

Zemtsovsky, Izaly. 2002. "Musical Memoirs on Marxism." Translated by Katherine Durnin. In *Music and Marx: Ideas, Practice, Politics*, edited by Regula Burckhardt Qureshi, 167–89. New York: Routledge.

RECORDINGS AND VIDEOS

Acuña, Claudia. 2002. *Claudia Acuña: Rhythm of Life*. Verve CD 314 589 547–2. Universal City, CA: UMG Recordings.

Alfonso, Carlos, et al. 1992. *Ancestros*. Qbadisc CD 9001. New York: Qbadisc. Originally released in 1987 on an LP of the same name, EGREM LD-4432.

———. 1993. *Ancestros II*. Qbadisc CD 9015. New York: Qbadisc.

———. 1995. *En los límites del barrio*. Artcolor CD 1A-501–36031 A. Havana: Artcolor.

Alfonso, Gerardo. 2000. *Recuento*. RedCasa CD, no number. Havana: Casa de las Américas.

Alfonso, Juan Carlos. 1991. *Si Dan . . . Den: Juan Carlos y su Dan Den*. Areíto LP LD-4708. Havana: Empresa de Grabaciones y Ediciones Musicales.

Álvarez, Adalberto. 1999. *Adalberto Álvarez y su son*. Sony Discos CD PWK 83563. Miami Beach, FL: P.O.W. Records.

Arcaño, Antonio. 1992. *Arcaño y sus Maravillas*. Areíto CD 0034. Havana: Empresa de Grabaciones y Ediciones Musicales.

Atkinson, Kim. 1996. *Mozambique Video Volume 1: Cuban Style in 3–2 Clave*. Sebastopol, CA: Pulse Wave Percussion Video.

Baños, René, et al. 1995. *Vocal Sampling: Una forma más*. Sire/Electra CD 61792–2. New York: Time Warner.

Barbería, Luis Alberto, et al. 1995. *Habana oculta*. Nubenegra CD 1.015. Madrid: Nubenegra.

———. 1997. *Habana abierta*. BMG Music Spain cassette 74321 493604. Madrid: BMG.

Barreto, Ray. 1973. *Indestructible*. Fania CD LPS 00456. New York: Fania.

Barreto, Ray, and Celia Cruz. 1988. *Ritmo en el corazón*. Charly Records CD 172. London: Charly Records.

Blades, Rubén. 1992. *The Best*. Globo Records CD CDZ-80718. Miami: Sony Discos.

Brouwer, Leo. n.d. *Grupo de Experimentación Sonora/ICAIC 3*. EGREM LDA-3460. Havana: Empresa de Grabaciones y Ediciones Musicales

Calzado, David. 1994. *Hey, You, Loca! David Calzado & La Charanga Habanera*. Magic Music CD C-0011–3. Barcelona: Cosmopolitan Caribbean Music.

———. 1996. *Pa' que se entere La Habana*. Magic Music CD C-0019–3. Barcelona, Spain: Cosmopolitan Caribbean Music.

Camerata, Romeu. 1996. *La bella cubana*. Magic Music CD C-0029–3. Barcelona: Cosmopolitan Caribbean Music.

Centro de Investigación y Desarrollo de la Música Cubana, ed. 1995. *Sacred Rhythms of Cuban Santería*. Smithsonian Folkways CD SFCD40419. Washington, D.C.: Smithsonian Institution.

Céspedes, Guillermo, et al. 1993. *Una sola casa*. Green Linnet CD GLCD 4007. Danbury, CT: Green Linnet Records.

Chirino, Willie. 1993. *South Beach*. Sony Tropical CD CDZ-81147/2–469613. Miami: Sony.

———. 1995. *Acere*. Sony Tropical CD CDZ-81713/2–469801. Miami: Sony.

———. 2001. *Afro-Disiac*. Latinum Music CD 94912–2. Miami: DLN Distribution.

Cortés, José Luís "El Tosco". 1993. *Llegó NG, Camará*. Artex CD CD-072. Havana: Artex/ Empresa de Grabaciones y Ediciones Musicales.

———. 1994. *Simplemente lo mejor de . . . NG La Banda.* Caribe Productions CD CD-9435. Havana: Empresa de Grabaciones y Ediciones Musicales.

Costales, Adolfo, and Tony Pinelli, eds. 1993. *Nueva trova: Selección de éxitos.* Artex CD CD-075. Havana: Empresa de Grabaciones y Ediciones Musicales

Cruz, Celia, et al. [1954]. *Santero.* Panart Nacionalizada LD-2060. Havana: Panart.

Dane, Barbara, prod. 1971. *Cuba va! Songs of the New Generation of Revolutionary Cuba.* Paredon Records P-1010. New York: Paredon.

Delgado, Issac. 1999. *La primera noche.* RMM CD 82272. New York: RMM Records.

Díaz Laportilla, Carlos. 2000. *Vocal LT.* Bis Music cassette CS-201, Colección Sésamo. Havana: Artex.

Estrada, José Luis, and Eugenio Carbonell. 1994. *Los Cachivache.* Noncommercially available demo recording. Madrid: Estudios Sonoland.

Fajardo, José. 1995. *Leyendas/Legends: Mister Pachanga and His Orchestra.* Sony Tropical CDL 81533/2-469746. Miami: Sony.

Fellove, Francisco. N.d. *Fellove: Conjunto Habana.* Areíto LP LD-3803. Havana: Empresa de Grabaciones y Ediciones Musicales.

Ferrer, Pedro Luis. 1994. *100% cubano.* Carapacho Productions CD CP-100101. Miami: Carapacho Productions.

———. 1995. *Lo mejor de Pedro Luis Ferrer.* BIS Music CD CD-123. Havana: Empresa de Grabaciones y Ediciones Musicales.

Formell, Juan, and Los Van Van. 1988. *Songo.* Mango LP MLPS 9825. London: Island Records.

———. 1997. *Te pone la cabeza mala.* Metro Blue CD 7243-8-21307-2-7. Madrid: EMI-ODEON.

———. 1999a. *Llegó . . . Van Van.* Havana Caliente CD 360571. Miami: Pimenta Records Corporation.

———. 1999b. *Los Van Van: 30 aniversario.* Caribe Productions cassette C-9555A and C-9555B. Havana: Caribe Productions.

García, Alejandro "Virulo", and Grupo Moncada. N.d. *La historia de Cuba.* Areíto LP LD-3741. Havana: Empresa de Grabaciones y Ediciones Musicales.

Hierrezuelo, Lorenzo, and Reynaldo Hierrezuelo. n.d. [early 1960s]. *Los Compadres.* Areíto LP LD-3639. Havana: Empresa de Grabaciones y Ediciones Musicales.

———. 1993. *Llegaron Los Compadres.* EGREM CD 0046. Havana: Empresa de Grabaciones y Ediciones Musicales.

Hinton, Carma, dir. 2003. *Morning Sun.* TRT Video. San Francisco: Long Bow Group.

Lavoe, Héctor. 1999. *Tributo a Héctor Lavoe, "La voz" con Los Titanes.* Discos Fuentes CD 11072. Miami: Miami Records.

Lay, Rafael. 1992. *The Heart of Havana, Vol. 1.* Orquesta Aragón. Tropical Series RCA CD 3204-2-RL. New York: BMG Music.

Linares, María Teresa, ed. N.d. *Antología de la música hispanocubana.* Areíto/EGREM LP LDA 3326. Havana: Academia de Ciencias.

Loyola Fernández, José, et al. 1996. *Música y revolución.* Producciones UNEAC CD CD-0206. Havana: Empresa de Grabaciones y Ediciones Musicales.

Mena Gómez, Jorge, et al. 1996. *Angelitos negros: Amor X amor.* Magic Music CD C-0028-3. Barcelona: Cosmopolitan Caribbean Music.

Milanés, Pablo. 1997. *Pablo Milanés cantautor: No me pidas (1977).* Universal CD LATD-40082. New York: Universal Music Group.

Muñequitos de Matanzas, Los. 1996. *Ito Iban Echu.* Qbadisc CD QB 9022. New York: Qbadisc.

Nocchi, Nicolás, et al. 2000. *Orichas: A lo cubano.* Universal/Surco CD 012 159 571-2. Miami Beach, FL: Universal Latino Music.

Pelladito, Justo, et al. 1997. *Cuba. Afroamérica: Chants et rythmes afrocubaines.* VDE-Gallo CD CD-959. Lausanne, Switzerland: AIMP and VDE-Gallo.

Pérez Prado, Dámaso. 1990. *Havana, 3 A.M.*: Pérez Prado and His Orchestra. BMG Music cassette 2444–4-RL (Tropical Series). New York: BMG/RCA.

Pérez Prado, Dámaso, et al. 1991. *Memories of Cuba: Orquesta Casino de la Playa (1937–1944)*. Tumbao CD TCD-003. Madrid: Camarillo Music.

Piñeiro, Ignacio. 1992. *Ignacio Piñeiro and His Septeto Nacional*. Tumbao Cuban Classics CD TCD-019. Madrid: Camarillo Music.

Puebla, Carlos. 1993. *Hasta Siempre: Carlos Puebla y sus Tradicionales*. EGREM CD CD-0083. Havana: Empresa de Grabaciones y Ediciones Musicales.

Quintana, José Luis "Changuito", and Rebeca Mauleón Santana. 1996. *The History of Songo/La historia del songo*. DCI Music Video VH0277. Miami: Warner Brothers.

Ramos, Eduardo, prod. 1998. *Antología de la nueva trova, vol. 1*. EGREM CD 0295. Havana: Empresa de Grabaciones y Ediciones Musicales.

Revé, Elio. 1993. *Papá Eleguá*. EGREM CD 0078. Havana: Empresa de Grabaciones y Ediciones Musicales.

Rodríguez, Pete "el Conde", et al. 1996. *Fania All Stars with Pete "El Conde" Rodríguez*, Fania CD 690. New York: Fania Records.

Rodríguez, Silvio. 1991. *Al final de este viaje*. Ojalá CD 0002. Havana: Ojalá Studios.

———. 1996. *Domínguez*. Ojalá cassette MC 0019. Havana: Ojalá Studios.

Rolando, Gloria. 1991. *Un eterno presente: Oggún*. Videoamerica S.A.; Artex S.A. Havana: Imágenes.

Ros, Lázaro. 1992. *Olorun 1*. EGREM CD 0013. Havana: Empresa de Grabaciones y Ediciones Musicales.

———. 1995. *Asoyí: Cantos arará*. OK Records CD-9476. Havana: Caribe Productions.

Ros, Lázaro, and Grupo Mezcla. 1992. *Cantos*. Intuition Records CD INT 30802. Mainz, Germany: Schott Music.

Rupérez, José Luis, ed. 2000. *Album de la revolución*. CubaSoul CD, no number. Madrid: Cuba Siglo XXI Music, under license from Empresa de Grabaciones y Ediciones Musicales.

Santos, John. 1982. Liner notes to *The Cuban Danzón: Its Ancestors and Descendants*. Folkways Records LP FE 4066. New York: Folkways Records.

Saquito, Ñico. 1993. *Goodbye Mr. Cat*. Rounder CD WCD-035. Cambridge, MA: World Circuit.

Silverman, Chuck, and José Luis Quintana. 1998. *Changuito: A Master's Approach to Timbales*. Miami: Warner Brothers Publications.

Strachwitz, Chris, ed. N.d. *La historia del son cubano: Sexteto Habanero (The Roots of Salsa Volumes 1 and 2)*. Folklyric Records 9054. El Cerrito, CA: Arhoolie Productions.

Strachwitz, Chris, and Avalos, Michael, eds. 1991. *Sextetos cubanos: Sones 1930*. Arhoolie Folklyric CD 7003. Selected recordings of the Sexteto Munamar, Sexteto Machín, Sexteto Nacional, and Sexteto Matancero. El Cerrito, CA: Arhoolie Productions.

Urfé, Odilio, ed. 1955. *Festival in Havana: Folk Music of Cuba*. Riverside Records LP 4005. New York: World Folk Music Series.

Urkiza, Pável, and Gema Corredera. 1995. *Trampas del tiempo*. Intuition CD INT 3179 2. Madrid: Nubenegra.

———. 1996. *Cosa de broma*. Intuition CD INT 3181 2. Madrid: Nubenegra.

———. 1999. *Síntomas de fe*. Manzana CD PLCD-229. Madrid: Manzana Producciones Discográficas.

———. 2004. *Art bembé*. Conspiradores CD lcd33. Madrid: Peer Music.

———, prod. 1997. *Habana abierta*. Ariola CD 74321 493602. Madrid: BMG Music.

———, prod. 1999. *Habana abierta: 24 horas*. Ariola CD 74321669332. Madrid: BMG Music.

Valdés, Jesús "Chucho". N.d. *Irakere Vol. 1: Selección de éxitos 1973–1978*. Areíto cassette C-4003. Havana: Empresa de Grabaciones y Ediciones Musicales.

———. 1999. *Indestructible*. P.O.W. Records CD PWK 83558. Miami Beach, FL: Sony.

Valdés, Merceditas. 1992. *Aché*. EGREM cassette C-230. Havana: Empresa de Grabaciones y Ediciones Musicales.

———. 1995. *Cantos afrocubanos: Merceditas Valdés con los tambores de Jesús Pérez*. Areíto cassette C-224. Havana: Empresa de Grabaciones y Ediciones Musicales.

Vanrenen, Jumbo, et al. 1989. *¡Sabroso! Havana Hits*. Earthworks/Caroline CD Carol 2411–2. New York: Caroline/Virgin Records.

Varela, Carlos. 1993a. *Carlos Varela en vivo*. Artex CD-074. Havana: Empresa de Grabaciones y Ediciones Musicales.

———. 1993b. *Monedas al aire*. Qbadisc CD QB 9010. New York: Qbadisc.

———. 1994. *Como los peces*. RCA International CD 25754. Madrid: RCA.

Various artists. 1994. *Despójate*. Caribe Productions CD 9430. Havana: Caribe Productions.

SHEET MUSIC

Almeida, Isabel Otilia. 1981. "Himno a la demajagua." Havana: Editora Musical de Cuba.

Almeida, Juan. 1981. "Este camino largo." Havana: Editora Musical de Cuba.

Díaz Cartaya, Agustín. 1959. "Marcha del 26 de Julio." Havana: Editora Musical de Cuba.

Ruiz Suárez, Rosendo. 1975. "Redención: Himno obrero." Havana: Editora Musical de Cuba.

Silva, Electo, and Mirta Aguirre. 1978. "Canción antigua a Che Guevara." Havana: Empresa de Grabaciones y Ediciones Musicales.

INTERVIEWS

All interviews were conducted by the author in Havana unless otherwise indicated.

Abreu Robles, Yaroldi. Professional percussionist. June 28, 2003.

Acosta, Leonardo. Musicologist and author. September 1, 1996, and February 6, 2001.

Blaha, Charles. Career diplomat, U.S. Foreign Service. September 3, 1996.

Bolívar, Natalia. Author and researcher on Afro-Cuban religions. October 1, 1996.

Bonne, Enrique. Composer and performer. Interview by Raul Fernandez for the Smithsonian Institute. December 15, 1999, Santiago, Cuba.

Calzado, David. Leader of the Charanga Habanera. October 9, 1996.

Carbonell, Walterio. Author. September 9, 1996.

Chailloux, Graciela. Historian. September 26, 1996.

Corredera, Gema. *Novísima trova* artist. July 31, 2001, Madrid, Spain.

de la Fuente, Yasmina. Wife of Rodolfo de la Fuente. June 19, 2003.

Díaz Ayala, Cristóbal. Author and musicologist. June 9, 1997, and March 12, 2002, San Juan, Puerto Rico.

Díaz Pérez, Clara. Musicologist. September 17, 1996.

Esquivel, Alexis. Visual artist. September 21 and 22, 1996.

Faya, Alberto. Musicologist and performer. September 2, 1996.

Fernández Pavón, Reynaldo. Author and composer. January 2, February 21, March 9 and 18, 1998; March 21, 1999, Philadelphia, PA.

Fernández Robaina, Tomás. Author and researcher. August 31 and September 25, 1996.

Ferrer, Pedro Luis. *Nueva trova* artist. September 18, 1996.

Ferrer Aponte, Jerry. Director of the Habana Ritmo. July 1, 2004.

Fontaine, Luisa. Housewife. September 19, 1996.

Fundora Dino, Melquiades. Flutist of the Orquesta Sensación. February 18, 2001.

García, Juanito. Director of the Conjunto Folklórico Nacional. June 24, 2003.

Giro, Radamés. Author and musicologist. September 6, 1996, June 22, 1997, and February 6, 2001.

Hernández Martínez, Isabelle. Musicologist. October 10, 1996.

Jimeno, Tomás. Percussionist. August 3, 1992.

Lapique Becali, Zoila. Author and researcher. October 3, 1996.

Linares, María Teresa. Musicologist. June 22, 2003.

Martínez Furé, Rogelio. Cofounder of the Conjunto Folklórico Nacional. July 3, 1998.

Menéndez, Lázara. University professor. October 5, 1996.

Menéndez, Pablo. Professional musician. September 10, 1996.

Neira, Lino. Percussionist and instructor at the Instituto Superior de Arte. September 19, 1996.

Orejuela Martínez, Adriana. Musicologist. September 18, 1996.

Orovio, Helio. Musicologist. September 26, 1996, and Febrary 9, 2001.

Patterson, Enrique. Author and researcher. October 19, 2000, Miami, Florida.

Pedrito, Justo "Pelladito". Percussionist and member of the Conjunto Folklórico Nacional. June 25, 1998.

Pedroso, Pupi. Keyboardist for Los Van Van and Los que Son Son. June 26, 2003.

Prieto, Jorge. Author and researcher. September 22, 1996.

Reyes, José "Pepe". Author and researcher. February 21, 2001.

Rodríguez, María Teresa. Housewife. January 12, 2001.

Ros, Lázaro. Professional performer and agent. October 4, 1996, Guanabacoa, Cuba.

Sosa, Cristóbal. Radio journalist. October 1, 1996, November 12, 1997, and February 18, 2001.

Valdés Santandreu, Celso. Violinist in the Orquesta Aragón. February 28, 2001.

Villa, Miriam. Housewife. June 25, 2003.

Villafranca, Elio. Professional performer. June 6, 2000, Philadelphia, PA.

Vinueza, María Elena. Musicologist. October 2, 1996.

Index

Page references for figures and examples are in italic.

Abakuá music: attitudes toward, post-1959, 198, 210–13; and *mozambique,* influence on, 183; in prerevolutionary period, 38, 199, 296n. 4; public performances in 1960s, 64

"Abuelo Paco, El" (Ferrer), 160–61

academias de baile, 33, 61

Acosta, Leonardo: on Amateurs' movement, 87–88; on capitalist music making, 19–20, 22; on mambo, 48; on music education, 188–89

Actas del folklore (journal), 75, 209, 298n. 18

Adorno, Theodor, 19

Africa, Cubans in, 86, 141, 214

African aesthetics in Cuban music, 44, 48, 50–53

Africans and African Americans in Cuba, 191

afrocubanismo, xii, 199, 207

Afro-Cuban music. *See also* Afro-Cuban musicians; Afro-Cubans; Conjunto Folklórico Nacional; religious music
—commercial genres: with religious themes, 199–201, 300n. 36, 301n. 43. *See also* chachachá; *conjuntos; danzón;* mambo; *mozambique; pilón;* rap music; *son; timba*
—noncommercial genres: and Afro-Cuban religions, role in, 197; and black identity, 196; attitudes toward, pre-1959, 38, 170–73, 176, 279n. 12; folklore ensembles, since 1990, 193–94 (see also *comparsas;*

makuta; religious music; rumba; *tumba francesa; yuka* drumming); government ambivalence toward, post-1959, 174–75, 186, 192–93, 294n. 5 (*see also* Consejo Nacional de Cultura; Partido Comunista de Cuba); government promotion of, early 1960s, 64, 81, 175; increased visibility of, post-1959, 175–77, 182, 190–94, *192, 205–7, 206,* 301n. 45; university courses in, paucity of, 188–90

Afro-Cuban musicians: and Amateurs' movement, involvement in, 86, 175–77, 195, 205; conga drummers, prerevolutionary, 44; in Conjunto Folklórico Nacional, 187–88; influence on development of Cuban music, 44, 52–53, 115, 125, 165, 170–71; and noncommercial genres, attitudes toward, 178–79, 181, 183–84, 185; performance opportunities in revolutionary Cuba, 64, 180–85, 196; salaries of, recent, 238–39; as semiprofessional, in 1950s, 36; women, 64, 128, 246. *See also* Afro-Cuban music; Afro-Cubans; Bonne, Enrique; Conjunto Folklórico Nacional; Izquierdo, Pedro; Mezcla; Ros, Lázaro; Síntesis; Valdés, Merceditas

Afro-Cuban religions: and Afro-Cuban music, 197; suppression of, pre-1959, 198–200. *See also* Palo; Santería

Afro-Cubans: definition of term, 267n. 1; historical study of, in Cuba, 189–90; publications about, 295n. 18; rap performed

341

Compositor:	Integrated Composition Systems
Text:	Aldus
Display:	10/13 Aldus
Printer/Binder:	Thomson-Shore, Inc.